VIOLENCE AND CULTURE

A Cross-Cultural and Interdisciplinary Approach

JACK DAVID ELLER

Community College of Denver

THOMSON

™

WADSWORTH

Australia • Canada • Mexico • Singapore • Spain
United Kingdom • United States

THOMSON

™

WADSWORTH

Violence and Culture: A Cross-Cultural and
Interdisciplinary Approach
Jack David Eller

Senior Acquisitions Editor: *Lin Marshall*
Assistant Editor: *Nicole Root*
Editorial Assistant: *Kelly McMahon*
Technology Project Manager: *Dee Dee Zobian*
Marketing Manager: *Lori Grebe Cook*
Marketing Communications Manager: *Linda Yip*
Project Manager, Editorial Production: *Catherine Morris*
Art Director: *Maria Epes*
Print Buyer: *Karen Hunt*

Permissions Editor: *Stephanie Lee*
Production Service: *Merrill Peterson, Matrix Productions Inc.*
Copy Editor: *Lauren Root*
Illustrator: *Patricia R. Isaacs, Parrot Graphics*
Cover Designer: *Patricia McDermond*
Cover Image: *Digital Vision/Getty Images*
Compositor: *Cadmus*

For more information about our products,
contact us at:
**Thomson Learning Academic
Resource Center
1-800-423-0563**

For permission to use material from this text or
product, submit a request online at
http://www.thomsonrights.com.
Any additional questions about permissions
can be submitted by email to
thomsonrights@thomson.com.

Library of Congress Control Number: 2004115136

ISBN 0-534-52279-3

**Thomson Higher Education
10 Davis Drive
Belmont, CA 94002-3098
USA**

Asia (including India)
Thomson Learning
5 Shenton Way
#01-01 UIC Building
Singapore 068808

Australia/New Zealand
Thomson Learning Australia
102 Dodds Street
Southbank, Victoria 3006
Australia

Canada
Thomson Nelson
1120 Birchmount Road
Toronto, Ontario, M1K 5G4
Canada

UK/Europe/Middle East/Africa
Thomson Learning
High Holborn House
50/51 Bedford Road
London WC1R 4LR
United Kingdom

Latin America
Thomson Learning
Seneca, 53
Colonia Polanco
11560 Mexico
D.F. Mexico

Spain (includes Portugal)
Thomson Paraninfo
Calle Magallanes, 25
28015 Madrid, Spain

To my father, a strong man
Who never raised his voice or his hand

Contents

PREFACE   xi

Chapter 1

Cross-Cultural Approaches to Violence: The Problem of Definition and Research   1

Defining Violence   4
    Force   5
    Intention   5
    Personhood   6
    Rationality   6
    Legitimacy   8
    Perspective   9
Analyzing Violence: Further Issues   13
    General Factors in the Creation of Violence   13
    The Group Effect   15
    The Will to Differentiate   16
    Cognitive Dissonance   18
    Desensitization   19
    Self-Esteem   20
Studying Violence: Opportunities and Challenges   21
    Definition and Operationalization   22
    Issues in Cross-Cultural Studies   23
    Methodological Issues in Large-Survey Research   27
Retrospect and Prospect   29

Chapter 2

Theoretical Approaches to Violence:
Biological, Psychological, and Social   *31*

Supernatural Theories   32
   Being(s) or Force(s) of Evil   32
   Human Nature, or Human Will   33
Scientific Theories   34
   Biological Theories   34
   Psychological Theories   39
      Psychoanalysis   40
      Behaviorism   41
      Frustration-Aggression Hypothesis   43
      Social Learning Theory   43
      Rational Choice Theory   44
   Social Theories   45
      Functionalism   46
      Functional Conflict: Simmel and Coser   48
      Conflict and Cultural Integration   49
      Conflict Theory   50
      The Value of Violence: Georges Sorel   52
Further Social Theories of Violence   53
   Socialization and Development of the Self   53
   Anomie Theory   55
   Labeling Theory   56
   Cultural Materialism   57
   Process Theory   58
Retrospect and Prospect   59

Chapter 3

Violence in Cross-Cultural Context:
Introduction and Nonviolent Societies   *61*

The Social Grounds of Violence and Nonviolence   62
Cooperation and Competition in Peaceful Societies   70
   Case Study 1: NONVIOLENCE IN THE SEMAI OF MALAYSIA   74
   Case Study 2: THE EVEN-TEMPERED UTKU OF NORTHERN CANADA   77
   Case Study 3: JAINISM—A RELIGION OF NONVIOLENCE   80
   Case Study 4: INVISIBLE VIOLENCE IN THE PIAROA OF VENEZUELA   82
   Case Study 5: THE FRIENDLY HEADHUNTING ILONGOT OF THE PHILIPPINES   84
Retrospect and Prospect   86

Chapter 4

Violence in Cross-Cultural Context: Traditional and Complex Violent Societies   87

Violent Traditional Societies   87
>   Case Study 1: SYSTEMIC VIOLENCE IN THE YANOMAMO OF VENEZUELA   88
>   Case Study 2: AMBIVALENT VIOLENCE IN THE GISU OF UGANDA   91
>   Case Study 3: VISIBLE AND INVISIBLE VIOLENCE IN THE MKAKO OF CAMEROON   92
>   Case Study 4: THE WARRIOR CULTURE OF THE CHEYENNE IN NORTH AMERICA   94
>   Case Study 5: VIOLENCE AND CULTURE CHANGE IN THE SURI OF ETHIOPIA   97
Violent Complex Societies   99
>   Case Study 1: SOCIETY AS ARMED CAMP IN ANCIENT SPARTA   99
>   Case Study 2: VIOLENCE, TRADITION, AND IDENTITY IN MODERN ALBANIA   103
>   Case Study 3: THE RITUAL OF THE BULLFIGHT IN SPAIN   105
>   Case Study 4: SOCCER HOOLIGANISM IN BRITAIN   106
>   Case Study 5: THE BEAUTY OF VIOLENCE IN TRADITIONAL
>   (AND MODERN) JAPAN   108
Retrospect and Prospect   113

Chapter 5

Gender and Intimate Violence   115

Conceptualizing Gender and Family Violence   116
    Definition and Operationalization   116
    Model and Theory   117
Gender Violence in Cross-Cultural Perspective   120
    Violence against Women in Non-Western Societies   120
    Case Study 1: BRIDES ARE BURNING—VIOLENCE AGAINST WOMEN IN INDIA   125
    Violence against Women in Western Societies   130
Child-Directed Violence   132
    Exceptional Forms of Child Abuse   133
    The Major Categories of Child Abuse   135
The Most Intimate Violence: Suicide   139
Hurting without Hitting: Structural Violence   140
>   Case Study 2: STRUCTURAL VIOLENCE AND THE ORDINARY LIVES OF THE
>   POOR IN BRAZIL   142
Retrospect and Prospect   147

Chapter 6

Religious Violence: Introduction   148

Groups and Believers   150

Religious Beliefs and Violence   154
    Religion as Explanation of Evil   154
    Religion as Justification of Evil   161
Sacrifice and Martyrdom   171
Retrospect and Prospect   174

Chapter 7
Religious Violence: Case Studies   176

Case Study 1: THE PERSECUTION OF HERETICS IN CHRISTIANITY   177
Case Study 2: TERRORISM AND SEPTEMBER 11   182
Case Study 3: APOCALYPSE SOON—POISON GAS, MOTHER-SHIPS, AND
             SOLDIERS FOR CHRIST   187
    Aum Shinrikyo: Apocalypse in Japan   188
    Heaven's Gate: Self-Destruction for the Next Level   190
    Soldiers for Christ   194
Case Study 4: SIKHISM—SAINT SOLDIERS   199
Case Study 5: WARRIOR CULTS—THUGS AND ASSASSINS   201
Retrospect and Prospect   203

Chapter 8
Political Violence: Introduction   205

Politics as a Macrosocial Factor in Violence   206
Understanding Political Violence   209
A Typology of Political Violence   213
    Polity versus Polity   214
    People versus Polity   217
    Polity versus People   229
    People versus People   233
Retrospect and Prospect   235

Chapter 9
Political Violence: Case Studies   237

Case Study 1: THE "REIGN OF TERROR" IN THE FRENCH REVOLUTION   238
Case Study 2: "THEORETICAL REVOLUTION"—BOLSHEVISM IN RUSSIA   246
Case Study 3: AT WAR WITH HISTORY IN BOSNIA   253
Case Study 4: "TRIBAL" GENOCIDE IN RWANDA   260
Retrospect and Prospect   266

Chapter 10

Violence in American Society: Introduction   **267**

The Scope of Violence in the United States   268
    The Uniform Crime Report   268
    The National Crime Victimization Survey   270
Explaining American Violence   273
    The Psychocultural Dimension   274
    The Macrosocial Dimension   280
        Urbanization   281
        Race and Ethnic Stratification and Competition   282
        Gender Relations   283
        History and Geography   284
    The Microsocial Dimension: Family   285
        Parenting and Child Abuse   286
        Domestic Violence and Spouse Abuse   288
Retrospect and Prospect   292

Chapter 11

Violence in American Society: Case Studies   **293**

Case Study 1: WORKPLACE VIOLENCE   294
    Type 1: INTRUSIVE VIOLENCE   295
    Type 2: CONSUMER-RELATED VIOLENCE   295
    Type 3: RELATIONSHIP VIOLENCE   296
    Type 4: ORGANIZATIONAL VIOLENCE   297
Case Study 2: SCHOOL VIOLENCE   299
Case Study 3: GANG VIOLENCE   305
Case Study 4: RIGHT-WING/MILITIA VIOLENCE   313
Case Study 5: AMERICAN PSYCHO—SERIAL KILLERS AND PSYCHOPATHS   321
Retrospect and Prospect   325

Glossary   **327**
Bibliography   **329**
Index   **339**

The Americas

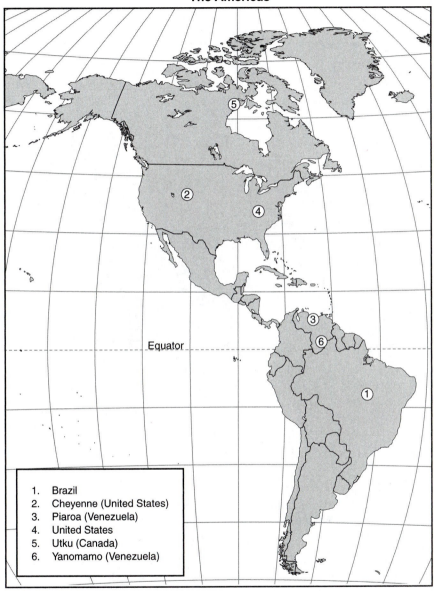

Equator

1. Brazil
2. Cheyenne (United States)
3. Piaroa (Venezuela)
4. United States
5. Utku (Canada)
6. Yanomamo (Venezuela)

Eastern Hemisphere

1. Albania	10. Mkako (Cameroon)
2. Bosnia	11. Papua New Guinea
3. Britain	12. Semai (Malaysia)
4. France	13. Spain
5. Gisu (Uganda)	14. Sparta
6. Ilongot (Philippines)	15. Suri (Ethiopia)
7. India	16. Russia
8. Jains (India)	17. Rwanda
9. Japan	

Preface — 2006

The world is a violent place. The world has always been a violent place. Whether it be lions chasing down zebras, countries marching off to war, or men battering their wives and children, the infliction of pain and suffering seems to be embedded in the very fabric of life.

Nothing seems more obvious than violence, and nothing seems more odious. Neither of these statements is true. Violence is actually a much more complex and contradictory phenomenon than it might seem. In fact, in many cases, and in many cultures, it is not considered a problem at all. In fact, not all violence is objectionable to all societies, and virtually no societies find every form of violence negative or antisocial. There is almost always some expression—and often many expressions—of violence that is considered "normal" or "legitimate" or even highly honorable, including self-defense, war, or professional boxing.

Perhaps today more than ever, it is critical to have a clear understanding of violence. To understand is not to condone; we can comprehend the sources of our own violence and still condemn it. In fact, it might be true that we can only condemn violence if we comprehend it first. However, the realm of violence, for all the attention it has received in recent scholarship, is surrounded by a haze of misunderstanding. Violence seems like something that "they" do, whoever this "they" may be. They may be criminals, or "evil" ones, or the "uncivilized." "We" do not engage in violence; we act for a noble cause, or because we were provoked, or because the situation demanded it. This book will shed some light on these views and dispel some myths.

Why is violence more of a problem today than in the past? Is there really more violence today than ever? Statistics show that the incidence of violent crime, as with other forms of crime, is actually dramatically lower in the United States than a decade ago, and it is obvious that marauding Huns and zealous crusaders have ceased to crisscross the globe. One reason for our newfound concern might be the destructiveness of our modern weapons. We can no longer afford the luxury that people indulged in, as late as World War I, if not later, of relishing fighting and conflict as the most glorious and honorable thing a man can do. Another reason might be our enhanced sensitivity to the feelings of others, our heightened intersubjectivity, that allows or forces us to "feel their pain" and deprives us of the innocence of ignorance. In any case, the "problem" of violence has expanded to include behaviors that we deemed completely normal not so long ago, like corporeal punishment of children, violence between spouses, or war.

To understand—and to intervene in—contemporary violence, two points must be established. The first is that violence, like all other human behaviors and institutions, is culturally relative. That is to say, it does not hurt less when a Yanomamo man pounds another man's chest than when an American man pounds a woman. However, the "value," or legitimacy, of the action differs greatly. The actions and practices that our culture calls violent other cultures call normal; the actions and practices that we now call violent we once called normal; and perhaps in the future many of the actions and practices that we call normal today will be rejected as violent and illegitimate. Therefore, it is difficult to compare and measure violence across time or cultures. In other words, what "counts" as violence depends on what standard we use.

The second point is that we cannot see something clearly unless we can compare it to something else. In this case, we cannot explain violence unless we can contrast it to nonviolence. Americans talk a lot about nonviolence, but most of that talk is mere wishful thinking. Nonviolence is the absence or cessation of violence, right? If we could just stop our fighting—if we could, as Rodney King once pleaded, "just get along"—everyone would live in peace, right? The answer is no, resoundingly no. Violence doesn't come out of nowhere. Its source may be biological, psychological, social, or more likely some combination of these factors, but it must be met at the source or it cannot be met at all. And as anthropologists know, you cannot tweak a cultural system in one spot and expect all the other spots to stay the same—or to change in the way that you desire.

This is why we will examine not only myriad versions of violence in the world but also some (of the very few) versions of nonviolence. We must ask ourselves the question, What are nonviolent societies doing "right" that we are doing "wrong"? If we are serious about reducing the violence in our lives, are we then prepared to make the changes to our value systems, our institutions, and our interpersonal relationships that are necessary to achieve this goal? If we find that there are consistent cultural and social foundations upon which human nonviolence is built, we cannot reasonably expect to build our own nonviolence without those foundations. And we may find along the way that our current foundations, consciously or unconsciously, foster the very outcomes that we bemoan.

In the end, we will find that humans as individuals are quite violent. Humans in groups are more violent, even if those groups are anonymous—crowds, for

hierarchy of violence : 4. *hung groups of ideologies + interests*
3 *human groups of group identity*
2 *Humans in groups*
1 *Individuals*

PREFACE   **xiii**

instance. Human groups with a group identity are more violent still, and human groups with ideologies and interests are the most violent of all. And it is not simply a matter of how much damage they do; it is also a matter of how they feel about that damage. Humans integrated into groups with identities, ideologies, and interests can be blindingly violent and walk away feeling good about it—or feeling nothing at all.

The Structure of the Book

This book surveys human violence from a wide cross-cultural and interdisciplinary perspective. Any single volume cannot hope to include all of the varieties of violence, nor all of the cultures, nor all of the disciplines that might relate to the subject. We have selected here an assortment of nonviolent societies to discuss (from among the very limited number of such societies) and a larger number of violent societies (but a smaller percentage, since they are more common) to compare them with. We have attempted to include past and present societies, "traditional," or small-scale, societies, and complex, or large-scale, societies. We have further focused on a set of instantiations of violence, from gender/domestic violence to religion-inspired violence to political and ethnic violence. No doubt there are others that could have been included.

Any single author or book has to carve out a manageable scope from a vast and interrelated territory. Accordingly, the disciplines represented in this book are preponderantly psychology, sociology, and anthropology, with some discussion of biological and "ethological" perspectives. Other disciplines, such as political science, criminology, and various more specialized theories are not a significant part of the present treatment.

In most areas, the analysis proceeds along a trajectory of paired chapters. The first two chapters provide the conceptual and theoretical underpinning for further discussion; they introduce the terms and factors that inform the study of violence, as well as raising the problem of operationalizing research on such a complex area of inquiry. Finally, they explore the theoretical options of the three major disciplinary approaches. No attempt is made to prove the "truth" of any one discipline or theory, but rather each is offered as adding a piece to the overall puzzle.

The next three chapters examine the psychocultural, microsocial, and macrosocial foundations of violence or nonviolence. Chapter 3 takes a look at the shared traits of nonviolent societies, Chapter 4 at the commonalities of violent societies. Chapter 5 focuses on the realm of gender and intimate—that is, intrafamilial—violence and nonviolence, where the three foundational levels of violence manifest themselves most personally.

The subsequent six chapters, grouped into three pairs, explore two new issues—ideology and interest. Each pair starts with a chapter presenting a general discussion and follows with a chapter of case studies. Chapters 6 and 7 consider religion as an ideological support for violence; although in no way assuming that all religions are violent or that all religious followers are violent, they do highlight the fact that religion can, in a unique way, provide the grounds for legitimate violence. Chapters 8 and 9 turn to political violence, covering a huge domain of nationalistic, ethnic, revolutionary, and counter-revolutionary conflict.

Chapters 10 and 11 apply everything we have learned along the way to the context of American culture, revealing the foundations and consequent expression of nonviolence and of violence in our society. The analysis of violence in America is deliberately saved for the end because the subject cannot be fully grasped without the preceding discussion and because it is almost impossible to view one's own society objectively. It is hoped that after examining violence from a wide variety of perspectives, readers will be able to view America anew.

The book does not make any specific recommendations for limiting violence nor outline unrealistic expectations for the future. Nor does it rule out hopeful possibilities: readers who work their way from start to finish will see for themselves what the construction of a truly nonviolent society might entail and seek to apply that knowledge. However, they will also learn that such awareness is not without its costs and consequences. It is possible that we are doomed to a certain level of "normal" or "background" violence as a modern society, however conceived.

CROSS-CULTURAL APPROACHES TO VIOLENCE

The Problem of Definition and Research

War. Terrorism. Ethnic conflict. Genocide and ethnocide. Mass murder. School shootings. Road rage. Workplace killings. Gang-related slayings. Rape. Assaults, attacks, abuse. Sometimes it seems like the whole world is a cauldron of violence or at least of seething hostility and grievance apt to boil over into violence at any time. Violence takes many different forms, yet in every case it seems to share some fundamental characteristics—harm, cruelty, destruction, domination, evil.

Many of us have been the victims of violence. Perhaps some of us have been the perpetrators of violence. Virtually all of us believe that we understand violence, even if we cannot clearly define or delineate it; like pornography, we "know it when we see it." But, like pornography, perhaps we do not really know it quite as well as we think. Perhaps it is not entirely objective and absolute and the same for all people in all times and places. Perhaps, to some extent, violence, like pornography and even like beauty, is in the eye of the beholder.

This is probably an unfamiliar and difficult concept to grasp at first sight. "Violence is violence," we are inclined to think. But things are not so simple: different individuals consider different things violent, different ages have considered different things violent, and different cultures today consider different things violent. When the United States went to war in World War II, we did not view ourselves as going off to commit violence. When citizens of ancient Sparta threw "unfit" babies off of cliffs, they did not see themselves as committing violence. When a Yanomamo man pounds the chest of another man or hits his wife, he does not deem himself to be committing violence. When eighteenth-century slavers captured and sold Africans as slaves, they did not regard themselves as committing violence. And when the 9/11 terrorists crashed airplanes into the World Trade Center, they did not feel guilty of committing violence. And in each of these cases, many people—at least in their own societies—held the same opinion.

1

In all situations in which we want to understand something accurately, it is necessary to start with definitions. A definition should be the *necessary and sufficient conditions* to distinguish something from all other things—necessary in that the phenomenon must have these qualities or else it is not the phenomenon, and sufficient in that no other qualities are required to set it apart from other phenomena. For instance, in the case of violence, we might emphasize the "objective" characteristics of the behavior; in other words, if someone gets hurt, then it is violence. On the other hand, we might emphasize the "subjective" characteristics; that is, if someone intended to hurt another person rather than doing so accidentally, then the behavior is violence. Or, finally, we might emphasize the "social" characteristics; as such, if a group shares certain values and norms that hold certain kinds of behaviors to be negative and hurtful, then the behaviors are violence, but if their values and norms hold the exact same behaviors to be neutral or insignificant or even positive and beneficial, then they are not violence. In other words, is all hurtful behavior therefore "violence," and is all violence negative?

As a first exercise, then, look at the list of items below, and answer for yourself which ones are violence and which are not—and why.

1. A strong wind knocks over a tree.
2. A beaver chews through a tree until it falls.
3. A lumberjack cuts down a tree.
4. A person puts a bomb in a tree and blows it up.
5. A flood kills a cat.
6. A dog kills a cat.
7. A veterinarian amputates a cat's damaged leg.
8. A veterinarian gives a sick cat a lethal injection.
9. A veterinarian gives a healthy cat a lethal injection.
10. A kid throws a cat out of a moving car.
11. A person kills bacteria by gargling with mouthwash.
12. Bacteria kill a person through infection.
13. A doctor kills a patient accidentally during surgery.
14. A doctor kills a terminally ill person intentionally after the patient requests it.
15. A doctor kills a person intentionally to collect the person's life insurance.
16. A doctor cuts off the foreskin of an infant.
17. A doctor cuts off the foreskin of an unwilling adult.
18. A doctor harvests organs to sell on the black market.
19. A person shoots another person while trying to rob him.
20. A person shoots another person in self-defense.
21. A person shoots another person while playing with a gun.
22. A person shoots another person while cleaning a gun.
23. A man forces a woman to have sex at knifepoint.
24. A man forces his wife to have sex with him by overpowering her.

25. A man insists that his wife have sex with him, even though she really doesn't want to.
26. A person poisons another person.
27. A person kills herself.
28. A woman kills her children.
29. A woman kills her children because she says God told her to.
30. A soldier kills another soldier during a war.
31. A soldier kills a civilian during a war.
32. A soldier kills a civilian during peace.
33. A society throws a virgin into a volcano to appease the gods.
34. A society destroys an enemy city under instructions from their god.
35. A person casts a sorcerer's spell on another person, but the second person does not get sick.
36. A person casts a sorcerer's spell on another person, and the second person gets sick.
37. A flood kills a man.
38. A tiger kills a man.
39. A man kills a tiger for food.
40. A man kills a tiger for sport.
41. A chess player defeats another chess player.
42. A boxer punches another boxer and knocks him out.
43. A hockey player checks another hockey player into the boards.
44. A hockey player slashes another hockey player in the face with his stick.
45. A man calls a woman a bitch.
46. A woman calls a man a son of a bitch.

There are no "right" or "wrong" answers here, and undoubtedly different survey-takers, especially in different cultures, would answer differently. Before you move on, review your answers and think about the distinctions you made.

Looking back now on the choices you made, ask yourself what the criteria or processes were that you used to make your determination. For example, did you evaluate numbers 19, 20, and 21 all as violence? If so, you have not distinguished between an accident, self-defense, and a crime. If you called both number 38 and number 40 violence, then you have not distinguished between human and nonhuman action. And if you answered yes to number 44 but no to number 43, then you have made a distinction between "legitimate" and "illegitimate" violence.

And that's OK. The point of this exercise is to explore where we as a society and you as an individual stand vis-à-vis violence. Probably, unless you are unique, you did not answer yes to every single item, yet every single item involved some kind of harm being done to some living being. If you answered no to any of the items, then in your view there are some instances in which harm to a living being does not constitute violence. If you answered no to any of the items from number 12 to the end, you believe there are some instances in which harming a human being is not violence. How do we make these assessments, and what do they say about us—and about violence?

Defining Violence

Webster's defines violence as "exertion of physical force so as to injure or abuse; ... injury by or as if by distortion, infringement, or profanation; ... intense, turbulent, or furious and often destructive action or force; ... vehement feeling or expression." The word comes from the Latin root *violare*, "to violate," which is probably significant. Glenn Bowman (2001: 25) expands this notion of violation to include the following:

- To break, infringe, or transgress unjustifiably
- To ravish or outrage (especially a woman)
- To treat irreverently, to desecrate, dishonor, profane, or defile
- To vitiate, corrupt, or spoil
- To treat roughly, to assail or abuse
- To break open, to interrupt or disturb, to interfere with rudely or roughly

That covers a very great range of behavior. Do we want to equate "dishonoring" someone with injuring someone—or dishonoring someone with dishonoring some belief or object—and do we want to respond equally to both: that is, do we want to put someone in jail for punching you or for calling you a name?

Definitions can be narrow or wide, strict or loose. If we define violence narrowly or strictly, fewer things will qualify, and that might be good; if we define it widely or loosely, more things will qualify, and that might be good too. Or either approach might be bad. For example, the definition above includes physical force, so if an injury or abuse does not involve physical force—say, if it is verbal or emotional or financial—then is it not violence? Is an armed robbery "violence" but a peaceful embezzlement not, even if the embezzlement results in much greater losses? The definition also draws attention to the emotional quality of violence, the "vehement feeling" associated with it. But is extreme emotion a necessary or sufficient condition of violence? If I attack you with no vehement feeling in my heart, is that now not violence? Or if I have a strong hostility toward you but do not act on it, is that still violence?

Things are getting a bit more complicated, and that is as it should be. In the real world, nothing is simple, least of all something like violence. Let us then make a stab (if you will forgive the "violent" metaphor) at laying out some key components of any approach to violence. They might include:

1. Force and the different kinds of force
2. Intention, or the subjective state of the perpetrator
3. Personhood, or whether only persons can be agents or victims of violence
4. Rationality/irrationality, or whether violence involves or requires a loss of control and of "clear thinking," whether it is "meaningless"
5. Legitimacy/deviance, or whether some injurious actions are acceptable and normal, and under what conditions we make the distinction
6. Perspective, or whether all parties in the situation observe and evaluate the situation in the same way

Force

Let us begin with the issue of force. Is force necessary and sufficient to qualify an action as violence? Let us agree that we are talking about physical force here. We have already made the distinction between "street crime," such as armed robbery, and "white collar crime," such as embezzlement; is the amount of physical force (or threatened physical force) more important than the amount of financial damage? In other words, if the robber steals $20 from us and our broker steals $20,000, which is more "violent"? Furthermore, is there a difference between "used force" and "threatened force"? Finally, are we going to limit "force" to physical force? If a man says to his wife, "Stay with me or I'll kill you" or "Stay with me or you'll never find anyone else who will love you," are these both "forceful" and both violent? If violence requires physical force, then we would be unable to call verbal abuse or emotional abuse or property abuse "violence." Again, that might be desirable, but it is a social choice we must make.

If by force we also mean "lack of options" or "lack of freedom to exercise options," then a lot more things become violent. Some social scientists use the term *structural violence* (see Chapter 5) to refer to circumstances that deprive people of choices and condemn them to unfavorable social positions. For instance, racial discrimination would be a kind of structural violence, as would poverty. If a white man beats a black man with a club, that is clearly violence. But if a white man has better access to jobs, education, or political office than a black man—or any man has better access than a woman—is that "violence", after a fashion? It certainly does do some harm.

Intention

The issue of the subjective state of the perpetrator of violence is also key. In our legal system and in our everyday thinking on the subject, a person must *intend* to do harm to be fully culpable for any harm he or she does. This is why juries attempt to get at the "state of mind" of the defendant, to decide whether the injury was *intentional* or *accidental*. To an important extent, one cannot commit violence or crime unless it is a voluntary and intentional act. That is to say, if I don't see you coming and swing my arm, resulting in your bloody nose, this would probably be seen in most courts as not a case of violence, although I am sure your nose hurt quite a lot. Or if a bad man grabbed my arm and swung it against my will, hitting you and resulting in your bloody nose, this would probably also not be seen as violence on my part (perhaps on the bad man's part, though). Finally, if the bad man told me to hit you in the nose or else he would kill my whole family, I would probably not be held responsible for violence, since my action was coerced. Thus, unintentional acts—whether an effect of accidental, uncontrollable, or coercive causes—might be said to inhabit a gray area in regard to violence.

Personhood

The survey earlier in the chapter raised the issue of personhood and whether only persons could be held responsible for violence. This is a moral issue: that is, are humans the only moral agents in the world, or are other beings—or even natural forces—morally responsible too? If a human smashes my house, that is probably violence. But if a tornado smashes my house, would it make sense to call the tornado violent? We do speak of "violent storms," but is this more than a metaphor? We speak of "nature's wrath," but more than likely, nature does not have any sentiment, wrathful or otherwise. Tornadoes are not angry or "vehement" when they touch down in a Midwestern trailer park, and lions are not angry when they kill zebras. Nor are bacteria angry when they infect us, nor are we angry when we take antibiotics.

If only humans can be agents of violence, can only humans be victims of violence? We probably hesitate more here. Torturing a human is definitely violence. Torturing a dog or cat more than likely feels like violence too. But what about torturing a fish? Putting a live lobster in boiling water is very likely torturous to the crustacean. What about torturing a carrot? What about all the poor germs that die when you gargle? If there is a line—and there almost certainly is—that separates harm to some life-forms as violence from harm to others as not violence, where is this line and on what grounds do we draw it?

Rationality

Rationality is one of the crucial areas for both a "folk" and a scientific understanding of violence. We tend to think that violence is, at least to a degree, irrational—that it emerges out of fits of rage or other highly emotional and not altogether controllable conditions. In law we distinguish "crimes of passion" and "temporary insanity" from other crimes and excuse them. Partly this is a matter of intentionality: if we are not in control, if we "lose our mind," we cannot be completely responsible agents. But this is also largely a matter of our illusions about crime in general and violence in particular—that no "normal" or "right-thinking" person "could do such a thing." It is a way of distancing ourselves from violence, of making violent people "the other," of insisting that *we* could never do such a terrible thing.

Roy Baumeister, in his book *Evil: Inside Human Violence and Cruelty* (2001), discusses what he calls the "myth of pure evil." In his analysis, this myth has several components:

- Evil involves the intentional infliction of harm on people.
- Evil is driven primarily by the wish to inflict harm merely for the pleasure of doing so.
- The victim is always innocent and good.
- Evil is the other, the enemy, the outsider, the out-group.
- Evil has been that way forever.
- Evil represents the antithesis of order, peace, and stability.
- Evil-doers are often marked by egotism.
- Evil-doers have difficulty maintaining control over their feelings, especially rage and anger.

In short, evil and evil-doers are anything but us. Evil is the "monstrous."

But as Baumeister and others have noted, violence is often, if not usually, anything but irrational or even highly emotional. It was Hannah Arendt (1969), the observer of World War II and post-World War II atrocities, who coined the phrase "the banality of evil" to highlight its frequently very ordinary and nonmonstrous character. Looking at Nazi war criminals like Eichmann, she was struck by their remarkable ordinariness. Eichmann was not a slathering demon, not a crazy person (as we picture Charles Manson to be), not the devil personified. Her point was that, in the right circumstances, it could have been you or me.

This disturbing and distasteful realization was given factual support by one of the most famous (and deservedly so) experiments in the history of psychology. Not long after World War II, using a process influenced by the very observations Arendt was making, Stanley Milgram (1963) conducted a series of studies on violence and authority. The experiments involved asking volunteers to administer electrical shocks to subjects as part of a "teaching" procedure. Of course, the experiments were not really about teaching, there were no subjects to be shocked, and the shocks were fictitious. However, the volunteers did not know any of this.

Brought into a scientific-looking laboratory, where a white-coated scientist stood by, volunteers were instructed to ask questions of a subject and give him or her a shock for each incorrect answer, and to increase the voltage for each subsequent incorrect response. The alleged subject would at first complain of the discomfort of the shock, then yell, then scream for release, and finally go silent if the voltage got high enough. Many volunteers seemed reluctant to give the higher shocks, and some appeared visibly upset by the whole affair, but under the "scientist's" gentle but relentless prodding—saying things like, "Please continue" and "The experiment requires that you continue"—a remarkably large percentage (65%) of volunteers administered the maximum shock. What Milgram concluded is that perfectly normal and "good" people could be made to perform acts of violence, even to commit potentially fatal violence, with the subtlest of pressures. The line between "good person" and "abuser" or "killer" was a fine one, and, under the right circumstances, virtually of any us could cross it.

Legitimacy

It might appear on the surface that violence is never legitimate and that any discussion of its legitimacy would be inappropriate, but such is not the case. The violence of soldier against soldier in war is, except to the most adamant pacifist, legitimate. The violence of victim against criminal in moments of self-defense is legitimate. The violence of defensive lineman against quarterback (short of "cheap shots" and late hits) is legitimate. And the violence of the lion against the zebra is legitimate.

The problem of the legitimacy of violence represents our first serious encounter with the "relativity" of violence—relativity in regard to individuals, situations, and societies. If I am a professional boxer (your opinion of boxing notwithstanding) and I don a pair of gloves, enter the ring, and punch my opponent, this is legitimate violence. If I go outside and punch a civilian, or go home and punch my wife, that is not. So it is not the action as such (punching someone in the nose) that is legitimate or illegitimate but rather the *action in a specific social context*.

Let us take a further look at the question from a historical and cultural perspective. In America today, shackling a man with chains around the ankles and forcing him to work all day is considered illegitimate and violent, but clearly two hundred years ago in some parts of the country, it was neither. Not only was it considered legitimate, but it was not even considered violence. In some societies today, it is considered legitimate for a man to hit, or in extreme cases to kill, a woman. In their traditional culture, as we will see later, the Yanomamo of Venezuela routinely practiced male-on-female aggression (as well as male-on-male aggression) in their everyday lives, and in "modern" and "civilized" parts of the world a woman can still legally and "legitimately" be beaten or killed by men for "crimes" like adultery or being the victim of rape, and to settle disputes between men, women can be forced to marry men not of their own choosing.

Although these actions may all seem very wrong to us, that is not the point. Relativitism tells us that what seems very wrong to one group may be completely "normal" to another. As we will learn below, this fact makes the cross-cultural study of violence difficult, since violence may not be defined or counted in the same way from place to place; whatever indicator we choose to count might not be counted—or it might not even count as an indicator—in a particular context. Thus, we cannot always assert that violence is deviance; in some cases, in our own society and any other, violence is normal. Besides, "deviance" is relative to the expectations and definitions of the society; some societies would consider football and war deviant and barbaric, whereas we embrace them but condemn bullfighting and spousal abuse (although the latter practice is all too frequent). In fact, these discrepancies raise the additional issue of ideal versus actual culture: we may condemn spousal abuse or rape or murder as deviant but still do a lot of it. We might even say (and will continue to observe as we proceed through this book) that American society tolerates, if not lauds, a certain amount of violence or, at least that it accepts a certain amount as the "cost," or trade-off, for some of our prized values and behaviors.

In the work of Arendt on violence, the issue of legitimacy figures prominently. Speaking of "political violence" or the violence that a government or leader employs against its own people, she notes that power and violence are not the same thing at all (Arendt 1969). As a political force, violence is in fact the opposite of power, which is "legitimate" in some way. Violence in her view is by nature illegitimate, the tool that rulers use when they have lost or never had legitimate power. (See Box 1.1.)

Perspective

As we have just seen, the issues of legitimacy and relativity raise the issue of context, which, as we will now discuss, raises the issue of perspective. The point here is that there are always at least two parties to every instance of violence—the perpetrator and the victim—whose perceptions of the situation may be profoundly different. As Baumeister (2001) argues, we tend to privilege the perception of the victim in our conventional approach to violence, but there are no automatic reasons why we should do so and some good reasons why we perhaps should not. First of all, the victim tends to see himself or herself as an innocent party to the violence, which may or may not be the truth. Second, the victim will naturally tend to have a more negative attitude toward the violence than the perpetrator. And third and most important, by dismissing any perception the perpetrator might have of the situation, we cut ourselves off from a critical source of information. Even worse, if we simply presume to know what the perpetrator is thinking—especially if we presume that he or she is not thinking at all, but merely acting like an irrational blood-thirsty monster—we are almost certain to get it wrong.

Significantly, there is often, if not always, a third party to violence (either literally or figuratively)—the "audience," the "public," or the "society"—that

"the banality of evil" re A. Eichmann 1963

1906–1975 Ger–Jewish pol. theorist U. Marburg → Bard Colley

1.1   *Hannah Arendt on Violence* *On Violence (1970)*

"Power corresponds to the human ability not just to act but to act in concert. Power is never the property of an individual; it belongs to a group and remains in existence only so long as the group keeps together. When we say of somebody that he is 'in power' we actually refer to his being empowered by a certain number of people to act in their name. The moment the group, from which the power originated to begin with ... disappears, 'his power' also vanishes. In current usage, when we speak of a 'powerful man' or a 'powerful personality,' we already use the word 'power' metaphorically; what we refer to without metaphor is 'strength.'

"Force, which we often use in daily speech as a synonym for violence, especially if violence serves as a means of coercion, should be reserved, in terminological language, for the 'force of nature' or the 'force of circumstances' ... that is, to indicate the energy released by physical or social movements.

"Authority, relating to the most elusive of these phenomena and therefore, as a term, most frequently abused, can be vested in persons—there is such a thing as personal authority, as, for instance, in the relation between parent and child, between teacher and pupil—or it can be vested in offices, as, for instance, in the Roman senate ... or in the hierarchical offices of the Church. ... Its hallmark is unquestioning recognition by those who are asked to obey; neither coercion nor persuasion is needed. (A father can lose his authority either by beating his child or by starting to argue with him, that is, either by behaving to him like a tyrant or by treating him as an equal.) To remain in authority requires respect for the person or the office, and the surest way to undermine it is laughter." (Arendt 1969: 44–45)

"Violence ... is distinguished by its instrumental character. Phenomenologically, it is close to strength, since the implements of violence, like all other tools, are designed and used for the purpose of multiplying natural strength." (46)

"Rule by sheer violence comes into play where power is being lost." (53)

"Power and violence are opposite; where the one rules absolutely, the other is absent." (56)

"Since violence always needs justification, an escalation of violence in the streets may bring about a truly [violent] ideology to justify it." (77)

> "Violence can remain rational only if it pursues short-term goals. Violence does not promote causes, neither history nor revolution, neither progress nor reaction; but it can serve to dramatize grievances and bring them to public attention." (79)

is, there are bystanders watching at the scene of the violence or there is a relevant social context of beliefs, values, and norms within which it occurs. Hence, in a real and crucial way, violence is a *performance* that social actors put on for themselves and others, whether they are aware of it or not. As such, all of the relevant social factors need to be included in a complete and accurate description and understanding of it; this is what anthropologist Clifford Geertz (1973) called, in a very different context, "thick description." Our description could be "thin" and objective: "That guy hit that other guy over the head with a chair." However, a thick description would integrate the perspectives of the victim, the perpetrator, and the audience, with their motivations, values, and understandings, to construct a full account of the incident.

As anthropologist David Riches (1986: 3) has written, "violence is very much a word of those who witness, or who are victims of, certain acts, rather than of those who perform them. . . . When a witness or victim invokes the notion of violence, they make a judgment not just that the action concerned causes physical hurt but also that it is illegitimate." Or, in other words, "when the term 'violence' is being used, attention should crucially be focused on *who* is labeling a given act as such and most especially their social position" (4). This leads to Riches' definition of violence as "an act of physical hurt deemed legitimate by the performer and illegitimate by (some) witnesses" (8).

As many social scientists and criminologists note, perpetrators of violence often do not perceive themselves as committing violence at all. This is not to say that their perception counts more than the victim's or the audience's, but it does not automatically count less either. Thus, perpetrators, as we will see in the course of our discussion, often see themselves as victimized too in some way—provoked into their response or assaulted to the point of "self-defense"—or as swept along by events or as acting out of some higher cause or good. All too often, they see the victims as either not really injured at all (or at least "not much") or as less valuable or even less human than themselves. And, as we said, if only humans can be victims of illegitimate violence, then less-than-humans or nonhumans cause us no guilt.

Finally, the victim's perception of degree of violation, however creditable, can be impeached by what Baumeister calls the *magnitude gap*. The magnitude gap reminds us that the importance and intensity of violence is almost always greater for the victim than for the perpetrator; that is, the victim's "loss" in the situation is almost always greater than the perpetrator's "gain." Of course, in some cases it is difficult to see what the gain might be at all; perhaps it is little more than honor. But if I kill you, my gain in honor is still arguably less than your loss in life. And if I steal from you, my gain in property or wealth is often less than your loss materially and emotionally. And, ultimately, I probably walk away and sleep well that night, whereas you might have anxiety and feelings of violation for days, weeks, or years to come. So if we take the victim's testimony to the exclusion of other testimony, we will get a somewhat skewed sense of the seriousness of the matter.

At the same time, it is in the perpetrator's self-interest to minimize the seriousness of the same affair, for a number of reasons. Riches mentions a few: that it is easier to justify actions if their consequences are minimal; that it is easier to excuse the actions if they appear involuntary or unavoidable or reactive; and that it is part and parcel of the violent act to attempt to influence and disrupt the victim's perception of it (the old "you really liked it" rationalization of the rapist). Schmidt and Schroder (2001: 3) make the following three observations regarding the "social construction" of violence:

> Violence is never completely idiosyncratic. It always expresses some kind of relationship with another party and violent acts do not target anybody at random (although the individual victim is likely to be chosen as representative of some larger category. . . .
>
> Violence is never completely sense- or meaningless to the actor. It may seem senseless, but it is certainly not meaningless to victim or observer. As social action, it can never be completely dissociated from instrumental rationality. . . .
>
> Violence is never a totally isolated act. It is—however remotely—related to a competitive relationship and thus the product of a historical process that may extend far back in time and that adds by virtue to this capacity many vicissitudes to the analysis of the conflictive trajectory.

To these general points the authors attach three elements of an "anthropological approach" to the study of violence:

> acts of violence are not sudden outbursts of aggressiveness devoid of historicity, meaning, and reflexivity. . . .
>
> violent imaginaries are not ephemeral constructions of fragmented subjectivities, nor are they the inevitable products of reified concepts such as 'cultural models' or 'traditions'. . . .
>
> violence is performed as well as imagined by reflexive, socially positioned human beings under specific historical conditions for concrete reasons. (Schmidt and Schroder 2001: 18-19)

This is a very (perhaps overly) complex way of saying that violence does not come out of thin air; that it is real-life, flesh-and-blood people who engage in it; that these people have their reasons for their actions, which are not abstract or purely conceptual; that these actors are at least partially aware of their actions and their reasons; and that the entire context of the violent episode must be considered in a full and useful account of the violence.

ANALYZING VIOLENCE: FURTHER ISSUES

It should be apparent by now that violence is not simple—not in its motivations nor its manifestations nor its meanings. It should also be apparent that, whatever the definition, violence is something that all humans engage in to some degree at some point in their lives. Violence is not just the province of the psychopath, the deviant, the monster, the "other." The expression of violence is a complicated (but not impossibly complicated) blend of basic human nature, individual personality, and social circumstances. None of these factors explains violence entirely, but none of them can be left out of a thorough explanation. Let us explore these issues further.

General Factors in the Creation of Violence

One of the main themes of our earlier discussion was that violence is not just something that bad people do. Of course, we can define a "bad person" as a "person who does violence," but this is not a useful definition because (1) it does not discover or attribute cause and (2) it makes us all "potentially bad people." An explanation does more than restate the obvious, or else it is merely circular: bad people do violence, and people do violence because they are bad.

Psychologists, sociologists, and anthropologists alike are putting less emphasis on what is inside the person (in most cases—there are of course psychopaths out there) and more on what is outside the person in getting to the root causes of violence. Few children are "born violent" (although, again, maybe some are). And violence, like any other form of deviance, is not just something that "they" do. It is something that we all do or can do. The traditional approach, that violence is something that "others" do but not us, is flawed, even false, and hints at the perspectival nature of violence: it is easier for us to see *their* violence than our own. Thus, rather than an absolute and "impermeable" boundary between the good "us" and the evil "them," all of the evidence suggests that the boundary is much fuzzier and more permeable than we think—and like to think.

The psychologist Philip Zimbardo (2000), picking up where Milgram and others left off, argues that violence or "evil" is less to be explained by the *dispositions* of individual agents than the *situations* in which individuals are placed. He identifies a set of variables that have the effect of making "good people" do "bad things," and the list is fundamental to any further study of violence and culture. It includes:

- Indoctrination into a rationale or justification, that is, an "ideology" that legitimizes violence
- Obedience to authority, with no opportunity for dissent
- Anonymity and deindividuation
- Diffusion of responsibility
- Gradual escalation of violence
- Dehumanization of the enemy or the victim

Of these, he emphasizes the potency of one above all the others: blind obedience to authority (see the discussion of the "true believer" in Chapter 6). He concludes, then, that it is critical to teach our children how to distinguish between just and unjust authority; if situations and ideologies can be our damnation, they can also be our salvation (19).

Baumeister (2001) compiles much the same list of danger signs in the creation of violent actors, with a couple of noteworthy additions. His version includes diffusion of responsibility; deindividuation; division of violent "labor"; dehumanization and/or demonization of the victim; separation of decision makers from those who carry out violent acts; egotism; and idealism. Most, if not all, of these characteristics are social or "external" rather than psychological or "internal"—and even the ones that are internal tend to be external initially. A person must learn to be egotistical or idealistic, and specific social forces are conducive to these mind-sets, as we will see. All in all, however ("spontaneous" violence excluded, such as when someone tries to take a baby's candy), violence tends to be explicable first and foremost in terms of social and cultural factors. Awareness of these is of paramount importance in understanding and responding effectively to such violence. Just labeling terrorists as madmen misrepresents them and misplaces our energies in addressing the problem their actions pose.

The National Center for Injury Prevention and Control (www.cdc.gov/ ncipc/factsheets/yvfacts.htm) has published an extensive list of "risk factors" that lead to violence, particularly youth violence, although most of them are general enough to relate to violence in all its forms. The factors break down into four categories: individual, family, peer/school, and neighborhood/community. *Individual risk factors* include history of early aggression; beliefs supportive of violence; engaging in antisocial behavior, such as setting fires and cruelty to animals; use of alcohol or other drugs; being a male; being involved in serious but not necessarily violent criminal behavior; and bullying or being bullied. *Family risk factors* include authoritarian attitudes; harsh, lax, or inconsistent discipline; poor monitoring or supervision; exposure to violence in the home; parental drug or alcohol abuse; poor emotional attachment to parents or caregivers; low family socioeconomic status or poverty; and antisocial parents. *Peer/School risk factors* include association with peers who engage in high-risk or problem behavior; low commitment to school; and academic failure. Finally, *neighborhood/community risk factors* include poverty or low economic opportunity; high levels of family disruption or transience; low community participation or socially disorganized neighborhoods, and exposure to violence.

The Group Effect

One of the most remarkable and compelling facts about violence is that groups tend to meet the above conditions even better than solitary individuals and that group violence tends to be more prevalent and more intense than individual violence. Groups do not necessarily have to be coordinated to share beliefs and values (see later discussion); rather, some of the most extraordinary and extravagant violence is committed by mobs and crowds, with little leadership and little shared identity. Observers from Freud on have commented on "group psychology" and the ease with which groups slip the normal bounds of social restraint and behave as if they have reverted to a more primitive emotional state.

It goes without saying that only groups can meet the criteria of diffusion of responsibility, division of labor, and separation of leaders from "ground level" violent perpetrators. But the very reality that groups provide a collection of individuals, no one of whom is solely responsible for the actions of the group, loosens the restraints on groups. A "fog of responsibility" develops, and even more significantly, a "fog of information"—members of the group may not know what the entire group is doing or what is being done in their name by other members. It is easier to "lose yourself" in the group or to dismiss your small role in the cumulative violence or in the culpability of the violence. As we all know, the common Nazi defense after World War II was "I was only following orders," which does convey a certain moral weight: as we noted earlier, one cannot be held morally responsible for an act if that act was involuntary or coerced.

The "just-following-orders" defense also highlights the separation of decisions from actions that charaterizes violence. The ground-level perpetrators are merely carrying out decisions that they did not make, and the higher authorities are merely making decisions that they did not carry out; each has his or her moral burden lessened accordingly. This disconnection between violent actions and their motivations is in fact part of an often much more extensive "division of labor"—not just between authorities and perpetrators but between various contingencies of perpetrators, no one of which has to follow through with the violence from start to finish. Dividing the business of violence into small, almost tolerable steps—like assigning different people in the concentration camp system to drive the prison trains, guard the inmates, perform the executions, bury the dead, and so forth—detaches any single individual from the reality of the whole enterprise. And, as we will see, detachment is one of those crucial emotional conditions for committing heinous violence against fellow humans.

Besides the specific traits that make violence "smoother" for groups, groups also tend to bring out general elements of human psychological and social behavior that contribute to the possibility and intensity of violence. Baumeister points out that groups "tend to be more antagonistic, competitive, and mutually exploitive than individuals. In fact, the crucial factor seems to be the perception that the other side is a group. An individual will adopt a more antagonistic stance when dealing with a group than when dealing with another individual" (2000: 193). Further, groups give a measure of moral authority that individuals lack. Finally, the group and its survival and success become an end in themselves, and individuals can take a threat to the group's cohesion as a threat to their personal existence or honor.

Clearly groups also present opportunities for blind obedience—in fact, they may attract those who are most prone to blind obedience—and for anonymity and idealism. The issue of idealism is critical and will be explored further in subsequent chapters, but it is a unique characteristic of groups, which often imagine themselves the bearers of some specially noble mission or value. The occasional individual may fantasize himself or herself on a mission too, but missions tend to be reserved for groups, and groups tend to reinforce the missionary quality of their actions. Indeed, violence in the name of an ideal "is nearly always fostered by groups, as opposed to individuals. . . . Whether one looks at religious warriors, members of Fascist or Communist groups, or modern members of street gangs, one finds the same pattern: The group is regarded as above reproach. The members of the group may sometimes think rather poorly of one another, but the group as a whole is seen as supremely good" (Baumeister 2001: 192). As such, the idealism of groups, as opposed to the idealism of individuals, "usually ends up conferring a right, a license, to hate" (ibid.).

The Will to Differentiate

Groups have specific dynamics that are conducive to violence. But why are groups so ubiquitous and powerful in human life? The dizzying diversity of cultures, and the rapidity with which humans who share anything at all in common—locality, language, physical characteristics, religion, interests, or what have you—will pull together and identify themselves as or with a group, makes us think that humans have a will to differentiate. By this we mean that humans seem to want and need to be an "us," not just a "me." In plainer terminology, we are a hopelessly social species. However, you cannot have an "us" without having a "them," and therein lies the problem.

Psychology has studied the human tendency to "attach" to other significant people for some time. John Bowlby (1969), in researching infant behavior, developed an entire "attachment theory" to describe the process by which humans grow strong emotional bonds to others—at first parents or caregivers—that long outlive their purely "instrumental" characteristics. Interestingly, the quality of the bond does not correlate directly to the quality of the care; humans seem to want to attach, and will attach, whether the caregiver is particularly "worthy" of attachment or not. Studies of nonhuman primates, and even of nonprimate species like ducks, have found similar tendencies to attachment (for example, Lorenz's famous duckling experiments). Most of the human research has focused on infancy, but there have been attempts to extrapolate research results to areas like political and national identity and ethnicity.

Taking this notion a step further, Henri Tajfel (1978; 1981) conducted a series of "minimal group experiments," in which he placed subjects into "groups" (fictitious, as it turns out) to perform various tasks and evaluate the performance of others. The imaginary groups were given neutral names like "red" or "blue," and "members" never met each other (because there were no others). Still, by the end of the experiment, subjects tended to demonstrate some preference for their "group" and some disdain for the "other group." For instance, subjects' evaluations of the performance of their own group were consistently higher than evaluations of the other group. Thus, the mere perception of membership in a group or category may be enough to instigate group formation and group judgment. He called his resulting theory *social identification theory* and described the process of social identification as occurring in three steps. First, *social categories* exist—reds and blues, Americans and Iraqis, Serbs and Bosnians, blacks and whites, and so on. Second, *social identification* takes place, and people come to identify with their category, to think of themselves as "a red" or "a blue." Finally, members use their identification for *social comparison*: they judge themselves in the context of their group and its standards, seeking to minimize differences between themselves and their group—and at least in some cases, maximize differences between themselves and other groups.

Sociologists have long talked about *in-groups* (the groups we as individuals belong to) and *out-groups* (the groups we do not belong to or consider "other"), but the implications for violence in group formation have only recently come to light. If we not only differentiate ourselves from "the other" but distance ourselves too, the potential for violence increases. This process can proceed far beyond this point. Ultimately, our inherently negative feelings and judgments of "them" (often based on no information whatsoever) can grow into a thorough dehumanization or demonization of "them." Only "we" are fully good and fully human, and "they" are something less—dogs, pigs, insects, worms, dirt, even devils. And the moral kid gloves are off when it comes to beings of lesser humanity: we may not be morally free to kill humans, but we are morally free to squash bugs, exterminate vermin, wipe the dirt off our (collective) shoes. Notice how common—and how potent—such dehumanizing language is for groups in conflict.

It is also much easier to commit violence against a group than an individual. Groups are relatively faceless (deindividuated). Not shooting until you "see the whites of their eyes" may lead to not shooting at all. Impersonal violence is less disturbing than personal violence for most normal humans, since we do not have to confront the fact that the "other" feels pain and has a family and loves his country and cause as much as we do. This is why wise leaders of violence do not allow followers to get close to the enemy, let alone befriend the enemy. It is hardest to hurt a friend, slightly less hard to hurt a fellow human, and least hard to hurt a nonhuman—or dehumanized—victim.

Cognitive Dissonance

Psychologists have learned that we humans have another strange quality about us that can be intentionally manipulated to inoculate us against qualms about our own violence. This quality if known as *cognitive dissonance*, which is our drive to make all of our experience consonant or consistent and to modify our perceptions if things get too dissonant. In other words, when we find ourselves in a situation that does not fit our expectations of ourselves or of others, we tend to "resolve" the "dissonance" by making a cognitive, or mental, shift. There are a couple of ways that this shift can go—we can change how we think about ourselves, or we can change how we think about others.

One of the prime directives of human life is for our lives to make sense, for our experience to be meaningful, and for that meaning to be consistent. Another prime concern is for us to feel good about ourselves, to feel we are good or competent people. But in a situation in which we are committing explicit violence, something has to give; we cannot maintain all of these positions simultaneously. We could, for instance, decide that the experience is not meaningful or consistent, but this could lead in the worst case to insanity. Sometimes, we use this escape hatch by blaming the situation for being "anomalous" or exceptional: "I am not usually like that, I don't know what happened." We might also choose to adjust our sense of ourselves, by admitting that we are violent and cruel people who like doing harm; this option is, however, extremely rare, as most perpetrators of evil see themselves as rather good people. In fact, if our violence is idealistic in nature, then we see ourselves as more than good people: we are *the* good people, the defenders of truth and virtue. So what usually happens, in situations of violence, is that we adjust our perception of the victim, seeing that person as, again, less than us, maybe less than human, and as deserving of a violent fate.

In short, the typical responses to cognitive dissonance are

1. Disengagement of the self—for example, telling ourselves that we were "not really there" (repression or dissociation), that we were not acting "in our right mind, " or that we had no choice
2. Emphasis on our own virtue—telling ourselves that we are doing a good work, that our cause is just, that our actions are necessary to bring about some greater good
3. Emphasis on the lack of virtue of the victims—telling ourselves that they deserved it, that they were "enemies of the people," that they were obstructions to the greater good or a better future, that they were sub-humans or demons

As various students of the human psyche and group phenomena have observed, these effects can be exploited to create a hostile and violent social reality and to create hostile and violent people. Often, those who want a revolution will start violence in the streets, as Arendt (1969) observed, to produce a violent ethos and a violent ideology; we might say that the violence precedes the reason for the violence and produces the reason for it. Savvy group leaders will use the "initiation" or "hazing" mechanism to inure members to violence and to secure their attachment to the group: "The group would not ask me to commit violence unless there was a good reason, and now I feel closer to the group because why else would I commit such violence myself?" is the desired psychological re-sponse. In the final analysis, the violence may be more important to the ideology than the ideology is to the violence—what counts is just getting people riled up and switching on all of the group-psychological mechanisms, regardless of their real purpose.

Desensitization

We are all aware of the concept and the power of desensitization; we fear its effect on children and ourselves from movies and cartoons and video games. The idea is simple: The first act of violence is the most difficult, and every sub-sequent act becomes more comfortable. So, if children see violence in the media or play violent games—on the computer or with toy weapons—the first step toward violence has been taken. Similarly, once the street-gang member, the soldier, or the revolutionary has committed his first aggressive act or taken his first life, violence becomes familiar, less disturbing, more tolerable.

There is good reason to believe that this process works and that people in authority take full advantage of it. Soldiers stick bayonets in dummies before they stick them in people. Medical students operate on cats and dogs, then cadavers, before they cut open humans, desensitizing them to blood. And, as we noted, gangs and clubs get members to commit petty acts before they ask them to commit major acts. Most humans, other than psychopaths, feel some sensitivity about the pain and suffering of others, but this sensitivity can be worn down with practice, gradually converting a normal person into a detached killer. As is probably well known, even psycho-killers often start their careers torturing or killing animals as children and, as they grow older, eventually graduate to humans.

And here is a final major component of the ability to inflict violence on others—indifference to the feelings of others. Individuals, groups, and societies that can easily put aside the experience of others, that can overlook the pain, the suffering, and the humanity of their victims, can commit violence against them much more freely. As we will see in later chapters, one of the key differences between violent and nonviolent parties is their degree of empathy and their interest in the well-being of others. If we take psychopaths as the most extreme manifestation of violent actors, a topic we will examine more closely in the final chapter of this book, we are not surprised to find that, "Compared to other people, they lack remorse, empathy, guilt, responsibility, emotional depth, and self-control" (Baumeister 2001: 221).

Self-Esteem

If you were to ask a person off the street about the typical perpetrator of violence, the answer would probably be that he or she suffers from "low self-esteem." This is one of the most pervasive and interesting myths in the understanding of crime and violence. In fact, the seriously violent have some of the highest—or most inflated—senses of self found among humans. Baumeister (2001) notes that in addition to lacking sensitivity, psychopaths are characteristically egocentric and grandiose.

We like to think that violent deviants must have low self-esteem, first, because we are inclined to blame all psychological problems on low self-esteem and, second, because it gives us a feeling of superiority over them. We are OK, but they have self-esteem issues. It is the same sort of misconception encountered previously, which holds that violent perpetrators must be crazy, bloodthirsty monsters. But we know now that a thin line separates us from them and that this line is often more about circumstances than personality; with some exceptions, violence is not committed by extreme people but by people in extreme situations. It is not, fundamentally, a "personality" problem.

If we actually look at the way violent individuals think and act, we find that their behavior really comes with (and from) a very high sense of their own worth and importance. If anything, their self-esteem is too high, giving them the impression that the feelings and suffering of others do not count for much. The two particular forms this exaggerated self-esteem often take are, as we mentioned earlier, egotism and idealism. If I am egotistical, only my thoughts and feelings and interests really matter, and others are at best a means to an end and at worst an obstacle to an end. Egotism tends to the dehumanizing thought patterns discussed earlier: "I am valuable, and you are not." Idealism tends to come with more "content"; that is, it is not just about me as an individual but about me as a member or representative or bearer of a higher group or higher message or higher good. The most dangerously inflated self-esteem is the self-esteem of the crusader or zealot, who thinks that anything outside his cause and community is wicked and must and will fall. Such a person can persecute and kill "righteously," because no calling is greater and no cost too great to pay for it.

In fact, if we reflect for a moment, it will become reasonable to view the ego of the chronically violent person not as low but as *fragile*. Violence more often emerges from *threatened* self-esteem than from low self-esteem. People with the highest opinion of themselves but the least justification for that opinion are often the first to commit violence in "self-defense." The husband who hits his wife because she does not show enough "respect"; the guy at the bar who starts a fight because someone looked at him funny; the religious zealot who persecutes others because he or she thinks everything outside their group is polluting; the political revolutionary who fears every independent thinker as a "counterrevolutionary"—these actions are symptomatic of threatened egotism and threatened idealism. These two self-esteem issues will help to explain, in our cross-cultural survey of violence in Chapters 3 and 4, why honor, pride, and male ego play such prominent roles in societies where violence is part of the everyday social fabric. The following section will flush out some of the issues and challenges in conducting research on violence in different social and cultural contexts.

STUDYING VIOLENCE: OPPORTUNITIES AND CHALLENGES

The process of collecting information always presents particular difficulties and challenges even when the subject of research is simple and clear to define. As we have seen, the definition of violence is slippery and evasive. Before we can analyze violence, we must determine what counts as violence. Then we must craft the proper tools and devices to capture the information we seek and to make the appropriate interpretive use of that information.

Violence is measured and catalogued in American society in many ways, which we will discuss in more detail in subsequent chapters. Measures of violence include crime reports to police, which are collated by the FBI, as well as official victimization studies (surveys done on the general public to learn how many of them have been victims of different sorts of crimes) and academic research done by psychologists and sociologists. Other sources of information include hospital records, social-service agencies, and other organizations that have frontline contact with offenders or victims. One of the most dismaying realities in this apparently straightforward process of information gathering is that the numbers generated by these various sources are usually quite at odds with each other. In addition to this problem is the very practical one that many crimes, violent and otherwise, go unreported. And what is unreported cannot be counted or analyzed.

Cross-cultural study of violence presents an even more daunting set of problems. First, other cultures and societies may not collect statistics on crime and violence at all. Second, what counts as violence and is documented as such may be very different from one society or culture to the next, including our own. Third, it can be extremely difficult to relate information pertaining to a variety of sociocultural contexts. Uncontrolled variables, faulty comparisons, and obscure causation may turn research results into pure guesswork. In this light, let us now consider some of the implications for studying and understanding violence in its different social forms and contexts.

Definition and Operationalization

Let us hope that we are sufficiently comfortable (or uncomfortable) by now with the problems of defining violence. Some of the issues we have examined so far are:

- Whose perspective and account of the violence is significant—the victim's, the perpetrator's, the audience's, or a combination of these?
- Do "legitimate" and "illegitimate" violence count equally?
- Is an act deemed to be violent within the context of study? (In one setting, punching someone may viewed as violence and in another as male horseplay or bravado.)
- Does only violence that is physical, as opposed to mental or emotional, count?
- Does only violence that does injury, as opposed to "harmless" violence, count?
- Does only violence that is intentional, as opposed to involuntary or accidental, count?
- Does only violence that is committed by and against humans, as opposed to that committed by or against other creatures, count?
- Is "mitigated" violence, such as self-defense, of equal significance as unmitigated violence?

And so on.

Until we have a settled and shared definition of violence, we really are just fumbling in the dark. We do not know what to collect or what to do with what we collect. And, as of now, we do not have a settled and shared definition. But let us proceed as if we did. After the subject of research has been defined, the next step in any procedure of data gathering is *operationalization*—that is, creation of the specific tools and measures to be used in gathering data. When we "operationalize" a topic, we choose *what will count* and *how we will count it*. For instance, in our data gathering on violence, we would probably elect to count violent acts resulting in death, as opposed to violent acts resulting in lesser injury or no injury. Say the specific phenomenon we seek to explore is "murder." First, we determine what will count as a murder. A car accident will not count. Suicide will not count. Killing in self-defense will not count. Killing while temporarily insane will not count. Any kind of accidental killing will not count. Killing by a dog or lion or tornado will not count. Killing of a dog or lion will not count. Many other incidents of death inflicted on one by the actions of another, or oneself, will not enter our equation.

Now, having selected our items, we must concoct instruments that will, with reliability and validity, get the information we have decided to get. In our own society, some of these decisions have already been made, and we have been collecting such information for decades. One basic device is the Uniform Crime Report (UCR), a compilation of police reports prepared annually by the Federal Bureau of Investigation (FBI). Of course, the validity of the UCR depends crucially on the quality and completeness of the reporting by local police departments. It also depends crucially on the willingness of the public to make such reports. It is entirely reasonable to assume that certain cases of violence, and certain categories of people, can be underrepresented in the report. In fact, it can be and has been argued that the very choice of items on the report—murder, assault, theft, auto theft, robbery, larceny, and burglary—tend to focus on lower-class and minority offenders in ways that inclusion of embezzlement or fraud would not. Another shortcoming of the UCR is that it does not collect a lot of contextual information about the crimes it describes. This and other deficits are supposedly filled by the National Crime Victimization Study, based on interviews with the public to determine the exposure to crimes that may go unreported and to collect other information about the details of these crimes; we will talk about this study in more detail in the final two chapters of this book.

Issues in Cross-Cultural Studies

Carol and Melvin Ember (1993) are the authors of a major review of the literature on the methods, findings, and challenges of cross-cultural research on violence. As they note themselves, fairly few such studies exist and those that do include relatively few variables. The authors also make a useful distinction between *cross-cultural* and *cross-national* research.

Cross-cultural research refers to comparisons of a phenomenon such as violence across all types of societies, from the smallest and most "primitive" to the largest and most "modern." This is the realm in which anthropology functions, and we will turn to it ourselves, starting in Chapters 3 and 4.

Significantly, cross-cultural research tends to favor small and nonindustrial societies, leaving out societies like our own; therefore, in a way, it is not as thoroughly comparative as it could be. Nevertheless, for understanding a phenomenon in depth, cross-cultural research is valuable, if not essential.

Cross-national research is the type with which we are more familiar, which compares rates and causes of a phenomenon like violence in various modern countries or nation-states. The difference between this sort of research and the cross-cultural variety amounts to more than a shift in subject. Cross-national studies tend to rely on data that are more quantitative—"objective" or numerical data of the sort collected by the UCR or Victimization Study mentioned earlier; on the other hand, cross-cultural studies tend to rely on more qualitative data, of the sort collected by fieldworkers doing their personal observations of a society. Anthropological fieldworkers, often if not ordinarily, do not have access to police records, court results, or other quantitative data because such facts may not even exist. However, Ember and Ember make the point that quantitative data may or may not be more accurate and trustworthy than qualitative data.

Therefore, a bigger problem with cross-cultural comparisons than the type of data they use is the particularity of each separate study that makes up the comparisons. Often or even usually, fieldwork is not done with the express purpose or goal of being incorporated into comparisons, so the operationalization of the variables in the study may be very specific to the society under investigation. Further, explanations of a phenomenon tend to be "intra-societal"; that is, they refer to various aspects of a particular society, which aspects might not exist or be relevant in another society. Finally, researchers never claim that the society or variable under consideration is "typical" or representative of other societies or situations, including whatever is available in their cross-cultural comparisons. This lack of control over variables and methods of data collection is potentially overcome, however, by the size and diversity of the sample. One of the main advantages, then, of cross-cultural research is that it draws on so many different sources and is more inclusive than any other type of research. Any one field study may be atypical or unrepresentative, but the sheer number of such studies, covering hundreds of different societies, tends to "smooth out" or "cancel out" the anomalies. Additionally, such comparisons may lead or force researchers to consider correlations and causes they had previously ignored or discounted and may produce surprising results simply because of their scale. Finally, there is no reason why cross-cultural studies must use only qualitative fieldwork data; with the purpose of comparison in mind, researchers can supplement traditional data with targeted quantitative information as well.

Ember and Ember state unequivocally that the two main challenges in cross-cultural research are definitions that fit the range of variation and operational measures that apply to the cases. They mention "homicide" as one term with a problematic definition. To us, infanticide is almost certainly a type of homicide or murder, but cross-cultural studies show that more than half of all societies practice it to some degree. One interpretation is that more than half of all societies commit child-murder; however, in many of those societies, their conception of infanticide is more along the lines of "postbirth abortion." As the authors assert: "It seems then that *when* a society socially recognizes a new person (before, at, or after birth) is related to whether or not infanticide is considered a crime" (Ember and Ember 1993: 220). However difficult this reality may be for us to accept, it raises the issue of the socially specific meaning of terms like "crime," "murder," and "person"—and highlights the fact that our definition of these terms is only one possible way of defining them, and probably not the most common way.

Even the killing of adults means different things in different societies and in different situations within societies. In many societies, killing members of one's own group or village was considered deviant, but killing outside one's own group was acceptable or desirable; it would be more akin to "war" than to "murder." In general, "some acts we call 'crimes' have no analogs in other cultures" (Ember and Ember 1993: 220), such as wife-beating, child abuse, and other kinds of violence that are "normal" in certain cultural contexts. We cannot apply our interpretations of these matters to them any more than they can apply theirs to us. One of the most important observations from this research is that not all acts of "violence," or even all acts of killing, are considered "abnormal" or "bad" or even "violent" in all societies. Usually, peace within the local community is encouraged (and often achieved), but violence against other communities may be condoned, as we just stated, and even violence against other groups within the local community may be accepted. If the community includes different families or lineages or other such groupings, people may not feel that all community members are "us," and violence is usually only proscribed against "us." Feuds, revenge killings, and other violent acts may make up the normal social structure not only of the multivillage society but also the village itself.

Reviewing the extant cross-cultural research, Ember and Ember notice a set of factors that seem to appear frequently enough to demand our attention. One is *child socialization* and violence. Three particular aspects of child rearing that seem related to violence are

1. Frustrating socialization
2. Conditions that may promote what has been called "protest masculinity"
3. Socialization for aggression (Ember and Ember 1993: 227–29)

Frustrating socialization refers to practices like harsh and punitive child training or low need-satisfaction (not fulfilling the child's needs). Protest masculinity arises when males feel the urge to forcefully express their sex- or gender-identity and importance, especially when that identity or importance has been somehow threatened by social circumstances. One of the leading such circumstances is father-absent households, which are common in many societies and not associated with poverty or dysfunction at all. In fact, one study of more than a hundred societies found a relationship between father absence (in the context of polygynous mother–child households) and violence, although we cannot rule out other confounding variables (Bacon, Child, and Barry 1963). Ember and Ember themselves favor the "socialization for violence" aspect, whereby a society more or less explicitly sets out to inculcate violent values and practices in children, especially in societies where war and warriors are prized. As they put it, "more war causes people to encourage more aggressiveness in their boys (to make them more capable warriors), and more socialization for aggression inadvertently causes more interpersonal violence (homicide and assault); in addition, war also has a direct effect on interpersonal violence, perhaps because war legitimizes violence" (Ember and Ember 1993: 224).

War, thus, becomes another factor in the prevalence of societal violence. By definition, war is violence, but war also appears to spawn violence in other ways, as alluded to earlier. Not only does violence occur during war but also after war:

> Whether a nation was defeated or victorious, homicide rates tended to increase following a war. These results ... suggest that a society or nation legitimizes violence during wartime. During hostilities societies approve of killing the enemy; afterward, homicide rates may go up because inhibitions against killing have been relaxed. . . .
>
> In the United States, for example, surges in violent crime rates occurred during the 1860s and 1870s (during and after the Civil War), after World War I, after World War II, and during the Vietnam War. (Ember and Ember 1993: 225)

They also single out *cultural patterns* of violence as well as *social structures* of violence. They note, for instance, that "societies with one type of violence have others" (225). Societies with higher incidences of war also have higher incidences of violent sports, beliefs in harmful magic, and more severe responses to crime. In other words, violence in one area of society is associated with violence in other areas; completely "contained" or "focused" violence is not the rule. Also, levels of violence are correlated with social factors like the size of the community, class stratification, gender inequality, and political integration beyond the community.

In conclusion, Ember and Ember (1993: 226–30) make the following recommendations for future cross-cultural research:

- More standardization of data collection and data operationalization.
- More emphasis on distinguishing the gender-role element of aggression. For instance, is aggression considered to be a component of the male role?

- More attention to male-female relationships as locus of social violence, particularly the spousal relation and other intrafamilial factors.
- More awareness of the importance of modeling and socialization—that aggressive role models produce more children prone to violence and that approval of aggression leads to more aggression. This modeling or valuing of aggression may be subtle or almost unconscious, but it is very effective nonetheless. Encouraging male sports, giving boys violent toys, even playing rougher with boys and teaching them to suppress their emotions can contribute to ultimately violent expression.
- More appreciation of the circular relationship between social factors and violence—that is, of the fact that size and complexity of society, the presence of violence, socialization toward violence, and other factors can be the cause of violence but are also the results of violence. Such insight might make it possible to explain violence and enable intervention, either at the point of socialization or the point of re-creation of social conditions that perpetuate that socialization.

Methodological Issues in Large-Survey Research

Rosemary Gartner (1993) expands on some of areas touched on by Ember and Ember, while discussing the opportunities presented by large-scale cross-cultural studies. As she notes, serious violence is comparatively rare, so large surveys document "enough of these acts for statistical analysis of trends over time and systematic comparisons of levels of violence across cultures" (199). Furthermore,

> Large-survey data allow consideration of properties of a culture or society that affect violent behavior but that can neither be reduced to individual or small-group characteristics nor uniquely identified in single-society studies. While rates of violent behavior are made up of the purposive actions of individuals, these actions occur in particular cultural, institutional, and structural settings and are shaped by group and systemic responses to them. Large-survey data are necessary for examining the processes that link violent behaviors at the micro-level with these macro-level influences. (200)

Some of the problems, however, that complicate such research, as we should expect by now, are:

- Assumptions about the equivalence of acts classified by various contributors in different societies
- Abstraction of violent acts from their interpersonal and cultural contexts
- Difficulties in documenting random and systematic measurement errors due to underreporting, misrecording, and overreporting
- Absence of information on forms of violence neglected by official data-collection systems

A number of devices exist to attempt to accomplish the goals of large-scale cross-cultural research on violence. For example, the United Nations has compiled data from its members since 1946, and in 1977 it began to conduct Crime Trends and Criminal Justice Surveys, gathering voluntary information on homicide, assault, sex crimes, robbery, and kidnapping among other crimes. INTERPOL, the International Criminal Police Organization, also collects and publishes data on violence, including murder (defined as "any act performed with the purpose of taking a human life" but excluding man-slaughter and abortion), rape, and other serious crimes. One vexing problem with the INTERPOL study is that not all countries participate and those that do participate do not do so regularly nor always send the same amount or quality of information, so each year's report suffers from the vagaries of that year's input. The World Health Organization prepares its own mortality statistics annually, based on information from forty to fifty countries, and other efforts like the Comparative Crime Data File (which includes facts on 110 countries) also collect their own data and distribute their own findings.

There are clearly benefits and liabilities to this type of research. The bene-fits are the scope and sheer volume of information. However, the liabilities concern the reliability and validity, and therefore the overall usefulness, of the end product.

> Violence that is noncriminal (e.g., official violence) or not direct and interper-sonal (e.g., delayed deaths from workplace hazards) is largely excluded from consideration. Moreover, the criminal and interpersonal acts of violence that are measured are subject to under-reporting, misclassification, and variations in classification. Because the extent of these errors is difficult to establish and no doubt varies across societies, correcting for them has not been possible. Consequently, most researchers view as untenable analyses that directly com-pare societies on their rates of such violent crimes as rape, assault, or robbery (Gartner 1993: 202).

Other countries also conduct victimization studies, but their methods and operationalizations are often so different that collating them into one big inter-national study is difficult, if not impossible. To compensate for some of these problems, a single unified International Crime Survey was undertaken in 1989 across fourteen countries (all Western—Australia, Canada, the United States, and eleven European countries). The ICS asked questions about three cate-gories of violence (robbery, sexual assault, and other assault), including loca-tion, harm done, and demography and lifestyle of the victims.

A few independent researchers have attempted to conduct their own cross-cultural surveys on violence. The Conflict Tactics Scales asks respon-dents to report on their own victimization of violence, including domestic vio-lence such as verbal abuse. At least a couple of surveys on the perception or definition of violence have also been done, including Newman's (1976) study of the perception of deviance across six countries and Archer and McDaniel's

(1989) analysis of high school students' conceptions of conflict resolution in eleven countries. Such studies expand the range of violent behaviors investigated but present obstacles in collating them to each other and to more mainstream "official" reports.

Notwithstanding the difficulties, these large-scale studies in concert have yielded some interesting results. One is that violent crime tends to be more prevalent in "less developed" countries than in "more developed" ones; the noteworthy exception is the United States, which has a violence rate greater than all other developed nations and many underdeveloped ones. Economic inequality, "broken" family structures, and "cultural support for violence" are all correlated to murder rates, especially in poorer countries, but "of the wide variety of political, economic, cultural, and social indicators included in these analyses, only one—income inequality—has shown a consistent (and positive) association with homicide rates" (Gartner 1993: 205). Unfortunately, studies with a very large number of entries ("large-n" surveys) lose much of their detail and contextual information, in contrast to "small-n" surveys, where more in-depth data can be collected on each incident. Such smaller studies "can devote more attention to cultural differences in the meaning and definition of violence" (Gartner 1993: 206). This research indicates that young people, urban people, and males are particularly common both as offenders and victims of violence.

RETROSPECT AND PROSPECT

Violence is many things to many people, and it is not a simple thing to understand, so it cannot be a simple thing to "fix." In some cases, it may well be a "fault" in the violent individual, but more often than not, research has suggested, it is an effect of social and cultural circumstances and of particular situations and variables. Even when it is the fault of individuals, we are still led to inquire why some societies seem to produce more such violent individuals than other societies do.

We have seen in this chapter some of the problems and challenges in defining and quantifying violence. We have also seen some of the basic "causes," or contributing factors, which we will look for throughout our review of diverse kinds of violence—familial, ideological/religious, political, and so forth—and examination of the violence that plagues American society. We can already identify four factors that play a central role in the formulation and justification of violence:

1. *Integration into groups*. Without going any further, the very existence and dynamics of groups increases the likelihood and intensity of violence.
2. *Identity*. When these groups are given a sense of "oneness," of common origin and destiny, the possibility of violence is even greater. Groups need

not have an identity at all for a "group mentality" to emerge (they can be mere mobs), but a shared identity secures the group in new and stronger ways.

3. *Ideology.* When identity groups possess a "doctrine" or "dogma" about the world and their place in it, violent action against other groups is likely; if these beliefs form a competitive and violent ideology, then such action is practically inevitable.

4. *Interest.* When a group has or thinks it has a common interest or interests—economic, territorial, political, and so on—and that others are a threat to those interests, then violence can appear to be an appropriate, if not inevitable, response.

Cross-cultural research has produced insight into the generation and function of violence, but there are many challenges to interpreting and using the information that has been gathered. Comparative studies point out connections that researchers might not have anticipated or been able to see at all if they had simply stayed close to home and only looked at our society or a few societies like our own. Of course, in a sense the work of observing and understanding violence cross-culturally is only beginning, and the present book is a contribution to that effort. Even so, Gartner (1993) has already found that certain sociocultural conditions seem to inoculate a society against interpersonal and collective violence, including

- Circumstances in which there is strong informal social control backed by highly consensual norms and values
- Circumstances in which individuals are linked in networks of communal obligation and mutual interdependence
- Circumstances in which social institutions encourage political integration and other relationships that crosscut exclusionary social groupings

"Societies with these characteristics," she concludes, "tend to have a collectivist or communitarian orientation that is reflected in their social, political, and economic ideologies and practices. This orientation may represent the sociocultural factor crucial to explaining well-known societal differences in violence" (208). The rest of this book will be an exposition and a test of this hypothesis. In the following chapter we will explore a variety of social-science theories on the causes and sources of human violence.

THEORETICAL APPROACHES TO VIOLENCE

Biological, Psychological, and Social

Every human society experiences violence of some sort or another—if not the violence of war and crime, then the violence of death and natural disaster. Every human society also tries to make some sense of the violence it experiences. Not all are "theoretical" about it, nor are all those that are theoretical necessarily "scientific" about their theories, but violence is inherently something that cannot be ignored and cannot be left alone. We try to find meaning in it, if only to "correct" or eliminate it. If the initial step in confronting any topic is definition, then the next step is explanation and hypothesis. Our definitions and explanations will determine our responses and policies—what kinds of interventions are necessary or whether intervention is necessary at all.

Analysts and scholars have attempted to observe and explain violence from a variety of theoretical perspectives. The two most general perspectives are the "internal" and the "external"—that is, whether the cause or source of violence is "inside" the violent individual (in his or her "mind" or personality or genes) or "outside" the violent individual (in the social situations, values, or structures in which he or she acts). These two overarching perspectives correspond roughly to biology and psychology on the one hand and sociology and anthropology on the other, with some interesting overlap in new disciplines like "sociobiology" or the study of how genes affect behavior. This chapter, therefore, will explore the range of theoretical accounts of violence from these fields, offering them as objectively as possible but with an eye to extracting from each what we can learn toward constructing a comprehensive understanding of the multifarious thing we call violence.

Before we look at the mainstream scientific theories of violence, let us consider some older, influential notions on the subject. Every human society has some conception of why humans do bad things to each other or of why bad things happen to people, even if not at human hands. Most of these conceptions, however, are not "scientific" in the sense of being based on careful and quantitative observation, methodological naturalism, experimentation, and cross-cultural consideration. Careful and quantitative observation means that people have attempted to set aside their preconceptions and prejudices and to take the facts for what they are, including measuring and counting behaviors and occurrences to obtain accurate information and arrive at reliable causal relationships. Methodological naturalism means starting from an assumption that human behaviors and consequences are determined simply by human beings. Experimentation, obviously, means deliberately setting up contrived situations and manipulating those situations in such a way as to "control" the "variables" that might influence the outcomes so as to identify regular relationships between conditions and results. And cross-cultural consideration means looking not just at your own society or societies very much like it but including other, even quite different, societies within our analysis. Naturally, throughout most of human history, humans have had little knowledge of or interest in other societies, either keeping at a safe distance from them or criticizing or condemning them as inferior, wicked, and maybe even less than human. However, as we learn from anthropology in particular, humans in all societies are just that—humans—and their behaviors and rules not only teach us about them but about ourselves, about the entire range of human potentiality and about ways of being that we may never have considered—or even known were possible.

SUPERNATURAL THEORIES

Most human groups have approached the problem of violence with a prescientific and even specifically supernatural outlook. From this vantage point, violence is more than just a natural or human phenomenon but a "spiritual" or nonhuman one. It becomes a result or manifestation of negative or destructive *intentional* (in the sense of having their own desires, "personalities," and intentions) realities that are in part within us and in part outside of us or beyond us. At bottom, violence is the expression of a nonhuman or superhuman malevolence (which may also explain human malevolence) referred to as evil.

Being(s) or Force(s) of Evil

One likely and common perspective is that bad things happen to people, and people do bad things to each other, because there are discrete beings or forces of badness or evil afoot in the world whose role and interest is to do harm. In the Christian tradition, evil is attributed to a single being of evil, Satan or the devil; however, at least some Christian traditions also recognize a more or less extensive set of evil beings such as demons. The devil and/or demons can cause harm either directly—by attacking people—or indirectly, by tempting people to evil or even "possessing" people and using them to do evil. In other societies, beliefs about evil or harmful spirits are different but common.

Spirits, such as spirits of various plants or animals or natural phenomena, may be wicked or mischievous or merely indifferent, but their invisibility, incorporeality, and power make them particularly threatening. In some societies, even the spirits of dead ancestors can be a problem, not so much because they enjoy hurting living humans as because they are unpredictable and capricious and outside of the realm of human rules and roles.

Not all societies believe that evil takes a "personal" form. Instead, evil may be an impersonal force, such as "bad luck" or "karma" or the misapplication of an otherwise positive or benign force like "mana" or "chi." In some societies, human beings may take advantage of supernatural forces through sorcery or witchcraft to do harm to other humans. Some religions even view evil not as a distinct force but as part of the inescapable fabric of reality. Buddhism for one sees the material world as a place of suffering by its very nature, where evil, sickness, sadness, decrepitude, and death reign. One cannot eliminate these truths, but one can respond to them.

With a supernatural attitude toward evil, violence is typically seen either as inevitable—we cannot stop the evil beings or forces from doing what they do—or as a temporary aberration that will be ended someday, when the being(s) and force(s) of good defeat the being(s) and force(s) of evil and establish a better way of life. In the former case, the most humans can hope for is short-term relief from violence and evil through ritual, offerings, sacrifices, prayers, and so on. In the latter case, humans can hope for much more—that, if they choose the "right side" and become "warriors" in the epic struggle between good and evil, they can eradicate evil and enshrine good. Interestingly, this process constitutes using violence to fight violence, and all the world is experienced as a place of fighting (see Chapters 6 and 7).

Human Nature, or Human Will

In the Christian tradition, the other essential source of bad or evil in the world is us—human nature and the exercise of human "free will." Christianity teaches that God gave humans free will, and with that will humans can choose to do either good or bad, and they often choose bad. There is, of course, still the being called the devil and his minions to tempt people to do wrong, but it is in the end always our choice and our fault. Even more, though, since the ancestors of all humans, Adam and Eve, chose bad in the beginning, then all of human nature—and even physical nature—is tainted and ruined by bad or evil. Thus, the Christian story goes, there was not even death or suffering or toil in the world until humans, by their rebellious and evil actions, brought them in. So, all the violence of the world—death, carnivorism, natural disasters, and all the rest—are somehow humans' doing.

Obviously, not all societies or religions believe exactly this account of humanity and evil. However, many if not most religions have some account of how humans and the world got to be the way they are, and since both humans and the world are ambivalent and complicated when it comes to good and evil, most offer some kind of explanation for why humans are bad or flawed and why the world is difficult and troubled. No matter what the specific explanation, it often comes down to choices that humans made in the formative period of the universe or to actions that the creator beings took to make the world and its human inhabitants the way they are.

From this standpoint, the goal of humans tends to be begging for forgiveness for their inadequacy and struggling to become better creatures. As fundamentally flawed, they cannot possibly fix their own problems or the problems they have caused, but they can hope for a "gracious" reversal of the "fallen" order of things and a reward some other day—in some other world—where pain and death and violence do not exist.

SCIENTIFIC THEORIES

These prescientific or supernatural conceptions are interesting and important, partly because they illustrate humans recognizing and struggling with the problem of violence or evil and partly because so many humans over the millennia have oriented their thoughts and behaviors in these terms. However, for a scientific understanding of violence, we must turn elsewhere. In recent, especially Western, history, people have looked instead to natural perspectives on human behavior in general and on violence in particular, and they have identified two overarching approaches:

1. An "individual" or "internal/mental/biological" point of view, asking what it is about specific individual humans that makes them act so.
2. A "group" or "external/social" point of view, asking what it is about human collectivities or circumstances that makes people act so.

Of course, no scientific theory can or does completely focus on one of these approaches to the exclusion of the other, and there are some theories that stand somewhere between or attempt to "bridge" the two. Still, it is a useful practice to orient our discussion around these two poles or tendencies. The former, the individual/internal/mental pole is represented by psychology and biology, while the latter, the group/external/social pole, is represented by sociology and anthropology.

Biological Theories

Biological theories of violence concentrate on the physical substrate of our nature and behavior. This substrate includes our brain, our body, our chemistry, and our genes, as well as more fanciful things like our facial features or the shape and texture of our skull. No matter what the specific emphasis of the theory, biological explanations look for what is "wrong with" the violent individual in terms of his or her physical characteristics.

Some of the earliest biological approaches to violence, and in general to crime and deviance, attributed it to physiological factors. For example, people often connected overall body morphology (the shape of the body) to antisocial behavior, dividing humans into categories of, say, endomorph (heavy and round), ectomorph (light and slender), and mesomorph (intermediate and muscular). Certain body shapes were simply more inclined toward deviance than others. This same folk approach to physical traits also developed explanations in terms of facial features (the old "shifty eyes" notion) and skull contours. The latter, known as phrenology, was actually a fairly elaborate "science" at one time, with detailed charts of the head and the various personality tendencies associated with them. By "feeling the bumps on the head" (more accurately, the protrusions and depressions on the skull), a skilled phrenologist could determine if you were the "criminal type" or not. Theorists have also laid blame for violence on things like too much testosterone or an extra Y chromosome.

In a more scientific vein, recent biological work has focused on the brain, both in terms of its physiology and its chemistry. Violence, along with other behavioral anomalies, has been studied as an effect of the physiology or function or health of the brain. For instance, chemical imbalances have been discovered to explain a number of negative behaviors, from depression to schizophrenia, and the appropriate drug therapies have been developed. Some have also attributed violence to the structure or the electrical functioning of the brain, leading to some dubious "cures." For instance, as we all know, two of the recommended treatments for violent behavior in not-so-remote history were electroconvulsive therapy (that is, "shock treatment"), which involved massive doses of electricity to the brain to disrupt its malfunctioning, and of course cutting out the offending parts of the brain, especially in the form of "lobotomy."

A final and controversial but promising application of the biological perspective to violence is *ethology*, or the evolutionary study of behavior. One of the great advantages of this approach to the problem of violence is a not only cross-cultural but cross-species comparison—one that makes us question whether violence is exactly a "problem" at all. Nature is innately violent: lions kill zebras, bacteria kill their hosts, and humans kill all kinds of things, including each other. The world that we live in seems almost to be designed for maximal violence and suffering. If something is this pervasive, there must be (1) some biological basis for it and (2) some adaptive reason for it.

There is no doubt whatsoever that species do harm to other species with impunity and that the continuation of nature depends on it—cats do not feel bad when they kill mice. It is a much more interesting and important task to consider the matter of intra-species aggression—that is, violence committed by members of a species against other members of the same species. The motivations can for the most part not be the same as inter-species aggression, which is usually for purposes of food. Such intra-species aggression can be between individuals of the same species but, significantly, can also be between *groups* of the same species. Such behavior is particularly relevant for human conduct.

Johan van der Dennen (2002) has written a major summary of the findings on "intergroup agonistic behavior" (IAB), which is defined as aggressive or violent interactions (for example, threatening; chasing; hitting; biting; injuring; and, in the extreme case, killing) between members of two or more spatially separate, distinct, and identifiable groups as members or representatives of such groups. Now, not just all species will or can demonstrate IAB, since not all species live in and act as groups; in fact, the study finds that the vast majority of species do not display IAB. Instead, the majority of their aggression is inter-individual, such as fighting over mates, food, or territory. This does not mean, of course, that non-IAB species do not do serious harm to each other on occasion. E. O. Wilson, the most prominent spokesman for the approach known as sociobiology, wrote that even nonhuman species showed infanticide, rape, mating violence, cannibalism, mutilation, and indeed killing: "Murder has now been observed frequently enough in gulls, hyenas, hippopotamuses, langurs, macaques, and some other vertebrates to suggest that it is both widespread and . . . far more common and hence 'normal' in these species than in man" (quoted in van der Dennen 2001: 3).

What most of this violence seems to share is a relation to reproductive fitness: committing violence against rivals, especially in the case of male rivalry, serves to reduce the fitness of the rival and/or enhance one's own fitness and/or reduce the number of the rival's offspring. Obviously killing other males or their progeny eliminates them from the gene pool, but merely chasing them away from the group, or wounding them, or exhausting them, can have beneficial effects for the winner. As a regular aspect of "natural selection," survival is all about reproductive success—individuals that are able to get the most food live the longest and breed the most (surviving) children, reproduce more of their own kind, and dominate the struggle.

It is a simple fact that males engage in more of this sort of behavior than females in virtually all species. Why is this? We might answer that males have more testosterone and are "naturally" more aggressive, but this is really just restating the question. Why do males have more of the aggression-making hormone, and why are they then more "naturally aggressive"? Again, an evolutionary answer makes the most sense. Males are willing to fight, to kill, and to risk mortal injury themselves because much more is at stake for them in the reproductive competition than for females. In most species, a female has no problem passing along her genes; essentially every female will breed at breeding time. However, since one male can fertilize any number of females, it is not necessary—in fact, not ordinary—that all males will reproduce. The dominant males will sire many more offspring than the recessive males, which is, from a natural-selection point of view, how it should be. But what this means is that, for males, the reproductive options are successful reproduction or genetic oblivion; those that do not win access to females disappear from the gene pool. Therefore the high-risk aggressive behavior of males is worth the risk, because if they fail to breed they are "genetically dead" anyhow. In other words, males are more "expendable" than females because most males will be genetically expended no matter what.

Looking now specifically at larger animals, in particular mammals, IAB has been documented in sixty-four species, *of which fifty-four are primate species.* Of the nonprimates, dolphins, hyenas, wolves, lions, and cheetahs have been observed to engage in intra-species intergroup aggression. Dolphins, for instance, are known to practice harassment of females by young males, who attempt to separate them from their group and even to "gang-rape" them. Packs of wolves will invade and attack other packs, and male lions will attempt to conquer and control another male's pride, often with lethal consequences. Lions, and also ordinary house cats, are likely to commit infanticide against the cubs or kittens of other males, making room for their own offspring.

Most such IAB, as well as most individual and intra-group aggression in the animal kingdom, is "ritualized" and not fatal. Animal behaviorists refer to the species-specific responses that put an end to the aggression before it goes too far as "inhibiting mechanisms." For example, when two cats are fighting, the battle usually stops before anyone gets seriously hurt when one antagonist rolls over and exposes its belly. The winner could easily now slash open the exposed area, but instead the gesture of surrender acts to "switch off" the aggression. Different species have different signals they send to indicate capitulation (think of humans putting their hands in the air or cringing on their knees), which signals usually end the confrontation. Thus fights do not go on very long, they are not ordinarily fatal, and they do not escalate into full-scale "war." In fact, intentional or orchestrated "war"—sustained violence between two communities of a species—is common in only two kinds of species: ants and higher primates.

Ant colonies have been observed to wage campaigns against each other that can last for weeks and that result in killing, cannibalism, parasitism, robbery, and even "slavery." "Genocidal" wars among ants make a certain kind of sense because of the low reproductive costs to ant communities: soldier ants are neuter drones that would not reproduce anyhow. Among primates, intergroup violence is seen in species from the most primitive, like lemurs, to the most advanced, like chimps and of course ourselves. In fact, there is a correlation between the "level of evolution" and the level of IAB, with chimpanzee violence resembling human violence rather closely—both demonstrating sustained war, murderous raids against other groups, and an exclusively male pattern of participation in the carnage (in a few lower primate species, females may be active in the violence too).

Within the primate category, IAB can take on a chillingly human aspect. Primatologists like Jane Goodall have described what can only be called "chimp warfare" with great surprise. Van der Dennen summarizes one such encounter as follows:

> Parties of up to ten males, sometimes accompanied by females and subadults, quite regularly patrol the boundaries [of the group's territory], keeping close together, silent, and alert, often stopping to listen intently, apparently actively searching for signs of neighbors. Sometimes they climb a tree to scout the "hostile" territory of the adjacent community, just like a human reconnaissance party might do.... If no members of the neighboring community are detected, the patrol may stealthily intrude into the "enemy" territory. When a fairly large "enemy" party is encountered both parties may engage in vocal and gestural agonistic displays, or one of them may charge and chase the other away, or both give up and return to their core areas. At other times, a party, upon spotting "enemies," may flee, thus avoiding encounter. When, however, small parties or single "enemy" chimpanzees, particularly anestrous females, are encountered by the "warriors," these may be severely and viciously attacked and killed. (van der Dennen 2002: 19–20)

In Goodall's investigations, she recorded five lethal attacks and thirteen other attacks that produced severe wounds and bleeding.

This brief description leaves the impression that chimp groups not only fight when they have to but actively seek out opportunities for conflict. This is precisely what the observers suggest—that the chimps "looked as if they were aiming for the best chance of encountering another group" (van der Dennen 2002: 20). Bygot adds that the attacks featured "unusual brutality and persistence":

> All observed lethal attacks were unprovoked and lasted at least ten minutes. The victim was deliberately held down by some of the attackers, and subjected to a treatment more brutal than any found in intracommunity aggressive episodes. As Itani (1982) phrased it: "antagonistic interactions of a group versus an individual, or a group versus another group, *with the intent to kill*, is peculiar to chimpanzee society." (Quoted in van der Dennen, 20; italics added.)

Interestingly but not unexpectedly, the most serious violence tends to be committed by males and against other males or against females that are not in their sexually receptive state; females are no doubt desirable to the males of the attacking group, and accordingly sexually receptive females are often led away or kidnapped to be integrated into the victors' community.

Significantly, gorillas, orangutans, and other higher primates do not exhibit these behaviors. What is different about chimps—and humans—that might account for this behavioral difference? Scientists speculate that it may have to do with the role of the males in the group. In other words, the characteristics that the most systematically violent primates—chimpanzees and humans—share are

- Male domination
- Male–male cooperation, especially social structures in which males band together in "discrete solidarity groups," or coalitions
- Territoriality and the willingness to fight and die for territory
- Treatment of females as a transferable or portable resource for males
- A kind of "ethnocentrism" that distinguishes members of our group from members of other groups
- A kind of "xenophobia" that makes members of our group averse or hostile to other groups
- An ability and willingness to ignore inhibiting mechanisms and practice violence and even cruelty well beyond the needs of the situation or the capabilities of other species

These are, of course, the very social characteristics that most human groups exhibit.

In conclusion, Konrad Lorenz (1966), of the duckling "imprinting" experiments, has studied aggression and noted the same critical features. Many species are violent toward their prey and toward their feeding and mating rivals, but few show the persistent and intense violence of apes and humans—the "most evolved" species. He acknowledges that the identification with an "us" and the discrimination against a "them" can inevitably lead to violence against strangers or outsiders and a dangerously close and closed bond among our "own kind" and that these two factors can enhance each other. He is also aware of that unique (or not entirely unique, since chimps do a certain amount of it) phenomenon of culture, which he calls "pseudo-speciation" or the creation of sets within species that distinguish themselves from other members of the same species. "The dark side of pseudo-speciation," he writes, "is that it makes us consider the members of pseudo-species other than our own as not human, as many primitive tribes are demonstrably doing, in whose language the word for their own particular tribe is synonymous with 'Man' " (83). Of course, we should add that the result of treating other pseudo-species (societies or cultures) as less than human is not restricted to primitive tribes by any means.

Psychological Theories

The other major discipline that tends to look for "internal" causes for human behavior is psychology. Psychology ascribes the bulk of human action to the "mind" or the "personality," which is not without its contact points to the external "objective world" (even psychologists accept that much of personality is learned) but which constitutes an inner reality from which behavior flows. It is also not without consequences that psychology originally grew out of biological studies of human behavior, including brain studies and studies of instincts and "drives." In this section we will look at a selection of specific psychological theories of violence and assess what they have to offer to an overall understanding of this pervasive phenomenon.

Psychoanalysis   One of the first comprehensive psychological theories of human nature was Freud's psychoanalytic theory. His view is a combination of instinct/drive thinking and a basic "social psychology" of how these instincts or drives are shaped by encounters with "objects," including other people. His theory also evolved over his lifetime, so there is no single version of psychoanalysis that quite captures every aspect of the perspective.

Generally speaking, psychoanalysis contains two major components: (1) instincts, or drives, which are natural, unstoppable directions of energy that control our desires and our goals, and (2) a tripartite division of "mind," which is an enduring but dynamic commitment or "canalization" of these drives, which results, in particular, from confronting and compromising with "reality." Let us discuss the mind first. Freud envisioned that human infants were creatures of pure desire; they want what they want when they want it. All of the impulses with which we are born, all of the stuff that makes us human, are part of the primitive, nonsocial part of the mind that he termed the *id*. However, no one can always have what they want when they want it, so the infant has to learn, to his or her great frustration, that there are ways to get what you want and times when you cannot have it. The part of the mind that develops to relate to external reality and arrange for the satisfaction of the id is the *ego*— the "I" or the part that feels the most like me to me. The ego is crafted as an interface between the deep and unconscious part of the personality and the external world. It is the "surface" of the mind, the "conscious" part. The ego knows how to compromise and wait and do other necessary and appropriate things, but the id knows none of this. It just wants. The third part of the mind is the "critical" or even "moralistic" part—like the internalization of a judgmental parent—called the *superego*. The superego keeps watch over the ego and provides a sort of inner voice, criticizing and judging it.

The id is, in his view, the most natural, spontaneous, and untamed domain of the personality; part of it cannot be acceptably expressed in public and part of it cannot possibly be brought to "consciousness." It is the "other" within us (*id* means "it" in Latin), containing not only the stuff that could not even theoretically be raised to the surface but also the stuff that has been actively pushed down into it or denied to exist. This process Freud designated *repression*, or the energetic suppression of elements of our own nature or experience. Freud's entire model of mind is a very energetic one, and repression requires a commitment of energy but is never entirely successful; it could not be, since the repressed contents are still undeniably instincts and drives. If sufficiently repressed, they will still manifest themselves in some way—often as dreams, neurotic symptoms, "slips of the tongue" (Freudian slips), or deviance. Violence and aggression, on this account, could be expressions of repressed id.

What exactly is down there in the shameful basement of the mind? The main contents are the drives or instincts. In Freud's first formulation of the theory, the drives amounted to a single force—the *pleasure principle*, or pleasure instinct. Mind exists to maximize pleasure and minimize pain. However, in his later work—especially after the shattering experience of World War I—the pleasure principle seemed inadequate to explain the amount and virulence of human destructiveness. He added a second instinct—the *death instinct*—to the forces of the unconscious id and also assembled a more sophisticated and metaphorical picture of the drives. The pleasure principle, *eros*, was not just about feeling pleasure and avoiding displeasure but about "integration" or "union." It was the part of us that wanted to unite with other humans—whether in love, sex, or community—and even to keep ourselves integrated as individuals. However, it was opposed by the death instinct, *thanatos*, that wanted not so much death as *disintegration*. The goal of the death instinct was to disunite, to disintegrate, to return the personality to a lower or even the lowest possible energy state, which would be passivity or death. It opposed the integration of the personality, which required enormous energy commitments, and it opposed the integration of the individual into larger social aggregates—couples, families, communities, nations, the human race.

Human existence, for Freud, was a constant and irresolvable tension between these two instincts—both real, both natural, both human. Furthermore, as humans advanced in the project of integrating ever larger groups, the death instinct had to be repressed more and more effectively. We could not discharge our aggression against our lover, or our family, or our society, or potentially our entire species, but still the instinct could not be eliminated or denied. Freud saw this instinctual blockage expressed in two particular forms—unusually vicious wars, like the World War I, and mental illness, which was basically the death instinct turned on the self. In other words, violence was natural and instinctive to humans, and it would be expressed, either against others or against oneself. And the more we denied and repressed it, the more forcefully it would return and the more deviantly it would manifest itself.

Behaviorism   Refusing to accept the "depth psychology" of Freudianism and its spin-offs, early psychologists suggested that such talk was mere pseudo-science, while others criticized it for being unobservable. We cannot see the mind—certainly not the id and the ego, the drives and instincts—so how can we measure it or test it or use it in any meaningful way? A predictable response to the perceived evasiveness and impracticality of psychoanalysis was a completely opposite approach, to disregard what goes on "in the mind" (in the extreme cases, even to deny that there is such a thing as mind) and to focus on what we could know and observe—namely, behavior. Not incidentally, all of the formative work in behaviorism was performed on animals (cats, dogs, pigeons, and the like), which presumably do not have an unconscious and an ego like humans, so applying the findings to us is problematic at best.

Among the key names in behaviorism are Ivan Pavlov, E. L. Thorndike, and of course B. F. Skinner. Pavlov, as everyone knows, was the psychologist who discovered the "conditioned response" in dogs that led them to salivate at the sound of a noise. Normally a noise would go off before feeding time, initiating a chain of events (noise—food—saliva). Pavlov discovered that even without the food the dogs would still salivate, as if they had learned to connect the noise with the food. The response, salivation, was a reflex to food, but salivating to the noise was a learned response, a conditioned reflex. By manipulating the circumstances, he also discovered several traits of such conditioned reflexes.

- *Extinction*—the conditioned reflex would fade away if the pairing of the unconditioned stimulus (here, the food) and the conditioned stimulus (here, the noise) ceased to occur. In other words, the behavior was temporary, lasting only as long as it was "reinforced" with real results.
- *Generalization*—the conditioned reflex would occur if the conditioned stimulus was similar, though not identical, to the original stimulus (i.e., a different but similar sound would give the same results).
- *Differentiation*—the animals could learn to distinguish between stimuli that were reinforced and those that were not.
- *Pathology*—if the animals were conditioned to respond to one stimulus but not another, and the two stimuli were modified to become confusing or anomalous (e.g., difficult to tell apart), the animals would show distress and "neurotic behavior."

Thorndike performed his experiments with cats, which had to find their way out of a specially designed box. His work suggested too that the animals hit on a solution to the "problem" by trial and error but that gradually erroneous behaviors would be extinguished and only successful ones would be retained. He called this process the Law of Effect—that is, only behaviors that have the desired effect are "learned" and preserved; ineffective behaviors are eventually lost. His second Law of Exercise went on to posit that a learned response will be stronger the more times it is used successfully.

B. F. Skinner is known as the arch-behaviorist for his insistence that behavior is everything and that "mind" is nothing. According to this perspective, which became known as the "black-box" view of behavior, a stimulus goes "into" the box of mind, something unknown and potentially unknowable happens "inside" the box, and then behavior comes "out" of the box. Along with "mind," Skinner discounted chimerical concepts like "personality" or "feelings" or "intentions"; only overt and observable behavior is meaningful and measurable. Accordingly, he saw all behavior as learning by means of reward and punishment. The behavior of animals (and humans, presumably) could be "shaped" by controlling the rewards. If a subject begins to exhibit a desired behavior (the experimental or therapeutic goal), the subject can be rewarded so as to produce more of that behavior. As the subject nears the desired behavior, responses closest to the goal are rewarded; until eventually, all undesirable behaviors are extinguished and the goal achieved. Skinner called this entire process *operant conditioning*.

Subsequent experiments that refined the variables proved that some forms of reinforcement—especially "intermittent" forms whereby the subject was not rewarded every time the stimulus occurred—actually made the reflex stronger. None of the experimenters studied violence or aggression as such, but the implications of these experiments are clear. First, violence, like all other behaviors, is learned. Further, it would be learned more strongly and practiced more often if it was "rewarded," that is, if it was successful in some way. The rewards might be money or power, praise, or merely a good feeling about oneself. Hypothetically, then, violent behavior could also be extinguished if it became ineffective. Finally, there was no need, in fact no advantage, to appeal to "violent personalities" or "violent instincts" or any other such mystical talk to understand and correct violence or any other form of deviance. By simply controlling the environment and making violence "profitless," we could weaken it to the point of disappearance. It might be worth looking at Skinner's utopian novel *Walden Two* to examine his idea of an engineered behaviorist society.

Frustration–Aggression Hypothesis   A hypothesis (not quite a full-blown theory) that in ways mixed the insights of psychoanalysis and behaviorism was the frustration–aggression hypothesis of John Dollard. He noticed, not unreasonably, that when a subject encounters an obstacle to achieving its aims, the frustration it feels at the experience can lead to violence. The aggressive response may be an attempt to remove or destroy the obstacle (like breaking down a barrier between a hungry man and his food), or it may simply be "letting off steam" from the buildup of frustration. Either way, it is possible to reconcile certain aspects of the two theories above by allowing that humans do have drives or instincts to reach certain goals but that when circumstances thwart their efforts they become hostile. Additionally, if aggression proved to be a good way to deal with obstacles, such behavior would be rewarded, reinforced, and repeated. This hybrid view explains violence as an intersection of instinct and experience without reverting to an "aggressive instinct."

Social Learning Theory   Dollard and his partner Neal Miller are largely responsible for a more general theory of which the frustration–aggression hypothesis is a small component. Called *social learning theory*, it attempts to incorporate the best of behaviorism—that behavior is in fact learned and rein-forced—but introduces a noninstrumental and purely "social" aspect to the process of learning as well. The researchers noticed, for instance, that indivi-dual animals did not have to learn responses all by themselves each time but that they could observe and learn from each other. If rats could learn by imita-tion and not just conditioned reflex or operant conditioning, then how much might humans learn from each other through sheer shared experience, verbal communication, and higher cognitive processes?

Albert Bandura is one of the key figures in applying this notion to aggres-sive behavior in humans. Observing and experimenting with children, he dis-covered that they would tend to imitate the behaviors they saw in models, whether those models were adults, peers, or fictional characters encountered on TV and elsewhere. *Modeling* was the central concept. Other humans (or humanlike beings, including cartoon or video-game characters) provided examples of how humans might or ought to behave. Children would see this behavior and "try it out," even when there was no particular instrumental value in the behavior (i.e., they were not going to get any particular praise or reward for doing so). The imitation of the behavior itself constituted a "rehear-sal" for the behavior, increasing its likelihood in the future. The behavior would stick, especially if some reinforcement did occur (say, they got some candy out of it or got some attention or praise from peers or superiors).

Bandura and his colleagues used various devices to test this process, giving children violent TV programs to watch or violent peers to play with. Then they observed the children in natural or experimental settings. In one study, they gave children a "punching clown" (the kind that bounces back up when you knock it down) after their violent social input, and the children were more aggressive toward the clown than other children who did not get the same input. It seems clear, then, that seeing violence and getting the opportunity to practice violence does in fact increase the likelihood of using violence—that violence is, at least in part, a learned behavior. Again, it need not even lead to any particular rewards—one of the fundamental aspects of social learning the-ory is that behaviors may be and often are learned for their own sake, because those are "the things we do"—but positive rewards can only serve to strengthen the behavior and make it even more likely and "normal." Ulti-mately, once we have learned violence from our models, we become models for others (particularly children), who observe and imitate our behavior. Vio-lence or any other behavior ends up as "our way" of being.

Rational Choice Theory   Finally, Albert Ellis and others have emphasized the rational element of human behavior—that is, that people choose their behaviors based on their assessments of the current circumstances and the best possible responses to those circumstances. In a sense, people perform a little "cost–benefit" analysis every time they do something, weighing the behavioral options and perceived outcomes and selecting the option that appears to offer the best overall outcome.

In such a model, termed *rational choice theory,* violence would be considered (by the violent actor) as a rational choice to his or her given conditions. Say, if the person is poor and has little prospect of getting a good job, he or she might turn to robbery or burglary, since it is the next best decision. Of course, if the theories discussed earlier have any value, the choice of violence might be a self-sustaining habit, as each violent performance is a rehearsal for the next. Also, if others in our experience have made the same choice, with some success, and if our own choice leads to reinforcement, then the choice of violence is highly predetermined. Still, rational choice theory says that violence would be a rational choice.

The import of this view is twofold. First, if violence is a choice, then violent perpetrators are certainly not irrational nor even abnormal; rather, what is deviant is not the individual but the situation or the decision-making process. In more favorable circumstances, the same individual would choose a "better" course of action. Second, therefore, there is a way to reduce or eliminate the violence from a social system: reduce or eliminate the situations that result in violent choices. If people are violent out of poverty, ameliorate poverty. If people are violent out of racism or male chauvinism, change those conditions. In this essentially optimistic view of the world, violence is not done by bad people but by people in bad circumstances. Give them more positive circumstances and they will rationally choose more positive behaviors.

Social Theories

The biological and psychological theories discussed earlier have zeroed in on "internal" factors that cause or promote violence, though not to the complete exclusion of "external," or social factors. In fact, even in the most "internal" of theories—psychoanalysis—the contact between the individual and the outside world affects his or her behavior in critical ways. In contrast to psychologists, sociologists and anthropologists have attempted a more thoroughgoing description of human behavior in terms of the systems and structures that surround and influence individuals. They give much less attention to "mind" or "personality," at least as original sources of behavior, and much more attention to society and culture, the behavioral structures and the "webs of significance" that exist before we are born and that persist after we die. We simply participate in them for a while and take most of our individual shape from them.

There are two general approaches that inform both sociology and anthropology, which is one reason why we will review these two fields together in this section. Another reason for doing so is that they share a set of conceptual tools, such as *group, norm, institution*, and of course *culture*. Both begin not with the individual but with the external influences on the individual—the norms and rules of his or her society, the groups of which he or she is or is not a member, the institutions in which he or she participates, and most fundamentally (especially for anthropology) the culture of his or her society. In the extreme case, the individual disappears as an individual and becomes, analytically, little more than a "position" or a nexus of roles in a social system, but both disciplines also consider how the individual is formed and shaped by the social forces that exist outside of him or her. Thus, although sociology and anthropology do not explore the "inner realm" of humans, they cannot ignore it either. They simply conclude that the inner realm is, at least to a large extent, an effect or product of the outer social world.

Functionalism   One of the two basic theoretical approaches in sociology and anthropology is *functionalism,* that is, the view that any "social fact" (a behavior, a group, a norm, an institution, etc.) has a function and can best be understood in terms of that function. The function is what the social fact does in society—what it achieves for society, its reason for being. For instance, the function of the economy would be to get people fed or to distribute scarce resources. The function of the family would be to bear and raise children, regulate sex, share labor, and provide love and companionship. These functions can be distinguished by the goals they achieve for individuals and by those they achieve for society as a whole.

It is easy to appreciate the needs individuals have and how social rules or norms or institutions might fill those needs, but it is less easy to grasp the "needs of society" and how violence might serve either. After all, is society not just the sum total of all the individuals in the group? And is violence not universally disruptive and "dysfunctional"? To both questions, some schools of sociology and anthropology say no. Society is actually more than the sum of its parts (individual humans), and it has its own needs and requirements. Perhaps the most fundamental of these needs is cohesion or integration—to get people to stick together as a society, to continue to exist as a society. It is always possible that individuals might be better able to meet their needs alone than collectively, yet everywhere humans do and must pursue their interests together as a society. And many things threaten the existence and persistence of society, not the least of which are the violent or conflictual behaviors that humans engage in: internal disagreements, crimes, wars, feuds, class differences, and so on. Yet functionalists find "functionality" even in these "disintegrative" activities.

The dean of sociological functionalism is Emile Durkheim, who discussed the integration of society in such classic works as *The Rules of Sociological Method, The Division of Labor in Society, Suicide,* and *The Elementary Forms of the Religious Life.* His central interest is social solidarity—the processes by which individuals cling together to constitute a society. Following Ferdinand Tonnies, he identifies two principal modes of social solidarity, referred to as

G

"mechanical" and "organic." Mechanical solidarity (*gemeinschaft*) exists when all members of a society are essentially "alike," that is, when there is a minimum of social differentiation. His model for such a case is "primitive society" (like the Australian aboriginals), who share a single "collective conscience" created in their close relationships and their religious rituals. Individuals are integrated by being basically the same. Organic solidarity (*gesellschaft*) is different, though, because according to this concept, people are divided into distinct "types" with distinct rules and roles yet cast into mutual dependence on each other. Modern societies with their class, race, gender, age, and other divisions represent this sort of solidarity.

It might seem at first glance that "mechanical" societies would be well integrated and "organic" ones less so, but this is not the case. Even before Durkheim, Herbert Spencer offered the analogy between a society and an organism. Society *is* an organism in the sense that it is composed of various systems (groups and institutions constituting "organs") that must work together for the functioning of each other and the whole. In a way, then, a society with a division of labor might be more integrated than one without, since we nonfarmers cannot live without the farmers who feed us. But society faces a problem: potentially destructive differences in ideals and interests pit one element of society against another. Durkheim admits this problem but finds that it is normally solved adequately by socialization; each person becomes "adjusted" to his or her "station" in society, accepts the legitimacy of social differences, and does his or her part for the good of the whole. That is, division normally produces solidarity. But not always.

Societies also produce a certain amount of "deviance," including crime, suicide, conflict, and violence. The question is whether these behaviors are functional too or whether they are dysfunctional. In a variety of ways, Durkheim and those who follow him suggest that they are actually functional. For instance, he cannot help but note that crime is omnipresent in all societies; therefore it is empirically or statistically "normal." Further, each particular society has its characteristic rate and distribution of crime, which is normal for that society. According to this view, the high incidence of murder in America is not deviance at all but an American norm. Beyond that superficial notion, he asserts that crime and conflict function to identify, clarify, and strengthen those very collective morals and sentiments that make society possible in the first place. The criminal or deviant draws down our condemnation precisely because he or she does not follow the rules, is not like us in critical ways. In fact, crime and conflict would not be deviant at all were it not for the very collective morals and sentiments that call them deviant. They presuppose social solidarity and also perpetuate it.

So, in one regard, crime and conflict mobilize society to activate and practice its collective conscience. On the other hand, deviance can represent a kind of "friction" that appears when the society and its divisions are not "working" or when those divisions are no longer perceived as equitable. Then, crime and conflict act as a kind of social "thermometer" that measures the health of a society. The crimes and conflicts are not dysfunctional as such but are rather the *symptoms* of a dysfunctional or at least changing society. The function, clearly, is to alert people to the threat to the health of the body social and to do something about it. Violence might be likened to a fever, which is not be hated but to be treated, not directly but at its underlying causes. Violence is a kind of "social purging," as when the sick body vomits, trying to disgorge something unsalutary from the system—so as to return to homeostasis and health.

Durkheim finds one other function for crime or conflict, and that is as a source of social change. Precisely because collective conscience is so strong, it often does not allow flexibility; the result can be social stagnation. However, deviance from the system can be the harbinger of a new system or at least a new norm or group or institution for the system; obviously, anything new will be seen as deviant to some extent. Thus, today's crime may be tomorrow's norm, and conflict or even violence may be "creative" in the end.

Functional Conflict: Simmel and Coser   Other sociologists carried the functional analysis of conflict further, most notably Georg Simmel and Lewis Coser; in fact, the work of the latter is a close reinterpretation of the former. Simmel wrote his seminal piece on conflict in 1908, in which he argued that conflict was a kind of social behavior like any other. All society, truth be told, is some combination of "positive" and "negative" forces, and the negative ones—usually seen as discordant or disintegrative—can be as important to the social system as the positive ones. Unity and discord, he writes, are not opposites at all; conflict may be not only a part of a social relationship but may actually constitute the relationship.

Simmel seems to accept the reality of an innate instinct or drive toward hostility in humans, which takes many forms: competitive and antagonistic games, legal conflicts (as in trials), conflicts over interests, conflicts between close or intimate people, and conflict between groups. However, in every one of these cases, individuals must "be in relation" in order to have conflict; conflict is a social relationship. He notes, interestingly, that individuals who have many factors in common may treat each other more roughly than individuals with less in common—what has come to be called the "narcissism of small differences."

We are particularly interested in what Simmel has to say about group conflict. He sees it as functional in a variety of ways. For one thing, conflict enhances one's awareness of the group and the values and interests of the group. It also leads to increased integration and centralization of the group; individuals and collectivities must put aside their differences and observe higher integration in order for the group to meet its challenges and reach its goals. Thus, an internal reorganization that is functional occurs within the group. Finally, the conflict identifies and strengthens the boundaries of the group, making it clear who is and is not within it.

There is a danger here as well, though. The group in conflict cannot allow much internal variation. Groups in conflict tend to be internally intolerant: "they cannot afford individual deviations from the unity of the coordinating principle beyond a definitely limited degree. The technique for this is sometimes an apparent tolerance which is exercised in order to be able to expel with all the greater decisiveness those elements which definitely cannot be incorporated" (Simmel 1908/1955: 93). In fact, such a group will risk ending up with a smaller membership if it can also achieve a tighter and more committed membership (as Lenin will urge: see Chapter 9). Also, such conflicts in which the "personal" element is minimized and replaced with a collective one tend to be more ferocious and intractable. Personal motives, Simmel argues, are ultimately more merciful and less radical than group motives; in the group "we sometimes abandon ourselves to it more extensively, passionately, and with more concentration" (38). This is particularly so, he notes, when the issues at stake are "truths" for the groups.

Coser (1956) fine-tunes Simmel's argument in a variety of ways, making the following claims:

- Conflict establishes and maintains boundaries between groups and societies.
- Conflict establishes and affirms group identity.
- Conflict is often more intense in close relationships than in distant or nonexistent ones.
- Conflict is often more intense when there are few internal differentiations than when there are many (the many differentiations can also be multiple ways of affiliating and "cross-cutting" potential conflicts).
- Conflict leads to increased internal cohesion.
- Conflict can create new norms and rules.
- Conflict in which individuals feel that they are fighting as representatives of groups can be more intense and radical than when they are fighting as individuals.

Conflict and Cultural Integration Traditionally, anthropology has tended to emphasize the stability, homogeneity, and discreteness of its subject societies—the small tribal societies with which it is most often associated. Evans-Pritchard (1951) in his summary of anthropological research stated as much when he claimed that the discipline aims to study "those societies which are structurally so simple, and culturally so homogeneous, that they can be directly observed as wholes" (8–9). However, it was already clear to workers in the field that few if any societies were really that homogeneous (versions of Durkheim's gemeinschaft) and in fact they did not have to be.

Ten years before writing *Social Anthropology*, Evans-Pritchard had collaborated with Meyer Fortes on *African Political Systems* (1940), in which they observed that many indigenous African societies appeared to be "an amalgam of different peoples" and that all except the Zulu and Bemba "are still today culturally heterogeneous" (9). Cultural diversity *within* a particular society became a more prominent and important issue. As Leach (1954) pointed out in Burma, a cultural zone like the Kachin Hills area "is culturally diverse and the political organization is structurally diverse (63)" and even worse, the cultural and structural variation do not mirror each other. He goes on to conclude "that the system of variation as we observe it now has *no* stability through time" (ibid.).

Max Gluckman (1956), working also in the African context, made the connection between social organization and integration on the one hand and conflict on the other. In his *Custom and Conflict in Africa*, he showed decisively not only that peace and stability are not necessary for social cohesion but that conflict could be socially integrating in its own way. All societies, he found, contain terms of hostility and competition, if not outright conflict and violence (like feuds and vendettas). These societies all contain internal differentiation, into kinship groups, age grades, gender groups, economic classes and castes, ethnic or national groups, and so forth. These differentiations pit people against each other in the same society as members of subsets with differing interests and loyalties. However, rather than blowing a society apart, these internal complexities actually provide a kind of "cross-cutting" organization in which individuals are bound to each other in diverse and even contradictory ways; this person may be my mate in one regard and my enemy in another. The central discovery of his study is, then, "how men quarrel in terms of their customary allegiances, but are restrained from violence through other conflicting allegiances which are also enjoined on them by custom" (24)—that is, that internal differences and even disagreements can be highly functional and integrative. As he concluded, "these conflicting loyalties and divisions of allegiance tend to inhibit the development of open quarrelling, and ... the greater the division in one area of society, the greater is likely to be the cohesion in a wider range of relationships—provided that there is a general need for peace, and the recognition of a moral order in which this peace can flourish" (25).

Conflict Theory   The second general theoretical approach, an alternative to functionalism, is *conflict theory*. Oddly, although conflict theory has treated conflict and violence as a central concept from its very beginning, in some senses it shares much of the attitude that functionalism does toward these phenomena. As we have seen, functionalism is often not "anti-conflict" at all. And although conflict theory disapproves in an important way of the present conditions in society that make conflict real and necessary, it is not opposed to conflict either and certainly views it as creative and even desirable. In ways—and more so for some than others—it positively celebrates conflict.

The father of all conflict theories is Karl Marx, who put conflict ぅ gle at the center of his analysis of society. In fact, after a brief introduction, ⅲ *Communist Manifesto* of 1848 reads:

> The history of all hitherto existing society is the history of class struggles. Freeman and slave, patrician and plebeian, lord and serf, guild-master and journeyman, in a word, oppressor and oppressed stood in constant opposition to one another, carried on an uninterrupted, now hidden, now open fight, a fight that each time ended neither in a revolutionary reconstitution of society at large, or in the ruin of the contending classes.

He closes the document with the following words:

> The Communists disdain to conceal their views and aims. They openly declare their ends can be attained only by the forcible overthrow of all existing social conditions. Let the ruling classes tremble at a Communist revolution. The proletarians have nothing to lose but their chains. They have a world to win. Workingmen of all countries, unite!

Historically, all societies, then, have been characterized by a social (class) distinction, whether it be master and slave, plebeian and patrician, lord and serf, and most recently capitalist owner (bourgeoisie) and capitalist worker (proletarian). This distinction depended on inequalities and produced tensions, which in fact served creative purposes; although class strife and other kinds of conflicts may not be particularly pleasant, they are productive. When those conflicts are resolved, new social formations are created.

One way or another, conflict theories—inspired by Marxism—believe that conflict is inherent to, if not beneficial for, human society, and they emphasize a dimension of social analysis that functionalism traditionally underestimated: *power*. If all individuals, groups, and classes in society do have needs and interests, not all of them have equal power to achieve those needs and interests. Power inequalities, resulting usually from other inequalities—specifically economic ones, between the owners of the productive resources and the workers who use those resources—result in inequalities of opportunity and thus of outcome. All of these things produce tensions and conflicts. Dominant group(s) will naturally try to influence society and will have more success than their rivals; society then will represent the interests and ideals of the dominant segment of society rather than an "objective" vision of society, and certainly not the interests and ideals of the dominated segment. In modern society, not only because of the dominant class's control of the economic capital of society but of the "intellectual capital" as well (schools, media, books, etc.), that class can have its way and lead the lower classes to think that this way is right and normal.

Therefore, conflict theorists tend to see violence in one or both of two lights. First, violence is the normal if not necessary application of the power of the dominant group against the lower groups; in other words, violence is oppression. Of course, not all the devices that keep the lower groups "in their place" involve violence; they are also controlled through ideology and social and economic resources. For instance, conflict theorists often single out religion as a tool of domination: if poor, powerless people are convinced that the gods want them to be poor or that it is their own fault that they are poor (say, through concepts like karma and reincarnation) or that they will be rewarded in heaven (where the last shall be first), they are more likely to accept the current situation. The use of social and economic resources involves everything from education and the media to jobs and property. If, for example, the poor can be convinced that it is possible to "work your way to the top," to "pull yourself up by your bootstraps," then they will struggle against the odds to do so and even feel guilty when they fail. But if this approach does not succeed, the dominant group has the violence of the police and the army as well as the "structural violence" of class and race segregation to achieve its interests.

The other view of violence is that it is an expression of the dissatisfaction of the lower classes, a rumbling of trouble to come, the harbinger of the next phase of social change. Violence becomes the cry of the oppressed against their oppression and thereby the motor of society and of history. Some conflict theorists, especially the more "activistic" ones, have seen such violence not only as tolerable but as highly desirable, since the dominant group will never surrender its privileges voluntarily. Thus, violent struggle, even revolution, is an acceptable and recommended course for resolving social contradictions. Such violence is not at all "abnormal" or deviant but is in fact fully justified and even welcomed. We will examine this subject further in the chapters on political and ethnic violence.

The Value of Violence: Georges Sorel   We might mention any number of "theorists" of violence, especially revolutionary violence at this point, and a number of them will appear throughout the rest of the book, in its discussion of religious/ideological and political violence. Here, we will consider one of the influential advocates of social violence, Georges Sorel (1961). In his book *Reflections on Violence*, first published in 1908, he recommends violence as the course, outlined by Marx, that would lead immediately to the reconstitution of society and the triumph of the workers. Even more emphatically, he makes the case that not only is violence of this sort ethical and moral but that its alternative is unethical and immoral.

Sorel lived and wrote in a time of social unrest, particularly among the working class (see Chapter 9). In response to the solutions reformers of various types were recommending, he rejected and despised those of the "parliamentary socialists," who wanted to work within the system to make incremental change. This approach, he argued, was not true socialism but a ridiculous middle-class parody of it. The only effective and legitimate action, in his view, was action taken by the working class itself, and that action had to include violence. Class war, he wrote, was "the point of departure for all Socialist thought" (Sorel 1908/1961: 132)—and Marxists theorists would do well to learn as much from the workers in the streets.

For Sorel, proletarian violence paves the way for the coming socialist revolution, and the fundamental form of proletarian violence is the general strike. He sees the general strike as the military tactic of the class war; it is the direct, physical confrontation between labor and bourgeoisie in which the workers not only express their interests but realize their identity. What is achieved is a clear contrast between the proletariat group and the bourgeois group; in fact, as Edward Shils writes in the introduction to the later edition of Sorel's book, Sorel approaches the socialist question with an emphasis on "tribal solidarity, intensely self-conscious and passionately sensitive to long-range ends" (Sorel 1908/1961: 17). He glorifies ultimate social distance between the two classes and ultimate hostility between them—a total "us-versus-them" mentality.

The general strike is the first step in the socialist revolution, which aims not at compromise with or reform of the system but at the obliteration of the system. It is a terrifying prospect, he admits, and will become more terrifying as it nears its goals. However, this terror, this violence, is more ethical than either of its alternatives. One alternative is the prolongation of an unjust system, with peripheral reforms steered by the middle class or by socialist "intellectuals." Here, nothing ever really changes. The other alternative is a brutal revolt of the kind seen in the French Revolution and later upheavals. These events, he says, were marked by a lack of military discipline and an uncontrolled lust for carnage. The workers' revolution will be a *war* carried out by military rules and with military precision; it will also carry with it the certainty of the goodness and success of its cause. Therefore, it will be the most ethical kind of violence and the most ethical kind of action.

FURTHER SOCIAL THEORIES OF VIOLENCE

Although functionalism and conflict theory dominate the social sciences and even tend to undergird theories that do not explicitly invoke them, sociology and anthropology have nonetheless generated a variety of other perspectives that offer new concepts and promise new insights. The following is a brief survey of a few of the more important and productive theories.

Socialization and Development of the Self

Both sociology and anthropology possess a concept of culture, although anthropology develops and uses it much more extensively. Culture is, in short, the learned and shared ways of thinking, feeling, and behaving in a society and the resulting products, or "artifacts," of its mores. Culture is most assuredly "outside" of the individual, at least initially. No baby is born with the language, morals, knowledge, or beliefs of his or her society or any society at all for that matter. Thus, by a process commonly called socialization in sociology or enculturation in anthropology, the new human observes the behavioral context of his or her fellow members of society, receives implicit or explicit instruction in the society's ways, imitates those ways more or less successfully and gets correction and guidance in this imitation, and eventually (if all goes well) "learns" the society's culture well enough to become a functioning member of the society himself or herself. In a word, what started as "outside" the individual ends up "inside" the individual as personality or the tendencies toward thinking, feeling, and behaving of the individual.

Sociology has taken this notion seriously from the time of some of the early theorists, such as George Herbert Mead and Charles Cooley. Both agreed that the individual begins life with little internal content or "self." This self—one's knowledge and awareness of who you are and what you are expected and able to do—develops through social experience and activity, especially through noticing the effects on and responses of other people in one's environment. Cooley used the phrase "looking-glass self" to express this process, in which an originally egoistic and unaware child begins to see himself or herself "as others see him or her," to pay attention to and internalize the responses, judgments, and attitudes of others. Mead referred to the same general process as "taking the role of the other," in which you acquire the ability to view yourself "from the outside," through the eyes of the other, as it were. This accomplishment, also known as intersubjectivity or reflexivity, depends even more on the reactions of some people than others, who are the *significant others*—usually family or peers or other important figures in the individual's social universe—who matter most to and affect the individual the most.

Accordingly, the people we spend a lot of time with and interact with count a lot toward what we are going to do and what we are going to become. We will belong to various kinds of groups from which we learn our values and beliefs and norms and against which we will evaluate ourselves. Significantly, we can divide these groups into *in-groups* and *out-groups*. In-groups are the groups to which we belong, in which we participate, and from which we tend to get most of our cultural knowledge and sense of self. In-groups are "us." Out-groups are "them"—the groups to which we do not belong, with which we interact infrequently, if at all. Most of the time, but not exclusively, we identify with, bond with, and orient ourselves to our in-groups. That is, our in-groups are our *reference groups*, the ones that we use as sources of our own behavior and identity and attachment (recall Tajfel's social identification theory in the previous chapter). However, this is not always and necessarily the case; people can also compare themselves to out-groups, attempting to behave like those others or to have what those others have. Such individuals may or may not be accepted by the out-groups, which sets up a dynamic of dissatisfaction, frustration, and possible aggression.

Differential association theory aims specifically to account for deviance and violence as a form of social learning. Sutherland and Cressey (1978), for example, emphasize that individuals acquire deviant and violent behavior through observation of and interaction with deviant others. Future deviants and violent offenders not only learn specific "techniques" but also more general motives, attitudes, and rationalizations. Essentially a kind of "culture of deviance/violence" is built up and transmitted, which is one approach to gang analyses. Thus, the behavior and the values from which it flows are not "deviant" from the perspective of the "subculture" but might be viewed as alternative paths to the same (or sometimes to different) ends. Especially when people cannot meet their needs by "socially acceptable" means (as Merton discusses; see following section), they may form or enter or be socialized into a group that possesses its own means.

Anomie Theory

Another way to look at violence as a cultural problem is the sociological concept of *anomie.* Durkheim himself discussed the concept of anomie, the social condition of the breakdown or absence of rules and constraints that occurs when society changes in such a way and at such a rate that the normal adjustments of people to their social positions no longer function. Robert Merton elaborated this notion. In his *Social Theory and Social Structure* (1949) he examined deviance in American society in terms of the overall structures of society. He found three key components in the American system: culture, social structure, and the egalitarian belief that holds everything together. Culture in his analysis includes things like the values and morals and expectations as well as attitudes and relations of wealth, power, and prestige. Social structure includes the actual groups and institutions that influence the possible opportunities that particular individuals and types of individuals legitimately have. Finally, egalitarian belief teaches that anyone can succeed if they merely strive hard enough.

In a well-adjusted society, these three components will support each other: the egalitarian belief will be justified by the social structure that allows individuals to achieve their culturally appropriate goals. However, when these factors lose their "congruence," rules and expectations no longer fit realities, and something has to give. The resultant condition is anomie, in which individuals must find another way besides the culturally prescribed one to meet their needs. One possibility, Merton admits, is surrender and suicide. For the majority of us who continue to struggle on, the main available forms of adaptation are conformity; innovation; ritualism; retreatism; and rebellion, or conflict/violence.

Labeling Theory

Sociologists like Frank Tannenbaum (1938) have insisted on the importance of social labels in the formation and encouragement of deviants and violent individuals. He highlights the way that society defines actions and then assigns those definitional "labels" to actors. In short, a delinquent becomes socially negative because he or she is defined as socially negative. When individuals act to make the "prophecy" borne by their label come true, the situation is bad enough; however, when a negative label is added to differential association— that is, when a person accepts himself or herself as bad and begins to associate with other bad people—the situation gets that much worse—fast. Tannenbaum refers to this process as "dramatizing evil," in which we tell stories and create scenarios about destructive behavior in such ways as to make it more likely. Thus, we—the audience—unwittingly produce our own social problems by defining certain acts as "bad" or "evil" and thereby castigating the actors as bad or evil as well. The individual actor being suggestible, he or she quickly embraces the label and identifies with it—and may even seek out more of it. The solution, he concludes, is to refuse to dramatize evil: the more we make out of it, the more we make of it.

Edwin Lemert (1951) and Howard Becker (1963) advanced the theory of social labeling. Lemert emphasized the "societal reaction" to deviant behavior, which tags a particular behavior and its perpetrators as deviant; this behavior and the reaction to it are termed "primary deviance." However, in a next step, called "secondary deviance," the perpetrators accept the identity of a deviant and commit themselves to deviance or violence as an adaptation to or defense against society's response to them. Thus, the reaction of society not only defines but encourages such conduct. For Becker, as the name of his book suggests, the socially constructed role or label of "outsider" or outlaw is key to the understanding of deviance and violence. He highlights the role of "moral entrepreneurs," who have the position or power of defining this or that behavior as deviant in the first place and distinguishes them from the others who never contributed to or accepted that definition. The social and legal outsider refuses to conform to this constructed version of right and wrong and voluntarily wears the mantle of "criminal" almost as a heroic gesture.

Two important experiments have highlighted the power of labeling for conflictual or even violent behavior. One is the famous "Stanford prison" simulation of Zimbardo (1973), who constructed a mock prison in a Stanford University basement and recruited ten "prisoners" and eleven "guards" randomly from a population of volunteers, mostly college students. Without training, the participants quickly settled into their roles, the guards becoming authoritarian and even abusive and the prisoners becoming resistant and gradually resigned and depressed. The guards began to dole out arbitrary punishments and degradations, and the prisoners sank deeper into disorganized thinking and emotional instability. The guards used familiar techniques to disempower and dehumanize the inmates, and conditions escalated so quickly that the experiment had to be terminated after only six days. The second experiment is a labeling game originated by Jane Elliott, which she has practiced on innumerable subjects—school children, public audiences, and corporate groups—since 1968 and which she calls "Blue Eyes, Brown Eyes." To begin the exercise, as she calls it, she divides her subjects, or participants, in Tajfelian manner—into two categories, the Blue Eyes and the Brown Eyes. Anyone with another eye color she labels "abnormal." Then she assigns each label a value: blue-eyed people are stupid, lazy, and untrustworthy, whereas brown-eyed members are the opposite: smart, hardworking, reliable. Not only do the subjects quickly begin internalizing their new roles, brown-eyes becoming more confident and dominant and blue-eyes regressing into more timid and self-effacing mannerisms; they even began to interact with each other on the new terms, the browns acting in an "arrogant, ugly, domineering, and overbearing" way toward their "inferiors."

Cultural Materialism

Moving in a radically different direction, the anthropologist Marvin Harris (1974) has claimed that all cultural behaviors, including war and aggressiveness, have "practical" material causes. We may not immediately see them; in fact, our cultural attitudes and values may obscure them, more or less intentionally. He is very leery of ideologies and beliefs that lead us to explain our behaviors in terms of feelings or motivations, instincts or "spiritual" causes. For instance, he analyzes violence in small-scale societies like the Yanomamo (see Chapter 4) of Venezuela or the Maring of New Guinea in relation to environment and population. Both societies fight periodic battles with members of their own society or other societies, in which considerable male casualties may be inflicted and other types of harm done (lands destroyed, women kidnapped, etc.). His argument is that the conflicts are based on such mundane concerns as protein supply: the Maring fight when their population (and that of their pig herds) are on the verge of exceeding the carrying capacity of their territory, and the Yanomamo have long since passed that capacity in regard to protein. In particular with the latter society, their transition from hunting to horticulture (of fairly low-protein foods like bananas and plantains) means that they long ago entered a cycle of acute resource competition. However, the reality of war in both cases is more subtle than that: the necessity of competition and conflict puts a premium on males as warriors and aggressiveness in those males, which leads to the depressed status of women. War does not directly kill women; rather, it calls for the production of more men, which indirectly kills females, as both societies practice female infanticide. What follows is a vicious cycle: "The fiercer the men, the greater the amount of warfare, the more such men are needed. Also, the fiercer the men, the more sexually aggressive they become, the more the exploited are the women, and the higher the incidence of polygyny"—which results in a shortage of wives and even more male competition and aggression (Harris 1974: 87).

Process Theory

Louis Kreisberg, in his *Social Conflicts* (1982), performs a systems analysis of intergroup conflict, finding a "cycle" of conflict that is distinguished by—and can perhaps be intervened in—a distinct set of phases. He also identifies the key variables in each phase of the rise and fall of conflict. A conflict breaks out when parties have, or feel they have, conflicting goals or incompatible objectives. In this first stage, the *basis for conflict stage*, internal (including instinctive) and interactional components figure in the establishment of a conflictual relationship. In the process, group boundaries get formed or reinforced and social organization within those boundaries is furthered. In stage two, *emergence of conflict*, the actual hostility takes shape. During this stage, three developments necessarily occur:

- A consciousness on the part of each group of themselves as a collective entity
- A grievance against the other group
- A belief that its grievance or dissatisfaction can be reduced by changing or eliminating the other group (Kreisberg 1982: 66)

The grievance at the core of such conflict can be related to deprivation (real, imagined, or relative), "rank disequilibrium," or "changes in attainments and expectations"—that is, actual improvements or declines in quality of life or hopes that improvements will come.

Stage three involves *pursuing conflict goals*, in which parties move to achieve their purpose for engaging in conflict. The specific factors that affect how a group pursues its goals include its traditions, history, and personality; its ideology; its social organization; and its resources. The responses that the rival or enemy makes naturally influence the course of the conflict, as well as the existence and actions of other parties. If conflict continues it may enter a stage of *escalation or de-escalation*, which will either intensify or "cool off" the conflict. He notes that once a conflict starts, it has a strong tendency to increase in magnitude. Expressing and acting on aggression leads to a justification of and commitment to the group and its cause. At the same time, a sense of "crisis" is fostered in which power is yet more centralized, members are increasingly radicalized, dissent is discounted and alternatives not considered, and a kind of absoluteness of thinking based "on stereotyped images of adversaries and on historical analogies" takes over (Kreisberg 1982: 166). At some point or another, the stage of *termination of conflict* arrives, which may be a result of a gradual de-escalation to the point of "peace"; of changes in the goals of the parties; of negotiation, resolution, or conversion or, ultimately, a result of victory or defeat. In the extreme case, the adversary is "eliminated" completely, either through integration into the victorious group or through physical liquidation.

RETROSPECT AND PROSPECT

 how does Gilligan's theory fit here?

In this chapter we have reviewed the contributions to a theory of violence from a variety of sciences, natural and social. One thing we know for sure is that violence cannot be completely "natural" or instinctive, otherwise all human groups would evince it equally, which they do not. Each theory we have seen has a specific perspective, and none quite tells the whole story, although each has an important piece of the puzzle. There are also some key areas of overlap. It seems, therefore, that a unified theory of violence would emphasize the following points:

- Violence, like all other human behaviors, has an "internal" or physical/mental/psychological and an "external" or social/cultural aspect.
- Violence is in a way part of the nature of humans, living things, and physical reality.
- The internal and the external cannot be completely separated in regard to violence. Individual humans commit violence, but when they do they constitute the "environment" for other humans—in other words, one person's internal state results in violent behavior that is experienced as external to another person, who may consequently internalize and imitate the violent behavior, creating an experience for another person, ad infinitum.
- Factors and forces motivate our behavior that we are sometimes totally unaware of. We tend to think of ourselves as free and willful persons, but in actuality we are shaped and pushed by social phenomena that we often cannot see and often could not understand or change if we could see them.
- We are fundamentally products of our experience. Violence, like everything else human, is largely learned. This learning tends to take place within discrete groups and to be transmitted through culture.
- Violence, although an inherently human phenomenon, takes different forms in different societies. Certain values, norms, institutions, and so on, promote violence, and others do not. We cannot approach violence as an isolated thing but must understand it as a part of, and a manifestation of, wider social factors. And we cannot hope to "cure" violence unless we really know what causes or fosters it, which requires as "cross-cultural" a perspective as possible.

- Finally, as we argued in the first chapter, what counts as violence will not even be the same from society to society or situation to situation. We cannot impose our definition or understanding of violence on other groups or societies.

With these points in mind, we can now commence the exploration of the realm of violence with some hope of drawing general and useable conclusions about it. Accordingly, in the following chapters we will examine violence and nonviolence in a wide variety of cultural settings and in the light of a wide variety of circumstantial variables, including familial, social-structural, psychological, ideological, and cultural factors.

VIOLENCE IN CROSS-CULTURAL CONTEXT

Introduction and Nonviolent Societies

In the first two chapters of this book, we confronted the diversity and difficulty in defining, operationalizing, and theorizing about violence. The crux of the matter is that how one defines, studies, and explains violence will affect two subsequent outcomes—first, how much of it we locate out there in society, and second, how precisely we intervene in it. If we define violence widely, the result is that we will catch a great deal of violence in our "net" of analysis, whereas obviously if we define it narrowly—or fail to define it at all, as many societies still do not or have only recently ceased to do—then we will conclude that there is little or no "problem" of violence. Ultimately then, what we consider to be the "source" or "cause" of violence will determine where (if anywhere) we put the effort of our intervention—whether into the supernatural realm, the mind, the body, or the culture and social structure.

We can go only so far in the presentation of generalities, however. If it is true, as we are sure that it is, that violence is related closely to the particular practices, values, and institutions of particular societies, then we must descend to that level of specificity. Thus, the bulk of the rest of this work will consist of close-up examinations of concrete societies (past or present) and their attitudes toward and practices of violence. Most critically, we cannot completely understand what makes for a violent society until we have examined nonviolent societies to explore the differences.

The present chapter will focus primarily on nonviolence. By any account, there are and have been relatively few profoundly nonviolent human societies, and depending on one's definition, there may be none at all. Certainly, no really peaceful societies exist among the world's modern industrialized states. Many people have made the erroneous assumption that not only are modern societies all (relatively) violent but modern society *introduced* or *caused* human violence. Steven LeBlanc (2003), in particular, criticizes the popular myth of the "noble savage" under which many laymen, and even many scholars, operate. Rather, as a practicing archaeologist, he argues that humans have been nonpeaceful in most times and places, that people "in the past were in conflict and competition most of the time" (8). This observation, this fact, does not change the reality that we will probably only find true human nonviolence in the cultural past, but it does change the cause of that nonviolence: it is not time itself that makes the difference but the specific and actual environmental and cultural circumstances in which nonviolent groups lived. With this knowledge, we can perhaps make some meaningful recommendations aimed at reducing the violence of our own societies; without it, we most certainly cannot.

THE SOCIAL GROUNDS OF VIOLENCE AND NONVIOLENCE

At the end of the first chapter, we were already in a position to name four factors that play a role in the incidence of violence—integration into groups, identity, ideology, and interest. Humans as a thoroughly social species inevitably and irretrievably manifest the first factor. The second readily attaches to groups (as we saw, real or imagined), and the third and fourth are not far behind.

The significant kinds of groups that humans do and must live in are not mere crowds or mobs or herds but *social groups*, which means that they, like the groups in which ants and the nonhuman primates live, have "rules and roles"—that is, standards and norms for behavior and "concrete" relationships between individuals and "kinds of individuals"—that define social categories or classifications and their behavioral norms. These category-specific behaviors may be instinctual (as in ants and bees) or they may be learned (as in humans and, at least to a degree, in other primates), but they make for a "structured" social community in which all members are not alike.

In applying this social perspective to violence, we should distinguish between three modes, or dimensions, of social reality that can vary independently but that are practically interconnected in any concrete human society. This interconnection is known in anthropological parlance as *holism*, the view that all of the parts of a society—its institutions, values, roles, and so forth—are to some extent networked with each other and, even more important, "consonant" with each other. The three modes, or dimensions, to consider are:

1. *Macrosocial*: These refer to the "large-scale" social structures and relations in a society, such as the economic system, the kinship and residence patterns, the political institutions, the leadership roles, and other constructs that affect all or major portions of the population of the society. They are the overarching terms within which people construct their social actions.
2. *Microsocial*: These are the "small-scale" and interpersonal social structures and relations through which people experience their societies. Examples of microsocial structures would be particular families,

neighborhoods, friendships, and classes. Microsocial relationships are obviously "local versions" or products of macrosocial rules and institutions (for instance, my monogamous marriage is an instantiation of the macrosocial norm of monogamous marriage), but never perfectly or simply so. The microsocial dimension is where individuals "work out" their social lives within the constraints of the macrosocial.

3. *Psychocultural*: These are the ideas, beliefs, and values that pervade and sustain the two levels of social structure. Individuals must be inculcated with particular ways of thinking, feeling, and acting—particular attitudes about what is "right and wrong," "good and bad"—which are the "rules" of the social "game." These psychocultural forces are primarily cultural, in the sense of being "public" and "outside" the individual's mind, but also psychological, in that they are internalized and learned through the process of socialization or enculturation (as we discussed in the previous chapter). Individuals are by no means automatons of their cultures, but they are constructed products of them, and they live their lives and form their actions within the "language" of their cultural values and possibilities.

Sociology and anthropology have shown that all societies have four analytically and functionally distinct areas, or "domains," each of which consists of some combination of specialized roles, values, and institutions. These four domains are *economics, kinship, politics*, and *religion* (sociology typically adds a fifth, *education*). For the purposes of this book, we will use these terms with the familiar meanings they have for most people. Economics refers to all the beliefs and practices about how people produce, distribute, and consume goods and services. Kinship refers to family and marriage beliefs and practices. Politics concerns how people establish and maintain social control and how they use power to achieve social order and social conformity to rules and norms. Religion refers to the beliefs and practices whereby humans orient to the nonhuman or superhuman world to bring that world into relationship with human society. Each domain contributes to the macrosocial structure.

Anthropology in particular regards these domains as not entirely "equal" in their determining, or "causal," importance. Economics in the broadest sense is taken as the "core" or "base" of society and culture—the most fundamental part that influences or shapes the other domains. How people produce in their environment—the kinds of work they do, the way they divide their labor, the way they form groups to perform this work, the way they produce and share wealth, the kinds of relationships and dependencies and inequalities that result—affect how they live together, how they rule each other, and even what they believe about the origins and "truths" of their society. There are four basic systems for performing these functions, each with a distinct consequence for the type and amount of violence and other cultural phenomena. The following list describes these four super-macrosocial systems and a few of their microsocial and psychocultural effects.

1. *Foraging, or hunting and gathering.* Foraging societies subsist by hunting wild game and gathering wild plants. They do not domesticate or control any of their food sources. They tend to live in small (usually five to fifty members), mobile, fluid groups called bands. Men generally hunt and women generally gather, and although meat tends to be a higher-status food, men produce less food in most cases than women; in some societies, women provide more than 75 percent of the band's nutrition. Therefore, although there is a gender division of labor, men and women are usually roughly equal. There is a status difference between young and old, but elders ordinarily cannot compel youngsters to do anything, since the groups are so fluid: if anyone is unhappy in the band, they can leave and join another band or start their own band. So, no individual has much more power than anyone else. Also, because foraging does not produce a surplus, no one has much more wealth than anyone else. Foraging produces a roughly egalitarian society of close family members with little or no violence. Until about ten to twelve thousand years ago, all humans lived in foraging societies, and a small number still do today.

2. *Pastoralism.* Pastoralism is one of the two original forms of domestication, drawing its primary food supply from domesticated animals. Pastoralism produces larger societies (hundreds or even thousands of members) because there is surplus food "on the hoof." Pastoralists still tend to be mobile, since they must move their herds from place to place in search of pasturage. Because of their mobility and their vulnerability to attack and robbery—and their propensity to attack and rob other societies—they tend to be warlike. Also, following from their foraging heritage, men usually own and control the animals, making for distinct gender inequality. In many such societies, men arrange marriages for the women in their family and exchange women for animals or other types of portable wealth. Society is therefore very male dominated. Male values of aggressiveness, fearlessness, toughness, and so on, are central to the society, and in some cases males organize themselves into age-based or other types of subgroups, such as warrior societies, to act as protectors and peacekeepers of the society. Violence is common and even valued.

3. *Horticulture.* Horticulture is the other of the two original forms of domestication, consisting of simple farming without the use of the plow, irrigation, fertilizer, or permanent fields. Horticulturists still need to be somewhat mobile, as their techniques tend to deplete farmland quickly and they must open up new land every few years or so. Even so, they often

have semipermanent or long-term villages near their lands, and they produce enough surplus to feed large groups and to support a small number of non-food-producing specialists, such as artisans or religious leaders. In many but not all horticultural societies, women play an important role in the economy, owning and controlling land and producing much of the food. Women's status is therefore often but by no means always higher than in pastoralism. At the same time, larger groups living in permanent close quarters to each other, together with concepts of private property in regard to land and surplus, lead to inequality in society and disputes and rivalries in the community. Chiefs, priests, and other kinds of low-level leaders appear to settle disputes and keep order, but there is often considerable internal strife. At the same time, many horticultural societies are not particularly warlike, and quite a few (see the discussion of Rwanda and Burundi in Chapter 9) have been conquered by pastoral or intensive agricultural societies and incorporated into complex stratified societies, often with themselves in the lower strata.

4. *Intensive agriculture*. Intensive agriculture is the most recent economic system, appearing in parts of the world only about five to six thousand years ago; in many places, it is still not the main economic system. It is a more complex type of farming, which uses plow and draft animals, irrigation, fertilizer, and permanent fields. As a result, much larger populations develop, containing thousands to millions of people. These populations are necessarily sedentary; in fact, one reason why the economy does and must intensify is that all the available arable land is in use; the only way to feed the growing population is to make the land produce higher yields. Private property becomes very important, and the large surpluses produced are siphoned off by an elite class that constitutes the "government" of the society. Government now is formalized, with a high chief or king in charge, and this government is necessary to organize the planning and labor required to run such a complex society. Therefore, economic and political stratification is extreme, with a rich ruling class, a poor working class, and potentially one or more classes in between. This form of politics is called the *state* and is warlike at its root (see Chapter 8). The first states in history, small independent cities or city-states in Mesopotamia, were constantly at war with each other and routinely conquered each other to assemble territorial empires. Men tend to be the leaders and to occupy all the key social positions—king, general, soldier, priest, merchant, and so forth. Inequality and violence are endemic in most cases. Almost all people in the world today are citizens of state-level societies, and all people are contained within some state, as states have claimed all the territory on the planet. States, then and now, are highly competitive over wealth, land, and resources, and they usually have standing armies and instill martial values in their men, if not also

their women. Until recently in all states, and still in many states, war is considered a glorious avocation.

Thus, we can see that there is a clear and consistent relationship between certain macrosocial structures—in particular economics and politics—and the kind and amount of violence. Allthough of course there is considerable variation within each type, since all of these types of societies are present in the modern world, we should expect to find predictable differences between them in their experience and attitude of violence.

Going beyond these crucial but general observations, we can ask more penetrating questions. What specific kinds of violence do different societies generate, and what is it about them that generates it? Marc Howard Ross, in *The Culture of Conflict* (1993), has conducted a large-scale cross-cultural survey of the sort discussed at the end of the first chapter to broach precisely these questions. He examined ninety different societies in regard to their quality and quantity of violence, identifying thirteen variables and their "amounts," or levels:

1. Local conflict—how commonly conflict within the local community occurs.
2. Intercommunity conflict—how commonly conflict between communities of the same society occurs.
3. Physical force—how often force is used by individuals involved in disputes, not institutionalized "official" force.
4. Extent of compliance with community norms and decisions by individuals.
5. Internal warfare—how often organized, systematic violence waged by one group in the society against another, or by individuals acting alone, occurs.
6. External warfare—how commonly war against other societies takes place.
7. Hostility toward other societies—the extent of measurable negative feelings toward outside groups.
8. Acceptability of violence directed against members of the local community.
9. Acceptability of violence directed against members of the same society outside the local community.
10. Acceptability of violence directed against other societies.
11. Conflict management—a society's dominant mode of dealing with conflicts when they arise: either contending parties are encouraged to find their own solution, new parties are easily drawn in and strong pressures are brought to bear for resolution, or authorities get involved and work to achieve a settlement.
12. Mediation, negotiation, or arbitration—how often third-party involvement without binding decision making or litigation is used.
13. Adjudication—how often binding third-party decisions with or without formal court systems are used.

Ross's results are shown in Table 3.1.

TABLE 3.1	CROSS-CULTURE MEASURES OF CONFLICT		
Variable	**Number of Cases**	**Percentage of Cases**	**Value**
1. Local conflict	4	4.4	Endemic
	20	22.2	High
	46	51.1	Moderate
	20	22.2	Mild/rare
2. Intercommunity conflict	25	28.1	Endemic
	23	25.8	High
	21	23.6	Moderate
	20	22.5	Mild/rare
	1		Not codable
3. Physical force	34	37.8	Often used
	32	35.6	Sometimes used
	24	26.7	Rarely/never used
4. Compliance with norms	43	50	High
	31	36	Moderate
	12	14	Highly variable
	4		Not codable
5. Internal warfare	31	36.5	Frequent
	14	16.5	Common
	10	11.8	Occasional
	30	35.3	Rare/nonexistent
	5		Not codable
6. External warfare	45	53.6	Frequent
	13	15.5	Common
	6	7.1	Occasional
	20	23.6	Rare/nonexistent
	6		Not codable
7. Hostility to other society	28	37.8	Extensive
	18	24.3	High
	17	23	Moderate
	11	14.9	Low
	16		Not codable
8. Acceptability of violence against community	0	0	Valued
	7	8.1	Accepted
	18	20.9	Tolerated
	61	70.9	Disapproved
	4		Not codable
9. Acceptability of violence against other communities	12	15.6	Valued
	28	36.4	Accepted
	10	13	Tolerated
	27	35.1	Disapproved
	13		Not codable

continued

TABLE 3.1 CONTINUED			
Variable	**Number of Cases**	**Percentage of Cases**	**Value**
10. Acceptability of violence against other societies	39	60.9	Valued
	16	25	Accepted
	3	4.7	Tolerated
	6	9.4	Disapproved
	26		Not codable
11. Conflict management	31	35.2	Find own solution
	27	30.7	New parties drawn in
	30	34.1	Authorities involved
	2		Not codable
12. Mediation	57	64.8	Often used
	19	21.6	Sometimes used
	12	13.6	Rarely/never used
	2		Not codable
13. Adjudication	27	30.3	Often used
	21	23.6	Sometimes used
	41	46.1	Rarely/never used
	1		Not codable

Adapted from Table 5.2 of Marc Howard Ross, *The Culture of Conflict*, pp. 78–80. Copyright © 1993 Yale University Press. Reprinted with permission of Yale University Press.

Even a quick pass through the table's data is highly informative. Violence is by far least common within the community, more common between communities of the same society, and more common and even valued between different societies. Overall, violence is surprisingly frequent: almost half of societies experience intracommunity conflict, and two-thirds experience interpersonal physical force sometimes or often.

Next, Ross proceeds to separate his variables into measures of internal and external violence. Items 1, 2, 3, 4, 5, 8, and 9 constitute the set of variables that determine level of internal conflict and violence, and items 6, 7, and 10 determine external conflict and violence. Societies that scored high overall in internal conflict obviously suffer more regular and more severe conflict. As Ross states,

> Legitimation and frequency of physical violence, feuding, and strong factionalism within and between communities all characterize the high-conflict societies, as does irregular compliance with local community norms and decisions. In these societies, intense conflict is a reality of daily life and organizes activities and perceptions. No phase of daily life—whether it is subsistence activities, the movement of people or goods, the socialization of children, ritual activities, or building a house—fails to be influenced by who are friends and who are foes and where any of them might be at a given time. (82)

Inversely, societies that are low in internal conflict, while still encountering situations that could lead to intense hostility, seldom see such hostility break out.

In low-conflict societies, differences that arise are often managed in such a way that rancor, polarization, and outright violence are avoided. Broadly based social identities often link people in the same community and between communities so that common interests are emphasized more than differences. Although conflicts develop, and some evoke strong feelings, the existence of cross-cutting ties leads to acceptable solutions before the dispute gets out of hand and violence escalates. (83)

Interestingly, there is a moderate correlation between incidence of internal conflict and external conflict but a good number of exceptions, so we cannot summarily conclude that societies with high internal violence will have high external violence and vice versa.

Finally, Ross performs some sophisticated statistical analyses on his data to test the relevance of three theories to the facts of violence. These theories are cross-cutting ties theory (the more social bonds there are that cross social boundaries, the less violence), complexity theory (more complex societies are more violent), and psychocultural theory (harsh socialization and gender conflicts increase violence, whereas mild and affectionate socialization deters it). He finds that *psychocultural factors are significantly related to the level of internal violence in a society*. "Specifically, the data show that the more affectionate and warm and the less harsh the socialization in a society, the lower the level of political conflict and violence" (99). Also, there is a weak correlation between cross-cutting ties and reduced violence: societies with more "multiple-reference groups" and fewer fraternal interest groups experience less violence. However, social complexity seems to have less relation to internal conflict, and other elements of cross-cutting ties theory, like intercommunity trade and marriage, are statistically insignificant.

As far as external conflict is concerned, Ross's analysis finds that all three theories have a bearing on its prevalence. Of the psychocultural items, harsh socialization, lack of affection, and male gender-identity conflict are all significantly related to external violence and war. Also, more complex societies demonstrate more external conflict. Finally, cross-cutting ties theory is supported, but only weakly, since such ties make a difference in "uncentralized" societies (those without a central government) but not in centralized ones. The ultimate conclusions Ross draws from his research are (1) that psychocultural factors are critical, in the sense that positive dispositions to violence are instilled by harsh parenting techniques, lack of emotion within the family, and physical punishment of children; (2) that cross-cutting ties within a community are effective for controlling violence within that community but have less effect on intercommunity conflict; and (3) that greater social complexity is correlated with both kinds of conflict but especially external violence—the larger and more internally differentiated the society, the more likely it is to engage in violence against its neighbors.

As a kind of coda, Ross also mentions that there are some societies that deviate from predicted frequencies of conflict based on their cultures and social structures. Within both realms of internal and external conflict, there are those with too much and those with too little conflict for their "type." Societies that are "underconflicters" internally tend to be in East Asia and North America, to have much more external conflict than internal, and to put their women in less politically active roles. Societies that are "overconflicters" internally tend to be in the Mediterranean and Pacific Island areas, to have roughly equally high amounts of external conflict, and to put their women in more politically active roles. Societies that are "underconflicters" externally tend also to have low levels of internal conflict, to have less contact with outside societies, and to have less emphasis on obedience and self-reliance in socialization. Finally, societies that are "overconflicters" externally tend to have much more external conflict than internal, to have more contact with outside societies, and to have more emphasis on obedience and self-reliance in socialization.

COOPERATION AND COMPETITION IN PEACEFUL SOCIETIES: CASE STUDIES

As we would expect from everything we have learned up to this point, nonviolent societies have some distinct characteristics in common, both in terms of their economic and social organization and their culture and cognitive/emotional concepts and practices. They tend to be small societies or small subsocieties of a larger society; there are virtually no nonviolent large states (if there were, some other state would have long ago conquered them). They also have similar attitudes toward issues like child rearing, the proper social relationships between members of the group or community, concern for each other's feelings, and cooperation and competition. In fact, Bruce Bonta (1997), in his own cross-cultural survey of the literature on violence and nonviolence, finds consistent patterns distinguishing violent and nonviolent societies in regard to this last item.

Bonta's research is a good general introduction to the discussion that succeeds it. He reports that there are more than forty societies in the world that have been described as nonviolent or peaceful, living in conditions with virtually or absolutely no violence. His study surveys twenty-five of them in terms of their practices and attitudes concerning cooperation and competition.* Before we continue, let us follow our own best practice by defining our terms. Bonta uses the word *cooperation* to mean that "people attain their goals only when other participants do also" and *competition* to mean that "people attain

---

*The twenty-five societies included in the analysis are the Amish, Balinese, Batek, Birhor, Buid, Chewong, Fipa, G/wi, Hutterites, Ifaluk, Inuit, Jains, Kadar, !Kung, Ladakhis, Lepchas, Mennonites, Montagnais-Naskapi, Nayaka, Paliyan, Piaroa, Semai, Tahitians, Tristan Islanders, and Zapotec. A number of these societies are described later in the chapter.

their goals only if other participants do not" (Bonta 1997: 300). He also adds a third possibility, individualism, in which "people attain their goals without affecting the goal attainment of others" (300).

Put quite simply, Bonta finds a dramatic connection between nonviolence and cooperation: twenty-three of the twenty-five societies surveyed "shun competition as inimical to their beliefs and firmly link it with aggression and violence" (301). This is indisputably a psychocultural issue. The obvious question, then, is, How do these societies inculcate and sustain personalities or values that minimize or avoid competition? Bonta looks first to child-rearing practices. One of the primary ways that societies appear to suppress competition or enhance cooperation, which may feel strange or almost unpleasant to us as Americans, is to prevent egoism and high self-evaluation. He notes that one common and remarkable child-rearing method in such societies includes withdrawal of affectionate treatment from children after the first few years. Very small children are cuddled and coddled, but somewhere in the range of two or three years of age, attention and "warmth" are withdrawn from the child, often fairly abruptly.

> From being the center of everyone's attention, the child suddenly gets little notice at all and is made to feel like a very insignificant member of the community. In some of the societies, adults and older children actively make sure the 3-year-old no longer has any illusions of special status; whereas in other societies, the child is simply ignored. To emphasize, in many of these societies the change is sudden and dramatic.
>
> In some of the societies, the child may go through a period of lengthy temper tantrums, almost all of which are completely ignored. But soon the point becomes clear—no one is special, stands out, or is above anyone else. ... [T]he 3-year-old learns that the individual cannot dominate others. A spoiled 5-year-old might lead progressively to an egocentric, dominating, competitive, aggressive, and perhaps even violent adult. (Bonta 1997: 302)

This might be regarded as a kind of *leveling mechanism,* which functions to render everyone equal and to prevent any individual from becoming or perceiving himself or herself to be superior to or more important than anyone else. Of course, a part of this phenomenon is based on the fact that, about two or three years into the life of the child, another child often comes along who demands the parents' attention and energy. But the practice is also clearly quite intentional and deliberate.

Accordingly, it is very important in most peaceful societies for individuals to be equal; such societies typically "value humility and modesty and do not tolerate achievement-oriented people," certainly not anyone who would attempt to dominate or boss around other people (Bonta 1997: 304). Adults of all ages and genders are roughly equal, and there tend to be no distinct economic or social classes anyhow; even the relations between adults and children are relatively egalitarian, with children often able to ignore or sidestep the authority of parents. The idea that one person would have power over another is often repugnant and believed to create resentments and social disruptions that are almost palpable. As a result, these societies produce members who are "reticent, cautious, and modest about personal achievement, and they avoid leadership, or at least the arrogance of leadership, as a major strategy to maintain peacefulness" (305).

Naturally, children are not encouraged to indulge in competitive play; as we saw in the last chapter, rehearsal and modeling of competition and aggression make the individual more prone to and capable of competition and aggression, and that is exactly the opposite of what these societies seek. In the peaceful societies surveyed, children not only do not see adults engaging in competition, but they do not themselves engage in activities of the kind that would lead to differentiation and hierarchy among children.

> Kadar children in southern India ... play without any element of competition such as hiding, catching, or running away—their games are based on simply enjoyment of the activities of the moment. When Chewong children spin tops, which they acquire from the more aggressive Malay people of Malaysia, they leave out the competition that characterizes Malay top-spinning games.
>
> Most of the games of the children in these societies are cooperative activities, which involve demonstrating physical skills, mimicking adult activities, or telling stories. Semai boys play at hunting, while girls play house; they swing on vines, jump down waterfalls, and play fantasy games. A favorite game among the !Kung children of Namibia and Botswana is *zeni*, in which the children use a stick to throw into the air and catch a weight that is attached by a thong to a feather. Although children exhibit widely differing abilities in the game, they do not compete: All play for the sheer pleasure of it. (Bonta 1997: 303)

It might be sufficient to model nonviolence for children and to induce rehearsal of nonviolence in them for the purpose of creating nonviolent people. After all, it is only too true that we become better at what we do over and over. People who practice being nonviolent will usually be nonviolent, and people who practice being violent will usually be violent. However, many peaceful societies do not leave the outcome to chance this way but rather take further steps to ingrain in their members an aversion to competition and aggression. Adult behavior toward children figures prominently in this process, again in ways that are anomalous and a little distasteful to the typical American.

An important component of this personality-shaping process can only be called the implanting of fear in the child. From the Inuit of the Arctic to the Ifaluk of the Pacific Islands to the Semai of Malaysia, children are taught to experience virtually a visceral discomfort and a mental anguish at the expression or even the thought of hostility and aggression. This reminds one of the movie *A Clockwork Orange*, in which the violent criminal was taught to feel sick whenever he engaged in or observed violence. The Ifaluk teach their children to be anxious and fearful around strangers or large groups of people. The result in this and other similar societies is a timid and even slightly scared individual who feels quite bad when he or she misbehaves or sees others misbehave. Individuals in some cases actually feel emotionally responsible if they perceive themselves to be the source of another person's trouble or emotional pain. Thus, nonviolence is not a "state" but an active process, a result of perpetual vigilance:

> Everyone always appears peaceful, but each individual has to be on guard constantly to not offend others, to actively keep the peace. This guardedness, a feeling of ambiguity about the intentions of others, is the result of psychological practices, but it is only effective in societies where there is already little or no ambiguity about violence, which is always rejected. (Bonta 1997: 303-4)

Of course, even nonviolent societies are not without their competitions, but the point is that they have developed strong controls—psychological and social—to limit the occurrence of these situations and to minimize the consequences of them when they do occur. Some achieve nonviolence and the avoidance of competition not so much through cooperation as through individualism: if individuals have little or no interaction with each other, there is little opportunity for conflict. For example, the Nayaka of India prevent trouble by abstaining from both competition and cooperation, thus keeping to themselves and moving away from potential conflicts when they arise. As a society, households do not share labor or exchange gifts; in fact, the only cooperative social unit of any significance is the husband–wife couple. "Even parent-child and sibling relationships are fragile and maintained only if they live in close proximity. The couple works together, bathes together, eats together, and sleeps together—they are inseparable" (Bonta 1997: 310).

The Buid of the Philippines are equally individualistic, with marriage as the only cooperative, if still fragile, relationship. Marriage in Buid society symbolizes personal autonomy and voluntary bonds, which are positive values; they value kinship, dependence, and permanent and involuntary relationships as negative. They take this social segregation to an extreme in that men who speak to each other do not even face each other, and individuals seldom speak directly to other individuals anyhow. Instead, they direct their comments to the group at large. Even when they do engage in mutual activities like farming, they all sit squatting and facing the same direction rather than each other and keep their conversation to a minimum. One might call this nonviolent strategy avoidance rather than individualism.

What these peaceful societies—cooperative and individualistic—have in common is a world in which violence is basically not experienced and is never experienced positively. Children do not see violent models nor suffer violence nor practice violence. In fact, anything that even remotely resembles violence, including authority, leadership, anger, or individual achievement, is anathema.

To boss someone around or to be or act better than them is essentially to do them harm; they take the notion that a sin committed in mind is a sin committed quite seriously. The psychological underpinning of this attitude is a personality type that is somewhat hesitant, even a little fearful, but not pathologically so. But together they do illustrate, first, that human nonviolence is possible and, second, that certain conditions appear to promote it. Let us now examine a few cases of nonviolent societies in more depth.

Case Study 1: Nonviolence in the Semai of Malaysia

[handwritten margin notes: band level — foraging + hort, unstratified, & competitive]

The Semai as described by Dentan (1968) are perhaps the prototype of a nonviolent society. Not only do they commit little or no interpersonal violence, but they even deny that they experience hostile emotions. Their self-perception is definitely that of a peaceful people.

The Semai are one of the numerous indigenous groups of the Malay peninsula, occupying the west-central area (in fact, Dentan distinguishes the western and eastern Semai culturally). They are a diminutive people with brown skin and vaguely Asian features, whose men stand less than five-and-a-half feet tall, and sometimes less than five feet. Interbred with Chinese, Malays, and others, they cannot be designated as a "race." Their homeland, a rainforest region with mountains running through the middle, is naturally hot and wet, with a relatively unhealthy atmosphere where tuberculosis, malaria, hepatitis, skin disease, and a host of other maladies are endemic. Infant mortality ranges from 25 to 50 percent. Yet, under these unsalutary conditions, peace reigns.

The Semai are a foraging people (men hunting in the forest with blowguns), with some horticulture in shifting fields that must be cleared every two or three years. There is no private ownership of land or other real property; rather, families "own" land if they were the ones who cleared it and who are currently using it. If, however, they abandon that land, others take it over and "own" it in turn. The attitude toward houses is the same: a family that leaves a house empty may find it occupied by others if and when they return, and they will simply look for other residence. Distribution takes the form of generalized reciprocity, in which individuals share goods without calculating their donation or expecting an immediate and equal return; not to share, they say, generates *punan*.

Semai marriage is very informal, and premarital or extramarital sex is common and not particularly serious. Consanguines (blood relatives) tend to live in the same household, typically numbering fifteen to fifty people, and each nuclear family has its own compartment in the structure. Interactions among consanguines are characterized by generosity, tranquility, trust, and sociality.

no competition

Case Study 1: Nonviolence in the Semai of Malaysia (continued)

However, "others," or *mai*—which can mean non-Semai or Semai of another settlement or region or simply (and most often) nonconsanguines—are not trusted and not to be relied on. *Mai* are deemed unpredictable and best left alone. Yet, since blood kin are prohibited from marrying each other, Semai must marry *mai*, sometimes from far-off settlements, so there is a certain tension in such marriages. Not unreasonably, postmarital residence is ambilocal, splitting time between the husband's and wife's family. The taboo on sexual intercourse for up to two years after giving birth creates a prime condition for extramarital affairs, as does spousal travel or sickness; however, such behavior causes little consternation, with the Semai expressing the sentiment that it is okay since it is "just a loan." In fact, to object to a spouse's sexual transgressions would be viewed as selfish and as generating *punan*.

Finally, Semai political organization is at the band level of integration, with fifty to one hundred members in a typical band. Like most band-level societies, "political" relations are egalitarian, with no real leaders or even superiors. Elders command more respect than younger people, yet the former cannot compel obedience from the latter: the "subordinates" can simply refuse an instruction with the attitude of "I *bood*," which translated roughly to "I don't feel like it." Public opinion and informal negative sanctions are the only real force of conformity in society. Trying to coerce someone to obey generates *punan*.

We have referred in various contexts to the Semai concept of *punan*. It turns out that this concept is central to Semai understandings of social behavior and social appropriateness. It helps to explain why they seldom hit each other—and never kill—and even claim not to feel anger. *Mai* feel and do such things, but not "us." *Punan* refers to a condition of making someone unhappy, especially by frustrating them. Both the offending act and the resultant emotional state are *punan*. Not only is *punan* an unpleasant condition to be in, but it is also believed to increase the parties' chances of physical injury, for example, by causing an accident. Thus *punan* has real physical consequences too. The following behaviors are *punan* and therefore negatively construed: being stingy, refusing a request, making a request for more than another can afford to give, directly repaying a gift, demanding privacy or excluding friends or kin from your space, and refusing to grant sexual favors (which applies particularly to women). However, pressuring a woman for sex is also *punan*, so sexual aggression by men is circumscribed, even toward their spouses, since both would feel *punan* from the experience.

Clearly, then, this concept leads the Semai to avoid a constellation of social interactions that would make each other feel bad and frustrated, especially the kinds of interactions that suggest a power or obligation inequality. If a person does get *punan*, he or she has a couple of choices. One option is to simply endure it in silence. The other option is to seek compensation from the offender, to "right" the social equilibrium between them. The damaged

Case Study 1: Nonviolence in the Semai of Malaysia (continued)

party may go to an intermediary to negotiate an apology or a gift, but such intermediaries are not very common in Semai society. Alternatively, the damaged party may simply look for an opportunity to take some belongings from the offender, hence making the point that an offense was committed and justice has been served. If both parties do not accept the resolution of the dispute, a quarrel may break out, but violence never ensues; even when drunk, Semai people may get loud but they do not get aggressive.

How do Semai instill these values in people? First and foremost, children are not exposed to violent models or lessons. Children do not observe adults hitting each other, nor are children physically punished. In fact, children are not disciplined firmly at all, and even parental orders can be refused with a mere "I *bood*." To pressure a child, as to pressure any human being, is *punan*. Adults instead use fear to attempt to scare children into respect and obedience: they are taught to fear *mai*, to fear violence, and to fear other social misbehaviors. When a child is doing something dangerous, parents may literally cry out, "Fear, fear!" This is not to say that Semai people live in a constant state of fear but that they learn self-control and moderation through a certain cautious approach to the physical and social world.

When children do manifest aggression, as all children do when small, parents do not punish the outburst but rather laugh it away or meet it with a mock threat. They may, for instance, fake a blow toward the child. Little ones also play games in which they fake attacks on each other; they may almost but not quite hit each other with a stick, or almost but not quite wrestle each other to the ground. In either case, the attack—and the defeat—is never quite delivered. There are no indigenous games that actually involve aggression or even competition.

Central to Semai conceptions of human interactions, whether between adults or between adult and child, is the value of noninterference, or "not bothering" other people. *Persusah* means to make trouble for someone, to make them unhappy, to meddle in their affairs. A good person does not *persusah* others; *persusah* is to cause *punan*. When someone does *persusah* another, the normal response is passivity or withdrawal. Because this notion of *persusah* is applied to everything from family members to politics, a climate is created in which violence or even competition or domination is unwelcome and almost impossible—in fact, almost inconceivable.

Dentan did note one anomalous manifestation of violence among the otherwise nonviolent Semai. During the communist insurrection in Malaysia, some Semai were involved in the fighting, and he reports that they became effective soldiers, almost fanatical ones. Some described themselves in retrospect as "drunk on blood," and they were even surprised themselves by their behavior, although not exactly upset by it. They just didn't know they had it in them.

Case Study 2: The Even-Tempered Utku of Northern Canada

As described by Briggs (1970), the Utku, one of the Inuit or Eskimo groups of northeast Canada, are another society that avoids violence through their cultural construction of personality and emotion and their enculturation processes. Like the Semai, the Utku are a foraging society, one, however, that is somewhat more male-dominated because of the restricted economic contribution of plant gathering (traditionally women's work) in an arctic environment. Still, this does not lead to extreme gender inequality. They too are a roughly egalitarian society, with band-level political integration and a very scattered settlement pattern, especially in the winter months. During those times, extended family groups live in isolated households, but in the summer various households will often congregate, which can be a mixed blessing.

The inhospitable nature of the arctic climate and the profound closeness of residence among the Utku leads to a social climate in which emotional control is highly valued. Of all virtues, an even temper and mild demeanor under difficult conditions are essential to life in the north. The social ideal is a person who is kind and concerned, helpful and generous, and sociable and never resentful or angry. Negative emotions such as anger or bitterness would be very corrosive in their society. The Utku actually fear and distrust people who do not explicitly show good will and happiness, with smiles, laughter, and joking. Unhappiness, interestingly, is literally equated with hostility. At the same time, people should not exhibit their emotions too openly, for this kind of demonstrativeness makes adults uncomfortable. The proper balance is captured in the term *kanngu*, referring to restraint and shyness or a desire to be appropriately inconspicuous.

One of the key psychocultural concepts in Utku life is *naklik*, which translates to feelings of love, concern, or protectiveness. Adults say that children inspire *naklik* in them. On the other hand, behavior that is not *naklik* includes greed and selfishness, reluctance to help or share and displays of ill temper, from mere sulking to clear violence. The three worst traits that an Utku can possess are bad temper, selfishness, and refusal to help others. The resulting positive feelings and behaviors that are constellated—involving restrained happiness and mild emotional openness manifested in generosity and helpfulness—are perceived as morally good. The opposing constellation of negative feelings and behaviors—involving overly open emotions of any kind and especially hostility and anger (*urulu* or *huaq*) including verbal

Case Study 2: The Even-Tempered Utku of Northern Canada (continued)

criticism and abuse—is perceived as morally bad. Antisocial, anti-*naklik* actions, from verbal roughness to physical violence, are said to make people unhappy, annoyed, and frightened and are not practiced even against children.

The processes by which the Utku establish these tendencies in their members are very much in line with the analysis of Bonta, discussed earlier, and in fact he refers to them in his research. Very small children, under five years old or so, are expected to be emotional—easily angered and frightened—because they lack *ihuma*, or reason, sense. Therefore, adults do not demand much from the youngest children, neither punishing nor encouraging their emotional displays. Utku parents say that there is no point in attempting to teach or discipline such children until they acquire *ihuma*. Rather, small children are to be guarded and loved (*naklik*) with overt affection, and adults show a real fondness and softness toward infants. If a little one does misbehave, the proper adult course is to ignore the behavior or laugh at it. Parents sometimes try temporarily to settle the children down with pleasant words or threats or promises, but the adults almost always end up capitulating to the child's demands.

However, past the age of unreason—some time after age five and certainly by age ten—a child is expected to have developed *ihuma* and with it self-restraint and an understanding of good Utku etiquette, and he or she must demonstrate emotional control. It is in this period, as Bonta notes, that the parents rather abruptly cease to demonstrate affection to the child, often transferring it to a younger sibling. Briggs describes in some detail the passing of the childhood of young Saarak, a daughter in her host family; as a new baby joined the group, she was losing to her infant sister some of the attention, the open demonstrativeness, that she herself had formerly enjoyed. This change was manifested in a general nonresponsiveness of the parents to Saarak's cries, a mild but growing critical attitude toward her immaturity, and even "games" that seemed to tease her into acceptance of her new (and permanent) station in life. In one such game, relatives would pretend to mistake Saarak for the baby Qayaq, calling the latter by the former's name (as if to remind her that she was not the baby of the family anymore). In another, adults would ask a question like, "Where is the charming little one?" and when Saarak pointed to herself and said, "Here," they would point to the baby and say, "No, here." Briggs continues:

> But when, after a few repetitions, Saarak had learned to point to Qayaq, then her interlocutors asked her: "And where's the other charming little one?" Then when Saarak docilely pointed to Qayaq, they would correct her: "No, here," pointing to Saarak herself.
>
> Finally, her family teased her with the question, "Where's the annoying (*urulu*) one?" and getting Saarak to point to herself. Subsequently, her mother told her, "You're not charming; you're an old lady," making the girl cry, only to be comforted while the mother laughed. (Briggs 1970: 153)

Case Study 2: The Even-Tempered Utku of Northern Canada (continued)

Bonta also mentions, and Briggs describes, some of the "games" of physical violence that are played by groups like the Utku.

> Although in Utku society, children are rarely the victims of genuine physical aggression, it does happen occasionally that adults play at physical attack with a small child, as they do with each other. The poking game . . . is such an aggression game, but that game is enjoyed by the child "attacked" as well as by the attacker—until, eventually, adults teach the child to flee in earnest. There are other games, much more rarely played, which the child clearly does not enjoy. These games are always kept within the most careful bounds, yet they are nonetheless striking in contrast with the usual pervasive gentleness. Indeed, the aggressive nature of the games is enhanced by the fact that the players never exert any force; the caution seems to cry danger. One old grandmother was particularly given to these games. "Hit me," she would urge, holding out her face toward her granddaughter; "hit me." The child, Rosi, who was Saarak's age, would hesitatingly stretch out her tiny fist and lightly touch her grandmother's cheek. Immediately, the old lady would tap Rosi's face with her own fist, then again hold out her cheek: "Hit me again." Another of her favorite pranks was to tap her granddaughter lightly on her back or leg when she was not looking, then pretend unawareness when the child turned to investigate. She would repeat the game until Rosi screamed in anger, whereupon her expressionless old face would wrinkle with laughter. (Briggs 1970: 101)

Saarak's parents also sometimes teased her, for example, offering food to her only to snatch it away when she was about to take it. Children also take some pleasure in hurting or killing small animals, including puppies, with their parents' approval. The overall message is an ambiguous one—that violence and emotional harm are not good but they happen and that as you grow you must learn to tuck away your feelings for fear of some unanticipated and unpleasant outcome. As Bonta (1997: 305) concludes: "This builds conflicting feelings of aggression and protectiveness. Complex messages such as those aroused by aggressive games, or the loving and destroying of the same [animal], create doubt in the child that society is predictable, people are always nonviolent and nurturant, and one is always secure."

If there is hostility or hatefulness in Utku society, and there is, it is downplayed within the family but allowed some expression against nonkin. People who are more distant relatives or nonrelatives can be, and are, the brunt of hostile talk, such as gossip and name-calling; especially popular epithets include "greedy," "lazy," "unhelpful," and the like. People can accuse them of stealing or other antisocial behavior. Still, even toward nonkin, physical violence is intolerable and virtually unknown to happen; about the worst thing anyone can do to anyone else is ostracize them. Interestingly, Briggs points out that the Utku are aware of the emotional differences between themselves and Westerners. They say that the non-Utku are liable to be emotionally volatile—easy to anger and easy to get over anger—while they themselves do not anger but do not forgive. In fact, Briggs' host family was particularly displeased with her, calling her annoying for getting agitated and critical, lying to them, and scolding them. At one point, they asked her to leave.

In conclusion, then, the Utku people display little anger and almost no violence, but they still must struggle to some extent with these emotions. The overall tenor of their society is determined by their concern for the feelings of others (that other people not be unhappy or lonely), their values of generosity and unobtrusiveness into others' lives (including that of their own children), a general "horror" at demonstrations of anger and violence, and a milder aversion to any strong overt emotion.

Case Study 3: Jainism—a Religion of Nonviolence

Many, if not all, religions talk about peace and love and harmony, but their talk is clouded and contradicted by other messages and ultimately by their actions. Few if any religions have ever achieved a genuinely pacifist ideology and lifestyle, and perhaps examining one that has will shed light on what really contributes to peace and nonviolence. Almost ironically, the name "Jainism" derives from the term *jin,* meaning "conqueror"; however, like the "Greater *jihad"* discussed in Chapter 6, this conquest is not of the enemy but of the vices and lower instincts within the individual, such as desire and hatred. A Jain is one who sets out, not to conquer a world but to conquer a self.

Jainism as a religion is comparable to Buddhism in many ways, and in fact both appeared at roughly the same historical moment as reform movements of Hinduism. It does not teach any belief about a god who is a creator or sustainer or destroyer of the world; rather, like Buddhism, it is essentially a discipline based on a set of spiritual principles. These principles include the distinction between the material body and a spiritual identity separate from that body. Mahavir, the first "Jain," who lived around 500–600 B.C.E., taught this discipline, although he is not credited with "inventing" it.

The goal of Jainism, as that of Buddhism and even that of Hinduism, is the purification and ultimate liberation of the "soul" from the physical body and thus the achievement of true self-knowledge (sometimes known as *moksha* or *nirvana*). The link between the soul and the body, and between this bodily life and past and future bodily lives, is karma, which in the Jain view is a literal physical thing, like "grains" or "atoms" of religious matter. The soul is in bondage because of karma, which leads to a materialistic orientation in life and inevitably to negative and violent thoughts and actions like anger, hatred, greed, and so on. These thoughts and actions

Case Study 3: Jainism—a Religion of Nonviolence (continued)

result in more karma, which accumulates like dirt or rust on the soul. If the goal is to escape the bondage of the physical world and allow the soul to know itself as the free, nonphysical entity that it is, then the path to this goal is the liberation of oneself from matter and from the consequences of material action.

As a discipline, Jainism consists of what is called the Five Great Vows, a code of conduct intended to minimize one's interaction with matter and the degrading results of matter. Number one on this list of behaviors is *ahimsa*, or nonviolence. Obviously, it includes proscriptions against killing or harming people, but it goes much further. In its most dramatic manifestation, it takes the form of radical dietary rules. Vegetarianism is the least of the rules. It goes without saying that humans should not eat meat (that is, the flesh of the "five-sensed beings" who are most closely related to us). Eggs too are living things, though without the full five senses, and so cannot be consumed, although milk is acceptable since it is not a being in its own right. Not even insects or "mobile beings" without all five sense are edible, and devout Jains will even wear masks, drink through strainers, and sweep the path in front of them with whisks to avoid swallowing or stepping on such beings.

However, even vegetables are living things, so the strictures of *ahimsa* apply to them as well. Cereals like rice and wheat are the ideal and "fully noninjurious food" among the "one-sensed beings" of plants, because the seeds are produced only at the end of the natural life of the plant; thus, no additional harm is done by eating them. So-called "dry-fruits" are acceptable for the same reason. Next in acceptability are the fruits that ripen on trees or that fall from trees of their own after ripening, as this causes no anguish to the plant. Least acceptable among the plant foods are ones that are taken from a living plant, such as leaves (like lettuce) or roots and tubers (like potatoes and carrots). These foods are living and feeling parts of one-sensed beings, the removal of which causes pain to the plant and may also harm small mobile beings that live within them. Consuming such foods brings anguish to the plant and karma to the person. In fact, the ideal Jain life would involve doing no harm at all to the environment, which would involve consuming no food at all. And this is indeed the preferred way to leave this life—by depriving oneself of all food and departing karma free.

In addition to this demanding virtue, the Great Vows include four others, of a more conventional variety. They are *saty*, or truthfulness; *achaurya*, or nonstealing; *brahmacharya*, or chastity; and *aparigraha*, or nonpossession and nonattachment. Notably, Jainism advocates classlessness and gender neutrality; Brahmans and untouchables are welcome alike into the faith, and men and women are equal in their quest for liberation. Also, religious tolerance (*anekantvada*, or nonabsolutism, and open-mindedness) prevents a militant us-versus-them worldview and removes some of the cause for religious disagreement and animosity. Finally, relativity (*syadvada*) leaves no space for extreme or unequivocal assertions.

Case Study 3: Jainism—a Religion of Nonviolence (continued)

What these vows and principles suggest is a way of life that focuses not merely on the interests and good of the self or even of the "community of the faithful" but literally on others—all others—no matter what their station or even their species. Like the Semai or the Utku discussed earlier in the chapter, peace and harmony come not just from doing right in one own's interest as from doing right in everyone's interest—and everything's. If the quest for salvation depends crucially on the well-being of others, then the motivations for violence are negated. Dehumanization is impossible; if anything, even the nonhuman world is humanized. Further, if the antagonizers of society, including class and gender, are minimized, there will be less occasion for fighting and violence. Finally, where tolerance and relativity are serious values, blind obedience and indoctrination—two of Zimbardo's key ingredients for violence—are deprived of a place to embed themselves.

Case Study 4: Invisible Violence in the Piaroa of Venezuela

As described by Overing (1986), the Piaroa are a generally nonaggressive society in the rainforest of Venezuela, living near the highly aggressive Yanomamo (see next chapter). Like the Yanomamo, the Piaroa are a predominantly horticultural society, which practices some hunting as well. However, that is about where the similarities end.

The Piaroa social world is almost totally devoid of physical violence. Children are never physically punished, spouses never hit each other, and people are typically appalled by aggressive displays. Instead, they value interpersonal moderation. They do not possess political leaders, similar to the band-level societies described above. Occasionally shamans may accumulate some political power, but the more powerful someone like a shaman becomes, the more humble he is expected to act. Violence is associated with domination, and domination is associated with coercion, all of which are viewed negatively.

In particular, killing by physical means is held to be unthinkable and is equated with cannibalism, the "consumption" or "destruction" of one's own kind. The Piaroa believe that killing/cannibalism would cause their own death by a kind of spiritual poisoning. For the Piaroa, in fact, all killing is a form of cannibalism, and all death is a result of being eaten. There is no such thing as a "natural" human death, but rather all death is the work of sorcery by external

Case Study 4: Invisible Violence in the Piaroa of Venezuela (continued)

societies. More than that, consuming plants and animals—and the culture itself that gives the knowledge and skills to do so—are violent, dangerous, poisonous. Although Piaroa society condemns physical, "visible" violence, it is awash in spiritual, "invisible" violence.

To understand this mind-set, let us consider Piaroa cosmogony. In the Piaroa creation story, there were two creator beings, named Kuemoi and Wahari. Kuemoi, the Master of Water, was a violent—even insanely violent—ugly cannibal, and Wahari, the Master of Land, was the creator of the Piaroa people. The two beings were rivals and sorcerers, competing for each other's domain. Invading Wahari's land domain, Kuemoi created fire, plants and animals, and the means for exploiting the latter (that is, "culture," the knowledge and skills of farming and hunting). Wahari, in addition to creating humans in his own domain, created fish and fishing in his rival's sphere. Perhaps more consequentially, though, he transformed the nonhuman species from their original spiritual and anthropomorphic forms into their present edible forms. By losing their humanlike form, plants and animals became proper food for humans.

The extreme and almost unbearably contradictory message in this tale is that poison is everywhere in the world. Culture is poisonous because it was created by a mad god who was literally poisoned himself by drugs at the time of creation. Food is also poisonous; animals and large fish are dangerous to eat, but so are small fish, birds, and even plants. Consuming any of these things is dangerous, not because they cause physical harm but because they cause spiritual, invisible harm. After all, animals and fish were formerly "people" who were transformed into nonhuman beings by the gods and who are jealous and angry for losing their human forms and their ability to have culture. Therefore, although we humans eat them, they try to avenge themselves by "eating" us.

The world, thus, is an inescapably violent and dangerous place. If we do not eat, we die, but if we eat, we may also die. Every choice, every step, is fraught with peril. Inherent to the Piaroa world is the tension between eating and being eaten, and both actions occur simultaneously and continuously. If a Piaroa kills an animal and eats it, it is possible for the animal's spirit to enter that person's body and begin to devour it. All consumption is cannibalistic: since the animals and plants were formerly people, we perform cannibalism if we eat them, and if one of them attacks us from inside, we are victims of cannibalism.

The job of the shaman is to constantly engage the spiritual forces of violence and disease. If a shaman believes that a person is occupied by a destructive animal or plant spirit that is consuming him or her from within, the shaman can call upon a special set of spirits to do battle with the evil spirit inside the victim—literally, to eat the spirit that is eating the victim! Life consumes life, spirit consumes spirit.

Case Study 4: Invisible Violence in the Piaroa of Venezuela (continued)

In other words, Piaroa existence amounts to a perpetual state of reciprocal cannibalism, and religion is a daily struggle against spirits and against nature—and against human violence. Any person who acts aggressively or shows a tendency to harm or dominate others is believed to be under the control of one of the poisonous forces of the world and is cordoned off from society until he or she learns proper conduct, particularly humility and mildness. This practice forces the more important or powerful members of society, especially shamans, into a state of contradiction. Because only shamans can keep the forces of culture and nature at bay, they are important and dominant figures in society. However, if they begin to act too self-important or bossy, people will suspect them of being under malevolent influence. Being most intimately and continuously in contact with the forces of violence and death, they must be extremely careful to maintain proper demeanor. Thus, the more powerful one is, the more humble and mild one must behave. In the end, violence in Piaroa society is always seen as coming from the outside—from forces spiritual, natural, or cultural—and this violence—the violence of life—is impossible to escape.

Case Study 5: The Friendly Headhunting Ilongot of the Philippines

As described by Rosaldo (1980), the Ilongot are what we would call "headhunters," since they would conduct raids to kill victims and sever their heads, but they are not otherwise what we would consider a violent people. Except for their occasional (sometimes once-in-a-lifetime) headhunting expeditions, they are generally a peaceful group. The unexpected violent behavior carries special meaning for the Ilongot and their overall notions of self and emotion.

The Ilongot number about 3,500 people living in around thirty-five dispersed settlements in the hilly jungle of northern Luzon, an island in the Philippines, just 150 miles north of the capital city of Manila. To call the settlements dispersed is no exaggeration, as they may be from a few minutes' to several hours' walk from each other. Economically, the men hunt in the jungle and clear gardens for the women, who practice horticulture, raising rice, sugar, bananas, and other crops. However, this division of labor according to gender is not absolute, each gender assisting in the other's activities from time to time. Marriages are monogamous and matrilocal, with households containing on average seven members and settlements up

Egalitarian
unstratified
non competing

Case Study 5: The Friendly Headhunting Ilongot of the Philippines (continued)

to ten households. Politically, the Ilongot too, like all of the other societies we have encountered so far, are egalitarian. Men are considered to have more "knowledge" (*beya*) than women and also more "passion" (*liget*). Accordingly, men have the right to command (*tuydek*) women, but in practice women are generally granted gender equality—they have influence in tribal decisions, can resist male commands, and are not subject to violence from men. Indeed, such violence is not only uncommon but disapproved of by society. The greater *beya* and *liget* of men is not considered to be an aspect of inherent gender superiority but a result of the more extensive travel and the more strenuous and dangerous tasks of men. As always, it is critical not to interpret these kinds of statements through the lenses of our own culture; it would be wrong to conclude that every difference necessarily constitutes an inequality or that such distinctions have the same meaning and repercussions in all societies.

Be that as it may, it is clear that *beya* and *liget* are central concepts in the Ilongot's psychology and social reality. They believe that the heart is the center of human feeling, will, and action and that all growing things, not just humans, have heart. Heart is thus not only a psychological or "internal" thing but also includes one's external and social activities, particularly *liget*, which refers to energy, anger, passion, movement, enthusiasm, violence, and so on. To have *liget* means to be ready to take action, to be forceful, quick-moving, even a little stubborn, and to overcome shyness, fear, and reservation. *Liget* is thus a generally positive quality. When born from insults, slights, and other insinuations of inequality or envy, *liget* makes the heart withdraw from social interaction and oppose another person. It is therefore also associated with separation, social confusion, and chaos.

But social withdrawal and social disruption are considered negative and are linked to bad feeling and to bad health. Health, happiness, and sociality are all interconnected in a positive way. *Sipe*, happiness, is taken as the opposite of *liget* and depends on active engagement in society. How is this duality of *sipe* and *liget* reconciled? The answer is through the concept of *beya*, knowledge or experience. *Beya* gives form, sense, and consequence to heart. "Good *liget*" is concentrated or focused by *beya* into productive activity—work, sexuality, strength and courage, and in some instances killing. Chaotic, unfocused *liget* is frightening and ugly, but harnessed *liget* is beautiful and intense.

What does this cultural psychology have to do with headhunting? The male headhunter is normally a bachelor and therefore young, possessing more *liget* than *beya*. Adult and married men may assist in the instigation, planning, and celebration of the kill, but they do not ordinarily participate in it. The hunt actually commences as an orderly and structured exercise, but once the killing starts, the youths may get into a frenzy of wild and intense pleasure—

Case Study 5: The Friendly Headhunting
Ilongot of the Philippines (continued)

the feeling of *liget*. The goal is to cut off a victim's head and throw it to the ground, and if someone else intercepts it then it is his kill, not yours.

The Ilongot, looking back on their headhunting past, say that the moment of taking an enemy's head was life lived at its fullest, the peak experience when *beya* or knowledge had arrived to the young man but *liget* had not yet started to wane. The hunters, called *gelasaget* or "anxious seekers," shared that term with—and were the same people as—the bachelors on the hunt for a wife. Both consummations of the search, taking a head and gaining a bride, ended the search, relieved the tension, but also marked the beginning of the decline of male energy or *liget*. As a man "settles down" and matures as a husband and householder, his *beya* grows while his *liget* declines. He may never take—or even desire to take—another head, but he would encourage and aid other young men in the full flower of their *liget* to complete their search for that one peak moment when knowledge and passion intersect.

RETROSPECT AND PROSPECT

This survey of nonviolent societies has been short, because truly nonviolent societies are rare in human history. It has not been exhaustive—other nonviolent societies exist, including the !Kung bushmen and the Australian aboriginals (who are nonviolent most of the time, although they are willing to fight and even kill under certain circumstances, particularly in reaction to a violation of religious taboos), but they are few in number. What do these societies share in common? They are not nonviolent because they have a different "nature" from us moderns; in fact, we all share the same basic human nature. Nor are they nonviolent because they are "primitive" or because they are "better than us" (the Jains are a distinctly modern community) and the differences between nonviolent peoples and ourselves are primarily social-structural and psychocultural in nature.

In examining these same aspects of characteristically violent (sometimes extremely violent) societies in the next chapter and throughout the rest of the book, we will see that violence is motivated by a vast (although not infinite) number of interests and forces. In the end, it is possible that the societies that avoid or escape or suppress violence (the verb you choose will depend on your theoretical attitude toward the "naturalness" of human violence) have discovered the few paths or even the single path to harmonious human social relations, whereas the societies that indulge in violence or suffer it exploit the human potentiality for violence in amazingly varied and creative ways. What that says about us as humans is worth serious consideration.

VIOLENCE IN CROSS-CULTURAL CONTEXT

Traditional and Complex Violent Societies

In the last chapter, we examined a sample of the few (much less than 1 percent) of the world's societies that are classified as nonviolent. We could not help but notice that even some of these societies practiced limited violence, including headhunting. At the same time, we noticed some commonalities between these societies in terms of their social arrangements and their psychocultural dispositions.

In this chapter we will examine a sample of the much more numerous and diverse violent societies of the world. We will divide this sample into "traditional" and "complex," or state-level, societies, and we will look in some cases at societies as a whole and in other cases at specific instances or expressions of violence in those societies. As we do so, we should expect to observe that different sets of macrosocial and microsocial structures give rise to different psychocultural values and dispositions. In those societies that at least accept if not prize violence, we will find increased size and stratification of society, competition, male domination, harsh parenting, multiple manifestations of violence (seldom do we get violence in only one form within a violent society), and prickly concepts of power, honor, and shame. In other words, we can expect not only to see the violence but to see why violence "makes sense" or is explicable to them within a particular social and cultural context. In fact, some of these violent societies will even regard their behavior not as "violence" at all and certainly not as a "social problem" but as good and normal conduct.

VIOLENT TRADITIONAL SOCIETIES: CASE STUDIES

In the first of the two sections in this chapter we will look at an assortment of "traditional," or small-scale, societies. In most cases we will be using reports by fieldworkers, whose assessment of a particular society as traditional may no longer apply. However, in a number of cases it will be clear that we are talking about contemporary circumstances. Also, as for nonviolent societies, our sampling is far from exhaustive but suffices to illustrate the sorts of violence that occur in traditional societies and explore their sociocultural context; not in every case is the society violent in every conceivable manner, and in a few they are at least somewhat aware of and troubled by the violence that they commit or that they are implicated in.

Case Study 1: Systemic Violence in the Yanomamo of Venezuela

As described by Chagnon (1968), the Yanomamo have become the best-known example of a violent traditional society in the literature of anthropology. They have become, fairly or unfairly, the very prototype of a "fierce people." At the time of Chagnon's research the Yanomamo numbered some 10,000 living in about 125 scattered villages, ranging from 40 to 250 people each, with 75 to 80 being the usual number. They are located in the jungle of southern Venezuela and northern Brazil.

The Yanomamo practice horticulture with some hunting; men plant gardens and hunt, while women cook and gather firewood and water. They are **polygynous** and **patrilineal**, with an ideal of village **endogamy.** The basic unit of each village is the lineage segment, a set of related men (fathers, sons, and brothers). However, brothers are competitors for wives, so relations between brothers, especially brothers of similar age, are not close; they are often jealous, reserved, and respectful rather than warm. Marriages are arranged by men, usually within the village but sometimes with other (hopefully larger) villages. Women do not like to be married off to men in distant villages, because men are generally cruel to their wives, and with no brothers nearby to protect them they have no defense against this cruelty. Even so, exchanging women with other villages is a good way to form alliances and to prevent attack, especially if one's village is small (less than eighty inhabitants). Villages of forty or fifty people have trouble supplying themselves with women and defending themselves against the predation of other villages. At the same time, villages of more than a hundred members tend to develop internal strife, especially over adultery, so there is a tendency toward fission when villages reach a critical size.

Yanomamo society is a hotbed of tension and conflict, and men are required to demonstrate their fierceness constantly both in the domestic sphere and in intervillage rivalries. Most of the conflict is related to gender and sex relations. It is very much a patriarchal society; women have no say in their own marriages and are essentially pawns or resources in the social and

Case Study 1: Systemic Violence in the Yanomamo of Venezuela (continued)

political maneuvers of their kinsmen. After marriage, women are expected to serve their husbands by cooking and collecting firewood and water for them. If a man returns home suddenly from a hunt or raid, his wife is required to run immediately and start cooking for him; if she is slow, he has the right to hit her. Usually such blows are administered with the hand or with a nearby piece of wood, sometimes with the sharp edge of an ax or with an arrow or a burning stick. The worst punishments are doled out for infidelity, which is common. Some men show their ferocity by applying serious punishments to even minor infractions, and some women actually admire their husbands for their meanness, as if his behavior illustrates that he is a strong man or a man who really cares about her. But women do not appreciate major cruelty and may enlist brothers (if they are available) to support her; in the worst cases, she may run away from the marriage.

Much of the violence and fierceness of men can be traced to gender inequality and to child enculturation practices. Female infanticide is common (although male infanticide is fairly common too). A woman may kill her new baby if it is born while she is still nursing another child, which can last for two or three years. The most frequent method of death is strangulation or throwing the baby against a tree, or sometimes it is simply abandoned. Often mothers do not kill their children outright but neglect them to the point of starvation.

Boys and girls are socialized very differently. Little boys are naturally encouraged to be aggressive. They are allowed to slap adults and to tease little girls. Fathers will actually often tease boys until the latter slap or hit them, at which point the adults cheer in approval. Boys are also free of adult responsibilities until their teenage years, while girls start to learn and practice their subservient domestic roles very early in life. By the time boys are beginning to pass into adulthood, girls may already be married with children of their own (married to much older men, of course).

Finally, children are not immune to the hostility of the village. Children in fact are often the targets of adult sorcery: shamans will send evil spirits to eat the souls of children from other villages, and one of the jobs of shamans is to protect local children from such attacks by other villages.

Yanomamo society has a variety of institutionalized forms of violence, on a continuum from least to most serious. At the "lowest" level of hostility is the chest-pounding duel, which takes place between different villages and usually follows on occasions of insult, gossip, accusations of cowardice, stinginess, or unfairness in trade. In these duels, two men—one from each village—step forward, and one presents his chest and dares the other to hit it. The hitter punches the left pectoral region of the challenger with his closed fist as hard as possible. The supporters of the challenger urge him to take another punch, and up to four blows will be delivered before the challenger gets his turn to become

Case Study 1: Systemic Violence in the
Yanomamo of Venezuela (continued)

the hitter. The new hitter then gets to punch his challenger as many times as the former was punched. If either fighter retires before the blows are evened out, he is replaced by another man from the same group, so the duel continues. The point of the exercise is merely to earn a reputation for fierceness.

Next in order of seriousness is the side-slapping duel. In this competition, a man lands a blow with his open hand to the side of the other man's body between his ribs and hip. This form of dueling is more dangerous, since major injuries and fatalities are more common, but it is also shorter in duration—when a fighter is injured, the battle is soon over. Third in intensity is the club fight, which is usually brought on by disputes over women. Adultery is frequent in society, partly because of the chronic shortage of women, especially in smaller villages, and partly because of the sex taboo that holds for the periods of pregnancy and nursing, which can last two or three years. Men during these times will often seek other women for sexual comfort—women who are married or engaged to other men. Such is an occasion for a club fight.

In a club fight, men grab large lengths of wood or logs and take turns hitting each other on the head. As in the chest-pounding and side-slapping combats, taking turns is an integral part of the violence. Rather than being embarrassed by their infidelities, many men proudly display their head scars, even shaving their hair short or off to make the scars more visible. If the sexual rivalries cannot be settled with a club fight, then village fission may follow.

Raiding other villages constitutes a further level of violent interaction in Yanomamo society. The objective of raids or "war" is to kill one or more of the enemy without being caught or losing any of your own men. Raids are usually fought for revenge, but they may also be conducted to capture women. They believe that large villages are right to raid smaller ones; weakness is an invitation to attack, and that is why showing strength and fierceness is key to survival, both individually and as a village. The ultimate form of violence is treachery (*nomohoni*), in which a group or village tricks another into an ambush of some sort. One example would be if a party or village draws another party or village out with an offer of trade or other peaceful interaction, then attacks and kills the men and steals their women.

New wars and treacherous attacks are not usually started over women, although the Yanomamo themselves claim that arguments over women are their primary reason for war. However, in practice accusations of sorcery, previous deaths and the demands of revenge, or serious club fights appear to be the instigation for most violent confrontations. However, once war breaks out, acquiring women from the rival becomes a priority. If women are captured, they are raped by all of the men in the war party and taken back to the village, where they can be raped by any man who desires to participate.

Case Study 2: Ambivalent Violence in the Gisu of Uganda

The Gisu as described by Heald (1986) number some 500,000 Bantu-speaking horticulturalists who are renowned for their violence. They are feared by their neighbors for their aggressiveness and even regarded as cannibals; within Gisu society itself, some clans are more feared than others and some are considered cannibals by others. Their reputation for violence appears to be well deserved: in the 1940s and 1950s, the murder rate within Gisu society was 8.2 per 100,000, which was the highest in Uganda, and in the 1960s it increased further, to 24 per 100,000, which was twice as high as any group in the country.

Interestingly, almost all of the violence in Gisu society is interpersonal—that is, between individual men—rather than intergroup; there is little or no "war," raiding, or feuding. Also, it is noteworthy that the Gisu, while they are certainly aware of their violent tendencies, are not proud of them. Rather than glorifying their own hostile behaviors, they will often criticize individual aggressors or killers as bad men, and they even go so far as to condemn themselves as a bad people. "But what can we do?" they say.

However, as ambivalent as they are about their aggressive side, the Gisu seem to perpetuate this aspect of their personality and society by continuing to value and inculcate what they call *lirima*. *Lirima* is the manly quality of violent emotion, a force that "catches" a man or "boils over" in him, driving his attitudes and actions. It is linked to anger, jealousy, hatred, and resentment and is associated with actual physical changes and sensations like a lump in the throat or a rush of adrenaline.

But *lirima* is not a totally wild emotion; having *lirima* also implies control, strength of character, courage, and determination. It is a quality that only men possess. *Lirima* allows men to overcome fear. As such, it is viewed positively, as essential to withstanding life's ordeals bravely, but it also makes for dangerous men. Because of the presence of *lirima*, the Gisu see themselves as plagued by violent men whose aggression can boil over at any time and is a permanent part of their personality. This kind of aggression is not culturally condoned.

It is, though, culturally constructed or inculcated. The Gisu do not believe that *lirima* is a natural or instinctive quality of men. Rather, it must be created or installed. The process by which *lirima*, or the capacity to experience *lirima*, is generated is the circumcision ritual. Between the ages of eighteen and twenty-five, young men are circumcised in a public ceremony. The initiates are required to stand in the compound of their fathers and to betray no fear or pain as the operation proceeds. If he successfully passes the ordeal, the

Case Study 2: Ambivalent Violence in the Gisu of Uganda (continued)

men cheer and the women sing, and observers congratulate him on becoming a man.

Circumcision and other such "rites of passage" are common in traditional societies, and they even persist in modern, large-scale societies like our own. Generally, as analyzed by Van Gennep and Turner among others, the idea of such rites is that they not only mark but actually accomplish a status change—from single to married or from child to adult, for instance. For the Gisu, though, circumcision effects more than a status change; it effects an actual physical change, instilling in the youth his ability to experience *lirima* or violent emotion. The entire point of the procedure is to induce and to prove the youth's *lirima*. In most societies that practice such bodily ordeals, for example, there is also a component of instruction or socialization into the rules and roles of adulthood. For the Gisu, there is no other real content to the ritual and no "teaching"; the only additional component is the awarding to the youth of certain implements of manhood, essentially consisting of farming tools—but not, curiously, spears or other weapons.

What we see then is a cultural contradiction or irony: Gisu literally create a kind of man that they do not particularly value or want and that they suffer from. At the very least, they accept the negative consequences of creating such men, brave and angry men, who will be a potential problem for society later on. They, apparently, do not perceive the irony in their own behavior, and it is difficult to imagine what they might think about it if they did.

Case Study 3: Visible and Invisible Violence in the Mkako of Cameroon

As described by Copet-Rougier (1986), the Mkako distinguish between visible and invisible violence, neither of which is "symbolic" but quite real. Traditionally, the Mkako were foragers with some horticulture of yams and bananas, although they are farmers today. They lived in separate villages of five hundred to a thousand members, each village containing several unequal patriclans. Generally, the largest of the resident patriclans was the dominant one. Such clans or even smaller **patrilocal** households were the main corporate groups in society, making village solidarity weak. There were no chiefs or central political institutions, making them a fairly classic "tribal" society.

Case Study 3: Visible and Invisible Violence
in the Mkako of Cameroon (continued)

Within the patrilocal households, which they refer to as "fires," all physical violence is forbidden except in funeral rituals and between husband and wife. Absolutely no fighting between adult males is permitted. The Mkako concept of violence or *sasur* is related to breath and dryness, and it is likened to an inexplicable force that arises without reason, such as a gust of wind. It is also related to excess and to heat, as opposed to *weinate* or peace and cool.

Physical or "visible" violence is restricted to outside the patrilocal community and figures as "war" (*ndjambi*). War against outsiders is acceptable, but war, including feuds and vengeance killings, within the community would split it in two, making an "outsider" of a former insider. During the course of external wars, war leaders (*bende*) may emerge who are believed to control magic, have the support of spirits, and control *duma*, an animatistic force something like mana. While the *bende* is successful he may begin to acquire the role of a chief, but his (inevitable) failure or the rivalries engendered by his success eventually lead to the collapse of his incipient power.

Mkako war, even though it is prosecuted against "others," is subject to rules, although in some cases few if any limits are applied. If the enemy is foreign (non-Mkako) or remote, any violence is permissible, including cannibalism. If the enemy is a neighbor, Mkako or not, then the scope of the violence depends on any existing blood relations between the warring parties. If there are consanguines in the opposing party, then the fighting ends when the first man is killed; if there are no consanguines on the opposing side, any level of violence is possible. However, no man can or will fight with a mother's brother or a sister's son, and the war is stopped immediately if such relatives exist on the other side. No one would kill or eat kin, literally or symbolically.

Although physical or visible violence is proscribed against the "in-group," it is possible and common to have "invisible" violence between or even within clans. Competition between elders of different clans is actually frequent and important and takes the form of witchcraft (*lembo*). *Lembo* may even be used against members of one's own "fire" and is the only acceptable intracommunity form of aggression. In fact, as has been noted in numerous societies, witchcraft works especially well against those who are closest to the witch in proximity and kinship, because these are the people who are in most direct competition with potential witches. Mkako witches practice *lembo* against kin, and the most likely way to be subject to *lembo* is to stay in the same "fire" with one's kin. However, leaving the "fire" does not offer any real protection, since the consanguineal bonds still exist. So blood relatives are never really free from possible *lembo* done by their kin; only mother's brothers and sister's sons are off-limits from witchcraft, as these are the men who are dearest to you and must protect you.

*Case Study 3: Visible and Invisible Violence
in the Mkako of Cameroon (continued)*

Lembo is conceived as a spider or a crab in the belly of the witch that kills by sucking the blood of the victim, a kind of invisible cannibalism. *Lembo* victims are usually the people with whom the witch is in competition; often the attack is directed toward the women or children of the competitor, but sometimes the conflict is immediately witch versus witch. In the latter case, the witchcraft duel becomes an invisible war that ends in the death of one of the witches.

In conclusion, the Mkako recognize two forms of violence, visible and invisible, each real and each with its distinct forces, leaders, and domains. In the realm of visible violence, war leaders or *bende* depend on their *duma* to battle external enemies. In the realm of invisible violence, witches depend on their *lembo* to battle internal enemies. It is worth mentioning that war leaders can also try to acquire invisible power to augment their visible power, but this inevitably fails, as all overt attempts at gathering power fail.

Case Study 4: The Warrior Culture of the Cheyenne in North America

As described by Hoebel (1960), the Cheyenne were traditionally a pastoral society living on the western plains of North America, in the area of present-day Colorado. "Traditionally" here, however, refers to a particular period in Cheyenne history, for scholars of Native American history have concluded that the Cheyenne, like other Plains Indian groups, resided much farther east at an earlier time, migrating westward under pressure from tribes that were themselves being forced west by white expansion. Probably inhabiting the wooded area in the vicinity of Minnesota until recent centuries, the Cheyenne still exhibit traits of their original horticultural culture. Arriving in the Great Plains and acquiring horses, the Cheyenne developed a classic buffalo-hunting adaptation. Unlike true pastoralists, who control and herd their domesticated animals, Plains buffalo-hunters never domesticated the buffalo but followed them and preyed on them for virtually all of their economic and religious needs. Men hunted on horseback with bow and arrow and spear, usually in groups; there were restrictions on solo hunting. Women gathered plant foods using a digging stick, leaving camp in small groups and eventually separating from the group to gather plants individually. As pastoralists, the Cheyenne had to be mobile, so their housing was portable and their camps temporary, and populations of camps were low, numbering no more than a few dozen. Land

Case Study 4: The Warrior Culture of the
Cheyenne in North America (continued)

was not owned but rather occupied and controlled by particular societies, so
the possibility of competition over land was very real.

Within Cheyenne kinship, marriage was polygynous but at the same time
matrilocal or **neolocal** (perhaps a vestige of their earlier woodland culture).
Marriage was a serious and formal business between two families, characterized by gift exchanges. Men sometimes spent years attempting to win their
brides. Because of the matrilocal tendency, the residential and corporate
group was a female-centered family, headed by the oldest active husband in
the group. Families were not equal but ranked on the basis of personality, hard
work, and property. Divorce was easy, and the **levirate** and **sororate** were
practiced.

Occupying a social level superior to that of residential families were **bilateral** kindreds, which were composed of relatives who helped each other in
collecting and sharing food, preparing for marriage, and conducting rituals
and which connected related family units. Related kindreds were further organized in "bands," ten of which were known to exist in Cheyenne society, each
with its unique name and subculture, based on personality, physical appearance, or behavior. Bands were **exogamous**, and new bands could form by fission. These bands ordinarily camped separately, but they could come together
in times of ritual or war to create a "tribal camp" that could contain much or all
of Cheyenne society.

Gender roles and personalities were not only distinct but unequal. Men's
work (hunting) was more prestigious than women's work, and men also took
on the important roles of war, ritual, and politics. Men were expected to be
slow to anger and to control their emotions but also to be aggressive and to
have a strong ego. Early accounts describe them as quiet, rational, and sexually
repressed. Women were also expected to be restrained, although less aggressive and "touchier." These traits were instilled during childhood through strict
instruction yet little or no physical punishment. Babies were carried by their
mothers at all times, but they were not comforted when they cried; rather, they
were left alone. Designed to teach that crying is bad and futile, this practice
produced a stoic attitude in the Cheyenne populace. Early in their lives children were assigned adult roles, and by age twelve or thirteen the sexes were
separated. Individualism and competition were important, praised, and
rewarded.

One special form that male aggression and competition took in Cheyenne
society was a set of nonkinship groups known as warrior clubs or "societies."
Originally, there were five male warrior societies, named Fox, Elk, Shield,
Dog, and Bowstring/Contrary, although two more—Wolf and Northern Crazy
Dog—were added later. Membership in a society was open to any man, and

Case Study 4: The Warrior Culture of the
Cheyenne in North America (continued)

the societies were not ranked formally, although their performance of specific tasks could earn them special status. Each society possessed its own symbolic objects, clothing, dances, and songs.

Each warrior society had four leaders—two head chiefs who were ritual leaders and two other chiefs who were the bravest men in the group—and together these society chiefs made up the war chiefs of the tribe. The chiefs' main duty was, naturally enough, war; they were also responsible for a kind of policing function during hunts and rituals and enforcement of "government" regulations. This government—known as the Council of Forty-Four—was composed of forty-four "peace chiefs" who kept the peace within the tribe and made decisions regarding camp relocation, war, and crime. Positions on the council were formal offices with ten-year terms, and council members, all former war chiefs and headmen of their families, represented their respective bands. Each band had roughly the same number of chiefs on the council.

Although the council was the highest authority in Cheyenne politics, peace chiefs did not enjoy unlimited obedience and were not wealthier than other citizens. In fact, peace chiefs were not expected to be authoritarian at all but to be kind, generous, and wise as well as brave. Their primary role was to make and adjudicate laws, which formally dealt with violence both toward humans and toward the buffalo. For example, fighting and even anger within the camp were proscribed, and killing within the group was deemed a serious offense: a killer was a "rotten" person who would cause people as well as animals to stay away. The penalty for killing was ostracism and exile (although perpertrators were sometimes readmitted to the tribe after a few years) and death if necessary. There were also strict rules against feuds and revenge among families, behavior that merely produced more "rotten" people. Suicide was also rotten, but sometimes women committed it as a form of protest, an act that brought shame on their families.

Another strict set of rules concerned hunting. As mentioned earlier, solo hunting was forbidden, in the belief that a single man hunting alone would spoil the hunt for the tribe. Laws specified how and when hunting should be performed. The warrior societies policed the hunts, punishing any infraction of the rules.

Finally, war was a regular and organized feature of Cheyenne life, but only when directed at other tribes. Cheyenne would fight to control land, to avenge past defeats and deaths, to steal horses, and particularly for individual glory and status. There were three types of war—private, club, and tribal. In private war, any man could lead a war party for the purpose of stealing horses or revengeful scalping of enemies , and men were usually eager to join such parties. In club war, men from a particular warrior society would plan and carry out a joint attack on enemies, usually for reasons of vengeance; each society

***Case Study 4: The Warrior Culture of the
Cheyenne in North America (continued)***

acted in its own interests and on its own authority, and such wars brought the society honor and prestige. In tribal war, the entire Cheyenne tribe planned and coordinated attacks, with all of the warrior societies participating.

In waging war, more important than actually killing the enemy was the demonstration of bravery and the winning of glory. The main goal was "counting coup," a coup being any brave action, such as striking an enemy, saving a friend, being the first to locate the enemy, charging the enemy by oneself, and the like. Sometimes this behavior was taken to the extreme, especially by the so-called Contraries, who would do things like ride into battle backward or without weapons. In fact, their contrary behavior extended into other domains of life: they would not marry or ever sit or lie on a bed, they lived alone, and they did everything in a manner opposite to that of regular people. Respected as warriors, they were otherwise pitied by their fellows. As a general rule, all young boys from the age of fourteen or fifteen would join war parties, and by age twenty were considered full-fledged warriors. They would take their part in wars, counting coup, showing bravery and gathering glory. In a Cheyenne war, if a man died without counting coup, the war was regarded as a failure, no matter how many enemy warriors were tagged or killed.

Case Study 5: Violence and Culture Change in the Suri of Ethiopia

As described by Abbink (2001), the Suri are a tribal society in southwestern Ethiopia near the border with Sudan, consisting of 26,000–28,000 pastoralists. They are a patrilineal and polygynous society, in which, as is typical of their kind, women have low social status. There are no central leaders or chiefs, but there are age grades and religious mediators, which for the sake of convenience we will call priests. There is little intermarriage with other tribes, and contacts with outside societies tend to be limited to trading and raiding. The Suri are in many ways a classic example of pastoralist society.

Traditionally, violent encounters with other tribes were frequent but ritualized. The Suri do not believe that humans are inherently or naturally violent but rather, unlike animals, naturally social and organized. However, if this sociality is threatened or betrayed, then force is a legitimate response. Traditionally, this force took a variety of forms, including raiding and ritual dueling. It was considered inevitable but under cultural control.

Case Study 5: Violence and Culture Change
in the Suri of Ethiopia (continued)

Raiding, for example, was held to be a "fact of life," and the objects of raids included cattle, pastureland, and water holes. There was no attempt to conquer other societies but merely to push them off of coveted territories, and in fact peaceful relations obtained between societies during quiescent periods. Raiding operated under specific rules, including the obligation to give the other side prior warning of an attack; prohibitions on burning pastures, poisoning wells, or killing cattle; and strict taboos on raping or killing women. Raiding was not a sustained form of aggression and was not intended to "wipe out" enemies; rather, it was considered an exciting activity to engage in for its own sake.

Dueling, on the other hand, was a public spectacle held in an arena in front of spectators, especially young single women. It was more sport or ritual than war, played in the name of the man's social or territorial group. It too had specific rules: no killing, only men of certain age levels would participate, and there were time limits and referees. If a death were to occur, the dueling match soon stopped and everyone went home. More important than success in the duels was the opportunity for showing off one's fighting prowess, and men displayed their scars proudly. The top winner of the day was carried to the admiring female fans on a platform, and girls would choose a man to have further contact with. Young ladies did not always choose the big hero of the day, but they never chose a noncombatant.

Such was the traditional situation of the Suri, when aggression and violence were constrained by rule and ritual. However, in more recent times, the character of Suri violence has changed drastically, mainly as a result of external contacts and pressures. These external factors include drought and famine that have struck the entire area; the acquisition of new weapons technologies, particularly firearms; "development" in the form of poaching and gold trading; and increasing contact with the outside world, including not only other neighboring tribes but the central government of Ethiopia. As a consequence, violence has not only escalated but traditional ritual restraints to curb violence have weakened.

For example, in the 1970s neighbors of the Suri, the Nyangatom, began using rifles to push them from the west, killing many of them. The Suri were compelled to yield ground and migrate eastward until the 1980s, when they too acquired rifles and employed them on their eastern neighbors. What had formerly been limited raids became more fatal and "total" war, resulting in the killing of cattle, the slaughter of entire villages, assaults on travelers and elders, and kidnapping and murder of young girls—formerly completely prohibited.

The age-grade system has also become a source of conflict. By controlling guns and the modern discourse of power, young male warriors attempt to resist the authority of tribal elders and delay their own passage into the elder age-grade, thereby prolonging the violent (warrior) stage of their life. Thus,

*Case Study 5: Violence and Culture Change
in the Suri of Ethiopia (continued)*

instead of experiencing violence as integral to a particular age grade or stage of life and as filled with ritual and symbolic significance, young warriors seek to achieve a new kind of prestige, based on the exploitive, practical benefits of violence. The consequence for Suri society has been an overall increase in the scope and intensity of violence.

VIOLENT COMPLEX SOCIETIES: CASE STUDIES

The societies discussed in this second section qualify as "complex" societies, because they have more elaborate and differentiated social and cultural systems than traditional societies, often containing more than one identifiable social-cultural group. Complex societies are not in all cases "modern"; some, such as ancient Sparta no longer even exist, while others like medieval Japan have changed dramatically. However, all complex societies, young and old, share certain common characteristics, as we will see in the case studies that follow. Examining only a few of the many possible examples that exist, we will continue to explore the manifold aspects of this worldwide phenomenon in subsequent chapters.

Case Study 1: Society as Armed Camp in Ancient Sparta

We are all familiar with the word *spartan* as an adjective meaning "frugal and simple to the point of discomfort." We also all have a vague notion of the "golden age of Greece," a time when the democracy and philosophy of Athens flowered in the ancient world. However, few people are aware that this golden age was in fact very brief—that in fact Athens was not the dominant city of the region for most of Greek history and that democracy and philosophy were not its sole cultural achievements.

Hundreds of years before the time of Socrates and Plato, Sparta existed as another major power, a city organized on very idiosyncratic principles and much admired throughout the region, even in Athens. Sparta was a city born in and for war. This is not entirely atypical of Greek and other ancient civilizations. The ancient philosopher Heraclitus called war "the father of us all, the king of us all," and Plato described it as "always existing by nature between every Greek city state." Greece in fact was a land of sovereign and often belligerent city-states; before Alexander the Great (330s B.C.E.) there was no

Case Study 1: Society as Armed Camp in Ancient Sparta (continued)

unified "Greek state," merely a common culture that valorized war. As Hanson (1999: 14) put it, "Most Greeks agreed: war was the most important thing we humans do. It was fighting . . . that best revealed virtues, cowardice, skill or ineptitude, civilization or barbarism." The Spartan version of war was conducted essentially by infantries of shield- and spear-carrying soldiers known as hoplites, citizen militias that fought in close formations such that each man's shield protected himself and his neighbor. Spears bristled from the phalanx or "stacks" of tightly formed men, and the struggle itself constituted basically a "shock collision" in which the opposing forces clashed head-on and muscled each other until one side or the other broke ranks and retreated; often the entire skirmish lasted less than thirty minutes.

This highly ruly, almost ritualized approach to war (see the discussion of the European "just war" concept in Chapter 6) was characterized by

- A formal declaration of war (required) and the formal breaking of existing truces or treaties (that is, surprise attacks were discouraged)
- Prebattle rituals, including animal sacrifices
- "Seasonal" war in the spring and summer, carried out only during the day and on specific and agreed-upon fields
- Limitations on the violence—retreating armies were not pursued, wounded captives were not killed, prisoners were often freed, and noncombatants, as well as temples and sanctuaries, were spared
- Postbattle relations that allowed the dead to be returned unmolested and the victor to erect a monument on the site that would not be desecrated by the loser
- Proscriptions on "war technology"—at least in the classical period, only foot soldiers were employed; archers, cavalry, and artillery were rarely used and actually looked down upon

Furthermore, such face-to-face, hand-to-hand combat necessarily called for a degree of discipline that all Greek cities aspired to but that only Sparta achieved, at least for a time.

Sparta was unlike any other Greek city in two regards: its total commitment to military discipline and its fundamental dependence on an enslaved local population. Slavery was by no means unique in the ancient world, but Sparta had built its economy and society on the backs of the conquered people of neighboring Messenia, over which it had gained control by means of deliberate aggression in the mid-700s B.C.E. The conquered inhabitants became known as "helots" (from *heilotai* for "those taken"), literal serfs of their Spartan lords. The helots were legally attached to the land and were obliged to pay tribute in kind. They were not, however, "personal property," as in the case of European medieval serfs, but rather "state property," serfs who worked for

Case Study 1: Society as Armed Camp in Ancient Sparta (continued)

and served the Spartan state, although under the direction of individual Spartan overseers. They had no legal or social rights and no freedom of movement, although they were allowed to sell any surplus at a profit and even to own land. They were even able to perform in battle, occasionally even as hoplites and later as rowers on ships, but they were never accepted as Spartan citizens and always looked upon with suspicion and a certain degree of fear.

This fear was justified, as the helots did not accept their serfdom passively. As early as 650 B.C.E., a long peasant revolt took place, one that deeply affected Spartan society. Sparta became an armed camp, a police state, highly conservative in its outlook, committed to an "austerity of life and devotion to duty" that made it stand out in the Greek world (Michell 1964: 26). As Michell (1964: 28) explains: "The Spartans lived on top of a volcano which might erupt at any time and safety was only to be bought at the price of unrelenting vigilance."

Few societies have attained the level of martial organization that marked Sparta. Everything about the society, from politics to education, was geared toward producing an elite cadre of selfless, brave, and capable soldiers. The Spartan soldiery constituted an upper caste most closely comparable to feudal Europe or Japan with their institutions and values of honor and self-sacrifice. They were called the *homoioi*, the "peers" or "equals." Their sole profession was war, and they were literally forbidden from undertaking "vulgar" activities like trade or industry; for those lower pursuits, the helots and the "second-class citizens," such as the *perioikoi*—the "dwellers on the outskirts" of the city and society—were intended. Of course, the Spartan elite depended critically on these lower castes to support and supply them, but that hardly led to a kinder treatment of the lower types.

The values of the *homoioi* were based on toughness, dedication to the group, and a simplicity of life that approached true privation. Homes and meals were to be minimal; women did not wear makeup or jewelry. The "finer things in life" were seen as turning a warrior soft; the sole point of battle was honor and duty. The worst thing a man could do was to show cowardice; it was said that the women of Sparta urged their men to return from war either with their shields or on them. A man who displayed fear in the phalanx, which not only risked his own life but his comrades', was shamed and disgraced (*atimia*): if he returned home he was shunned as the craven coward that he was, and he might never find a wife or husbands for his daughters if he already had them.

To instill the proper skills and values, an intense regimen of training virtually from birth was established, emphasizing physical fitness and obedience. According to various ancient sources such as Plutarch, newborn males were inspected by city elders, and weak, unhealthy, or deformed babies were left to die. To fortify the strong, babies were bathed in wine and then given into their

Case Study 1: Society as Armed Camp in Ancient Sparta (continued)

mother's care for the first six years of life. At age six, boys were taken from their families and assigned to barracks, where they were enrolled in youth squads, or *ilai*. So began their military careers. By age ten they were engaging in competitive exercises and contests. They were also assigned to a junior mess hall, since all males of warrior age took at least their dinner meal in a military-style dining hall.

At age twelve, worthy males entered the serious stage of their training, in an institution that became known as the *agoge*, or military school. They were subjected to all manner of martial discomfort: they went barefoot, were given a single piece of clothing without undergarments, and slept on beds of rough reeds. They were offered unappetizing and inadequate diets and encouraged to supplement their fare by stealing—the one warning being that if they were caught, they would be punished twice, once by their victim and a second time by their superiors. From this time and throughout their education they were submitted to contests and competitions, both physical and otherwise. Some involved beatings and floggings, in which the "student" who endured the most torture won a prize; in such trials, deaths were not unknown. Other tests included music (mostly vocal) and dancing (or what in at least some cases might be considered marching). Each year a fight was held in which contestants formed two teams and met each other "with astonishing ferocity, 'using their hands, kicking with their feet, biting and gouging out the eyes of their opponents in the attempt' to drive the opposing side into the river'" (Michell 1964: 191). A "ball game" appears to have had no rules at all other than fighting over a ball until time expired, at which time the team holding the ball was declared the winner.

It has also been noted that a sensual if not sexual relationship was allowed if not encouraged between the young trainees and their seniors. Each youth was assigned a guardian (*erastai*, or "lover") from among the older male elites. This guardian oversaw his training and took a personal interest in him, which, according to at least some sources, included a homosexual interest. The point in raising this issue is neither to laud nor condemn the practice but to notice how far the Spartans were willing to go to generate a male camaraderie that would carry over onto the battlefield. Men were no doubt more willing to go to extremities for friends than for mere acquaintances, and for lovers than for mere friends.

At age eighteen, males became adults and active members of the army, although not yet as frontline soldiers. Six years of active duty led to "graduation" to the status of *eiren* or full-fledged soldier. This was the height of their military service, when wills were tested and reputations were won. From the mid-400s to the mid-300s or so, the Spartan army was the warrior class of ancient Greece—first helping to repel the Persian invasion, then turning into an enemy of Athens and conquering it around the turn of the century.

Case Study 1: Society as Armed Camp in Ancient Sparta (continued)

Meanwhile, at age 30 a man reached full citizenship and accepted his place in the *ecclesia*, or general assembly, a sort of "lower house" in the government. At this age he would move out of the barracks and live with his wife, if he had one, although he would still dine at the *syssition* or *phedition*, that is, the mess hall. Members of a *syssition* were required to attend and contribute to it, and they would vote to admit new young members based on the quality of those junior candidates.

The Spartan system was a successful one but a fragile one, in two senses. First, it depended on a small minority of men who relied on a large servile population. In fact, sources indicate that the number of Spartan elite males was never very large and actually declined throughout the period in question. Past a certain minimum number, they could not keep their hold on their helot population. Second, it depended on an indifference—a "spartan" attitude—toward the wealth that war won for them. Only while the soldiers maintained their self-denial did they maintain their discipline and fortitude. However, the victory over Athens was the beginning of the end for them, and by 371 B.C.E they were defeated at the battle of Leuctra, from which they never rose again. Loss after loss followed until Alexander's Macedonian army, with superior numbers, weapons, tactics, and discipline, put an end to Spartan and all other Greek independence.

Case Study 2: Violence, Tradition, and Identity in Modern Albania

As described by Schwandner-Sievers (2001), the power vacuum left with the fall of communism in Albania in the 1990s forced the Albanians to search for other sources of order and meaning. Under communist domination, traditional practices and cultures in Albania, as in other communist states, had been suppressed or replaced; the ideology of communism insisted that traditional cultures were at worst bourgeois creations designed to keep the proletariat from realizing their true international identity and at best vestigial distractions from the future communist worker identity (see Chapter 8 and Chapter 9). Either way, they were a form of "false consciousness" and were to be ignored and supplanted by more "modern" and "scientific" identities, specifically class identities.

At any rate, in Albania as in many formerly communist societies, the ready material for the subsequent social order was the suppressed and maligned tradition, which still lay dormant in the memories of many of the older residents (communism having only been imposed after World War II), as well as in the

Case Study 2: Violence, Tradition, and Identity in Modern Albania *(continued)*

works of anthropologists, who had collected traditional data, and of missionaries, for example the Franciscans in Albania, who also had kept records of traditional practices. In particular, in Albania, this traditional organization was based on the concept of *kanun*, or regional sets of rules and values, often expressed in proverbs.

The *kanun* of different parts of Albania vary, but there are some general shared characteristics. *Kanun* tend to employ dualistic symbolism, expressed as "black" and "white," contrasting a trustworthy "us," who need and deserve protection, with an unfaithful, dangerous, and treacherous "them," who can be rightfully assaulted or expelled. In this setting, "us" tends to refer to local patrilineal groups but can be extended by marriage or by reconciliation to include other groups outside the lineage. The positive relation to the in-group is encapsulated in the concept of *besa*, which is derived from the word for "oath" and which relates to hospitality, protection guarantee, alliance, honor of the house, and similar sentiments. The opposite of *besa* is *pabese*, which means unfaithful or untrustworthy. *Pabese* people can be targets of robbery, feuding, woman-kidnapping, and intervillage violence, including expulsion from the land. In fact, violence between *pabese* is normal and even virtuous.

Kanun, as with cognate concepts in many other Mediterranean societies, is centrally concerned with honor—the honor of the individual man, his family, and his village. If honor is threatened, violence is not only appropriate but probably necessary. As mentioned above, much of *kanun* morality is captured in proverbs, such as "Blood for blood," "The soap of a man is his gunpowder," and "The wolf licks his own flesh but eats the flesh of others." Accordingly, if another man or family or village starts a conflict, especially if the blood of a *besa* man or family or village is spilled, the revenge attacks are acceptable and valuable to restore the "balance of blood." Alternately, young men may organize violence against other villages simply to acquire prestige and prove their honor, guaranteeing feelings of dishonor in the subject village if not a subsequent counterattack. Individuals and groups who have been so dishonored are fair targets for public ridicule, ostracism, and assault—as for the Yanomamo, the perception of weakness invites more abuse. Although the issues of honor and dishonor do not generally concern women at the macrosocial level, they often do affect them at the microsocial level: for example, a woman whose family has been dishonored or has shown itself unable to protect its own will be significantly limited in her marriage prospects. Nobody wants to marry into a family without honor.

If honor is lost, there are two main ways to restore it. The first is through a ritual of forgiveness, in which the dishonored family or group must show extreme generosity. By making such a gesture, their honor rises in the eyes of witnesses. The second, more obvious, course is counterviolence, in which the

Case Study 2: Violence, Tradition, and Identity in
Modern Albania (continued)

dishonored party "washes his blackened face," especially killing a member of
another group during a feud.

Kanun is clearly a concept of limited scope, aimed at integrating people at
the family or village level but not beyond that; also, it is as much a disintegrative
force as an integrative one. However, in recent times, its application to new
and large constituencies—including gangs; mafia-style crime syndicates and
black markets; "security committees," or what have sometimes been called
"police gangs"; and even regional politics—has produced mixed results.
Whether it is sufficient to build a national culture and politics on it is question-
able, but it is understandable how people would turn to such a piece of their
"cultural capital" and attempt to make as much use of it as possible.

Case Study 3: The Ritual of the Bullfight in Spain

Stylyzed violen

On the surface, a bullfight is a situation in which a man intentionally hurts and
kills an animal in front of an approving crowd. However, as described by Marvin (1986) Spaniards do not think of the bullfight as violence (*violencia*), or
even as a fight (*pelear* or *luchar*) but as a "running of the bulls" (*la corrida de
toros*). In fact, if asked about the violence of the bullfight, Spaniards will make
the distinction between violence and cruelty (*crueldad*), the latter of which
does not apply to the event.

Clearly, fighters and the audience consider violent acts in the bullfight as
necessary, acceptable, and appropriate for the situation; however, there should
not be any sign of anger or aggression in the matador. In fact, violent or cruel
acts are considered disruptive, inelegant—the very opposite of what a good
corrida de toros should be. Rather, there is an elaborate protocol of "ritualized
violence" that makes a bullfight not only acceptable but beautiful.

The point of the contest is not the killing of a bull; that would be easy and
would not require all the pomp and symbolism. The point is how the killing is
accomplished—with skill, grace, and courage, that is, in a "civilized" manner. The
bullfight embodies the values of male competition in defense of male self-image
and honor, and in the mind of the observers the ultimate vindication of honor lies
in physical violence, which must be public to be effective. In other words, *la
corrida de toros* epitomizes the situation in which a man is forced to confront
another man in public, something like an American Wild West "showdown."

The matador plays the role of the honorable man in public. He is not
a "fighter" or a man with a reputation for violence, and he is not an "athlete."

Case Study 3: The Ritual of the Bullfight in Spain (continued)

He is not necessarily aggressive or muscular. He does not even instigate violence but merely responds to it; he is not even supposed to indulge in self-defense but rather in mastery of the "other male" and in the redirection of its energy and violence against itself. The bull is angry and ferocious, but the man must be composed and poised. He must show calm, skill, and self-control—able to master not only the bull but the whole violent situation without becoming violent himself.

From the matador's perspective, as well as that of the audience, the goal is not to make the animal suffer, and no one in the crowd enjoys the suffering that takes place; in fact, earlier practices like hamstringing the bull, using attack dogs, and putting gunpowder charges in its flesh have been eliminated. What is important is how the man in the arena comports himself—his style and aesthetic sense, the graceful harmonious relationship between man, cape, and bull—in a word, his "grace under pressure." He is to master the bull, leading it where he wants to without getting emotionally involved or losing control.

The kill is certainly the most dangerous and skilled moment in the event, in which the man is required to lean over the oncoming horns and slide a sword between the victim's shoulder blades. However, the matador may not use his sword to weaken the bull or defend himself, and the man who executes a bad or sloppy kill is called *asesino* ("murderer"), not a champion. Further, getting wounded is no sign of prestige but evidence of weakness or blunder.

Fans of *la corrida de toros* consider boxing to be distasteful, although they admire the matador. Why would a man want to humiliate or be humiliated by another man in public? To be violent and aggressive is uncivilized, a quality of animals but not of humans—it is to become like an animal. The bullfight is an occasion to transcend man's animal nature and display all of the elegance, poise, and emotional stoicism that distinguishes a man of honor from a man of anger.

Case Study 4: Soccer Hooliganism in Britain

As described by Dunning, Murphy, and Williams (1986), soccer hooliganism, or more-or-less organized violence at soccer matches, has been a problem in Britain since the 1960s, before which time British crowds were famous for their orderly behavior. However, in recent decades intranational and international soccer matches have come to be regular venues for planned and ongoing conflicts between fans and supporters of the various sides, and hooligans have organized themselves into "crews" or "firms"—with names like Anti-Personnel Firm (Chelsea), Gooners (Arsenal), or Bushwhackers (Milwall)—to realize their hostile intentions.

Case Study 4: Soccer Hooliganism in Britain (continued)

Hooliganism varies from mild manifestations like swearing and general bois-
terousness to major outbreaks of violence. Fans have run onto the field to disrupt play as well as started serious fights in the stands with fans of the other team
or with rival gangs or crews. These exchanges include fistfights, bottle throwing,
knife fights, and projectile attacks (pelting the other side with everything from
innocuous objects like plastic cups to life-threatening objects like darts, broken
seats, bricks and concrete, fireworks, and occasionally crude bombs).

Confrontations can and do occur during the matches, but large and more
destructive conflicts tend to take place afterward. The situation can start with
a "run," or rush, of hundreds of male fans along the streets looking for rivals to
assault. Hard-core hooligans tend to operate apart from the main body of the
group and to use tactics to outflank the police, who attempt to prevent or contain such incidents. If the crews are successful, then usually a series of violent
skirmishes ensues, in which rivals are attacked individually or in small groups,
cars are overturned, and the like.

Many young men view fighting as an important part of a soccer match, as
important as the action on the field, and they come prepared to have a good
fight. Each organized "crew" has its own distinctive songs and chants, and they
direct them and other gestures at their rivals, often investing more attention to
the taunts than to the game. The songs and chants include challenges to fight,
threats and boasts, and regular references to terms like "hate," "surrender,"
"kick," and "die." Frequently these provocations will be accompanied by syn-
chronized mock-masturbatory gestures.

Who are the men who engage in this behavior, and what is their motivation? Studies of arrested hooligans have shown that more than 80 percent of
these men are either lower-class workers or unemployed. The experience of
the lower class in Britain, as in many parts of the world, is characterized by
four features—age grading, sex segregation, territoriality, and ethnic solidarity.
In fact, in regard to the last feature, some members of soccer crews have been
connected to right-wing racist organizations, but at the same time blacks and
Asians are finding their way into various crews, and white firms often turn on
each other, so race or ethnicity are not key elements in soccer-crew behavior.
Rather, age, gender, and territory appear to be key.

Age grading tends to occur spontaneously from the fact that children are
sent into the streets to play at an early age without adult supervision. Young
children essentially come to constitute a subculture of their own and develop
values and bonds to each other that they do not share with other age groups or
generations. Sex segregation begins to occur not long after, as young girls are
drawn into the home and traditional female roles, leaving behind the "street-
corner society," which becomes increasingly and then almost solely male.
Without parents or girls around, groups of young males develop their own

Case Study 4: Soccer Hooliganism in Britain (continued)

standards and procedures of prestige and hierarchy, typically based on aggressiveness and strength. They organize themselves into gangs or crews, often centered on a small number of boys with a distinct reputation for toughness, strategy, and leadership. These values and behaviors are further reinforced by encouragement from adults to be tough and "stand up for themselves," as well as by rough child-rearing and by observations of adult models of public aggression, including family feuds and vendettas. For the street-corner boys, aggression is learned and rewarded.

Territoriality develops as gangs of single-generation, single-sex young people grow up together, share the same neighborhood and have little contact outside of it, and come to identify with their neighborhood (think of Tajfel's social identification theory). Young aggressive males attach their identity and their status—a competitive and threatened identity and status—to their community and, often enough, to the sports team of their community. Naturally enough, crews in the same neighborhoods or cities sometimes compete with each other for prestige and reputation, but when the threat or challenge comes from the outside—from a different city and its soccer team, for example—these competing crews will unite (in what has been described as an "ordered segmentation" system) to "defend their territory" against the outsider. In other words, the next crew over in the same neighborhood or town is "other" or "them" to us until the crew from a remote town comes into our space, at which time all of the local crews aggregate into a new and large "us" as opposed to the new and remote "them." When the remote "them" leaves again, our temporary "us" alliance collapses and the local rivals return to being "them."

Case Study 5: The Beauty of Violence in Traditional (and Modern) Japan

> The Way of the Samurai is found in death.
> —*Hagakure*

For a thousand years, from the ninth century until 1868 (the beginning of the "modern," or Meiji, era), Japan was a feudal society, often warring internally. Out of this social and political landscape, seasoned as it was with Shinto, Confucian, and Buddhist teaching, arose a culture in many ways similar to European feudalism of the same era but in other ways remarkably distinct, especially in its attitude toward death.

Case Study 5: The Beauty of Violence in Traditional (and Modern) Japan (continued)

Even before the elaboration of the warrior code that would come to be associated with the samurai, Japan was characterized by a high degree of stratification, filial loyalty, male domination, and reverence for leaders, particularly the emperor. Even during the times of the shoguns or military warlords, the emperor was still the focal point of obedience, even if not of actual power and law. In fact, since the seventh century, the imperial family and system were believed to be the creation of the sun god Amaterasu and the emperor himself to be a living god—a position that was only officially disavowed after the defeat of World War II.

During this feudal age, with the emperor primarily a figurehead or symbol of Japanese identity and unity, the real power fell to various squabbling local leaders or families. Each of these regional powers depended on a system of property-tied lords, or *daimyo*, and the vassals they could call upon to fight for them. These warrior-vassals, akin to the knights of contemporary Europe, were referred to as "those who serve," or *samurai*. They were a small number of high-status "professional" fighters who formed the upper caste of an extremely hierarchical society, with farmers, artisans, and merchants laid out below. In fact, they were traditionally forbidden to engage in trade or industry as an activity beneath them and were discouraged from seeking any monetary gain from their conquests. They made war out of loyalty to their masters and for the sake of honor.

Like the medieval knights, the samurai developed and practiced a code of "chivalry" known as *bushido*, or "the way of the warrior." It was a more or less complete set of standards for everything from combat to personal comportment to courtly love. These standards are probably most clearly spelled out in the book of the samurai known as *Hagakure*, transcribed in the early 1700s by Tsuramoto Tashiro from conversations with a retired samurai master named Yamamoto. This document emphasizes the centrality of death in the life of the true warrior. But death was only part of a complex of values revolving around duty, honor, discipline, dedication to one's master, a sense of impermanence, and even a notion of beauty.

As the modern commentator on the *Hagakure*, Yukio Mishima, has stated, its message comes down to three key philosophies: a philosophy of action, a philosophy of love, and a philosophy of life (1977: 41–42). The attitude toward action is that the samurai should act quickly and decisively, even without "thinking" in the usual sense. As the *Hagakure* advises, "When meeting difficult situations, one should dash forward bravely and with joy" (Tsunetomo 2002: 45). Or again, "The Way of the Samurai is one of immediacy, and it is best to dash in headlong" (60). *Bushido* is not a thinking man's philosophy; it is not given to contemplation and speculation. In fact, it is critical of the intellectual, whose ruminations may confuse the direct simplicity of duty and action.

Case Study 5: The Beauty of Violence in Traditional (and Modern) Japan (continued)

The second philosophy, that of love, reflects a combination of Confucian social order and knightly "chivalry." "Romantic" love, which has even been analyzed as a recent invention in Western societies (see De Rougemont 1956), was not the point, or at least to the extent that it was romantic, such love was to be as chaste and unrequited as the love of knights for their ladies. It was not a half-bad thing to die for love. However, as Mishima points out, love of a man for his fellow man was regarded as a higher and "more spiritual" love than that of a man for a woman (there are also some obscure lines in *Hagakure* about male love), and "the truest and most intense form of human love develops into loyalty and devotion to one's ruler" (Mishima 1977: 42).

Finally, the philosophy of living is that life is short, all things are imperma-
nent, time is insignificant, and it is better to die quickly than to linger. Again, *Hagakure* is clear: "When it comes to either/or, there is only the quick choice of death. It is not particularly difficult. Be determined and advance" (Tsunetomo 2002: 17). Here we see once more the urge to action, which is not only decisive but beautiful. Mishima writes that "we must recognize that when a human being tries to live beautifully and die beautifully, strong attachment to life undermines that beauty" (1977: 21–22). We can hear the Buddhist influence in these sentiments, in which detachment from life is the purest form of existence.

Since *bushido* is a "metaphysics of death," it is no surprise that the theme of death reverberates through it and that the samurai is called upon to keep the idea of death before him at all times. *Hagakure* admonishes the warrior:

> In constantly hardening one's resolution to die in battle, deliberately becoming as one already dead, and working at one's job and dealing with military affairs, there should be no shame. (33) The Way of the Samurai is, morning after morning, the practice of death, considering whether it will be here or there, imagining the most sightly way of dying, and putting one's mind firmly on death. (73)
>
> Meditation on inevitable death should be performed daily. Every day when one's body and mind are at peace, one should meditate upon being ripped apart by arrows, rifles, spears and swords, being carried away by surging waves, being thrown into the midst of a great fire, being struck by lightning, being shaken to death by a great earthquake, falling from thousand foot cliffs, dying of disease or committing seppuku at the death of one's master. And every day without fail one should consider himself as dead. (164)

Indeed, to avoid death, or merely to avoid a fight—either for oneself or others—is a form of shame. The document tells a story of two samurai who started wrestling until some onlookers pulled them apart. The elders and masters judged that the onlookers were wrong to interrupt a good

Case Study 5: The Beauty of Violence in Traditional (and Modern) Japan (continued)

fight: they were banished from the realm, and the two combatants were executed (137).

Mishima admits that a kind of nihilism lies at the heart of the way of the samurai—not nihilism in the sense that nothing matters but in the sense that nothing is very real. Life is a "puppet existence," an illusion. It is so brief that to cling to it is to corrupt the purity of life. This is one reason why the cherry blossom is such a powerful symbol in Japanese thinking (and perhaps flowers in our own culture): it is exquisitely beautiful and perfect, but only for a short time. Maybe all perfection is transient, and transience is a condition of perfection. Mishima, who himself committed ritual suicide in 1970, maintains even that a person "must die for love, and death heightens love's tensions and purity. This is the ideal love for *Hagakure*" (1977: 24).

It is not even so much a matter of choosing death, since death is obligatory for the samurai. It is his vocation. He might choose the timing or manner of death, but he has already committed to death by his profession; he is, as the master taught, already dead. Notice that the death that the samurai meditates on is not the death of his enemy but his own. Hence the unique valorization of suicide in the *bushido* code. Death, beauty, and honor or shame are all bundled together. For a samurai to avoid death would be a huge shame, and some forms of death are more honorable and beautiful than others. No doubt, the best death comes to the warrior in battle. However, not all are lucky enough to die at the point of a foe's sword. Some have the misfortune of living long and declining lives; others have to watch their lords die before them. Still others make grave errors or commit dishonorable acts that call for expiation. For all of these occasions, there is ritual suicide.

We are all familiar with the Japanese practice of "harikari," or what is more accurately named *hara-kiri* or *seppuku*. *Hara-kiri* is a word derived from *hara*, for "abdomen," and *kiri*, for cutting or splitting. *Seppuku* is the term for self-disembowelment. The significance of this practice is that the soul was believed to reside in the belly, so that death by assault to the stomach area was the most "spiritual" of deaths. *Seppuku* might be called for if a samurai's master died, as an act of devotion; such a suicide was referred to as *oibara*. A samurai might merely offer his life as a sign of loyalty to this lord, a practice called *chugi-bara*. If the death penalty were being meted out to a samurai, then the (voluntary) execution ceremony was a *sokotsu-shi*. And if the samurai were killing himself as a gesture of resentment or hatred or protest, then this act constituted *munen-bara* (Seward 1968). In all of its forms, it was a culturally weighty gesture.

Case Study 5: The Beauty of Violence in Traditional (and Modern) Japan (continued)

Ideally, *seppuku* would occur in the evening in a *daimyo*'s estate or in a garden. The honored victim would be given a formal banquet some days before the ceremony, and the death itself would be held on a ritual tatami mat of specific dimensions. He would be offered a short knife (just under twelve inches long) wrapped in thin paper, which he should grasp and plunge into his abdomen, cutting from the lower left to the upper right. A particularly brave samurai would add a slight upward cut at the top, called *jumonji*. Then, as a final honor, his death would be hastened by the intervention of an assistant, called *kaishaku-nin*, who would deliver a decapitating stroke with a specialized sword. If the condemned man cravenly refused to commence his own death or tried to escape, or if a dishonor was to be dealt, then decapitation without *seppuku* would take place.

In a few ways, other nonsamurai would emulate the behavior of the warriors. Particularly in the case of star-crossed lovers, double suicide (*shinju*) was one sign of their love. Instead of using a sword (the prerogative of a samurai), they would often tie a rope around the waists together and throw themselves off a cliff or into the sea. Seward suggests that this act conferred "the sense of joyful fulfillment in sacrificing one's like for an ideal ... a worthwhile death" (1968: 75). It might also be interpreted as a desperate act of protest against an impossibly rigid social system that offered no other options.

Although ritual suicide was banned by the Tokugawa shogunate in 1663 as a waste of valuable lives, it continued both to occur and to carry cultural meaning. In fact, in the relative peace that reigned from the mid-1600s to the mid-1800s, it may have been one of the few ways for a samurai to demonstrate his values and achieve the perfection that their code imposed on them. Some of the behaviors seen in World War II— from the death-dives of the kamikazes (the "divine wind") to various acts of ritual suicide by soldiers and generals—indicate that its significance persisted into recent decades. In fact, some analysts like Brian Moeran claim to be able to see the same themes and values in today's Japanese popular culture, for example its movies in such genres as *jidaigeki* or "historical" or "period" films, *yakuza* or "gangster" films, and the violent and pornographic style known as "eroduction." In all of these and others, apparently gratuitous torture and killing, often with a sexual tone, is studied in extreme detail and almost with affection. Moeran suggests that all of these forms echo the *bushido* values of death, honor, and beauty, through the experience of impermanence: "the appreciation of beauty, the sexual climax, and the attainment of selflessness when face to face with

Case Study 5: The Beauty of Violence in Traditional (and Modern) Japan (continued)

death, are all moments when language is driven from man's mind and time is conquered" (1986: 116). They would be a manifestation of that nihilistic, fanatical self-destructiveness that *Hagakure* lauds and that the paragons of virtue, the samurai, strove for in other, more dramatic times—all that is left of the pursuit of beauty in an age of peace and luxury.

RETROSPECT AND PROSPECT

It is unclear whether mankind is born violent or nonviolent, if either. What is clear from the two most recent chapters is that individuals can be made violent or nonviolent, depending on what influences they are exposed to.

It would seem a foregone conclusion that the way to produce a violent person and society would be to practice violence, and the way to produce a nonviolent person and society would be to practice nonviolence. But that is easier said than understood or done. In nonviolent societies, as we have seen, the standard constellation of overarching social institutions that regulate interpersonal microsocial relationships also represent and instill the values and personality traits characteristic of nonviolence. Thus, macrolevel phenomena, such as foraging economies and acephalous ("leaderless") politics, along with microlevel phenomena, such as parent–child warmth and sibling pacificity, and psychocultural phenomena, such as emotional aversions to seeing or causing discomfort, lead to and reproduce the nonviolent ethos from which they are also born. To appropriate a phrase from Bourdieu (1977), these social structures, which are already structured, act as structuring structures for the enculturation or socialization process, which in turn perpetuate and sustain the original structured structures.

Likewise, violence is created, sustained, and reproduced by violent macrosocial, microsocial, and psychocultural forces. Specifically, as compared to nonviolent societies, violent societies characteristically include more productive (and thus stratifying) economic systems, such as pastoralism and intensive agriculture, and more centralized political systems. They also include male-oriented corporate bodies, such as patrlineages, warrior clubs, and age sets. Microsocial influences include sexist familial relations, harsh or inconsistent parent–child relations, and a generalized spirit of competitiveness. This competitive spirit informs the psychocultural realm, where rank, power, honor, shame, "face," and revenge serve as strong motivators, especially for men. It would be hard to imagine how violence would not follow from such a setup.

At a more general level of analysis, we have seen how two (of four) factors in the creation of violence produce their effects. The first is integration into groups and the attendant generation of an us-versus-them situation. With some (often major) exceptions, violence is more common and intense against "them" than among "us," and the very existence of such groupings leads to conflictual competition. Particularly when males are organized into mutually competitive and antagonistic corporate bodies within a society, these bodies and the males in them are thrown into hostile relations. Whether the group is a Cheyenne warrior society, a Yanomamo village, or a British soccer crew, makes little difference. However, give those integrated groups a shared and valued identity—the second factor—and aggression and violence grow accordingly. Of course, such groups are almost never without such identity, except in the lab (as in Tajfel's experiments); in fact, it is often the identity that causes the integration. At any rate, if we are the X lineage or the Y crew, with our history and symbols and memories and territories, and so forth, and you are not, then violence between us is almost invited. What remains for us to examine in the following chapters is the effect of the other two factors—ideology and interest.

CHAPTER 5

GENDER AND INTIMATE VIOLENCE

One generalization that we have been able to make so far is that "external" violence is more common than "internal" violence—that is, that the amount and intensity of violence tends to increase the further one gets from one's "own kind." Violence is typically most legitimized against "the other," and the more remote the "other," the more legitimate the violence. Thus, if we were to rank the legitimacy of our violence against others, that against members of other societies would be most legitimate; that against members of other segments (e.g., villages) of our society would be less so; that against members of our segment of our own society even less so; and violence against members of our own kin group least so. Therefore, we would expect to find the family and the residential unit to be the most tranquil and benign social group of all. However, this is not always what we find, for a variety of reasons, not the least of which is the extreme vulnerability of some of its residents.

Deborah Prothrow-Stith has said it succinctly (1991: 145): "Violence is a problem that begins at home." Richard Gelles and Murray Straus (1988: 18) maintain that "You are more likely to be physically assaulted, beaten, and killed in your own home at the hands of a loved one than anyplace else, or by anyone else in our society." The "you" in this statement, though, is a particular one; some individuals in the family are more liable to be subjected to this treatment than others. Nijole Benokraitis (1993: 13) puts the final piece of the puzzle in place: "The home is one of the most physically and psychologically brutal settings in society, especially for women, teenage girls, and young children"—and also, as discovered more recently, for the elderly and the disabled

Entire books have been written about gender, domestic, and/or intimate violence; even subtopics such as spouse abuse or violence against children fill volumes or even multiple volumes. Therefore, we can only manage here an abridged discussion of the shocking yet all too familiar phenomenon of gender and intimate violence. In this chapter, we will consider various theories

115

and explore the macrosocial, microsocial, and psychocultural factors of this behavior worldwide, reserving our focus on violence in American society for the last two chapters of this book. The following discussion will include an in-depth look at violence—both direct and indirect, or "structural"—against women and children.

CONCEPTUALIZING GENDER AND FAMILY VIOLENCE

Any reasonable analysis of a problem like violence against women or other "intimates" must start with a clarification of terminology and methodology, as we have insisted throughout this book. Not every instance of a woman being struck or even killed is necessarily an instance of "gender violence," for men have gender too and so must be included in the definition. Rather, we are concerned primarily here with situations in which a woman, a child, or another such dependent (occasionally a man) is harmed by a person who knows the victim well and who, in ordinary circumstances, ought to be responsible for and interested in the health and well-being of that victim. Therefore, our discussion will not consider every case in which a woman or child is harmed (for example by a stranger), nor will it be limited to talking about women and children, since other "intimates" like the elderly are also potential victims of gender and intimate violence.

Definition and Operationalization

The definition, then, of such concepts as "gender violence" or "intimate violence" can vary, and the broadness or narrowness of the definition will articulate what "counts" as violence and thus calls for a response. Gelles (1997: 14) defines violence as "an act carried out with the intention or perceived intention of causing physical pain or injury to another person." This is at once a narrow and a broad definition—narrow in its limitation to the type of harm done and broad in the scope it lends to the amount of harm done. In other words, he only includes physical injury, but that injury might be severe, minor, or—theoretically—not physical at all but only "intended." In fact, he goes on to distinguish between violence and "other harmful but nonviolent coercive acts" (16), which would potentially include verbal and emotional abuse.

Whatever the accepted definition of violence, the term *gender violence* suggests that the behavior to which it refers is directed at a victim because of his or her gender or carried out by a member of the opposite gender. Although this conventional definition is useful, it does not cover same-sex violence, such as that between gay or lesbian partners. Finally, we could expand the concept to include more adequately "intimate violence" or "family violence," as Wallace does when he defines family violence as "any act or omission by persons who are cohabiting that results in serious injury to other members of the family" (1999: 3). Then we might also subsume spousal violence, parental violence, sibling violence, and elder violence under one category; furthermore, recognizing violence of omission as well as commission allows us to incorporate neglect as well as bodily harm. However, not all "intimates" or even "family" necessarily cohabitate, as for example in the case of dating violence or violence between estranged or divorced couples, so here too we still face difficulties.

These sorts of questions make a difference, of course, in terms of how we go on to operationalize "domestic" violence. How do we count it, and how do we decide what to count? People aiming to study gender/intimate violence rely on a variety of measures. Police and justice reports are, naturally, an important source of information, as are medical or institutional reports and surveys—hospital records or data kept at social service agencies or safe houses, for example. These kinds of data, however, are often not conclusive but rather only suggestive, because what is true at one agency or house may not be indicative of an entire community or society. Also, researchers may find useful data sifting through information collected and catalogued for other purposes, such as anthropological ethnographies and the Human Relations Area Files, a database of cross-cultural studies. In America a wide range of specialized organizations exist to monitor domestic violence and advocate for its victims, including the National Coalition against Domestic Violence, the National Victim Center, the American Association for Protecting Children, the National Center for Elder Abuse, and so on. In addition, specific measurement tools have been designed to quantify domestic violence. One of these is the Conflict Tactics Scale (CTS) implemented by Gelles and Straus (1988), which includes items of increasingly serious violence from throwing objects at the victim to pushing and shoving up to using a weapon. Other researchers, such as Propper (1997), have criticized the CTS for lacking context (e.g., allowing no provision for self-defense) and for ignoring degrees of severity or injury (e.g., how hard a blow was delivered). Undoubtedly, no measurement tool is perfect.

Model and Theory

Not surprisingly, there exists a great array of approaches to and perspectives on gender/intimate violence, as for all forms of violence. The general theoretical approaches include

1. *Psychiatric/personality theories.* These theories emphasize the pathology of the victimizer's personality—for instance, mental illness, personality disorder, psychopathy or sociopathy, and of course drug or alcohol addictions.
2. *Social learning theory.* As explained in Chapter 2, social learning theory stresses the behavioral models that the abuser had the opportunity to observe. Presumably, if a person sees abusive or violent behavior as a

child, that person might imitate such behavior as an adult. This pattern inevitably leads to a "cycle of violence," in which the habit or tendency is passed on over generations.

3. *Situational theories.* Situational perspectives, in particular the stress-and-coping model, look outside the individual, and sometimes even outside the family, for environmental factors that make violence more likely. These stressors may include low family income, unemployment, low education, personal or family illness, and so on. In this view, people who are not ordinarily violent might turn to or be pushed to violence by their circumstances, particularly if (1) they lack other coping skills and (2) the culture authorizes such responses, the prevailing value system prescribing, for instance, "spare the rod and spoil the child."

4. *Ecological theories.* Ecological approaches attempt to situate the individual and family in the wider context of community and society. For instance, a "mismatch" between the family and its neighborhood or community could result in violence.

5. *Sociobiology.* Sociobiological theories locate the "causes" of most behaviors in genetic sources. That is, they try to find the "adaptive value" of the behavior—why natural forces might actually select for it. One hypothesis is that male aggression, as we saw in Chapter 2, is a natural phenomenon and would naturally be turned on a male's own kin group on occasion.

6. *Feminist theories.* Feminist perspectives may hold a negative attitude toward male nature and instinct (the "males are costly" view), or they may emphasize the cultural values, practices, and institutions that support male social power, that is, patriarchy. They may see domestic violence, which is disproportionately male-on-female violence, as one component of a much larger system aimed at the subordination of women.

7. *Social exchange theory.* This is the preferred theory of Gelles and Straus, who argue essentially that people use violence in the family or with loved ones because they can, that is, "people would only use violence toward family members when there are rewards for violent behavior and when the costs of violence do not outweigh the rewards" (1988: 23). Violence is, in their view, a rational choice made by the abuser.

The theory that Gelles and Straus adopt merits a moment's reflection. What they say is that "costs and benefits" are the first step in the "calculation" of the aggressor: if there were nothing to be gained from it, the behavior would stop. However, they set that calculation within a more robust social analysis that involves such considerations as the "effective social controls"—or lack thereof—that would normally restrain violence; in fact, the absence of any external controls such as law or police intervention, and the presence of positive values that sanction violence, enter into the calculation. Further, certain microsocial qualities of the family unit itself contribute to the prevalence of violence within it, such as privacy and of course the "structural inequality" between its members; thus, when the external society is perceived as having no business interfering in "family business" or when women and children are lower in power and prestige than men, there are few disincentives to using violence. As we have noted repeatedly, macrosocial influences such as the honor concept or practices such as the dowry will also affect the calculation.

Among the early researchers of gender/intimate violence is Lenore Walker, whose pioneering work *The Battered Woman* (1979) describes the cycle of spouse abuse. The three-phase process begins with the tension-building stage, in which little actual violence may occur but intrafamily pressures are mounting. Phase two is the actual battering incident, which may be quick and sudden or prolonged over a period of hours or days. This is followed by phase three, a period of kindness and even contrition that lasts for a while but is eventually succeeded by another tension-building stage. Edward Gondolf (1989) distinguishes between different types of abusive males, such as the "sporadic batterer," who is ordinarily calm but explodes without warning into violence; the "chronic batterer," who is continuously abusive, verbally and physically; the "antisocial batterer," whose violence spills out beyond the family into his general dealings with society; and the "sociopathic batterer," who is an extreme version of the antisocial type.

Finally, Donald Dutton (1995) has not only elaborated the types of batterers but determined frequencies for each, while relating them to the wider context of power relations. In fact, he posits that gender/intimate violence is ultimately about "psychologically and physically trying to control their victims' use of time and space in order to isolate them from all social connection, both past and present. It was an all-out attempt to annihilate their wives' self-esteem, to enslave them psychologically" (Dutton 1995: 13). The types Dutton describes and their frequency are:

- Jekyll and Hyde type, around 30 percent, who are cyclical abusers, alternately violent and pleasant.
- "Psychopathic wife assaulters," around 40 percent, whose general psychological problems make them unlikely to change or improve. He further observes that at least some of this type literally have different physical reactions to their violence; they, like the psychopaths we discuss at the very end of this book, stay unusually detached from their actions—oddly "cool" and unaroused.
- "Overcontrolled wife assaulters," around 30 percent, who are more mildly out of touch with their feelings, avoidant and passive aggressive. Two subtypes he identifies are the "active" controller, or control freak, and the passive controller; the latter is relatively unemotional but rigid in sex role attitudes and verbally aggressive.

We will return to these and other considerations when we attend to American violence later in this chapter and in later chapters. First, though, let us take a look at domestic/family violence in other societies and cultures in the light of our discussion thus far.

GENDER VIOLENCE IN CROSS-CULTURAL PERSPECTIVE

As we established in the previous two chapters, nonviolence is the exception rather than the rule among the world's cultures, and no societies are utterly without violence or hostility. Beyond that fact, certain social and cultural conditions contribute to the pervading atmosphere of violence that will also inevitably contribute to the particular incidence of gender and intimate violence; some of the factors we have discovered already are male dominance, male–male bonding, hierarchy/stratification, a concept of honor that is tied to the protection of family resources (including women), as well as other culturally specific values and practices. It is to such universal and local variables that we must look for an understanding of the prevalence of interpersonal violence within the groups that should, for all intents and purposes, be the most nurturing.

The best-studied area of gender/intimate violence cross culturally is wife abuse. Nevertheless, investigations into and concern over spousal violence are still very uneven between cultures and are not always the main focus of domestic violence. In fact, Gelles and Cornell (1983) note that research outside the English-speaking world tends to focus more on child abuse than on spouse abuse. The reasons for this focus are not altogether clear but might relate to cultural notions of appropriate parental behavior as opposed to appropriate husband behavior—the latter allowing a much higher level of "normal violence." Indeed they find that the United States, Canada, and England take the most inclusive view of spouse abuse, whereas African and European countries have the narrowest definition (thus excluding many actions Americans would deem "abusive"), with Japan and India lying somewhere between the two extremes (Gelles and Cornell 1983: 10). Summers and Hoffman (2002) inform us that Thailand does not even have a term for domestic violence and therefore collects no data on it, whereas in Italy the official definition of wife abuse requires that the woman "must show physical proof and her injuries have to take forty days to heal" (xv).

Violence against Women in Non-Western Societies

A number of very useful syntheses of cross-cultural information on wife abuse are available. In the introductory chapter to one of them, Brown (1999) notes that the values of societies differ enormously on the question of maltreatment of women: some disapprove of even minor aggression, some condone relatively mild violence but disdain severe abuse, and some allow what we would judge to be extreme forms of violence. They further conclude that certain factors play a role in determining the level of violence, such as:

- Younger wives are more likely to be abused than older ones
- Women who are denied an important economic role in society are more likely to be abused
- Women who are isolated from their own kin by marriage residence are more likely to be abused
- Women who are "hidden" behind a wall of domestic "privacy" are more likely to be abused
- Women who live in societies that deny them the status of "autonomous adults," especially where their identity (legal or social) is dependent on or merged into the man's are more likely to be abused.

Finally, the violence of men toward women in many cases is not entirely about the male–female relationship; rather, a man often practices violence toward women as a gesture to other men, "to establish and assure his position within the male peer group," in other words domestic abuse, as in the case of the Yanomamo above, is a way for a man to guarantee "avoidance of ridicule and his position as 'a man among men' " (Brown 199: 14). This situation will only apply when and if men ridicule each other and jockey for social position and when wives are pawns in such power games.

Draper (1999), writing on the !Kung, shows us that traditionally women were exposed to violence from men (both husbands and fathers) but this exposure was never systematic or extreme. Significantly, the !Kung were a foraging society (like the Semai and Utku, whom we encountered in Chapter 3), a socioeconomic system closely associated with relative social equality and peacefulness. But economics alone cannot protect women from harm; Draper finds that a set of customs and practices shielded women from the worst abuses of men, such as typical monogamy (i.e., rare **polygyny**), **bilateral** kinship, a generally nonhierarchical society, and an ethos to avoid overworking women on the basis of their reproductive value. These institutions plus their overall nonviolent value system gave men "no social entitlement to physically chastise wives; when spouses fought, it was looked on as shameful and stopped as quickly as possible" (Draper 1999: 58).

The Wape and the Nagovisi (both of New Guinea) are horticulturalists; horticulture is an economic system also regularly (although not always by any means) associated with relative gender parity. Mitchell in particular, in describing the Wape, points to cultural and enculturation practices and values that instill equality and mitigate against violence. These include a tendency to minimize gender differences and a lack of any notion or habit of gender segregation or female "contamination." Women are the main economic providers (not uncommon in horticulture), and they enjoy considerable freedom in their marriage choice; they can even voluntarily leave an abusive marriage, and they remain in contact with their own kin after marriage. Most remarkably, women maintain strong female–female corporate bonds and may actually intervene as a group by surrounding the house of a bickering couple, clubs in hand.

Like the Semai and Utku (and the !Kung), the Wape practice emotional control, especially any emotion that might lead to violence. Parents ignore their children's hostile behavior, and the young ones "soon learn that public aggression is an embarrassing and nonrewarding activity" (Draper 1999: 102)—a fact that alters the "exchange value" of domestic violence to which Gelles and Straus (1988) refer. For good measure, the Wape secure their behavioral system with a religious view that constrains violence: they believe that the ancestral spirits linger near lineage lands, which is a strong sanction against hostility and violence since a disturbed ancestor may seek vengeance against a perpetrator by damaging his or her garden or person. The Wape actually hold rituals of conciliation for the benefit of the ancestors to announce that the parties are once more friends and to ask the spirits to refrain from harm.

Among the Nagovisi we find the recognizable pattern leading to nonviolence. Like the Wape, they are farmers; they live in **matrilocal** and **matrilineal** kinship groups, giving women prominence and position. They too ignore aggression in children, and accordingly the youths usually do not hit each other nor engage in competitive or threatening activities. Parents do not physically punish children under the age of five, presumably because they, like the Utku and the Wape, believe that such young ones do not yet possess the reason necessary to imbibe the lesson. Also like the Utku, verbal aggression is not unknown, but it almost never escalates into physical abuse. More incredibly, even severe verbal abuse can be punished with a fine, and women are at least as skilled in the art of verbal repartee as the men—in other words, they can hold their own in a battle of words.

However, nonviolent societies are the exception rather than the rule. Likewise gender/spousal nonviolence is rare. Most societies practice one or more kinds of spousal abuse in various social contexts and in relation to various cultural norms and values, and these violent societies tend to share certain common features. For instance, nearly all of the Kaliai women of New Guinea explain that they expect to be beaten by their husbands during their lives. They do not look forward to it, but they along with the men "uphold the right of a husband to hit his wife for cause" (Counts 1999: 76). Cause for them includes adultery or just flirting, publicly shaming the man, fighting with co-wives (in a polygynous society), or merely failing at her normal domestic duties. The major macrosocial institutions of society, such as **patrilocality**, **patrilineality**, and **bridewealth**, all function to the advancement of men. Not surprisingly, children learn to be aggressive early, and parents look on approvingly as youngsters fight each other. More surprisingly, women internalize much of this violent ethos, hitting their children, their husbands, and their co-wives; however, standing up to a husband's abuse is considered improper and can earn another thrashing. Most tragically, many women regard suicide as an acceptable, even honorable, alternative to a violent marriage.

Among the Bun, also of New Guinea, children play argumentative and aggressive games with each other, and parents interact violently with children by hitting, throwing things, and verbally attacking them. The result is the creation of men who abuse women but also of males and females alike who are "assertive, violent, volatile people" (McDowell 1999: 88). On the Marshall Islands, the people of Ujelang Atoll tease children and teach them to throw rocks at each other; mothers threaten their children with violence. Still more, men are valued as warriors and are expected to initiate confrontations with each other. The two ways that a man can show his ferocity are war and women—and they use the same word, *torinae*, for both. Women, interestingly, are believed to have their own hidden talent, although a malign one, in the form of evil magic; this magic, flowing from women, is regarded as the source of most violent forms of human misfortune—meaning that, while women are practically the victims of much violence, they are ideologically the cause of it.

Mushanga (1983: 140) surveys twelve traditional African societies and finds that, while violence within the family is hardly restricted to wives, it is certainly most targeted at them. In only one instance are wives not the primary victims of familial violence (the Abakiga/Kigezi people); in all others, they tie or exceed all other kin relations for percentage of family violence directed at them, ranging from a low of 23 percent to a high of 95 percent (the Abasoga). Among the Abakiga/Kigezi, the highest rate of victimization is actually against sons, with fathers close behind. And interestingly, the second most common pattern after wife abuse is brother and father abuse; among the Ankole, for example, brother abuse and wife abuse are equal at 23 percent, and father abuse comes in at around 10 percent. Therefore, where there is violence, there is often widespread violence; however, in the Abasoga, who outscored all other societies in the survey on wife maltreatment, there was zero reciprocal (that is, wife-on-husband) aggression, indicating a much worse circumstance for women than when there is some mutuality in hostility.

The conditions in India and the Middle East are if anything even more negative. Hegland's (1999) account of an Iranian village highlights a society in which women have virtually no rights whatsoever. Everything in this society favors men, who are raised to be violent and domineering; they learn early on "to devalue women and their activities, to use violence to get what they wanted, and to demonstrate the power and strength required for political survival" (238). The control over women's lives is nearly total. A woman is required to be a virgin at the time of marriage. She is under the authority of her male relatives until she marries, at which time that authority transfers to her husband; so complete is it that her own father cannot step in to minimize the husband's abuses against her. Women may not work outside the home as it shames her husband or family, and the men beat their wives as well as their own sisters if they dare to challenge the patriarchal system. Women are so little valued that, as one informant told, "When I was born, the minute they told my mother it was a girl she began to cry bitterly" (237).

There are numerous sources for such attitudes and behaviors, including macrosocial ones like the base economic system (especially pastoralism) and the dominant political system. Another of these sources is religious authority. Although this is not the only word the Muslim scriptures have on the subject, the Qur'an does appear to justify and has been used to justify male domination and punishment of women. One passage (surah 4:34) states: "Men are the maintainers of women because Allah has made some of them to excel others . . . ; the good women are therefore obedient . . . ; and (as to) those on whose part you fear desertion, admonish them, and leave them alone in the sleeping-places and beat them; then if they obey you, do not seek a way against them." Another verse, (surah 24:31) seems to endorse the *purdah* custom, in which women are kept covered in public and only shown to their husbands in the privacy of their own homes.

Recently such attitudes and the violence they produce have been exported to Western societies with the immigrants who hold them. For instance, English authorities reported at least twelve cases in 2002 of what might be called "honor killings," in which women are murdered by their own family members for perceived conduct that brings shame to the family. This conduct can include premarital sex, dating outside the religion or nationality, and sometimes even victimization like rape (a woman is often blamed for somehow causing the rape or is a disgrace to the family no matter how it happened). In one particularly stark case, a Kurdish Muslim was arrested for stabbing to death his sixteen-year-old daughter because she was dating a Christian boy and becoming "too westernized."

The situation for women is comparable in India and in the Indian component of Fijian society. On Fiji, where a large Hindu population has settled, the **patrilineal** and **patrilocal** patterns of northern India are reproduced. This includes a social world in which men and women both "accept, seldom question, and even occasionally sanction men's right to control 'their' women by the occasional slap, punch, or push" (Lateef 1999: 226). In fact, it is the "abnormal" or "deviant" man who does not hit his wife, for he demonstrates to society that he cannot control his family nor defend his honor. Most unusually from some points of view, older women are likely to cooperate in the abuse of younger women, especially mothers-in-law against their daughters-in-law. This practice has been criticized as a case of failure to act along gender-solidarity lines, but rather it should be seen as success in acting along kinship lines; the mother-in-law feels her loyalty to her son, not to her fellow woman. Brown (1997) has even coined the term "mother-in-law belt" to refer to that swath of the globe from West Africa to East Asia where young married women suffer

under the hand of an authoritarian and often cruel mother-in-law, wh(
pates in if not instigates the mistreatment of the bride.

This is perhaps most dramatically and tragically the case in India, especially northern India, where a long tradition of male domination and mother-
in-law tyranny reigns. Miller (1999) finds that female intrahousehold status is
lower in North India than anywhere else on the subcontinent, with little value
placed on and few freedoms or alternatives given to women. They suffer from
low education and employment, village **exogamy** (which separates them from
their kin), **hypergamy** (which attempts to marry them "up" to higher-caste
men, sometimes at any cost), and a dowry custom that can severely disadvantage the woman and her family. The result, particularly in the first years of a
marriage, can be a highly unpleasant home life for the new wife—or much
worse, as the following case study shows.

Case Study 1: Brides Are Burning—Violence against Women in India

A drum, a peasant, a Sudra (laborer), an animal, a woman—all of these are fit
to be beaten.
    —*Sixteenth-century Hindu document*

Pay 500 rupees now or 50,000 in 18 years.
    —*Advertisement for an Indian abortion clinic*

In 1987 a great stir was caused in India by the case of a young wife, eighteen-
year-old Roop Kanwar, immolating herself on her dead husband's funeral pyre.
One cause of the stir was the suspicion that the woman had not committed the
act entirely voluntarily; she may have been forced or even drugged. The other
cause was the reaction of her community to her suicide, which was jubilant. To
many, including some members of her own family, she had committed the traditional and ultimate act of *sati*, or purity, by joining her husband in death.
The villagers referred to her as *Sati Mata* (Pure Mother) and gathered to celebrate and chant around her death site for days. Their chants included slogans
like, "One, two, three, four, all hail Roop Kanwar" and "As long as the sun and
moon remain, Roop Kanwar's name will remain" (Sen 2001: 5). A kind of
"cult" of the purified Kanwar developed, with some people claiming that the
sati, now something like a saint, could cure any ailment as long as one had faith
in her. There was a national outcry against what seemed to many as a barbaric
and anachronistic practice, but in response local politicians created a committee called *Sati Dharam Raksha Samiti* (Keepers of the *Sati* Tradition) "to perpetuate their celebration of the widow's death" (33).

Case Study 1: Brides Are Burning—Violence
against Women in India (continued)

The key to understanding this reaction is that *sati* is in fact a tradition, virtually a ritual duty, among at least some groups in India. The act can be partly traced to religious myths, for example the story of Sita who was challenged to pass safely through fire to prove her "purity" and chastity to her husband, the culture hero Rama, or the story of Sati Devi, the loyal wife of Shiva, who threw herself into a ceremonial fire. These are powerful models and charters for female behavior, but they beg the question of why women's purity, chastity, and loyalty are such an important issue and why widows in particular are such a center of focus in this society.

To say that women are subservient to men in many cases or that women are lower in status would be an understatement. As one contemporary Indian woman said, "It is my duty to serve my husband and live by his wishes. If God gives me the gift of *sat* [purity] when the time comes, I will gladly follow him in death as I have in life" (Sen 2001: 176). However, not all of the deaths of wives in India are so voluntary; there is also an epidemic of bride murders of uncertain proportions. By some estimates there are at least 2,000 wife murders, so-called "dowry deaths," per year, with two per day in New Delhi alone (Stone and James 1995: 127). Sen reports almost two thousand such deaths in 1987 and over five thousand in 1991 (Sen 2001: 184). The most common form of such assaults is burning by dousing the woman with kerosene and setting her on fire or by pushing her into a kerosene flame (since many Indian households cook over open kerosene stoves). These attacks often pass for accidents, partly because accidental kitchen burnings do occur and partly because law enforcement authorities are slow to respond to claims of intentional homicide with female victims. As one Indian lawyer states, the police are corrupt at best, especially in instances of domestic violence, and the court system has "a gender bias that is so deeply traditional, it makes one despair" (77).

The presence of "dowry deaths" speaks to a complex and interrelated set of values and practices in regard to women, marriage, family, property, and social status. In parts of India, particularly the Northwest, **dowry** is a common (though recently outlawed) component of marriage. Dowry is the practice of sending a new bride into her marriage with some money or property supplied by her family. In some cases, observers have described dowry as the woman's early inheritance (her share of the family wealth prior to her parents' death), but in the present case this seems like an inappropriate characterization, since the woman does not in fact receive or benefit from the inheritance; rather, it is transferred directly to her husband. Thus, as Madhu Kishwar (1986) concludes, dowry in the Indian context really has the effect of disinheriting women and promoting their economic dependence on men.

*Case Study 1: Brides Are Burning—Violence
against Women in India (continued)*

The custom of giving dowry puts women and their families in an awkward
and difficult situation in a variety of ways. It is an enormous financial strain on a
woman's family, especially if they are not rich. A family with daughters,
particularly if they cannot offer ostentatious dowries, does not have "great
expectations" for those daughters or their own social mobility. This is a significant
problem due to the preference for "hypergamy" or "marrying up" of a daughter
to a higher-caste husband, who may demand a sizable dowry for the favor of marrying into the lower-caste family. Not surprisingly, there is a disincentive to raise
daughters and a strong incentive to raise sons; sons, after all, will bring in riches
from their wives' families. This sentiment is captured in a proverb that goes,
"Raising a female child is like watering your neighbor's plants." The almost inevitable consequence of this system is a definite preference for male children,
which is achieved through neglect of female children, selective abortion, and
female infanticide. The result is a disproportionately low number of females to
males in society—a ratio as lopsided as 917 females to every 1,000 males—and a
profound devaluation of the females that do survive. As Sen (2001: 82) puts it,
"Many Indian women tend to tolerate their daughters but, without exception,
adore their sons." This might seem to work against the dowry system, since fewer
women are competing for more men. However, in fact, Stone and James (1995)
argue that, since brides are really just chasing after high-status husbands, and
since weakening of caste restrictions has put more low-status brides into the
competition, even suspected dowry murderers succeed at finding second wives.

This was likely a problem for women in the premodern setting, but it has
become more so, not less, in modern urban circumstances. Dowry, the monetary value of which was formerly set by convention and included mostly hand-
crafted family goods, has become an indeterminate and ever-expanding
economic requirement often expressed in manufactured goods like televisions,
appliances, furniture, jewelry, vehicles, and cash. A man may naturally
demand as much dowry from a woman's family as he can extract, and he may
even "blackmail" her family into supplying additional dowry by suggestions
that she will be better treated if he receives more or even threats that she may
suffer if he does not. As one woman who survived a burn attempt told:

> One year of my marriage has not passed when my in-laws and husband started
> giving me trouble every day for more dowry. My mother-in-law started telling my
> husband, "Leave this woman and we will get you another one, at least the other
> party will give us more and better dowry than what these people have given us.
> What her parents have given us is nothing. Moreover, this girl is ugly and she is
> dark." (Quoted in Stone and James, 128)

In the worst-case scenario, the undervalued bride is actually killed, leaving the
man free to marry again and collect another dowry.

Case Study 1: Brides Are Burning—Violence against Women in India (continued)

It might seem as if this were a behavior more suited to the distant past than to the present day. However, the truth is that dowry death, and even the reemergence of *sati*, are distinctly modern phenomena. Account after account suggests that dowry death along with other forms of violence against women occur predominantly in urban and suburban settings among middle and upper-class or caste families. The practices are spreading into the rural and "traditional" areas of India as well, although lower class/caste and rural women have an advantage of sorts, that their labor outside the home is still valued, so they are somewhat more valuable alive than dead. And the husband's mother is often complicit in this abusive relationship, sometimes believing that the wife is "not good enough" for her son and sometimes considering the wife to be "hers" to use and to train, is the chief tormentor or instigator of unrest, as seen in the quotation above. In fact, Indian mothers-in-law (but not only Indian ones) may take it as their duty to "socialize" the new bride into her role in the family and society; this "socialization" may take the form of orders, criticism, gossip, overwork and denial of basic necessities like food, and actual physical abuse and punishment. The outcome is women oppressing other women in the interests of men in what Fernandez (1997: 439) calls the "reproduction of their own subordination."

Still, one might expect women's status to improve after they have been in the husband's family for a time and particularly after they have borne some sons to that family. Such was indeed the case in the traditional context: a young wife had little or no status, but over time she grew to become the senior woman in the household and the mother of many sons, acquiring status indirectly from her male heirs. However, in the modern scene, with its emphasis on smaller families and capitalist commodities, this one last lever of potential female value has been removed; being a mother, even of sons, does not guarantee safety let alone status in her adopted household. In fact, while it is still the case that new brides are in the most mortal danger, today older brides, including mothers and pregnant women, are suffering assaults in remarkable numbers.

Since many men and their families are no longer as interested in children as formerly, the woman has only a single remaining point of value in their eyes—her dowry potential. This last source they will sometimes exploit vigorously, to the extent of murder. One of the true tragedies of this situation is that families of some women, and perhaps even some women themselves, accept this in relation to the alternative, which is to have a class of unmarried (single, divorced, or widowed) women in society. An unmarried woman is a social problem, a shame and dishonor; as Kishwar (1986: 5) says, "most parents would rather see their daughters dead than to have them get a divorce and return

Case Study 1: Brides Are Burning—Violence against Women in India (continued)

permanently to the parental home." This observation ties together the practices of *sati*, dowry murder, female infanticide, and other forms of violence and abuse against women, including wife battering and "selling" daughters into sex slavery and prostitution: an unmarried adult woman is unacceptable to certain components of society, and they will do anything to avoid having an unmarried adult woman in the family.

So the prejudices against women are expressed in many ways. A woman who gets divorced is viewed with suspicion; the first assumption is that she must have done something to "deserve" getting thrown out by her husband. Her "reputation" and that of her family is ruined, and she is obviously no longer "pure" and "chaste" and "virginal," so her marriage prospects are dim to nonexistent. Her family is probably unwilling to provide a second dowry to marry her off, even if they could afford it and find a man willing to shoulder the burden of her. And she cannot support herself with paid work. One might suspect that widows would merit some better treatment for their loss and, in the case of older women, their seniority. The opposite is true: among the upper-class northern Indian groups like the Rajputs, a widow "must always be the last to eat and so must eat alone, apart from the rest of the family. She must never be seen in public. She cannot attend social functions, not even those involving only the family. She must keep her head covered at all times. She is, for all intents and purposes, a social outcast" (Sen 2001: 28).

One of the most incredible consequences of this virtual taboo on unmarried adult women is the communities of impoverished women that form in various places in India, including the holy city of Benares, where thousands of widows are

> driven out of their homes or with no means of support congregate . . . to eke out a miserable existence, poorly fed, poorly clad, unwanted, uncared for and unloved. They beg or subsist on crumbs doled out to them as charity, live in inhuman conditions, and die unlamented. Given no choice, they consider this wretchedness as punishment for the offense of having outlived the men they were married to.

> Cities like Benares and Brindavan are said to be "not just dumping grounds for widows but recruiting grounds for brothel keepers." Preyed on by relatives, cowed down by priests and persecuted by society, many widows have been driven to prostitution to keep body and soul together. In contrast, when one upholds the values of chastity and prefers immolation as a *sati*, she commands admiration for her "courage"—small wonder, then, that some widows not only went to the pyre apparently voluntarily but even insisted on their right to burn with the bodies of their husbands. (Sen 2001: 196)

Violence against Women in Western Societies

It goes without saying that violence against women is not restricted to the non-Western world. America actually has a notably high rate, and other Western or westernized societies have an equal or higher incidence, although inconsistent definitions and record-keeping systems make precise measurement difficult. Nonetheless, the data suggest a pattern of rampant gender/intimate violence in countries like our own—including our own.

As we mentioned, spousal abuse is recognized more overtly as a problem in the English-speaking world than elsewhere. According to Rawstone (2002) two women are killed by a male partner in England and Wales every week (as opposed to four per day in the U.S.); in addition, as many as a quarter of all English women experience intimate violence at some time in their lives. Almost half (47 percent) of all English female homicide victims are killed by a current or former male partner, versus 8 percent of male victims. The data are consistent in Australia, where 23 percent of women in a marriage or other long-term intimate relationship reported abuse by their man. A 1999 study indicated that 60 percent of female homicide victims were killed by an intimate male, compared to 11 percent of male victims who were killed by an intimate female (Pickering 2002). In Canada, a 1999 survey showed that 89 percent of family violence reported to police was male-on-female violence (Buset and Pepler 2002). The Republic of South Africa, which defines "domestic violence" very broadly—to include assault, intimidation, stalking, property damage, and entering a residence without permission—reports that 25 percent of women are victimized by a husband or boyfriend every week (van der Hoven 2002).

Since all of these societies, as well as the United States, were former British colonies, and since Britain draws much of its culture from more ancient sources—Roman and Christian—it is critical to examine all of these influences. According to English common law, wives and offspring were considered to be property of the male head of the family. In fact, the famous "rule of thumb" refers to the precedent that a man could hit his dependents with a stick that was no thicker than his thumb. This patriarchal pattern in turn emanates from Roman custom and law, specifically the *patria potestas* that granted men the right of life and death over their families. Marriage as an institution awarded the husband rights over his wife, and childbirth established his rights over his children—the same rights he had over his other property, his slaves, and his tenants. Among these rights were the power to disinherit, to dispose, to sell into slavery, or even to kill members of his household.

Religious beliefs and values coming from the Judeo–Christian tradition reinforced many of these views and customs. Males were also regarded as dominant, and ancient polygyny in the Torah/Old Testament period together with a preference for male heirs served to suppress female status. The very account of the male being created first and the woman coming "from" him, together with the woman's culpability for the "fall," more than suggested the inferiority of women; Genesis 3:16 clearly informs women that "thy husband ... shall rule over thee." The New Testament is equally direct: "For the husband is the head of the wife, even as Christ is the head of the church: and he is the saviour of the body" (Ephesians 5:23). Of course, a man is to love and protect his wife, but a wife is to serve and obey her husband. Still, there was little doubt who was in charge or what his rights were. In Cherubino's famous medieval "Rules of Marriage," he writes: "Scold your wife sharply, bully and terrify her. If this doesn't work, take up a stick and beat her soundly, for it is better to punish the body and correct the soul than to damage the soul and spare the body.... Then readily beat her, not in rage but out of charity and concern for her soul, so that the beating will redound to your merit and her good." Many a man has delivered many a lashing with precisely that spirit.

Other Western societies evince a habit of gender and intimate violence that has reportedly only increased in recent years. In Germany in 1999, 27 percent of murders were between related individuals, and women were the victim 52 percent of the time; as Jolin and Webke (2002: 42) note, women "are usually assaulted and injured at home by men they know. Men, however, are attacked in public places by other men who are strangers to them." According to Voigt and Thornton (2002), Russian women are three times more likely than American women to be victims of spousal homicide; at the same time, violence against women has no social category of its own and is tucked into such categories as "light bodily injury" or "hooliganism." Slovenia also does not designate domestic violence as a distinct crime, and its Law on Personal Data Protection actually precludes collecting information on such behavior without the parties' consent; even so, it is estimated that some 60 percent of family violence victims are female, which means that 40 percent are not (Pagon, Mesko, and Lobnikar 2002). Finally, in Japan, where Western ways mix with traditional ones, men are allowed wide latitude in the treatment of their wives; domestic violence is viewed as a private matter between husband and wife, not as a social problem, and no one outside the family has a right to interfere in its internal affairs. Accordingly, one-third of Japanese women who file for divorce mention spousal violence (mostly pushing, grabbing, pinching, slapping, and threatening) as a reason, and half reported at least one, and sometimes many, incidents of verbal/emotional abuse (Watanabe 2002).

Finally, not all gender/intimate violence occurs within the marital relationship. It is common for ex-spouses to seek out and injure or kill their divorced or estranged former partners. New attention has been turned to dating violence, including but not limited to date rape; a significant proportion of young women and men report abuse at the hands of their boyfriend or girlfriend. Other novel forms of victimization, to which the legal system was not always ready to respond, include stalking and its twenty-first-century variants, including spying, intercepting telephone or email messages, or posting damaging information or pictures on the internet.

CHILD-DIRECTED VIOLENCE

Gender violence and child violence cannot be completely dissociated, first because many of the children who are abused are female and second because, within the household, women and children alike tend to share a vulnerability to violent males. This is not to say that all maltreatment of children comes at the hands of men; indeed, it does not. Nevertheless, in a violent family it is often both women and children who are at risk, and in a violent society there is often no important distinction made between women and children when it comes to inflicting harm.

Indeed child-directed violence is often a part of the cyclical pattern of spousal abuse because, obviously, abusers must learn their violent ways as children. Thus, the Yanomamo, the various societies of New Guinea, the Iranians, the Indo-Fijians, the British soccer hooligans, and Americans alike instill violent behavior in their children by practicing violence on them and encouraging violence among them. David Levison (1983) has studied the relationship between wife beating and child-directed violence and discovered a significant but not entirely straightforward correlation. His analysis of forty-six societies sorted them into those that practice wife beating rarely, infrequently, frequently, and commonly and ones that practice corporal punishment of children rarely, infrequently, frequently, and commonly. He found that infrequent or rare wife-directed violence was related to infrequent or rare child-directed violence, but frequent or common spouse abuse was not significantly related to the frequency of child abuse. In other words, we typically find nonviolence in both areas and seldom find child abuse without wife abuse (only five out of the forty-six societies). We do, though, find rare/infrequent child punishment paired with frequent/common wife abuse; of the nineteen societies that demonstrated higher rates of spouse abuse, twelve were identified with lower rates of child punishment and only seven with higher rates. In other words, societies that perpetrate violence on children tend to perpetrate it on women too, but it is common to be violent toward women without also being violent toward children. Either way, the family becomes a school for young ones to learn their future violent roles.

Abuse of minors includes an astonishingly wide range of behaviors, which fall under the four general categories of neglect, emotional abuse, sexual abuse, and physical abuse (even to the point of death). Neglect alone can take many forms, including denying the child food and other care, rejecting or ignoring the child, exposing the child to an unsanitary or dangerous home environment (e.g., one with drugs or alcohol), or abandonment. Some, if not all, of these behaviors are emotionally abusive as well, if we consider emotional abuse to be any behavior that harms the youngster's feelings, psyche, or self-esteem; it could even be directed at a child's property or pet. Physical abuse, too, takes myriad forms, from grabbing and spanking to beating, and can be administered by the father, mother, or an older sibling (not to mention more distant relatives, neighbors, or friends). Fatal violence to a child may be the end result of a long train of abuse, or a single severe episode, or an intentional act of infanticide (involving most often but not universally, as we have seen, females). More controversially, some experts define certain forms of child abuse as the result of ritualistic violence, including satanic cult ritual. In fact, after investigating some high-profile cases, the Ritual Abuse Task Force in Los Angeles established an official definition of ritual abuse in 1989.

Exceptional Forms of Child Abuse

The term *child abuse* also refers to more exotic and unfamiliar expressions of violence, including child labor, child prostitution, child marriage (which is deemed completely normal in many societies), infanticide, child sacrifice, child abandonment to the streets, and child participation in war. Markham, Lindsey, and Creel in a 1914 study claimed that 2 million American children were working at adult jobs in factories and fields, and the novels of Charles Dickens often highlighted the same issue. These observations led to the passage of child labor laws in the United States and other countries. Today an untold number of children worldwide still work from young ages, which interferes with their education and growth. A significant proportion of these youths, males and females, are implicated in the international sex trade, in which men from developed countries travel to places like Thailand or Cambodia for sex with minors. Some of these children are abducted or picked up after being abandoned by their parents, but some are sold or offered into service by their parents, with or without a full understanding of their fate.

In many societies children, especially girls, are married at very early ages, often to men decades older than themselves. This practice is, in many instances, a perfectly acceptable cultural norm in such societies and would never qualify as "abuse." For some Middle Eastern and Central Asian societies, the marriage might be arranged as a settlement of a dispute between two families, as in the case of a murder or other affront to a family's "honor." Often enough, it is simply the normal order of things, older men getting the first choice of young girls as wives. Uzodike (2000) tells the story of a twelve-year-old girl who was married to a much senior man (a Fulani pastoralist in Nigeria) and repeatedly ran away from him. After the final escape attempt, the husband cut her leg off, causing her to bleed to death. The girl's father saw no fault in the husband's action. Finally, marrying a maiden to the man who raped her is a frequent proper resolution to the social problem of rape in contemporary and ancient societies, including ancient Hebrew society.

Infanticide is a practice found not only across human societies but throughout the natural world. Hausfater and Blaffer (1984) have assembled much of the cross-cultural and cross-species knowledge on intentional child-killing, finding that it takes place among birds, fish, large mammals (such as lions, bears, and wild dogs), and nonhuman primates as well as humans. They identify five general reasons why parents (and occasionally siblings) destroy their own kind:

> (1) *exploitation* of the infant as a resource, usually cannibalism; (2) *competition for resources*, where death of the infant increases resources available to the killer or its lineage; (3) *sexual selection*, where individuals improve their own opportunities to breed by eliminating dependent offspring of a prospective mate; (4) *parental manipulation* of progeny, where parents on average increase their own lifetime reproductive success by eliminating particular offspring; . . . [and] (5) *social pathology* for cases where infanticide on average decreases the fitness of the infanticidal individual. (Hausfater and Blaffer 1984: xvi)

They conclude that most human infanticide constitutes parental manipulation of reproduction, especially when practiced by the mother.

Accordingly, two particularly common contexts in which humans commit (more or less "normal") infanticide are resource shortage and "defectiveness" of the child. Perhaps not surprisingly, human infanticide is especially frequent in foraging societies, where small populations and widely spaced births are desirable. In a study by Daly and Wilson (1984), they report that of sixty societies analyzed and the 112 circumstances for infanticide cited between them, 56, or exactly half of the circumstances cited, involved "maternal overburdening." Their research also confirms general findings that "defective" babies are more subject to selection by infanticide; twenty-one of the thirty-five societies in the study that gave rationales for infanticide cited destruction of deformed or seriously ill children. As we saw in Chapter 4, the Spartans had this practice, which is apparently an age-old and widespread phenomenon. Roman law provided for the killing of defective offspring; Table IV of the Twelve Tables, Rule 1 states: "A dreadfully deformed child shall be quickly killed." The third-century writer Soranus in an opinion called "How to Recognize the Newborn that is Worthy of Rearing, " said that it should be "perfect in all its parts, members, and sense . . . its ducts, namely of the ears, nose, pharynx, urethra, anus are free from obstruction . . . [and] the natural functions of every member are neither sluggish nor weak." By Roman custom, an imperfect child could be rejected and disposed of by its father.

"Defectiveness" is a culturally relative term. In a large number of societies, twins are regarded as unnatural and defective in some way: Daly and Wilson found that fourteen of their thirty-five infanticidal societies dispose of one or both twins, and Dickeman (1975) likewise reports that eighteen out of seventy societies surveyed destroy one or both of twins. Also, adultery or the inability to establish paternity may render an infant "socially defective" and unrearable: Daly and Wilson's data show that 20 of the 112 reasons given for infanticide involve the failure or refusal of any man to accept paternity, and fourteen of the thirty-five societies provide for infanticide if the mother is unmarried. Overall, infanticide is surprisingly regular in human societies. In one last study of more than one hundred societies, 36 percent were noted to practice it commonly and 12 percent occasionally; in only 2 percent was it uncommon and 9 percent never used (Divale and Harris 1976). The cross-cultural comparison yielded even more interesting results: it was common in 100 percent of the Asian societies in the survey, compared to 58 percent of the African societies (although the other 42 percent had no data available), but only 22 percent of Oceanian and 25 percent of South American societies.

To choose just one more item off our list, although it is not exactly an issue of "intimate" violence, nevertheless children suffer from the violence of war both as innocent victims and as combatants. According to the International Committee of the Red Cross and UNICEF, some 300,000 children are being used as soldiers in conflicts around the globe. Particularly when these conflicts involve ethnic and religious groups in extreme and impoverished conditions, as they do in much of Africa, Asia, and Latin America, child recruitment into armies is ordinary. In many cases, children as young as ten enthusiastically join fighting forces to protect their families, villages, and cultures; in others, they are conscripted or abducted into service. One notorious instance is the Ugandan rebel group known as the Lord's Resistance Army, which has reportedly kidnapped as many as 20,000 youngsters, boys as soldiers and girls as concubines. An uncounted multitude of other children are exposed to the dangers of militant brigades, mines, orphan status, displacement into refugee camps, and the disruption of their educations and childhoods.

The Major Categories of Child Abuse

Clearly, like gender/spousal abuse, the phenomenon of child abuse is diverse and complex. A single cross-cultural and cross-national definition is probably treacherously difficult if not impossible. For instance, the U.S. Child Abuse Prevention and Treatment Act of 1996 defined it as "any recent act or failure to act on the part of a parent or caretaker which results in death, serious physical or emotional harm, sexual abuse, or exploitation [and] any act or failure to act which presents an imminent risk of serious harm." The African Network for the Prevention and Protection Against Child Abuse and Neglect expands the definition to include

> the intentional, unintentional, or well-intentioned acts which endanger the physical, health, emotional, moral, and the educational welfare of the child. These acts are those unacceptable normally to the community; in some cases, however, such acts include behaviors that may be accepted by the community but may endanger

the well-being of the child, although the child may or may not perceive these acts as abuse. (Quoted in Uzodike 200: 331)

Although this wider definition may be desirable and even necessary, it does raise the problem of who precisely will decide which acts are abusive, if not the local community. Does a cross-cultural and international standard exist? All we do know is that different cultures define, value, and respond to child abuse differently. According to Todorova (2000), for example, Bulgaria has made no attempt to formulate a legal notion of child abuse, and other countries have only recently enacted laws or begun keeping meaningful statistics.

Most classifications of child abuse—scholarly, medical, and legal—distinguish four major categories: physical abuse, sexual abuse, emotional abuse, and neglect. Physical abuse is probably the most overt and deadly of the forms of child-directed violence (although children can be dramatically harmed and even killed by any form of abuse). As we have emphasized repeatedly, physical abuse is by no means a recent phenomenon, although its identification as a "social problem" is. That is, many actions that other societies take that would be "abusive" in our eyes, are fine in theirs, and many actions that we took unproblematically in the past feel "abusive" by today's standards (e.g., paddling children in school). As early as the mid- to late 1800s child physical abuse was becoming a social issue in Western societies; in 1874, the case of eight-year-old Mary Ellen Watson, who was starved and beaten by her adoptive parents, drew national attention. However, it was really the work of Kempe et al. (1962) that gave child physical abuse its prominence as a social issue.

In 1962, C. Henry Kempe and his associates coined the term *battered-child syndrome* to describe the constellation of injuries they were observing in clinical practice. They conducted a nationwide survey of seventy-one hospitals covering 302 cases of child injury, 33 deaths and 85 permanent brain injuries; they also surveyed seventy-seven district attorneys prosecuting 447 cases, including 45 deaths and 29 brain injuries. What they found was a consistent pattern of signs in the children's symptoms, such as lack of hygiene, general poor health, malnutrition, multiple soft-tissue injuries (especially on the arms and legs, indicative of grabbing), repeated traumas to the same bodily zones, recurrent bruising, and a contradiction between the clinical data and the reports of the parents. The most affected children were the youngest, under three years of age. The parents too showed typical characteristics: low intelligence, alcoholism, marital instability, minor criminal activity, immaturity and impulsiveness, self-centeredness, and promiscuity; they had often been abused themselves as children.

Since clinical attention has been focused on child battery, a variety of other kinds of abuse has surfaced. One of these is the so-called *shaken-baby syndrome*, in which an infant is shaken vigorously, generally by a caretaker in an attempt to stop its crying. The syndrome manifests in such symptoms as brain swelling and damage, bleeding under the skin, blindness, hearing loss, speech and learning difficulties, developmental delays, and in extreme cases, paralysis and even death. Medical specialists commonly see burns, both "pattern burns" from hot objects (from cigarettes to irons or radiators) as well as "water immersion" burns (from being placed in too-hot water).

One of the oddest abusive behaviors to come to light occurs as result of a mental disorder, the *Munchhausen syndrome by proxy*, whereby parents fake illness in their children precisely for the purpose of getting medical attention. Roy Meadow (1977) was one of the first clinicians to identify this behavior, when, in the course of treatment of a six-year-old child who was repeatedly brought in by her mother for examination, it was discovered that the mother was replacing the girl's urine samples with her own to fake an infection. Since then, many other cases of the syndrome have been observed, in which parents have not only simulated illness in their child but actually harmed, smothered, or poisoned the child.

Cross-culturally and transnationally, the details of child physical abuse vary but the main facts remain the same. In Hungary, for instance, 80 percent of child murders are committed by a parent or step-parent, and child abusers tend to be poorly educated, unemployed, poor, and in large families (Kerenzsi 2000). Even more informatively, Kerenzsi (2000: 201) reports that "hitting children is socially acceptable.... Physical punishment is the habitual experience of children." Similarly, Bulgarian society has traditionally combined two deadly values—absolute control by the parents over the children in which corporal punishment is normal and a "closed" attitude toward the family in which no one outside the family can interfere with the parents' choice of child-rearing methods. Matsushima tells that traditional Japanese society gave parents "absolute control over children [who] could force their children to beg, or sell them to show-tents or brothels" (2000: 232). Finally, Nigerian customary law allows parents to "have the unconditional right to apply physical chastisement for the upbringing of children" (Uzodike 2000: 339).

Child sexual abuse can be widely or narrowly defined. If we limit its definition to actual intercourse or other inappropriate but distinctly "sexual" activity between a caretaker and a child, then its occurrence is relatively rare, although still much too frequent. But if we extend the definition to include things like marrying underage girls to older men, then child sexual abuse is a much more common but also much more "normal" phenomenon in many societies. In the United States and in other societies that keep statistics, sexual abuse is low in incidence, constituting 10 percent of child abuse cases in the United States, 16 percent in Australia, 5 percent in Hungary, and 5 percent in Japan. Victims are disproportionately female, and perpetrators are disproportionately male and friends or family members. Whether it is on the increase or our attention and methods have improved is not certain: either way, Finland, for instance, reported a 300 percent rise in child sex abuse in the short period between 1984 and 1991 (Taskinen 2000).

Virtually no society regards incest as an acceptable behavior, but even so many forms of unacceptable sexual behavior continue to be performed. Uzodike (2000: 332) explains that "rape, defilement, and indecent assault of young girls are far more common in Nigeria and, until recently, were not seen as child abuse even though people find such acts deplorable." According to the International Women's Health Coalition, almost half of all first sexual encounters for women are forced. Other more extreme or more culturally specific phenomena like child prostitution or what has been called "female circumcision" or "female genital mutilation" occur less frequently in the world, although in regard to the latter, "to the people who practice it, there is nothing abusive about it" (Uzodike 2000: 336).

Child emotional abuse is by some measures the most common form of child abuse but also the most elusive form. Again, it is difficult both to define and to collect data on emotional abuse: is it abusive to call a child a name, or to tell him or her that he or she is stupid, and how would we count the instances of such behavior? The problem is evidenced by the great disparities between statistics on emotional abuse, ranging from 31 percent of child abuse in Australia to 6 percent in Japan (with America coming in closer to the Japanese figure). Does this mean that the Japanese are much kinder to their children than the Australians or that conduct that is regarded as abusive by Australians is considered nonabusive by Japanese? Furthermore, physical and sexual abuse (and neglect) are no doubt emotionally damaging as well, so it is difficult even to separate out the emotional from the other aspects of harm. Likewise, neglect is a relative term, depending on what the standards of parenting and of living are in a society. For example, here Australia and Japan reverse positions, with 40 percent of Japanese child abuse cases involving neglect and 25 percent of Australian (and fully 63 percent of American). These wildly different numbers probably tell us more about the observers of child violence than the perpetrators of it.

Even so, there are extreme forms of child neglect that nearly everyone can agree on. One is child abandonment. Todorova and Kerezsi tell us that abandonment is a huge problem in southeastern Europe, virtually a normal part of their culture. In Bulgaria, 30,000 children reside in "orphanages" but only 4 percent of them are actually orphans; the rest have one or both parents alive and known (Todorova 2000: 48). In Hungary, which reports neglect as its single largest category of abuse (48 percent), over 24,000 children are also institutionalized, 60 percent of them Romany, or "gypsy," despite the fact that they compose only 5 percent of the country's population (Kerezsi, 192). And from Brazil to Africa children are often dumped on the streets by parents to fend for themselves as street urchins—begging, stealing, selling drugs, prostituting, and so forth. In some Latin American countries, governments have performed sweeps of city streets to round up stray children, and the problem has intensified in Russia since the fall of the Soviet Union.

The Most Intimate Violence: Suicide

If by "intimate" we mean close to the individual, then there is no more intimate form of violence than self-directed violence. "Auto-violence" can range from pulling out one's hair and cutting oneself to ending one's own life. Yet even here, we cannot eliminate cultural differences. In America we hold suicide to be criminal and immoral; in traditional Japan, as we learned in Chapter 4, it was regarded as a great honor, even a duty, in some cases, and as we will discuss in the next chapter, at many moments in Western history it has been celebrated as the highest form of spiritual expression and accomplishment (in the form of martyrdom).

In America, suicide is predominantly a male phenomenon. Men in all age categories kill themselves at rates between four and ten times that of women. Whites also commit suicide at higher rates than blacks, although the differences are still most pronounced in men (white men having the highest rate of all). And perhaps surprisingly, suicide is not a behavior ascribed to the young, despite the fact that teen suicide gets so much attention and is in fact relatively frequent: according to a national survey in 2000, three million teens contemplated suicide and one million attempted it. Still, the rate of successful suicide is lowest for men while in their teens and climbs steeply with age, occurring about 30 percent more often in the age range of thirty-five to forty-five and three times as high after age eighty-five. For women the highest rate is in the age range of forty-five to fifty-five, after which it levels off, dipping near to the rate of teen suicide. Interestingly, suicide rates peak for black men at an earlier age (twenty-five to thirty-four) and then steadily decline. Finally, not surprisingly suicide is related to external, macrosocial factors, as Durkheim noted in his classic study of the subject: historically suicide was far more common in the United States in the first decade of the 1900s and in the 1930s and dropped dramatically in the 1920s and 1950s, to its near-record low today.

It is worth noting at this point in our discussion that in other societies characterized by macrosocial institutions of abusive behavior, suicide is accepted or becoming accepted as form of escape. Recall that some analyses of Japanese ritual suicide (whether of warriors or of star-crossed lovers) link it to the repressive social norms of the time; also, Western literature has often celebrated couples who choose to die together when they cannot live together, like Romeo and Juliet. In sexually repressive societies, including Muslim and Chinese, women are once again turning to suicide in greater numbers. In such places as Afghanistan, in an ironic twist on the Hindu practice of burning a bride, women are choosing to take their own lives by burning themselves up. This behavior is particularly acute among young women who are attempting to avoid an arranged marriage and who have no other good social options. In a

2002 news article a twenty-seven-year-old Afghani woman, wrapped in bandages after a failed suicide attempt, was quoted as saying, "All Afghan women have a dark future. Now we have peace, but we still have family problems" (Reitman 2002). Similarly, women—especially rural women—in China are killing themselves in astonishing numbers. According to the data contained in another news article written in the same year (Fackler 2002), the suicide rate for Chinese rural women under forty years of age is three times the official rate in China (67 per 100,000 versus 21 per 100,000), more than three times the rate in Japan (18.8) and almost six times the rate in the United States. (In 2000, according to the World Health Organization, the highest national rate was Lithuanian men at 75.6 per 100,000.) Altogether, almost 160,000 Chinese women die from suicide annually, and suicide is the leading cause of death for Chinese people under age thirty-five—and that is according to official Chinese figures, which are notoriously optimistic. The reasons are not hard to identify: low status compared to men, arranged marriages, kidnapping of women as wives, and female infanticide, all adding up to a precarious life. (Recall that traditional China was the land of female footbinding.) As one local woman stated, "In rural villages, girls aren't made to feel wanted or loved. They never feel their life is valuable" (Fackler 2002). And the preferred suicide method: drinking pesticide.

HURTING WITHOUT HITTING: STRUCTURAL VIOLENCE

Nobody forces these unhappy women to drink poison or light themselves on fire, yet they are just as injured, sometimes just as dead, as if someone had. Yet in another way, in a sense someone—or something—did drive them to do it.

Most of the discussions of violence focused on familiar and "traditional" forms that involve someone raising a hand or a weapon to someone else—usually to a victim with less physical strength and less social means. However, not all violence requires an angry hand or even an intention to do harm. Some, perhaps much, violence and harm in the world is done without even a knowledge of doing it, by means of the institutions, practices, and structures of society. We refer to this as *structural violence*. Structural violence is the harm, including physical harm and death, that occurs as a result of the very rules and arrangements of society—the power inequalities, gender relations, class stratification, race and ethnic differences, and other basic disparities in society. These disparities privilege some people and disadvantage others, according to their position in the structure.

We can think of structural violence first and foremost in terms of its macrosocial dimension. Institutions such as polygyny, dowry, and patrilocal residence create a circumstance favoring male power and opportunities over their female counterparts. Values placed on one gender, one race, one religion, one age, vis-à-vis the other(s) produce and maintain potentially destructive relationships between them. Differential access to the tools and techniques that contribute to success and comfort in life—including education and health care—negatively impact those who are denied them. And behaviors and practices, which sometimes those people perform unconsciously, have consequences for strangers and loved ones alike that no one perhaps intends but that are real nonetheless.

Structural violence, by definition, falls inordinately on the poor and the weak. In all too many instances, the victims are women and children. For example, Kati Marton (2004), chair of the International Women's Health Coalition, informs us that women make up 70 percent of the world's poorest citizens. They also make up two-thirds of the world's illiterate adults. In some parts of the world, more than half of the women are unable to read, often because they are denied meaningful education of any kind. The highest rates are reported in South Asia, followed closely by the Middle East and Sub-Saharan Africa. Some of the very worst cases are Senegal, Benin, and Mauritania, where, according to the United Nations agency UNESCO, more than 70 percent of women (and nearly half of men) cannot read. Overall, one-third of the world's female population is illiterate.

Illiteracy is both an indicator and a cause of many of the other forms of structural violence in the world. Poor people, especially women, cannot get the health care that they need or want. Some of the poorest countries in the world have the highest rate of HIV infection (up to 40 percent of the entire population in some southern African states). For reasons of education, money, and cultural and religious values, women often cannot obtain contraception and so continue to have many (and unhealthy) babies; in the worst cases, 20 percent of all babies die in their first year of life because of lack of medicine and simple food. Marton (2004) estimates that 350 million women who desire birth control cannot acquire it and that 19 million have unsafe abortions each year; 13 percent of female deaths occur during pregnancy or childbirth. It has been documented that a little education reduces pregnancies as well as infant mortality.

Other practices that might seem remote from end-result health and quality-of-life issues have a profound effect on them. In India, for example, more than 90 percent of female AIDS cases appear in monogamous wives. This remarkable fact has been attributed to the desperate behavior of prostitution among some of the poorest women as well as to the behaviors of some of the men, most notably truckers, who visit prostitutes and take home infections (Cowley 2002). In the United States itself epidemiological researchers have recently turned their attention to the "carrier" behavior of truckers and other long-distance transmitters, including truck-stop prostitutes.

Case Study 2: Structural Violence and the Ordinary Lives of the Poor in Brazil

> Don't pity the infants who died here on the Alto do Cruzeiro. Don't waste
> your tears on them. Pity us instead. Weep for their mothers who are
> condemned to live.
>   —*Shantytown mother, Brazil*

Scheper-Hughes (1992) describes structural violence as it is experienced by
the women and children of a shantytown in the sugarcane region of northeast Brazil. In the town of Bom Jesus da Mata, some five thousand poor
laborers occupy the hillside squatter settlement of Alto do Cruzeiro. Most of
the men of the *bairro*, as it is called in Portuguese, are seasonal sugarcane
cutters; some are municipal laborers. Some of the women work too, often as
domestic servants in the homes of the upper classes, although many also take
in laundry. These people are part of a great social shift in the last half-cen-
tury, in which former rural residents (*matutos*, or "forest dwellers") migrated
into towns following the "modernization" of the archaic and semifeudal
sugar production systems of the eighteenth and nineteenth centuries. The
result has been the creation of, as Eduardo Galeano called it, a "concentration camp for more than thirty million people" (quoted in Scheper-Hughes
1992: 32).

To understand the plight of the *matutos*, it is important to remember that
Brazil was colonized by the Portuguese beginning in the 1500s and that large
feudal-style sugar plantations were established in the northeast. By 1630 there
were 144 such plantations in the state of Pernambuco alone, and because of
the labor shortage, African slaves had to be imported. Traditional sugar production was profitable enough but inefficient and irrational. When slavery was
abolished in Brazil in 1888, many of the social relationships and institutions of
slave society persisted, including the power and ownership of prominent
families and the paternalistic relations between these owners and their workers. However, if anything, the circumstances of the freed workers actually
deteriorated as slave labor was replaced by wage labor and the traditional
sugar mill was replaced by the modern industrialized sugar factory. At first,
workers were paid a small wage and allowed to occupy the owner's land and
cultivate a small garden for their own use. But as the "modernization" of the
industry proceeded, owners aimed to bring even these small plots into "production," and so starting in the 1950s the tenant farmers were evicted from
their land and forced to congregate in urban ghettos like Alto do Cruzeiro.

This modernization marked the end of the "semi-independent peasantry,"
who now became nothing more than wage-laborers with no property and no

Case Study 2: Structural Violence and
the Ordinary Lives of the Poor in Brazil (continued)

supplemental income or food sources other than their (inconsistent) employment. Furthermore, all of their needs became "modernized" as well, so that
they had to purchase all food and other supplies with cash and could neither
produce their own nor approach their patron for assistance. They had become
true "proletarians." At the same time, the wage they could earn typically could
not feed an Alto household; in the late 1980s food for a family of six cost the
equivalent of four times the minimum wage, and many men did not earn the
minimum wage, at least not year round. "The net result is misery and a constant scramble among all household members, including children, to find sup-
plementary wages" (Scheper-Hughes 1992: 46).

Hunger and thirst and their attendant consequences—including weakness, illness, and premature death—are an epidemic problem in the shantytown. Yet, this huge segment of society (over 50 percent of the population of
the town of Bom Jesus da Mata) is virtually invisible to the happier classes of
the town, and when they are seen, they are misunderstand and castigated for
their own poverty. As one city official said:

> There is no hunger, no real hunger, in Brazil. But the people eat poorly. They have
> bad dietary habits. For instance, the rural workers don't have the custom of eating
> fresh vegetables, fresh meat, fresh poultry, or even fresh fruits. Their diet is all
> carbohydrates—manioc, *farinha* [flour], beans, bread, spaghetti, cornmeal. Meat
> and fish are only "residuals" in their diet. . . . There is no children mortality on the
> *usina* [sugar property]. We have reduced child mortality to two percent through
> immunizations and supplementary food programs for mothers and children.
> (Scheper-Hughes 1992: 62)
>
> There is not so much poverty in Brazil as there is poverty of spirit, which is
> worse. Poverty of spirit—which you find among the rural workers—means that
> one is unwilling to improve one's condition. It means that one does not hunger
> after the better, the finer things in life, that one is content to live and let live.
> The *matuto* is soft; he doesn't like to work hard. He is not ashamed to ask for
> things, to beg. (63)

This ignorance of and indifference toward the poor—nobody works harder
than a sugarcane cutter—would be bad enough if only the rich held this attitude, but unfortunately the poor themselves have accepted this evaluation and
tend to blame themselves for their lot.

To the urban middle class, the poor "are seen as a kind of modern-day pla-
gue, an unruly cancerous growth, an infectious epidemic inflicted on the more
healthy and sound social body of the community" (Scheper-Hughes 1992: 91).
Even to themselves, the *matutos* "are the little people, the no-account people,
those whose features, clothing, gait, and posture mark them as anachronisms
in modern Bom Jesus" (88). They must struggle, starve, beg, and occasionally
steal because they have no other options.

Case Study 2: Structural Violence and
the Ordinary Lives of the Poor in Brazil (continued)

So the squatters suffer, and their suffering merely annoys the "decent folk" of the town. Hunger is the defining experience of the shanty settlement. It is "constant and chronic," with the average cane cutter consuming 1,500–1,700 calories per day while doing physical labor beyond the comprehension of most modern people. Thus, they are always hungry and often on the verge—or across the verge—of starvation. The symptoms of this slow relentless starvation are stark and include weight loss, lightheadedness and faintness, depression and mood swings, and a gradual wasting away physically and mentally. These symptoms have been lumped together under the term "Brazilian melancholy" and often attributed to racial and genetic causes, in particular the "miscegenation" of the races.

The structural violence of poverty and chronic hunger takes its toll on all in the *bairro*, but most of all it afflicts the children. The average baby on the Alto weighs 5.5 pounds at birth, as opposed to the average town baby, who weighs 7.7 pounds. Alto children often have their growth stunted by malnutrition, resulting in short adults. Alto children and adults are sickly. And predictably, child mortality is unusually high. Before the "modernization" of the sugarcane industry, child mortality was high but was linked to typical causes like infectious disease, and it was shared equally by all races and classes. However, since the 1970s it has become restricted particularly to the poor and the nonwhite and has shown itself to be linked to diet more than to disease. Even worse, mortality has been concentrated onto the very youngest of the young, infants under one year old. A 1989 survey illustrated that 49.5 percent of all deaths on the Alto do Cruzeiro were babies under twelve months of age; in other words, "infant death has come to replace child death almost completely" (Scheper-Hughes 1992: 296). If babies can survive their first year of life, they have a much better chance of living to adulthood, but by then the other health affects are set and irreversible.

Meanwhile, the syndrome of the sick baby is a stalking horror in the Alto. Scheper-Hughes (1992) describes it thus:

> I have seen Alto children of one and two years who cannot sit up unaided, who do not or cannot speak, whose skin over the chest and upper part of the stomach is stretched so tightly that every curve of the breastbone and the ribs stands out. The arms, legs, and buttocks are discolored. The bones of the hungry child's face are fragile. The eyes are prominent, wide open, and often vacant; sometimes they have sunk back in the head. The hair is thin and wispy, often with patches of baldness, though the eyelashes can be exceptionally long. In some babies there is an extraordinary pallor, a severe anemia, that lends the child an unnatural, waxen appearance that mothers see as a harbinger of death. (146)

Case Study 2: Structural Violence and
the Ordinary Lives of the Poor in Brazil (continued)

Again, even worse than the physical effects are the psychological ones, including the self-blame that the poor engage in, echoing the victim blaming that the fatter classes engage in. The *matutos* see their smallness, their sickliness, their inability to cope with life's struggles as evidence of the inherent "weakness" of their "breed" or "race." They accuse themselves as being inferior people, rather than people in inferior circumstances.

Among the odder and sadder aspects of their "folk diagnoses" of themselves, they see themselves as "nervous" rather than malnourished. They refer to themselves as "shaky" or "weak" or "irritable" or "off-balance" or literally paralyzed. They sometimes say that they are tired, dizzy, confused, sad and depressed, "wasted." The complete list of symptoms of *nervos* (Scheper-Hughes 1992: 80) includes headache, dizziness/faintness, sensations of heat or cold, confusion or madness, darkened vision or spots before the eyes, vomiting, nausea, buzzing in the ears, pounding in the chest, seizure, breathlessness, stomach ache, back ache, itching skin, shaky hands, weak or trembling legs, insomnia, weakness, and, most ironically, loss of appetite.

The poor on the Alto do not completely connect their symptoms—symptoms of starvation—to their hunger and diet. First, recall the official above who accused the *matutos* of poor eating habits. This is largely true but not voluntary. They long since lost their subsistence gardens, so many vegetables have fallen from their diet. They cannot afford meat, and it is generally unavailable in their neighborhood markets anyhow. All they can afford or acquire are the heavy, starchy foods like beans, rice, pasta, and flour or meal. Then, driven to fill their bellies with something that will "stick to their ribs," they have learned to devalue fruits and vegetables as "weak" or "light" foods, ones that just leave you hungry for more. At least starchy foods "kill hunger," although they do not nourish. Worse still are the foods that merely "fool hunger," like sugar, sugar water, and manioc flour. Adults will sometimes consume—or feed their children—sugar water or manioc paste when there is nothing else to eat. Your appetite is curbed, but you are starving for nutriments inside. This behavior includes substituting sugar water or manioc paste for mother's milk and baby formula.

In addition, *matuto* health has become "medicalized" by the modern establishment, in such a way that a person who shows up at a clinic (and the number of clinics has jumped by 1,000 percent) presenting the symptoms of *nervos* is usually diagnosed as "sick" rather than 'starving' and given medicine rather than food. "Nervous" women and children are more often given tranquilizers and sleeping pills than the food (and the contraceptives) they really need. This sword cuts in two deadly ways: first, people spend precious money on expensive medicines when they could use it on comparably cheap food,

Case Study 2: Structural Violence and
the Ordinary Lives of the Poor in Brazil (continued)

and second, it again mystifies or disguises the real source of the problem. If people are "sick" rather than "starving," then their problems are somatic rather than social. Sick people need their bodies healed, while starving people need society reformed. Ultimately, it is one more way of shifting the burden of their suffering onto the poor rather than recognizing it where it is—they are poor sickly people, not people in a poor sickly society.

So, deathly hungry children get medicine but are denied food. This is partly an outcome of the medicalization of poverty, but also partly a spontaneous response to the high death rate of infants. Parents have learned not to invest too much in babies, especially in their first year of life. Children die, and they have resigned themselves to that reality: "A child died today in the *favela*. He was two months old. If he had lived he would have gone hungry anyway," said one mother (Scheper-Hughes 1992: 268). And just as the *matutos* blame their physical and racial inferiority for their plight, so they blame the baby's own "will" or "desire" for its premature death. Babies suffer their own distinct set of symptoms as their health declines. Scheper-Hughes gives the following qualities of what she calls "doomed child syndrome": gradual wasting, weakness, lethargy or paralysis, retardation, pale or blotchy skin, sunken eyes, screaming, fits and seizures including head-banging, rigidity of the body, and explosive vomiting and diarrhea (367). A baby in this state does not have long to live.

Such babies, rather being given special attention and care, are the ones shown indifference and neglect. They are not abused, but they are simply not expected to live. Even more so, they are not believed to want to live. These doomed children, they say, lack a "will to live," a "vital life force." They are born "weak" or "nervous." As one mother stated, "they come into the world with an aversion to life. . . . Food doesn't interest them; it doesn't hold their attention. You see, they are neither here nor there" (Scheper-Hughes 1992: 368). Such little ones are born dying. Their "aversion to food," a symptom of starvation, is taken as a reason to starve them. And so they die, in prolific numbers: the average woman surveyed by Scheper-Hughes had had 9.5 pregnancies but only 4.2 living children.

The violence to which the poor of Bom Jesus da Mata are exposed is not all structural, of course. There are "real" threats too, not the least of which are the police and the *vigias* (municipal guards or watchmen), who exploit, beat, arrest, and "disappear" them. The poor live a life of fear—fear of being killed, fear of having their children kidnapped, fear of being abducted for organ trafficking, fear of being buried in pauper graves, fear of having to go to a hospital or morgue to identify a body, fear of not recovering a body at all, and generally a fear of being rushed, ignored, shooed away, and not taken seriously as human beings. But

Case Study 2: Structural Violence and
the Ordinary Lives of the Poor in Brazil (continued)

between the actual episodes of literal violence, the specter of structural violence is always there, weakening them, making them unable to respond to, control, or even understand their plight. They are sick, starving, insecure, and passive; in other words, you do not have to be physically beaten to be beaten down.

RETROSPECT AND PROSPECT

Although nearly all societies are hostile and aggressive toward those far from them, some—in fact, very many—are hostile and aggressive toward those closest to them. How to explain this puzzling, rather self-destructive behavior? As we have seen, the violent behaviors of a society tend to be related to each other. It is unusual for violence to be directed only toward certain people or perpetrated in certain situations and not others. Also, children who become violent adults must have learned their violent behavior by modeling it—on behaviors observed, most certainly, at home. Finally, the experience and expression of "closeness" and "otherness" are relative. To egotistical and self-referential men in a male-dominated society, women and even their own children can be "other." Certainly women who come from another family (as they all do) or village can be regarded as foreigners within the family.

Additionally, various psychocultural values and tendencies and macrosocial institutions and practices shape microsocial interactions in the domestic arena. If women are unequal and disempowered, then women in the home will be unequal and disempowered. If children are considered property or exploitable assets, then one's own children are considered property and exploitable assets. And if men band together to control the group's wealth while competing to manage its power, then women will necessarily be out of both and, even worse, may be one means men use to display their power to each other.

Ultimately violence may begin at home. Ultimately, it may have to end at home. In this and the preceding two chapters we have examined the basic social and cultural foundations of violence and nonviolence. Never forgetting where the roots of violence lie, we now turn to the discussion of ideological and political violence. Then, in the last two chapters, we bring our analysis "home" to America—to explore the roots of our own violence.

RELIGIOUS VIOLENCE

Introduction

very smart description

> Men never do evil so completely and cheerfully as when they do it from
> religious conviction.
> —*Blaise Pascal*

> With or without religion, good people will do good, and evil people will do
> evil, but it takes religion to get good people to do evil.
> —*Stephen Weinberg*

Looking around the world at the dawn of the twenty-first century, it is difficult
not to see the footprint of religion in many if not most of the violent acts or
situations of the day. Whether it is the Israel–Palestine conflict, the al-Qaeda
terrorist attacks, or fundamentalist Christian assaults against gay men or abortion clinics, religion seems to motivate many people to destructive behavior.
Throughout history, as the Crusades, the Inquisition, the witch trials, the
burning of heretics, the missionary conquest of traditional peoples, anti-
Semitism, and many other examples illustrate, religion has been at the center
of violence even in Christianity, which prides itself on being the religion of
love.

There are some people who think that religion is the source of all violence
in the world. There are others who think that religion is the source of all good
in the world, including morality, charity, scholarship, and "family values." No
doubt, both statements are exaggerations. Religion is a source of great good,
and it is a source of great evil. It inspires people to love and to hate, to kindness
and to killing. Nor is it the sole source of either. Humans have hurt and killed
each other for many things, including money, land, emotions, and ideas, and
they will continue to do so. But there is also no doubt, as Pascal and Weinberg
observe, that there is something distinct about religion, something that is
uniquely conducive to violence in the name of goodness.

What is this something, and is it really unique to religion? We have
already seen that groups are more dangerous than individuals, even if they
are "minimal" groups or even imaginary groups; the very integration into

148

groups elicits a different kind of behavior from humans than individuality. Give those groups an identity and a pattern of interaction, and the incidence of violence increases. Give those groups institutions and values that accept and promote, and the incidence of violence only increases again.

Religion, however, introduces the third factor that we have identified as laying the basis for violence—*ideology*. By ideology we do not mean merely "ideas" and certainly not "false" or, worse, deceptive and mystifying ideas (as in the Marxist use of the term). An ideology might be true, but its truth status is not the point. An ideology for our purposes is a more or less complete and all-encompassing system of ideas, a comprehensive view or even "theory" of thought about what humans should be and do and how it should all be manifested in society. An ideology not only offers to explain much if not all of life and reality but also to provide an authority and authorization for that explanation (whether it be nature, "history," or the supernatural). As such it tends toward absolutism—being the one and only answer—and toward idealism—that it is all right and everything else is all wrong. These two tendencies obviously lead to a serious potential for a radical dualism in the world, between those who are "with us" and those who are "against us." Finally, as Chalmers Johnson (1966: 83) has put it, ideologies "are incipient value structures"— potential or future sources of values, truths, and goals, perhaps the bases of entirely new future societies.

Religion is hardly the only sphere that provides humans with ideologies, and we will examine the political side of ideology in Chapter 8 and 9. That is, religion is not the only source of a "cause" or a "mission" within which to do violence. Even so, not only is religion particularly effective at providing a cause, but the one it provides is uniquely resistant to outside influences and organizes around a uniquely "ultimate" set of claims, authorities, and consequences. Plus, it has shown itself to be especially resilient and enduring in the modern world, where it was once expected to wither and decline.

The point is not that religion is bad but rather that it can be a singularly "good reason" for committing violence in some cases. Mark Juergensmeyer (2000), a writer on religious violence and terrorism, specifies four elements that create a vital link between the two:

1. The transcendent moralism with which such acts are justified,
2. The ritual intensity with which they are committed,
3. The familiar religious images of struggle and transformation—concepts of cosmic war—within which they are interpreted, and
4. The perception that their communities are under attack—are being violated—and that their acts are therefore simply responses to the violence they have experienced. (12)

These elements, together with the stakes of the cosmic struggle, mean that "losing the struggle would be unthinkable" even while it "is blocked and cannot be won in real time or in real terms" (161–62), resulting in a confrontation that may be defensive yet vicious in its means and "final" in its goals. When we add to or refract this experience with mundane but potentially life-and-death political interests, it should not be hard to see how violence is enabled.

GROUPS AND BELIEVERS

Religious groups are groups first, religious second. Yet, not all scholars of the group phenomenon have made a dramatic distinction between the two. Gustave Le Bon (1896), one of the classic students of group behavior, suggested that all human crowds have certain characteristics that he considered "religious." This religious sentiment, he wrote, is constituted of such features as

> worship of a being supposed superior, fear of the power with which the being is credited, blind submission to its commands, inability to discuss its dogmas, the desire to spread them, and a tendency to consider as enemies all by whom they are not accepted. Whether such a sentiment apply to an invisible God, to a wooden or stone idol, to a hero or to a political conception, provided that it presents the preceding characteristics, its essence always remains religious. The supernatural and the miraculous are found to be present to the same extent. (63)

In such circumstances, he continues, "Intolerance and fanaticism are the necessary accompaniments of the religious sentiment. They are inevitably displayed by those who believe themselves in the possession of the secret of earthly or eternal happiness" (64). In other words, not only is a radical exclusion—an us-versus-them—established, but "we" are endowed with all goodness and rightness and "they" with all badness and evil. They are reduced to an anonymous and less than human mass—enemies of the "true people," that is, us. These sentiments, he concludes, "necessarily lead those imbued with them to pitilessly extirpate by fire and sword whoever is opposed" to their identity, their doctrine, and their aims (69).

Eric Hoffer (1966/1951), in his study of the psychology and sociology of "true believers," shows that it is not unique to religion but any "mass movement" that makes humans more ready to "kill for the cause." In fact, Hoffer wrote his short treatise during the early years of the cold war and immediately after World War II, so his focus is more on communism and Nazism/Fascism than on religion. Any of these and similar causes can radicalize people, preparing them for extreme intergroup behavior.

> All mass movements generate in their adherents a readiness to die and a proclivity for united action; all of them, irrespective of the doctrine they preach and the program they project, breed fanaticism, enthusiasm, fervent hope, hatred and intolerance; all of them are capable of releasing a powerful flow of activity in certain departments of life; all of them demand blind faith and single hearted allegiance. (xi)

Hoffer argues that there are certain kinds of messages that are likely to motivate mass movements and that there are certain kinds of individuals who are likely to be attracted to mass movements. The striking thing is that the appeal of a movement, whether it is Christianity, communism, or Nazism, has little or nothing to do with the details of its "content" or doctrine. The point is not the specific creed—definitely not its truth or even its intelligibility—but its *certainty*. It claims to be "the one and only truth." Certainty, Hoffer writes, does not need or want understanding, only belief and faith; the true believer should turn off his or her critical-thinking mind.

> The effectiveness of a doctrine does not come from its meaning but from its certitude. No doctrine however profound and sublime will be effective unless it is presented as the embodiment of the one and only truth. . . . It is obvious, therefore, that in order to be effective a doctrine must not be understood, but has to be believed in. We can be absolutely certain only about things we do not understand. A doctrine that is understood is shorn of its strength. . . . The devout are always urged to seek the absolute truth with their hearts and not their minds. . . . If a doctrine is not unintelligible, it has to be vague; and if neither unintelligible nor vague, it has to be unverifiable. . . . To be in possession of an absolute truth is to have a net of familiarity spread over the whole of eternity. (80–81)

True believers, true converts to the cause, are able to shut their eyes even to contradictions to the "facts" they are fed, let alone to the suffering they create.

Insofar as the specific teachings of the movement are important, they usually speak of some better or perfect future state—a state that will be a vast improvement over the miserable present and that is worth sacrifice, *any sacrifice*, including the sacrifice of the present and all of the other people who are committed to the present condition of things. Such people are "enemies of the revolution," counterrevolutionaries, and obstacles to the imagined future. The particulars of this future are varied and often vague, referring perhaps to a "workers' paradise" or "glorious Reich" or "city of God." In fact, Hoffer suggests, the vaguer the details of the goal, the more likely that the movement will endure—since followers can never know for sure when the goal has been reached.

In order to detach people's attention from the present and direct it to the future, the present must be denigrated. Things as we currently know them are typically criticized as corrupt, fallen, evil, or decadent; therefore, followers' efforts and aspirations should focus on another time—either an idealized future or even an idealized past. And the movement must do what is necessary to make all of these claims seem true, including actualizing its own dogma by making life in the movement as "dour, hard, repressive, and dull" as possible. Hence the life of the follower is often spartan and self-deprived, not only as a result of the "austerity" of conflict but as a method for making the present more dissatisfactory and therefore the aims of the movement more meaningful.

This deliberate debasement of the present and all of the forces and agents of the present—the "system," the "satisfied man," the "counterrevolutionary"— creates an absolute rift between *us*, the people of the movement and of the future, and *them*, the people of the "establishment" and of the present. *We* are good and visionary, *they* are bad and reactionary. And this rift assembles us into an effective and often fanatical social group, a mass movement.

The kinds of people who are drawn to mass movements also give those movements some of their distinctive and more sinister qualities. First of all, potential converts to a movement must experience deprivation to some extent in the current order; social scientists have long known that dissatisfaction or deprivation can lead people to social change, even at great effort and cost. However, this deprivation is "relative" in two senses: first, what seems adequate to one person, group, or time may feel deprived to another, and second, the most effective agents of change are not the abjectly and hopelessly deprived but those just deprived enough to have some hope of achieving their goal. This has been referred to as the crisis of "rising expectations": completely downtrodden slaves and serfs are less likely to revolt against their burdens than those who have had a taste of a better possibility. This is why the middle classes have often been revolutionary.

Next, potential converts are those who wish to toss off their own personal failings and wrap themselves in a banner of something larger and more effective than themselves. Included in this cast of characters are "the poor, misfits, outcasts, minorities, adolescent youth, the ambitious (whether facing insurmountable obstacles or unlimited opportunities), those in the grip of some vice or obsession, the impotent, the inordinately selfish, the bored, the sinners" (Hoffer 1966/1951: 25). The problem with this motley list is that these folks, experiencing failure and frustration, do not seek more freedom but rather more un-freedom, both for themselves and for others. They want order, perhaps revenge, perhaps anonymity, but not freedom—not for themselves and certainly not for the enemy, the unredeemed. These members are least likely, therefore, to represent the kind of movement that most of us would like to see.

The potential members of a movement must be changed into actual members, and after that they must be motivated to act according to their new commitments and in concert with their new fellow members. In other words, they must be unified and mobilized. Hoffer points to a number of unifying forces, including imitation, persuasion and coercion, leadership, joint action, suspicion, and hatred. The role of joint action is crucial. As he noticed, and others have also emphasized, the simple fact of doing things together has a community-building aspect: "Even mere marching can serve as a unifier" (Hoffer 1966/1951: 121). This is why mass movements spend much of their time in group behaviors like singing, chanting, repeating oaths, celebrating symbols, hazing each other, and yes, marching. These elements should never be ignored in any group phenomenon.

Such movements demand a central unifying figure, a charismatic champion, a "leader" (duce, fuehrer, or prophet). The qualities of a mass movement leader differ significantly from those of a typical leader. Intelligence, nobility, and originality need not be among the former and in reality may be detrimental. Instead, leaders of mass movements tend to have and to be best served by the following traits:

> audacity and a joy in defiance; an iron will; a fanatical conviction that he is in possession of the one and only truth; faith in his destiny and luck; a capacity for passionate hatred; contempt for the present; a cunning estimate of human nature; a delight in symbols (spectacles and ceremonials); unbounded brazenness which finds expression in a disregard of consistency and fairness; a recognition that the innermost craving of a following is for communion and that there can never be too much of it; a capacity for winning and holding the utmost loyalty of able lieutenants. (Hoffer 1966/1951: 114)

Obedience to this larger-than-life figure, this potentially infallible and even God-sent messenger and savior of "the people," is desirable and likely. Questioning and reasoning on the part of the rank and file are discouraged; the leader and the movement are always correct (see the discussion of the French and Bolshevik Revolutions in Chapter 9).

Finally, Hoffer insists on the value of good old-fashioned hatred in organizing and mobilizing the true believer.

> Hatred is the most accessible and comprehensive of all unifying agents.... Mass movements can rise and spread without belief in a God, but never without belief in a devil.... That hatred springs more from self-contempt than from a legitimate grievance is seen in the intimate connection between hatred and a guilty conscience.... To wrong those we hate is to add fuel to our hatred.... The most effective way to silence our guilty conscience is to convince ourselves and others that those we have sinned against are indeed depraved creatures, deserving every punishment, even extermination. (1966/1951: 91)

This hatred can and should be put to use, for, as Arendt also reminded us, violent action can breed hatred and fanaticism where it did not exist before; on the principle of cognitive dissonance as well as the "embodiment" of doctrine, hateful behaviors—the more audacious the better—can spawn hateful attitudes and beliefs.

To end up where we began, the role of certainty and faith in one's own certainty energized the entire system.

> Faith organizes and equips a man's soul for action. To be in possession of the one and only truth and never doubt one's righteousness; to feel that one is backed by a mysterious power whether it be God, destiny or the law of history; to be convinced that one's opponents are the incarnation of evil and must be crushed; to exult in self-denial and devotion to duty—these are admirable qualifications for resolute and ruthless action in any field. (122)

~ Gilligan

If we are totally right, they must be totally wrong. If we are totally good, they must be totally bad. If we represent love, they must represent hate. Indeed, if we are truly human, then they must be something other than, something less than, human. They must be the totally *non-us*, the totally "other." There is nothing that is not acceptable or appropriate—nothing too extreme or inhumane—when perpetrated against *them* by *us* in full *faith* of our righteous and in the name and the pursuit of *our good*.

RELIGIOUS BELIEFS AND VIOLENCE

Many beliefs and convictions provide the conditions we have just described, but none provides them better and more purely than religion. Religion offers the unverifiable doctrine Hoffer addresses that must be accepted on faith. It generates a community of believers, an *us* and a community of nonbelievers, a *them*. It orients toward a vague and possibly unreachable ideal future state and supplies the leaders and offices that keep people propelled toward that state. Finally and most distinctively, it sets the ultimate stakes in the movement and the confrontation the "other"—unlike political movements such as Nazism and communism, the stakes are eternal and supernatural, and failure is not an option. Eternal spiritual rewards and punishments can motivate in ways that temporal and practical ones never can.

Religion as Explanation of Evil

Whatever your religious convictions and whatever your definition of evil, there is no doubt that negativity exists in the world. People do bad things to each other. Nature does bad things to itself (lions kill zebras, etc.). And nature does bad things to people (floods, hurricanes, droughts, etc.) Evil may just be a "perspective" (again, the lion does not think of itself as being evil, and obviously floods do not think at all), but from our human perspective, there is surely a lot of undesirable stuff going on in our world.

No religion can ignore the fact of the undesirable, the destructive, the "evil" in the universe. In fact, most if not all religions think actively about this problem and approach it in two ways—first, by explaining evil and, second, by justifying evil. As explanation, religion is merely accounting for a fact: there is bad stuff, and it does not seem to disappear or diminish. Religion could not ignore this fact and still be relevant to our lives. As Elie Wiesel (1990: 53) said, "evil, like good, is infinite, and ... the two are combined in man. He could have gone on to say not just man but nature itself, and sometimes even the gods.

Different religions and types of religions predictably handle the problem of evil differently. In fact, it is less of a problem for some than for others. For example, animistic religions, which posit spiritual forces or beings in various plants, animals, and natural phenomena (e.g., the sun, the wind, the rain, the thunder, etc.) can explain the problem fairly simply in terms of good spirits and bad spirits. Evil—bad luck, sickness, death—is the work of the bad spirits. Religions that emphasize ancestor spirits can do something similar: there may be good ancestors or bad ancestors, or the ancestors may be capricious, or they may be unaware of their effects on mortals. Some societies blame misfortune on human spiritual agents such as witches and sorcerers. Polytheism takes the solution to a higher level, offering good gods and evil gods; perhaps one god gives life, and another god gives death.

Monotheism has a more serious problem, depending on how it conceives of its god. If that god is a mixed personality, a doer of good and of evil, there is not as much of a problem as when the god is supposedly omnibenevolent. The former kind of god is the creator of all things, good and bad. At least in spots, this is how the Old Testament god is described: "I form the light and create darkness: I make peace and create evil: I, the Lord, do all these things," prophecies Isaiah (45:7). The book of Job is centrally concerned with the problem of evil, which the Old Testament god at least passively unleashes on Job. Consider it a test or a punishment, but Yahweh is behind bad as well as good; in fact, when questioned by Job on His goodness and morality, Yahweh merely thunders back that Job has no right to question Him, and Job acquiesces.

Anyhow, throughout the early Judeo–Christian writings, Yahweh is described or describes Himself as angry and jealous; Exodus 15:3 states, "The Lord is a man of war: the Lord is his name," and the chronicles of the Lord and his people testify to this fact again and again. (See below for some selections from the Judeo–Christian scriptures on evil and violence.) For believers who accept their god as multifaceted—as good and bad—this makes sense and solves the whole problem of where evil, violence, and war come from.

However, religions that try to purge their god of all negative and destructive characteristics are in more of a bind, since negative and destructive forces and events persist. Christianity is such a religion, as are some other latter-day "religions of love." If love and goodness and justice are all that the god is interested in and do, then why is there evil and misfortune in the world? The god may be loving and good and just, but the world evinces little love and goodness and justice. Why?

One possible and common solution is to fault humans. Humans are frail and flawed, and humans have freedom to choose their actions; it is the pursuit of human free will that leads people to commit acts of harm against each other. This explanation surely accounts neatly for most "moral evil" or person-on-person violence and cruelty, but it does not automatically account for "natural evil," such as the suffering inflicted by floods and droughts nor the suffering inflicted by nonhumans on humans and nonhumans, like lions killing zebras or, for that matter, killing people.

However, in some religious traditions, including the Judeo–Christian one, human free will is given even greater explanatory power. According to the account in Genesis, the original version of creation did not contain death nor suffering nor even predation; lions ate plants, it is presumed, although the plants still presumably suffered from being eaten. At any rate, after the "original sin" and the "fall" of the first people, not only humanity but the very physical world were cursed to suffer and to die:

> And unto Adam He said, Because thou hast hearkened unto the voice of thy wife, and hast eaten of the tree, of which I commanded thee, saying, Thou shalt not eat of it: cursed is the ground for thy sake; in sorrow shalt thou eat of it all the days of thy life; thorns also and thistles shall it bring forth to thee; and thou shalt eat the herb of the field; in the sweat of thy face shalt thou eat bread, till thou return unto the ground; for out of it wast thou taken: for dust thou art, and unto dust shalt thou return. (Genesis 3:17–19)

So, in a word, it is man's fault too that lions kill zebras, the land sprouts weeds, and life is difficult for everything, ending painfully for all. (See Box 6.1.)

6.1 | A Sampling of Violence in the Judeo–Christian Scriptures

And the Lord spake unto Moses, saying, Bring forth him that hath cursed without the camp; and let all that heard him lay their hands upon his head, and let all the congregation stone him.

And thou shalt speak unto the children of Israel, saying, Whosoever curseth his God shall bear his sin.

And he that blasphemeth the name of the Lord, he shall surely be put to death, and all the congregation shall certainly stone him: as well the stranger, as he that is born in the land, when he blasphemeth the name of the Lord, shall be put to death. And he that killeth any man shall surely be put to death.

And he that killeth a beast shall make it good: beast for beast. And if a man cause a blemish in his neighbor; as he hath done, so shall it be done to him.

Breach for breach, eye for eye, tooth for tooth: as he hath caused a blemish in a man, so shall it be done to him again. . . .

And Moses spake to the children of Israel, that they should bring forth him that had cursed out of the camp, and stone him with stones. And the children of Israel did as the Lord commanded Moses. (Leviticus 25:10–23)

And while the children of Israel were in the wilderness, they found a man that gathered sticks upon the sabbath day. And they that found him gathering sticks brought him unto Moses and Aaron, and unto all the congregation. And they put him in ward, because it was not declared what should be done with him.

And the Lord said unto Moses; The man shall be surely put to death: all the congregation shall stone him with stone without the camp.

And all the congregation brought him without the camp, and stoned him with stones, and he died; as the Lord commanded Moses. (Numbers 15:32–36)

And they warred against the Midianites, as the Lord commanded Moses; and they slew all the males. . . .

And the children of Israel took all the women of Midian captives, and their little ones, and took the spoil of all their cattle, and all their goodly castles, and all their goods. . . .

[Moses said] Now therefore kill every male among the little ones, and kill woman that hath known man by lying with him.

But all the women children, that have not known a man by lying with him, keep alive for yourselves. (Numbers 31: 7–18)

If thy brother, the son of thy mother, or thy son, or thy daughter, or the wife of thy bosom, or thy friend, which is as thine own soul, entice thee secretly, saying, Let us go and serve other gods, which thou hast not known, thou, nor thy fathers;

Namely, of the gods of the people which are round about you, nigh unto thee, or far off from thee, from one end of the earth even unto the other end of the earth;

Thou shalt not consent unto him, nor harken unto him; neither shall thine eye pity him; neither shalt thou spare, neither shalt thou conceal him;

But thou shalt surely kill him; thine hand shall be first upon him to put him to death, and afterwards the hand of all the people.

And thou shalt stone him with stones, that he die; because he hath sought to thrust thee away from the Lord thy God, which brought thee out of the land of Egypt, from the house of bondage. (Deuteronomy 13:6–10)

When thou comest nigh unto a city to fight against it, then proclaim peace unto it.

And it shall be, if it make thee answer of peace, and upon unto thee, then it shall be, that all the people that is found therein shall be tributaries unto thee, and they shall serve thee.

(continued)

6.1 A Sampling of Violence in the Judeo–Christian Scriptures (continued)

And if it will make no peace with thee, but will make war against thee, then thou shalt beseige it:

And when the Lord thy God hath delivered it into thine hands, thou shalt smite every male thereof with the edge of the sword:

But the women, and the little ones, and the cattle, and all that is in the city, even all the spoil thereof, shalt thou take unto thyself; and thou shalt eat the spoil of thin enemies which the Lord thy God hath given thee.

Thus shalt thou do unto all the cities which are very far off from thee, which are not of the cities of these nations.

But of the cities of these people, which the Lord thy God doth give thee for an inheritance, thou shalt save alive nothing that breatheth:

But thou shalt utterly destroy them; namely, the Hittites, and the Amorites, the Canaanites, and the Perizzites, the Hivites, and the Jebusites; as the Lord thy God hath commanded thee:

That they teach you not to do after all their abominations, which they have done unto their gods; so should ye sin against the Lord thy God. (Deuteronomy 20:10–18)

Now these are the nations which the Lord left, to prove Israel by them, even as many of Israel as had not known all the wars of Canaan;

Only that the generations of the children of Israel might know, to teach them war, at the least such as before knew nothing thereof;

Namely, five lords of the Philistines, and all the Canaanites, and the Sidonians, and the Hivites that dwelt in mount Lebanon, from mount Baal-hermon unto the entering in of Hamath. (Judges 3:1–3)

God is my strength and power: and he maketh my way perfect.

He maketh my feet like hinds' feet: and setteth me upon my high places.

He teacheth my hands to war; so that a bow of steel is broken by mine arms. . . .

I have pursued mine enemies, and destroyed them; and turned not again until I had consumed them.

And I have consumed them, that they could not arise: yea, they are fallen under my feet.

For thou hast girded me with strength to battle: them that rose up against he hast thou subdued under me.

Thou hast also given me the necks of mine enemies, that I might destroy them that hate me.

They looked, but there was none to save; even unto the Lord, but he answered them not.

Then did I bear them as small as the dust of the earth, I did stamp them as the mire of the street, and did spread them abroad. (II Samuel 23: 33–43)

That whosoever would not seek the Lord God of Israel should be put to death, whether small or great, whether man or woman. (II Chronicles 15:13)

O daughter of Babylon, who art to be destroyed; happy shall he be, that rewardeth thee as thou hast served us. Happy shall he be, that taketh and dasheth thy little ones against stones. (Psalms 137:8–9)

Withhold not correction from the child; for if thou beatest him with rod, he shall not die.

Thou shalt beat him with rod, and shalt deliver his soul from hell. (Proverbs 23:13–14)

Every one that is found shall be thrust through; and every one that is joined unto them shall fall by the sword.

Their children also shall be dashed before their eyes; their houses shall be spoiled, and their wives ravished. . . .

Their bows also shall dash the young men to pieces; and they shall have no pity on the fruit of the womb; their eye shall not spare children. (Isaiah 13:15–18)

So shall it be at the end of the world: the angels shall come forth, and sever the wicked from among the just,

And shall cast them into the furnace of fire: there shall be wailing and gnashing of teeth. (Matthew 14:49–50)

Source: King James Bible.

A twist on this conception that is employed by Buddhism is to describe the world and human life as unpleasant and flawed not so much by human actions at its origin but by human attitudes toward existence and action in the present. Thus, when Gautama Buddha became enlightened, he discovered that all of existence is *dukkha*, or "suffering," literally, "broken." This is the First Noble Truth. To be born is *dukkha*, to die is *dukkha*, to be separated from the things we enjoy is *dukkha*, to be in contact with the things we dislike is *dukkha*. It is not humanity's responsibility that existence is *dukkha*, but there we are. However, we by our attitudes perpetuate this suffering through the Second Noble Truth, which is attachment or desire; when we attach ourselves emotionally to our lives, we expose ourselves to this suffering. The solution is the Third Noble Truth, which is detachment; if we detach ourselves from our own lives, we isolate ourselves from suffering. Good and bad may come our way, but they do not disturb our peace. Finally, the Fourth Noble Truth, the so-called Eight-Fold Path, lays out the specifics of living an enlightened, detached life.

Another possible explanation for the violence and suffering of the universe besides human causation, and one that the Judeo–Christian tradition also exploits, is the activity of a second force or principle in the universe, one of evil and destruction. This "dualistic" solution depends on an evil personage such as "satan" or the "devil." Originally, *shaitan* from the Hebrew meant nothing more than "adversary" or "enemy" and sometimes even referred to emissaries of Yahweh who were not his enemy at all. Satan makes a dramatic appearance in the Book of Job, where he engages in a bet with Yahweh that results in Job's suffering, with God's complete permission and encouragement. However, as we noted, when Job complains of the injustice of his fate, Yahweh does not make the excuse that the devil made him do it.

Christianity picks up and extensively develops the idea of Satan, ascribing almost all ills to the devil or one of his minions. Now, two new elements have entered the story. First, Satan is virtually a "second deity," a dark lord to complement or offset the lord of light. He becomes not only God's adversary but nearly his equal. Second, the forces of evil are multiplied, so that now there are any number of demons in Satan's employ that persecute humanity. Practically all bad things can be attributed to some demonic figure or force, from bad luck to sickness to death.

This idea is not, of course, unique or original to Christianity. Perhaps the first distinctly dualistic religious vision was that of Zoroaster or Zarathustra, who believed in a universe with two equal forces—light (Ahura Mazda) and darkness (Ahriman or Angra Mainyu)—at odds with each other. Angra Mainyu is a kind of "countercreator" or "anticreator" who is responsible for bringing the serpent, plagues, "plunder and sin," unbelief, "tears and wailing," and the 99,999 diseases into the otherwise perfect creation of Ahura Mazda. Accordingly, the two gods or forces are perpetually at war, making of creation and particularly the human aspect of creation a battleground.

> Ahura Mazda is Lord! Ahriman he keeps at bay, he holds him back. May Ahriman be struck and defeated, with devs and drujs, sorcerers and sinners, kayags and karbs, tyrants, wrongdoers and heretics, sinners, enemies and witches! May they (all) be struck and defeated! May evil rulers not exist, (or) be far away! May enemies be defeated! May enemies all not exist, (or) be far away! (*Khorda Avesta*)

> We worship Obedience the blessed and the stately, who though lofty and so high, yea, even to the girdle, yet stoops to Mazda's creatures, who thrice within the day, and three times of a night, will drive on to that Karshvar Hvaniratha, called the luminous, as he holds in both the hands and poizes his knife-like battle-

ax, which flies as of itself, and to cleave the Daevas' skulls, to hew down Angra
Mainyu, the wicked, and to hew down Rapine of the bloody spear, to hew down
the Daevas of Mazendran, and every Demon-god. For his splendor and his glory,
for his might. . . . (*Yasna Avesta*)

Thus all of religion and all of human existence is or should be directed toward
combating Angra Mainyu and his forces of evil, and all humans are in fact warriors in the struggle between light and darkness.

Naturally, such a war-oriented religion is going to end with an epic battle, as
is evident from the final book of the Christian scriptures, the book of Revelation,
which foretells of a time when Satan will mount his ultimate attack and prevail
for a time. Of course, the forces of good must inevitably succeed, and the believers will be rewarded for their fidelity, but not before a lot of nonbelievers and
innocents are slaughtered. The story cannot possibly turn out well for everyone.

Religion as Justification of Evil

Religions, wherever we find them, must make sense of what really is, including
pain and death, injustice, and war. They must not only make it seem real and
tolerable but also justifiable and acceptable. Although to explain is not necessarily to justify, something cannot be justified unless it can be explained;
further, if it can be explained as a consequence of one's own actions, or as part
of a divine plan, or as an intrinsic aspect of existence, then it is by default justified. This includes, necessarily, human evils such as violence, persecution, and
war. How then can men use religion to do the evil that they do?

The *Bhagavad Gita*, the most famous and popular of the Hindu scriptures,
makes this point clearly. In this tale, the warrior Arjuna finds himself on the eve of
battle looking across the field at his enemies, who include some of his own kinsmen. He cannot find it in his heart to fight and kill his own family and is about to
throw down his bow and arrow in desperation, when his chariot driver, the god
Krishna in disguise, begins a discourse on the proper actions of a righteous man.
Arjuna is a member of the *kshatriya*, or noble/warrior caste, and his duty is leadership and war, and no one can find fault in him for executing his duty. Rather, the
fault would be to refuse one's duty, which would condemn one yet again to a
demotion in the great cycle of *samsara* or life/death/rebirth, which is the greatest
evil. But even more than this, Krishna instructs the reluctant warrior about why
neither he nor any man should worry about taking a human life, since the

> wise man understands the true nature of life, suffering, and eternity:
> Thou grievest where no grief should be! thou speak'st
> Words lacking wisdom! for the wise in heart
> Mourn not for those that live, nor those that die.
> Nor I, nor thou, nor any one of these,
> Ever was not, nor ever will not be,
> For ever and for ever afterwards.

All, that doth live, lives always! To man's frame
As there come infancy and youth and age,
So come there raisings-up and layings-down
Of other and of other life-abodes,
Which the wise know, and fear not. This that irks—
Thy sense-life, thrilling to the elements—
Bringing thee heat and cold, sorrows and joys,
'Tis brief and mutable! Bear with it, Prince!
As the wise bear. The soul which is not moved,
The soul that with a strong and constant calm
Takes sorrow and takes joy indifferently,
Lives in the life undying! That which is
Can never cease to be; that which is not
Will not exist. To see this truth of both
Is theirs who part essence from accident,
Substance from shadow. Indestructible,
Learn thou! the Life is, spreading life through all;
It cannot anywhere, by any means,
Be anywise diminished, stayed, or changed.
But for these fleeting frames which it informs
With spirit deathless, endless, infinite,
They perish. Let them perish, Prince! and fight!
He who shall say, "Lo! I have slain a man!"
He who shall think, "Lo! I am slain!" those both
Know naught! Life cannot slay. Life is not slain!
Never the spirit was born; the spirit shall cease to be never;
Never was time it was not; End and Beginning are dreams!
Birthless and deathless and changeless remaineth the
    spirit for ever;
Death hath not touched it at all, dead though the
    house of it seems!
Who knoweth it exhaustless, self-sustained,
Immortal, indestructible, —shall such
Say, "I have killed a man, or caused to kill?"

Nay, but as when one layeth
His worn-out robes away,
And, taking new ones, sayeth,
"These will I wear to-day!"
So putteth by the spirit
Lightly its garb of flesh,
And passeth to inherit
A residence afresh.

I say to thee weapons reach not the Life;
Flame burns it not, waters cannot o'erwhelm,
Nor dry winds wither it. Impenetrable,
Unentered, unassailed, unharmed, untouched,
Immortal, all-arriving, stable, sure,
Invisible, ineffable, by word

And thought uncompassed, ever all itself,
Thus is the Soul declared! How wilt thou, then,—
Knowing it so,—grieve when thou shouldst not grieve?
How, if thou hearest that the man new-dead
Is, like the man new-born, still living man-
One same, existent Spirit- wilt thou weep?
The end of birth is death; the end of death
Is birth: this is ordained! and mournest thou,
Chief of the stalwart arm! for what befalls
Which could not otherwise befall? The birth
Of living things comes unperceived; the death
Comes unperceived; between them, beings perceive:
What is there sorrowful herein, dear Prince?*

Thus, since the true essence of a person cannot be killed, and since the body is a mere temporary receptacle for that essence, then the fate of that body is of little import. Thus suffering is not suffering at all. What is there sorrowful herein, indeed?

The point is that religions, especially warrior religions (which most if not all of the major world religions are), make the justification of violence quite easy. They do so by

1. Creating the conditions in which violence is acceptable and even necessary, for instance, by constructing it as part of a larger and more critical struggle between spiritual forces, in which we humans are acting in the interests of and on behalf of a mighty and good force against another mighty but evil force
2. Creating a totalizing "us" and "them" and imputing "us" with all goodness and "them" with all evil, and
3. Raising the stakes of our actions and choices—of obedience to the will and interests of the religious forces—to the ultimate level, and providing the ultimate authority for those actions and choices, for in the name of God or truth or goodness or heaven, what actions are *not* justifiable?

This phenomenon is particularly evident in dualistic traditions, like Christianity and Zoroastrianism, where the entire ethos of the religion is that we are at war already. This conception exploits the relativity of violence, which almost always allows war as an acceptable circumstance for justifiable violence. If we are only fighting and harming combatants, that is all right. But if the entire nonbelieving world is combatants, then what violence is not justifiable? It is not ours to stop and question or ponder the morality of our behavior; in fact, it is not ours to make or even understand the struggle that we are in, for it is a fact of reality, not of our doing. Our duty is to take a side and obey. To paraphrase Arthur Koestler,

---

*Source: Translation by Edwin Arnold, 1885; available at http://www.sacredtexts.com/hin/gita/index.htm.

who was speaking of the communist movement, the front line is no place for discussions, and wherever a believer happens to be, he is always on the front line.

This calls for an examination of the concepts of "just war" and "holy war."
These notions are much on the minds and tongues of people in the early
twenty-first century. People sometimes find the terms a bit self-contradictory:
how can religion, which is supposedly a matter of love and peace, advocate
and justify violence and war? But this thinking is obtuse, since religion, including Christian religion, has advocated and justified war repeatedly throughout
its history. Any religion, but especially an old and large world religion, is a complex and sometimes conflicted thing. Christians may remember the messages
of peace in their scriptures but simultaneously forget the messages of violence;
it was Ecclesiastes (3:1–9) that said,

> To every thing there is a season, and a time to every purpose under the heaven:A
> time to be born, and a time to die; a time to plant, and a time to pluck up that
> which is planted; A time to kill, and a time to heal; a time to break down, and a
> time to build up; . . . A time to love, and a time to hate; a time of war, and a time of
> peace.

Islam, similarly, is a religion that talks much about, even bases its name on,
peace. The name "Islam" comes from the Arabic root *salaam*, which means
"peace" as well as "submission." A Muslim is one who attains peace by submit-
ting to the will of God (Allah), who is the ultimate author of all order and law
in the universe. Yet this religion too recognizes the need for struggle, even war,
for the cause and has even given the world the concept of *jihad*, which we will
discuss much more deeply below. For those Christians who might at this point
celebrate the peacefulness of their own religion and the violence of Islam, they
should take note that *crusade* has roughly the same meaning as *jihad*.

Religion is, finally, also more than mere spiritual concern but also a matter
of politics and other facets of power and conflict. But religion's inherent potential for violence comes from splitting the world into two opposing worlds, to
ascribing nonbelievers to the opposite world, and to attributing to themselves
and their world the "moral upper hand." All too often, the peace, love, and toleration of which a religion speaks is intended, explicitly or implicitly, *only for
other members of that religion*. This is a fact that should not be overlooked.
When the injunction is to love your neighbor or even your enemy, there is no
doubt that the assumption is that your neighbor or even your enemy would be
a co-religionist. There is no passage in any world religion's scripture that says
that one should love the nonbeliever, the infidel, the idolater. You should love
all of "us," indeed, but none claims that you should love all of "them" nor make
peace with them.

Accordingly, Christianity has a decidedly pacifist side to it, which cannot
be denied. All religions do: peace among us, nonpeace toward them. However,
at least to a degree, this pacifism was an effect of social and political realities as

much as or more than an intrinsic quality of the religion. Christians were definitely out of power for the first three centuries or so of their existence. Early Christians did not serve in the armies of the states that ruled them, mostly prominently the Roman Empire, nor did they hold office nor seek other worldly power. Again, this was not altogether their choice. Their "conscientious objection" to politics and the military was a result of their social ostracism and persecution as much as a conscious choice of their own. But indeed, a current runs through Christianity not only of pacifism but also of "otherworldliness" that led and still leads many to reject politics and government, armies and taxes, and even social action and reform. This is the current that refers to "being in the world" as opposed to "being of the world."

Hence the notion of two worlds, however those two worlds might be construed. The first world, the world of greatest concern, is the world of the "church" or the "elect" or the "saints," and so forth. The second world, the object of indifference if not disdain, is the world of the nonbelievers or the pagans or the carnal or the satanic. Augustine, the early church father, developed this idea extensively in his *City of God*, likening the two worlds to two cities, the *civitas dei*, or "city of God," and the *civitas terranae*, or "city of the world." The worldly city is the inferior of the two, the realm of strife and conflict and evil and unbelief, a realm fundamentally different from and antagonistic to the city of God. There could be no "normal relations" between these two domains.

This type of dualistic thinking builds conflict and confrontation into the foundations of the system. Although the two cities may not be, at least at all times, in open war with each other, they are certainly and irrevocably antagonists, with the potential for actual conflict and violence ever present. Therefore, Christianity includes a notion of "holy war," or crusade (from the Latin *crux* or "cross"), and of Christians as warriors ("onward, Christian soldiers"). First and foremost, like the Zoroastrians, Christians see themselves as warriors against the forces of evil, of Satan and his demons. However, the demonic/satanic forces manifest themselves in many ways, including unbelief and rejection of Christian truth and authority. These forces could even be responsible for Christian heresy, that is, alternate beliefs that are still recognizably Christian; we will return to this subject below. Non-Christians—including among others Jews, Muslims, pre-Christian pagans, and atheists—were often perceived as the very hands of Satan on earth and treated accordingly. Violence was not to be used for offensive purposes, especially for "spreading the faith," but the distinction in practice was often subtle and easily lost.

Under the influence of their newfound political power as the official religion of the Roman Empire (after the third century C.E.) as well as of analytical and legalistic tendencies of Greco–Roman culture, thought began to focus less on "holy war" and more on "just war." In other words, under what conditions was war justified, and how should a just war be carried out? There was never a moment's consideration that all war was unjustified or that war should be abandoned. Again, Augustine and subsequently Thomas Aquinas gave much attention to the question and arrived at some characteristics of a "just war":

- It must be declared by a legitimate authority, political or spiritual.
- It must be conducted with the right intention.
- It must be the last resort.
- It must be prosecuted in proportion to the threat and goal (in other words, no unnecessary use or level of violence).
- It must have a reasonable chance of success.
- It must be fought with all possible moderation (in other words, there should be "rules of war," including nonviolence against noncombatants, prisoners, etc.).

For example, when the actual Crusades were launched against Islam in the late eleventh century, the church did not justify those wars in terms of spreading Christianity but rather in terms of repelling attacks against what they understood as Christian territory, of punishing the attackers, and of reclaiming land, property, and populations that had been unjustly seized in those attacks. In other words, they were merely defending themselves, which made their response just. Besides, God wanted it: Deus lo volt. No doubt, the Muslims and other local peoples did not see it this way.

But it should be obvious that in practice virtually anything can be interpreted as a "just cause" for a "defensive war" in the name of religion. The very existence of another faith can seem like an offense, especially if that other faith is on the move, evoking a "defensive" response. Likewise, the existence of wrongdoing within the faith, in terms of heresy or blasphemy or sin, can be perceived as "offensive" and therefore as an appropriate cause for reaction. Finally, righting other "wrongs," such as the loss of one faith's own "sacred territory" or "birthright" or other property, or even just confronting those who reject the faith, takes on the air of "defense." An illustration of this last point is the famous "Requerimiento" that European explorers/conquerors used to justify their campaigns against indigenous societies like the peoples of the Americas. Upon arrival, a priest in the troupe would read a statement informing the locals that the Europeans had come to establish true religion and invite the natives to accept the authority of the Pope and the crown. This invitation, in Latin, was normally not accepted by the inhabitants, placing them in the position of enemies of the government and the religion, subject to conquest accordingly.

In other words, though religious violence is nonetheless destructive, it is easily justified as self-defense. The full rejection of religiously motivated war in Christendom only occurred after the shocking experience of fratricidal conflict across the continent (particularly the Thirty Years War, which ended in 1648) and the realization of the impossibility of enforcement of unanimity and orthodoxy on the flock. Heterodoxy (differences in belief) and sects of all kinds proved that they were here to stay; tolerance, then, became an undesirable necessity, though not at first a true virtue.

In Islam, the discourse of war, while divergent in some ways, was and is consonant with Judeo–Christian ideas and practices. They are all monotheistic religions, worshipping ostensibly the same god, and viewing the world as a battleground between good and evil in which all individuals must struggle with his or her place in that cosmic conflict. Islam, however, has one aspect that Christianity does not, which is that it was from the very inception a political as well as a spiritual force. While Christianity eschewed political power, Islam was a political and legal system even during the lifetime of the Prophet. There is, therefore, no tradition of "separation of church and state" in Islam to match the (partly traditional and partly quite modern) European/Christian version.

Like Christianity, Islam takes a dualistic approach to reality, dividing it into a "domain of peace" (*dar al-islam*) and a "domain of conflict" (*dar al-harb*). The *dar al-islam* is the realm of true religion and submission to the one true god and his will and laws; again, the very concept of *islam* derives from peace through submission. The *dar al-harb* is a realm of trouble, strife, and injustice, since it does not follow the ways of the one true god. It is a world or a life of false and wasted effort, even when it is not actually violent, because it does not obey Allah's will; it, like Augustine's "city of the world," pursues the wrong goals and is forever in conflict, internally and externally, because it is not rightly directed by and to god.

The *dar al-harb*, understandably, is in perpetual and inherent contradiction if not open conflict with the *dar al-islam*. This contradiction may not always be a state of war, but it is always a state of tension. The only way that this tension can be relieved once and for all is by the elimination of the *dar al-harb* and its integration into the realm of true religion, submission, and peace—that is, of Islam and the *sharia* law that it prescribes. Thus, the "struggle" against unrighteousness and unbelief, even within oneself, becomes a central feature of Islam. The term for this struggle is *jihad*.

Jihad is a much-misunderstood term, like crusade. When we use "crusade" in English, we do not always mean a holy campaign. For instance, when we hold a "crusade against multiple dystrophy," we do not think we are in a spiritual battle. However, even this crusade has some qualities of the "holy war" in our focus, commitment to succeed, and moral rectitude. *Jihad* is similar. Strictly speaking, it means something like effort or struggle, not war or violence as such (*qital* in Arabic). In fact, Islamic tradition recognizes four kinds of *jihad*, divided into the "Greater" and "Lesser" categories. The Greater *jihad* consists of three of these kinds: (1) *jihad* of the heart, of moral reform of the self; (2) *jihad* of the tongue, or proclaiming God's word and working to spread it; and (3) *jihad* of the hand, or doing good works in accordance with God's will. Only the Lesser *jihad* speaks of the *jihad* of the sword, or fighting the enemies of Islam.

However, again, as in Christianity, this mandate can and its application can be interpreted in many ways in practice. The Qur'an says, for example, that "idolatry is worse than carnage" and instructs believers as demonstrated in Box 6.2.

6.2   *Religion and Violence in the Qur'an*

And fight in the way of Allah with those who fight with you, and do not exceed the limits, surely Allah does not love those who exceed the limits.

And kill them wherever you find them, and drive them out from whence they drove you out, and persecution is severer than slaughter, and do not fight with them at the Sacred Mosque until they fight with you in it, but if they do fight you, then slay them; such is the recompense of the unbelievers. (sura 2.190–191)

And fight with them until there is no persecution, and religion should be only for Allah, but if they desist, then there should be no hostility except against the oppressors. (sura 2.193)

[P]ersecution is graver than slaughter; and they will not cease fighting with you until they turn you back from your religion, if they can; and whoever of you turns back from his religion, then he dies while an unbeliever— these it is whose works shall go for nothing in this world and the hereafter, and they are the inmates of the fire; therein they shall abide. (sura 2.217)

Those who believe fight in the way of Allah, and those who disbelieve fight in the way of the Shaitan [satan]. Fight therefore against the friends of the Shaitan; surely the strategy of the Shaitan is weak. (sura 4.76)

Surely those who disbelieve spend their wealth to hinder (people) from the way of Allah; so they shall spend it, then it shall be to them an intense regret, then they shall be overcome; and those who disbelieve shall be driven together to hell.

That Allah might separate the impure from the good, and put the impure, some of it upon the other, and pile it up together, then cast it into hell; these it is that are the losers.

Say to those who disbelieve, if they desist, that which is past shall be forgiven to them; and if they return, then what happened to the ancients has already passed.

And fight with them until there is no more persecution and religion should be only for Allah; but if they desist, then surely Allah sees what they do.

And if they turn back, then know that Allah is your Patron; most excellent is the Patron and most excellent the Helper. (sura 8.36–40)

So when the sacred months have passed away, then slay the idolaters wherever you find them, and take them captive and besiege them and lie in wait for them in every ambush, then if they repent and keep up prayer and pay the poor-rate, leave their way free to them; surely Allah is Forgiving, Merciful. (sura 9.5)

O you who believe! The idolaters are nothing but unclean. . . . (sura 9.28)

O you who believe! fight those of the unbelievers who are near to you and let them find in you hardness; and know that Allah is with those who guard (against evil). (sura 9.123)

Surely Allah loves those who fight in His way in ranks as if they were a firm and compact wall. (sura 61.4)

Obviously, then, Muslims are no more or less likely to exercise their capacity to perceive threats and affronts to their religion as "offenses" that merit a "defensive" answer than Christians or other believers. Note that there is even an indication of a "just" or appropriate level of force or violence—that one should not, for instance, "exceed the limits" nor continue to fight against those who desist in their "persecution" of the true faith or who accept it themselves.

Although the Western, monotheistic religions are particularly prone to this manner of thinking, they are by no means the only ones that indulge in it. Even Hinduism and probably most religions engage in a degree of "two worlds" thinking, which inevitably pits "us" (the good and true) against "them" (the evil and false). As a final illustration, the *Bhagavad Gita* discusses its own version of the two-worlds model (see Box 6.3).

6.3

The Divine and Demoniac Natures: Bhagavad Gita, Chapter 16

Pride, arrogance, conceit, anger, harshness, and ignorance—these qualities belong to those of demoniac nature, O son of Prtha.

The transcendental qualities are conducive to liberation, whereas the demoniac qualities make for bondage. Do not worry, O son of Pandu, for you are born with the divine qualities.

(continued)

6.3   The Divine and Demoniac Natures: Bhagavad Gita, Chapter 16 (continued)

O son of Prtha, in this world there are two kinds of created beings. One is called the divine and the other demoniac. I have already explained to you at length the divine qualities. Now hear from Me of the demoniac.

Those who are demoniac do not know what is to be done and what is not to be done. Neither cleanliness nor proper behavior nor truth is found in them.

They say that this world is unreal, with no foundation, no God in control. They say it is produced of sex desire and has no cause other than lust.

Following such conclusions, the demoniac, who are lost to themselves and who have no intelligence, engage in unbeneficial, horrible works meant to destroy the world.

Taking shelter of insatiable lust and absorbed in the conceit of pride and false prestige, the demoniac, thus illusioned, are always sworn to unclean work, attracted by the impermanent.

They believe that to gratify the sense is the prime necessity of human civilization. Thus until the end of life their anxiety is immeasurable. Bound by a network of hundreds of thousands of desires and absorbed in lust and anger, they secure money by illegal means for sense gratification. (verses 4–12)

Thus perplexed by various anxieties and bound by a network of illusions, they become too strongly attached to sense enjoyment and fall down into hell.

Self-complacent and always impudent, deluded by wealth and false prestige, they sometimes proudly perform sacrifices in name only, without following any rules or regulations.

Bewildered by false ego, strength, pride, lust and anger, the demons become envious of the Supreme Personality of Godhead, who is situated in their own bodies and in the bodies of others, and blaspheme against the real religion.

Those who are envious and mischievous, who are the lowest among men, I perpetually cast into the ocean of material existence, into various demoniac species of life.

Attaining repeated birth amongst the species of demoniac life, O son of Kunti, such persons can never approach Me. Gradually they sink down to the most abominable type of existence. (verses 16–20)

---

*Source: Translation by Edwin Arnold, 1885; available at http://www.sacredtexts.com/hin/gita/index.htm.

Although this manifestation of the us-versus-them view does not advocate violence as such, it certainly does create the conditions for an indifference to, if not acceptance of, violence, as we noted in our discussion of the theme of the Gita earlier.

SACRIFICE AND MARTYRDOM

Two remaining manifestations of righteous violence deserve our attention. In his classic study of *Violence and the Sacred*, Rene Girard (1977) draws together many of the points we have been making in this chapter, with a special reference to sacrifice. Many religious traditions have incorporated sacrifice—including human sacrifice—with more or less emphasis, and sacrifice is clearly a form of harm in which a victim suffers and dies for some religious purpose. Old Testament Judaism was a highly sacrificial religion, with specific and detailed rules relating the proper choice and handling of animal and plant offerings; Yahweh was said to enjoy the smell of burnt sacrifices. In many pastoral religions, animal (especially cattle) sacrifice is a prominent feature, and the human sacrifices of the Aztecs are infamous, though hardly unique. Christianity itself has a human sacrifice—the self-sacrifice of God in the person of Jesus—as its central and paradigmatic event.

Girard understands sacrifice in particular, and religion in general, as a phenomenon precisely about violence—not just doing violence to the victim but communicating something about, and controlling or channeling violence in, society. Violence is a fact of life, he says, including social life. The world is both a welcoming place and a destructive place; no religion worth its salt could ever deny the latter. However, violence unchecked, allowed to proceed without barriers, eventually leads to "an interminable, infinitely repetitive process" of vengeance and countervengeance that cannot be stopped, since every violent act calls for a violent response, that calls for yet another violent response. This cycle of vengeance would be the undoing of society.

Thus, Girard argues that we misinterpret sacrifice as a cultural act when we view it as a "theological" act, that is, as one ordered by the gods or one that placates the gods or mediates with the gods. Sacrifice is not about the anger of the gods but rather the anger of humans in social groups. In sacrifice, "society is seeking to deflect upon a relatively indifferent victim, a 'sacrificeable' victim, the violence that would otherwise be vented on its own members, the people it most desires to protect" (Girard 1977: 4).

The key to the meaning and the success of sacrifice, then, is the "sacrificial substitution"—the replacement of an intentional victim for the natural victim, which would otherwise be *ourselves*. It is the turning away or projection of violence from *us* to some specific and appropriate *them*.

> The victim is not a substitute for some particularly endangered individual, nor is it offered up to some individual of particularly bloodthirsty temperament. Rather, it is a substitute for all the members of the community, offered up by the members themselves. The sacrifice serves to protect the entire community from its own violence; it prompts the entire community to choose victims outside itself. The elements of dissension scattered throughout the community are drawn to the person of the sacrificial victim and eliminated, at least temporarily, by its sacrifice. (Girard 1977: 8)

Naturally, for this psychological/sociological/symbolic substitution to work, the victim must be not-us but at the same time not-too-different-from us. It must possess certain qualities or characteristics that make it a suitable substitute for our true target—ourselves or each other. A rock has few of the desirable qualities of a sacrificial substitute, and a plant has only a few more (which is why Yahweh disapproved of vegetables as good sacrifices). An ideal substitute victim needs to be as close to us as possible without being us.

What kinds of beings satisfy the symbolic needs of sacrifice? Animals are good, plants are less good, and certain classes of humans may be best of all. These classes of humans include "prisoners of war, slaves, small children, unmarried adolescents, and the handicapped"; in some societies, even the king was a routine sacrificial victim (Girard 1977: 12). What do these classes have in common? All of them obviously have the requisite similarity to us to be recognized as substitutes for us, but simultaneously "between the victims and the community a crucial social link is missing, so they can be exposed to violence without the fear of reprisal" (13). In other words, they look like us, but they are not us, and none of us will mourn their death nor seek to avenge it.

Girard sees this relationship between religion and violence going far beyond the practice of sacrifice:

> Religion invariably strives to subdue violence, to keep it from running wild. Paradoxically, the religious and moral authorities in a community attempt to instill nonviolence, as an active force into daily life and as a mediating force into ritual life, through the application of violence. (1977: 20)

> *Religion* in its broadest sense, then, must be another term for that obscurity that surrounds man's efforts to defend himself by curative or preventative means against his own violence. (23)

More than likely, he overstates his case, for not all situations of sacrifice or religion in general seem related to anger or social turmoil; some are quite mundane and routine. Still, sacrifice and religion fulfill a social function; they are simply not the only possible fulfillment of that function. In societies that have institutional mechanisms to punish violence once and for all and thus halt the cycle of violence that would rend society, the threat is diminished. The particular type of mechanism that Girard refers to is a judicial system—a formal criminal-justice system. When there is only one institution that has the legitimate right to seek vengeance and retribution on behalf of the group, then there is no reason or even possibility of an escalation of violence. However, in the absence of such a system, as in the case of small-scale and traditional societies, other means—ritual means—must be employed, ones that accomplish the same goal while obscuring that very goal in a mystery of symbolic meaning. And there is some corroborating evidence for this argument: Wallace (1966) in his renowned analysis of religion advances cross-cultural data to suggest that societies with "political" institutions tend to take recourse to religious solutions (for example, witchcraft accusations) much less than societies without them. In passing it is worth noting that more complex and differentiated societies (those with class or "ethnic" diversity) tend also to rely on religious methods of integration, including pantheons of multiple gods and supernatural bases for morality.

One final arresting example of holy violence is the voluntarily self-inflicted variety, which is commonly referred to as martyrdom. In general, martyrdom is "dying for the cause." In the next chapter we will see two examples of people willing to die for their beliefs—Islamic suicide bombers and Heaven's Gate members. There have been many others, from Masada to Jonestown. Nor, again, is religion the only cause for which one might sacrifice oneself. Giving one's life out of patriotism is a form of sacrifice, as is dying for a principle. Lacey Baldwin Smith (1997), in his historical study of martyrdom in Western civilization, maintains that Socrates was the first martyr because he died by choice (rather than escape) to be true to his beliefs and to make a public and eternal statement about life, death, and conviction. Others since have died for country, class, culture, and untold other causes.

However, a martyr is just a suicide victim with a cause to justify it, and not only does it evince a cause but it is often believed to *prove* the cause. It can also be used as a path to one's higher glory. As the early church father Tertullian argued, "The only key that unlocks the gates of Paradise is your own blood" (quoted in Smith 1997: 92). Christianity, not inexplicably, was particularly inclined to the virtue of martyrdom early in its history, partly because it was offered so many opportunities for it (by Roman persecution) and partly because of the very paradigmatic act mentioned above: if Jesus suffered and died for truth, then that is what followers should do too. Another Church founder, Cyprian, said that "death makes life more complete, death rather leads to glory" (91). St. Euphus stated it most succinctly when he said, "I want to die; I am a Christian," as if those two things are synonymous (95). Thus, Tertullian could not only seek death but urge it on others: "seek to die a martyr." And of course, the more painful and prolonged the death, the better for the cause: "those whose victory is slower and with greater difficulty, these received the more glorious crown" (92). Cyprian believed that not only was the martyr himself or herself rewarded for the act of self-destruction but that others witnessing it would be convinced of the truth of the cause due to the conviction of the martyr. However, as Chesterton has observed, "Persecution does not prove either side to be right; it proves that both sides are in desperate earnest" (Smith 1997: 185).

Christians are not the only ones to indulge in the process of death for a holy cause. Islam among other religions has a tradition of martyrdom too, as we know from the 9/11 attacks in America (see the next chapter). The attackers were promised eternity in paradise for doing God's will. Jeffrey Goldberg (2000), in his fascinating piece on the "education of holy warriors" in Pakistani madrasas, gives us a sense of the psychology of the martyr complex. He asks a young male student (all of the students are young males) how his family would feel if he died in a religious cause. "They would be very happy," he said. "They would be so proud. Any father would want his son to die as *shaheed*" (Arabic for "martyr").

Which takes us, in conclusion, to the characteristics of the individuals who would sacrifice themselves—and often enough others—to die for a belief. What drives humans to such extremity? Smith (1997: 15) offers these features: a "sense of uniqueness and destiny," a felt obligation "to take upon themselves the burdens of mankind," a distinct lack of apathy but also of tolerance, the incapacity "of accepting compromise or accommodating to the needs of others," a detachment from "friend, family, or community" (think of Nechayev, the revolutionary in Chapter 8), a refusal to make any "concession to the world" based on their "higher allegiance," and their certainty that they act "upon the knowledge that they are God's or history's instrument for achieving or defending absolute truth." In other words, martyrs might be regarded as the ultimate egoists and idealists.

RETROSPECT AND PROSPECT

It seems Girard is correct that religion has violence—an awareness of violence, a response to violence, a propensity for violence—at its very core. At one level it accepts violence as a component of physical and social reality even as it deflects that violence away from society, or at least away from "us." It establishes the condition in which humans could construe violence not as an aspect of ourselves but of the natural or the supernatural world. It also establishes the condition in which participation in violence—against "the other" and even against the self—can be a virtuous, even necessary undertaking. Especially religions that perceive the world as a cosmic battleground to begin with will see struggle and conflict not only as the "nature of things" but as the road to the "final solution" of this battle.

Specific doctrines can enshrine a martial and destructive spirit more than others, but in the end it is not, as Hoffer and others suggest, so much about the doctrine itself as the very existence of some doctrine. Ideology has its own inherent extremism: everything is at stake, and it is at stake *now*. There is no time to consider other alternatives, and there are no other alternatives worth compromising: how do you negotiate with evil or with the Devil himself? This battle is to the death, and death can be a good thing. What better way to die than fighting on the side of Right?

The next chapter will explore some detailed cases of religion-inspired violence in the present and past. The two subsequent chapters carry the discussion to the realm of political ideology and its resultant violence. Ideological violence is not always carried out in the name of God, but it is almost always carried out in the name of *something*. When it is not God, it is often perpetrated in the name of "the people"—whoever that people may be—the nation, the class, the ethnic group, the cultural group, or what have you. Perhaps what is most interesting about the modern world, and what will emerge from our studies, is that religion has taken on the character of politics, and politics has taken on the character of religion, to such an extent that it is impossible—perhaps unnecessary and inappropriate—to distinguish them. If you are dead from my cause, it really does not matter any more what my cause was.

RELIGIOUS VIOLENCE

Case Studies

If groups are inherently confrontational and dangerous, then groups with exclusivist and absolutist belief systems are still more so. The anthropologist Desmond Morris (1977: 149) has said that religion is such a system because its "cultural isolating mechanism demands social separation from those who worship in a different manner. It creates sects and breeds sectarian violence." To say this is neither to comment on the truth status of any religion nor to distinguish religion utterly from other group phenomena and ideological systems. In the previous chapter we noted how Le Bon (1896) and Hoffer (1966/1951) find that all mass-movement types of groups have absolutist and intolerant aspects to them, and we will explore this fact in the next two chapters in regard to political, nationalist, and ethnic groups and violence.

Yet there is no arguing against the fact that religion has taken a prominent and growing center in contemporary international violence. According to Magnus Ranstrop (2003), an expert on international terrorism, the number of fundamentalist religious movements of all types around the world tripled from the mid-1960s to the mid-1990s. At the same time, the number of religiously inspired terrorist groups grew from zero to about one-quarter of all known terrorist organizations. In the period from 1970 to 1995, religious groups accounted for over half of the total acts of world terrorism.

The case studies in this chapter are not limited to terrorism or to the present day. They range over such disparate phenomena as the violence against heretics throughout Christian history, the classic terrorist attacks against America on September 11, a variety of apocalyptic groups, and sects that practiced violence "for a living." The common thread, again, in these cases will be the sense of a divine mission, obedience to authority, demonization of "the other," and the sense of being in a war— even a cosmic war—that only we can win. That is, in the end, they will combine all three factors of integration into groups, identity, and ideology—in these cases, an ideology that legitimizes and virtually demands a violent response.

Case Study 1: The Persecution of Heretics in Christianity

Intolerance and even violence against religious dissenters far predates Christianity, although Christianity has extensively indulged in it. In fact, in the vast majority of societies, great and small, belief is truth and truth is social order. To disbelieve is to be wrong, and to be wrong is to threaten the established order of things, spiritual and political. Conformity of opinion and action is the foundation of law and order; dissidence is disruption and disorder. No wonder then that even democratic Athens condemned Socrates to death for impiety and corrupting youth by asking troubling questions and spreading doubt about the gods.

At any rate, since Christianity is first and foremost a belief *about* and a belief *in* the person of Jesus and his saving mission, belief—*correct* belief—is crucial to the religion. Alternate beliefs were "heresy," from the Greek *hairesis*, meaning "to choose or take for yourself," and practitioners of alternate beliefs were considered heretics. Orthodoxy was established by the Council of Nicaea in 325 C.E., which settled a variety of disputes within Christianity, especially that Jesus was at once wholly human and wholly divine and that God was three-in-one (the "trinitarian" solution). All other opinions on the matter instantly became heterodoxy, dissent, and heresy. This included of course all non-Christian religions—especially Judaism (which by denying Jesus denied God) and all shades of paganism—as well as other interpretations of Christianity, of which there were legion. Docetists believed that Jesus was purely divine and not human; Gnostics believed that only they possessed the "mysteries" of Jesus and could be one with him; Arianism taught that god was not three but one, that there was no biblical authority for the trinity concept (replacing it with a "monarchian" or "unitarian" conception). These were among, and the most durable of, the wide assortment of local variations of Christian understanding. Early on, even before Nicaea, Christians were arguing with and condemning each other for false doctrine, as in Hippolytus's *The Refutation of All Heresies*, Irenaeus's *The Detection and Refutation of False Knowledge*, also known as *Against Heresies*, Tertullian's "Prescription Against Heretics," and so forth.

When the state legalizes one view of religion, all other views become "outlaw" or even "criminal," so once trinitarianism and the "dual nature" of Jesus were settled, other opinions became civil matters, punishable by the state. Starting, then, with the Arian controversy, bishops who advocated Arianism were deposed, books were burned, and lives were threatened. As Leonard Levy, a scholar of the history of blasphemy and heresy, writes: "Thus, for the first time, Christians began to persecute one another for differences of opinion and faith. Constantine's edict fixed the precedent for temporal punishment of

Case Study 1: The Persecution of Heretics
in Christianity (continued)

offenses against the true Christian faith"(1993: 42). In fact, temporal punishments would not take long to transform into capital punishment; the code of
emperor Theodosius (380 C.E.) established Christianity as the sole religion of
the realm and set penalties for disagreement from the official version, which
came to include restriction from office holding, fines, confiscation of property,
banishment, torture, and even death for Christian heresy and prohibition of
other religions altogether. In 385 C.E. Bishop Priscillian of Spain and six followers had the dubious honor of becoming the first Christians to die over
theological disputes, by decapitation. They would not be the last. As Levy
concludes: "Religious intolerance became a Christian principle" (44).

And it should not be imagined that persecution and intolerance were
attitudes that were foisted on the church by a zealous state. Founding church
leaders like Tertullian, Augustine, and Aquinas saw great virtue in the elimination of schism as well. Tertullian positively delighted at the prospect of the
damnation of sinners, disbelievers, and the wise and mighty:

> How shall I admire, how laugh, how rejoice, how exult, when I behold so many
> proud monarchs, and fancied gods, groaning in the lowest abyss of darkness; so
> many magistrates who persecuted the name of the Lord, liquefying in fiercer fires
> than they ever kindled against the Christians; so many sage philosophers blushing
> in red hot flames with their deluded scholars; so many celebrated poets trembling
> before the tribunal, not of Minos, but of Christ; so many tragedians, more tuneful
> in the expression of their sufferings. (Quoted in Freke and Gandy 1999: 243)

Augustine later advocated the death penalty for heretics but left it to the state
to carry out the punishment. For him, religious crimes were much greater
threats than property or violent crimes; rejection of the faith was much more
serious than rejection of the law. Physical death as a penalty was simply not a
big deal, since, as Augustine rationalized, we are all bound to die sometime;
but as for heretics, he wrote, "we fear their eternal death, which can happen if
we do not guard against it and can be averted if we do guard against it" (quoted
in Levy 1993 : 48). In other words, executing heretics was not only doing a service to church and state by disposing of a divisive character and returning the
faith to purity, but it was doing the heretic a favor by saving his soul. Therefore,
he could make the distinction between "an unjust persecution which the
wicked inflict on the Church of Christ, and . . . a just persecution which the
Church of Christ inflicts on the wicked." Or again, the church could persecute
"out of love . . . to reclaim from error to save souls" (ibid.).

Several hundred years later, in the mid-1200s, Thomas Aquinas picked
up the issue again, accepting the definition of heresy as an intentional
choice of "false or new opinions" in regard to faith. Only the Pope could
determine correct faith, and any deviation from his authority constituted

Case Study 1: The Persecution of Heretics
in Christianity (continued)

"a species of unbelief" (ibid., 51). He distinguished several species of unbelief, including but not limited to heresy, paganism, Judaism, apostasy, and blasphemy. He recognized that, conventionally, blasphemy—a capital offense in the Christian Old Testament—referred to speaking an insult or curse against God, but this extended for him to utterances of untrue beliefs. In other words, someone who spoke something false or erroneous about God also took his name in vain, and therefore heresy was a kind of unbelief and unbelief was a kind of blasphemy. All were worse than any temporal crime one might commit, and since many temporal crimes were met with capital punishment, heresy and blasphemy even more so should receive the ultimate punishment. In his own words, heretics "by right . . . can be put to death and despoiled of their possessions by the secular authorities, even if they do not corrupt others, for they are blasphemers against God, because they observe a false faith. Thus they can be justly punished more than those accused of high treason" (ibid., 52).

The Jews, as non-Christians, were inherently subject to intolerance and abuse, and doubly so because of the association between them and the death of Jesus in the minds of Christians. However, a more ominous problem for Christianity from the 1200s through today was the appearance and stubborn endurance of various incorrigible dissident or "protest" sects of Christianity, even long before there was a "Protestant" movement. Deviant Christian beliefs and sects were popping up with more and more frequency and vigor, and the church was constantly fighting such outbreaks like they were brushfires. As early as the 1200s a movement known as the Free Spirits spread across Europe, because its followers often adopted a wandering, preaching-and-ministering lifestyle. Free Spirits subscribed to a loose bundle of beliefs concerning the freedom of the soul or spirit, such that every person's soul was one with God and could be or had been perfected by God. Sometimes they would claim that they *were* God or that they contained God. And since they had a direct communion with or revelation from God, they did not need to wait for resurrection or salvation, and they did not need a religious institution to teach them about faith or to arrange for their eschatological salvation. They were free and perfect now, here on earth, and since they were perfect they were no longer capable of sin, so they often practiced lying, cheating, stealing, adultery or public fornication, nakedness, and other kinds of unconventional behavior generally referred to as "antinomian." They were widely acclaimed to be insane, and some perished in prison, but most were burned for their heresy.

And the Free Spirits were not alone in their fate. There was a flood swelling that would break soon in the form of the Protestant Reformation. It built up over time, producing the likes of Peter Waldo, John Wycliffe, Jerome of Prague, and Jan Huss. They and their followers were hounded, executed when

Case Study 1: The Persecution of Heretics
in Christianity (continued)

possible, and even on occasion burned posthumously. But the offense of doc-
trinal schism and multiplication would not abate. It is no wonder at all that the
Holy Inquisition first appeared in Europe around this time (early 1200s) as the
antiheretical arm of the established church. While it took many forms over the
centuries before it was dismantled only in recent history, its purpose was to
root out and vanquish heresy, and its very institutionalization was testimony to
the level of concern felt in the church over the burgeoning protests.

The swell of "protest" broke through the dam with Martin Luther, who
launched the Protestant Reformation officially in 1517. This opened the door to a
virtually unlimited number of new forms of Christian belief and behavior (many
of which still survive today), heated up the animosity and violence within Christendom, and revived the term and charge of blasphemy in Europe. Luther himself was an adamant, even fanatical, anti-Catholic; he condemned the church as
the whore of Babylon and the Pope as the anti-Christ. He was naturally branded
a heretic by the Church, as were all "protesters" against Catholic authority of the
time; since that term was used against him, he needed to find another term to
hurl back at the Church, and "blasphemy" was there to be put back into service
again. To him, the Mass was blasphemy. The Pope and the papacy were blas-
phemies; the institution was "full of blasphemous lies" and "terrible idolatry."
Catholics who did not convert to Lutheranism were committing blasphemy and
should be excommunicated or exiled. Within twenty years of his original insurrection, in 1536, he called for imprisonment and execution for Catholic blasphemers.

Luther thought that everyone who went back to the source for himself
would end up sharing Luther's views and interpretations. They did not.
Instead, dozens if not hundreds of new Christian sects emerged, each with a
different attitude toward some aspect of the faith but each with the same attitude toward other sects—condescension or even condemnation. Arianism
appeared again, still teaching that the doctrine of the trinity was nonscriptural
and that many of the Church practices, like baptizing in the name of Jesus,
were unprecedented and wrong. They took a unitarian rather than a trinitarian
view of God, and they would eventually become known as the Unitarians. Perhaps the other most despised sect of the early 1500s was Anabaptism, meaning
"rebaptism." The Anabaptists believed that the Catholic practice of infant baptism was unscriptural and vain; infants, being innocent, did not need baptism
for salvation, and baptism prior to an individual's understanding of and commitment to the faith was pointless and wasted. Anabaptism was known for its
pacifism and what we might call today its "conscientious objection." It held
that no true Christian should bow to the state, only to God; members refused
to take any oaths of allegiance to the state, serve in the army, accept the death
penalty nor even pay tithes or church taxes. Other sects, such as the Quakers,

***Case Study 1: The Persecution of Heretics
in Christianity (continued)***

the Shakers, the Ranters, the Levelers, the Diggers, the Calvinists, the Methodists, and many more eventually took and continue to take shape.

It is predictable that the Catholic church and the state authorities would see this as a challenge and a dangerous precedent, and accordingly Anabaptists were called heretics and often burned at the stake. The odd thing, perhaps, is that Luther joined in the condemnation of these dissidents, originally calling for their incarceration, physical mutilation (such as boring a hole through the tongue with a hot poker, to symbolize the horrible talk that the criminal engaged in), and exile. In 1530, he endorsed the government's death penalty for Anabaptists, labeling them blasphemers. The Jews too were blasphemers to him, and he recommended that their synagogues and books be burned, their homes, money, and property taken or destroyed, their rabbis prohibited from teaching, and their use of the word "God" outlawed on penalty of death. He said that he would gladly put them all to forced labor or exile, or cut their tongues out and forcibly convert them to Christianity (by which he of course meant Lutheranism).

What followed were generations of religious war. The first round was fought by the dominant power, Spain under Charles V, the defender of the Catholic faith, against Protestant heresy mainly on German soil. But unlike previous schisms, this one would not die, partly for political reasons—local German princes saw religion as a means to claim and establish temporal independence in their domains, to escape the control of the centralized Church. At any rate, Catholicism capitulated in 1555, in the Peace of Augsburg, in which Catholicism and Protestantism (by which we and they mean Lutheranism) agreed to "tolerate" one another. A local prince could choose between the two faiths and establish it as the religion of his realm. Any subject unhappy with his liege's decision was at liberty to migrate to another princedom. Cities where both religions existed would tolerate both, and proselytization was forbidden; ideally, the two faiths would hold their current positions and leave each other alone. If this seemed like a reasonable settlement and the first occasion of "toleration under fire," it was fatally flawed both due to the proselytizing nature of both sides and to the exclusion of any other sects from the "peace." All versions of Christianity besides Catholicism and Lutheranism were still regarded as heresy and still subject to persecution.

The peace held for about sixty years, awkwardly, until the Thirty Years' War (1618–48), which ravaged central Europe and cost approximately 7 to 8 million lives (Dunn 1970: 76). Even during the central European peace, religious wars had convulsed France (Protestant Huguenots versus Catholics) throughout the latter half of the 1500s. Eventually the Thirty Years' War ended with the Peace of Westphalia (1648), which guaranteed once again the right of existence to Catholicism, Lutheranism, and Calvinism, at the local monarch's discretion.

Case Study 1: The Persecution of Heretics
in Christianity (continued)

Greater measures were taken this time to ensure the liberties of the "nonestab-lished" two religions in each territory, but other sects, such as the Anabaptists, were still left out of the equation and still exposed to persecution. Toleration, grudgingly won, was still applied in only limited way: Catholics, Lutherans, and (now) Calvinists tolerated each other, but none of them tolerated anyone else.

Case Study 2: Terrorism and September 11

Americans who were alive on September 11, 2001 will always remember that date. Some claim that the world was changed on that day; more likely, Ameri-cans discovered for themselves what the world has known and experienced for a very long time. Some, like American Christians Jerry Falwell and Pat Robert-son, harshly blamed secularism—a lack of religion—for the events; immedi-ately after the tragedy, Falwell, in conversation with Robertson on the latter's "700 Club" television program two days later said:

> Pagans, and the abortionists, and the feminists, and the gays and the lesbians who are actively trying to make that an alternative lifestyle, the ACLU, People for the American Way, all of them who have tried to secularize America—I point the fin-ger in their face and say "you helped this happen."

Falwell subsequently apologized. His apology message read, in part:

> I apologize that ... I singled out for blame certain groups of Americans. This was insensitive, uncalled for at the time, and unnecessary as part of the commentary on this destruction. The only label any of us needs in such a terrible time of crisis is that of "American." I do not know if the horrific events of September 11 are the judg-ment of God, but if they are, that judgment is on all of America—including me and all fellow sinners—and not on any particular group. In conclusion, I blame no one but the hijackers and terrorists for the barbaric happenings of September 11.
>
> We know ... that "The Almighty has his own purposes," but ... "The judgments of the Lord are true and righteous altogether."

Notice how, even in this backhanded apology, religion is still the prism through which the events are seen and explained. Either God used violence against us to teach us or punish us, or God allowed violence against us as a removal of his protection, or the hijackers and terrorists were acting out of their own (barba-ric) religious beliefs. No matter what, God is involved in some way, and the judgments of God, even the violent ones, are true and righteous.

We do not know what God was doing that day, but we do know what man was doing. A group of religious zealots committed suicide and mass murder

Case Study 2: Terrorism and September 11 (continued)

for a mixture of religious, social, and political reasons. These men were Muslims, which has led all to the conclusion that Muslims are violent or that Islam is a religion of violence; even Falwell again stated this position in a *60 Minutes* interview in October 2002. "Muhammad was a terrorist," he said, whereas Moses and Jesus were men of peace.

The point of the present discussion of 9/11 is not to suggest that Islam is any more prone to violence than any other religion. It is indeed prone to violence. So is Christianity. So are all religions that see the world in black and white terms, in which we are the one and they are the "other." However, 9/11, while it was a complicated response to a complicated situation, was religious as much as anything else.

Contemporary Islamic violence is a fascinating and incendiary mixture of religious belief and passion and political complaints and objectives. Islamic militants like Osama bin-Laden and his al-Qaeda organization offer a variety of grievances against the West in general and the United States in particular. The most persistent and aggravating one is the existence of the state of Israel in what they consider to be Muslim land and the continued support for that state of Western powers, most extremely, the United States. They believe that Arab states would have long since destroyed Israel, in any of the wars from 1948 to today, without the aid of America. Furthermore, when America does attempt to intervene in regional conflict as a broker of peace, we are always seen as a dishonest and not an impartial broker, taking Israel's side and working for Israel's benefit.

A second grievance is the perceived Western and American support for regimes in the area that are quite unpopular among many Arab citizens and that are often quite un-Islamic or even anti-Islamic. Many Muslims, militant or otherwise, would point to Egypt and Saudi Arabia as governments that have little legitimacy in the eyes of many of their own people and that would quite possibly fall without American props. That Egypt has conducted very successful antiterrorist campaigns, and that Saudi Arabia conducts at least half-hearted ones, is remembered.

A third grievance is the Gulf War and subsequent sanctions against Iraq. This is seen as naked aggression against a Muslim state, and Islamic extremists sometimes claim that millions of Iraqi people are starving and dying because of the decade-long embargo, a dubious claim at best. They also see the ratcheting-up of war propaganda (which turned into a real shooting war by March 2003) by the U.S. administration against Iraq a decade later as simply another instance of American anti-Islamism. Surely, Falwell's remarks about Muhammad and Islam cited earlier, which were broadcast in the Arab world, do not help our cause much. Associated with the two wars against Iraq is their offense at stationing of foreign troops in Saudi Arabia, the birthplace of the Prophet and his religion. Islamic militants see this in religious terms as blasphemy and in political terms as colonization.

Case Study 2: Terrorism and September 11 (continued)

Finally, there is the cultural complaint against America and the West—that we are a secular, corrupt, and corrupting culture that threatens their own traditional and stable society with our irreligion, loose morals, women's rights, and music, television, computers, and so forth. In a way, the struggle is nearly as much a cultural as a religious one. However, all of these factors must be seen through the lens of the decline of Islamic power since the 1700s or so, the colonization and exploitation of the region by foreign Western powers, and the even older "clash of civilizations" between Christianity and Islam epitomized in the Crusades and perpetuated by the impolitic comments of Falwell and others.

Extreme violent acts make no sense and generally have no place without such "political" factors, even in the name of religion. If Christianity and the West were leaving Islam and the Arab world alone, religious differences by themselves would probably be insufficient to generate suicide attackers. However, the two together—religion and politics—make an explosive mix, in which the politics often gets lost and only the religious message gets through. Consider this statement by Sulaiman Abu Ghaith, a spokesman for al-Qaeda, which was issued shortly after 9/11 (see Box 7.1).

7.1   ### *Statement of Sulaiman Abu Ghaith to Muslims*

Peace be upon Muhammad our prophet and those who follow him.

I direct this message to the entire Islamic nation, and I say to them that all sides today have come together against the nation of Islam and the Muslims.

This is the crusade that Bush has promised us, coming toward Afghanistan against the Islamic nation and the Afghan people. We are living under this bombardment from the crusade, which is also targeting the whole Islamic community.

We have a fair and just case.

The Islamic nation, for more than 80 years, has been suffering. The Palestinian people have been living under the Jewish and Zionist occupation; nobody moves to help them. Here we are, this is an Arab land, this is a land that is being desecrated, people have come to take its wealth.

The nation must know that 'terror' and the terror of the United States is only a ploy. Is it possible that America and its allies would kill and that would not be called terrorism? And when the victim comes out to take revenge, it is called terrorism. This must not be acceptable.

(continued)

7.1   *Statement of Sulaiman Abu Ghaith to Muslims (continued)*

America must know that the nation will not keep quiet any more and will not allow what happens against it. Jihad today is a religious duty of every Muslim, if they haven't got an excuse. God says fight, for the sake of God and to uphold the name of God. The American interests are everywhere all over the world. Every Muslim has to play his real and true role to uphold his religion and his nation in fighting, and jihad is a duty.

I want to talk on another point, that those youths who did what they did and destroyed America with their airplanes did a good deed. They have moved the battle into the heart of America. America must know that the battle will not leave its land, God willing, until America leaves our land, until it stops supporting Israel, until it stops the blockade against Iraq.

The Americans must know that the storm of airplanes will not stop, God willing, and there are thousands of young people who are as keen about death as Americans are about life.

The Americans must know that by invading the land of Afghanistan they have opened a new page of enmity and struggle between us and the forces of the unbelievers. We will fight them with the material and the spiritual strength that we have, and our faith in God. We shall be victorious.

The Americans have opened a door that will never be closed.

At the end, I address the sons and the young Muslims, the men and women, for them to take their responsibility. The land of Afghanistan and the holy warriors are being subjected to a full crusade with the objective of getting rid of the Islamic nation. The nation must take up its response and in the end I thank God for allowing us to start this jihad. This battle is a decisive battle between faithlessness and faith. And I ask God to give us victory in the face of our enemy and return them defeated.

Further indication that the attackers themselves were acting on explicitly religious impulse can be found in the attack plan, a four-page document that was discovered some time after the attacks. The plan contains a list of activities to perform in the days and hours leading up to the final event, many of which are distinctly devout in nature, such as:

- "Read a verse from the Qur'an and recognize the meanings and what God prepared for the believers in endless happiness for martyrs."
- "Remind yourself to obey God this night since you will face critical situations that require believing and obeying 100 percent, so teach yourself . . . for the job you are about to carry out."
- "Pray all night and insist on victory, absolute liberation."

Case Study 2: Terrorism and September 11 (continued)

- "Know that what happens to you, it's only a test from God, that he will raise you one step and clean your bad deeds."
- "When you arrive [at the airport], say your prayers. And smile, be satisfied, because God is with the faithful and He is guarding you, although you don't feel it. Say the prayers; God makes us triumph. . . . Look cheerful and satisfied, because you're doing a job which is loved by God, and you will end your day in heavens where you will join the virgins."
- "When you board the plane and before you step in, read your prayer and repeat the same prayers we mention before, when you take your seat. Apply the rules of the prisoners of war. Take them prisoner and kill as God said; no Prophet can have prisoners of war. Open your chest welcoming death in the path of God and utter your prayer seconds before you go to your target. Let your last words be, 'There is no God but God and Muhammad is His messenger [the Islamic creed].' Then, *inshallah* [God willing], you will be in heaven. When you see the infidels, remember that the enemies of Islam were in the thousands, but the faithful were victorious" (Source: U.S. Department of Justice).

How is such a mind-set possible? We have seen that exactly such a mind-set is uniquely possible for the true believer. In fact, as Hoffer wrote, all such extreme movements produce believers who are ready to die and to kill for the cause; all of them have the potential for "fanaticism, enthusiasm, fervent hope, hatred and intolerance" (1966/1951:75).

The final ingredient that leads to extreme action is a war-time mentality. As we observed in the previous chapter, participants in religious or other kinds of mass movements usually see themselves not as aggressors but as defenders. They are the ones who are aggressed against. They are merely protecting themselves, responding to a war that they did not start but cannot shirk. We see this war-time and self-defensive mentality in bin Laden and other militants. As bin Laden stated in a CNN interview in 1997:

> We declared jihad against the U.S. government because the U.S. government is unjust, criminal, and tyrannical. It has committed acts that are extremely unjust, hideous, and criminal whether directly or through its support of the Israeli occupation. For this and other acts of aggression and injustice, we have declared jihad against the U.S., because in our religion it is our duty to make jihad so that God's word is the one exalted to the heights and so that we drive the Americans ways from all Muslim countries.

Nearly a year later, in early 1998, he issued a statement calling for attacks on all Americans—combatants and civilians alike—as a religious duty of Muslims:

> We—with God's help—call on every Muslim who believes in God and wishes to be rewarded to comply with God's order to kill the Americans and plunder their money wherever and whenever they find it. We also call on Muslim *ulema*

Case Study 2: Terrorism and September 11 (continued)

[religious authorities], leaders, youths, and soldiers to launch the raid on Satan's U.S. troops and the devil's supporters allying with them, and to displace those who are behind them so that they may learn a lesson.

> The ruling to kill the Americans and their allies—civilians and military—is an individual duty for every Muslim who can do it in any country in which it is possible to do it, in order to liberate the al-Aqsa Mosque and the holy mosque [Mecca] from their grip, and in order for their armies to move out of all the lands of Islam, defeated and unable to threaten any Muslim.

Finally, in an escalation of anger and rhetoric, by the end of 1998 bin Laden was justifying the acquisition and even use of weapons, including nuclear weapons, in the prosecution of this "just war":

> Acquiring weapons for the defense of Muslims is a religious duty. If I have indeed acquired these weapons, then I thank God for enabling me to do so. And if I seek to acquire these weapons, I am carrying out a duty. It would be a sin for Muslims not to try to possess the weapons that would prevent the infidels from inflicting harm on Muslims.

> If I seek to acquire such weapons, this is a religious duty. How we use them is up to us.

Case Study 3: Apocalypse Soon—Poison Gas, Mother-ships, and Soldiers for Christ

As we have seen, people with a cause and a grievance are people prone to violence—and the greater the cause or the grievance, the greater the capacity for destruction. There is one other aspect of the particularly religious character of much of historical and modern violence that needs to be emphasized, however, and this is the phenomenon of *eschatology*, which makes up a critical part of the Christian message and increasingly of other religious messages too, as we will see in the case studies that follow.

Eschatology (from the Greek *eschaton*, or "end") refers to beliefs about the end of time, the end time, that is, about how the world as we know it will end. Christianity has a highly elaborated eschatology, prophesied throughout the scriptures but made most explicit in the final book of the New Testament, the Book of Revelation. When the end comes, a cataclysmic conflict will put the world through incomprehensible suffering, killing off the vast majority of humans and scarring the earth, until the complete and final victory of the good side, God's side, over the bad side, Satan's side, and the establishment of new order inhabited only by the winners of the conflict, the righteous warriors, whose victory was always assured.

Case Study 3: Apocalypse Soon—Poison Gas,
Mother-ships, and Soldiers for Christ (continued)

As we observed in the last chapter, the experience of humankind has been a volatile one. Soldiers on the march see enemies everywhere, find battles to fight, and accept orders unquestioningly. However, when this war is interpreted as *the* war—the ultimate war, the final war, cosmic war—the stakes are highest, the enemies fiercest, defeat least tolerable. And when the consummate battle is near, or already under way, there are no noncombatants and all weapons are useable.

Eschatological thought is not unique to Christianity; Islam possesses it, as does Judaism in a less developed state. Hinduism teaches about a cycle of cosmic declines and rebirths, and Maya religion foretold an end to time too. However, Christian ideas and conceptions of the "end of the world" have become particularly common currency in the modern world, and the conditions of that world—with its nuclear and environmental threats, its unhappy ethnic groups and marginalized classes—make that message more appealing, and seem more imminent, than ever. Finally, by the process of syncretism, Christian images have been effectively alloyed with other religious and social concepts—from karma to UFOs—to produce some odd but deadly combinations.

Aum Shinrikyo: *Apocalypse in Japan*

The world remembers March 20, 1995, when a sect in Japan released a nerve gas called sarin into the subways of Tokyo, killing twelve people and injuring over five thousand. Why would anyone do such a pointless, harmful, and ineffective thing as this? The answer is that it was not at all pointless and that the harm was a—if not the—point, and its ineffectiveness was not at all the predicted or desired result of the action.

The world soon learned that the gas release was a deliberate attack by a group known as Aum Shinrikyo, led by a blind guru named Shoko Asahara. Asahara, born Chizuo Matsumoto in 1955, had been a religious seeker since early in life, moving through various "New Age" and Eastern beliefs and groups, picking up ideas about natural foods and Chinese medicine and karma along the way, until he found and joined the Japanese "new religion" called Agonshu. Agonshu taught that bad karma held believers back from true enlightenment and that this karma could be alleviated through meditation and suffering, including the imposed suffering of others.

In 1984 Asahara formed his own group, and in 1986 while in India, he supposedly achieved enlightenment. The following year he named the new group Aum Shinrikyo—Aum after the Hindu mantra "om" which is the sound of totality, of the creative and the destructive forces of the universe, plus *shinri*, which is Japanese for "supreme truth," and *kyo*, for "religious teaching." Like many new sects, Aum Shinrikyo was born in controversy and struggle, and the group saw these challenges as the reactions of a hostile world against their truth; the result was to make the sect more militant, fostering its sense of embattledness and aggressiveness.

A militant Aum Shinrikyo was not destined to be a pleasant thing, given its belief structure. These beliefs focused on two areas: the person of Asahara as a unique being, and the eschatological predictions it made and the solutions it offered. Asahara claimed, for instance, that he possessed special DNA and that he had even done blood tests to prove it. Further, he maintained that he was a higher being, an inhabitant of a superhuman nonmaterial plane of existence. Therefore, he could see and know things that other mere humans could not, including the unfolding of the end time. Naturally, he also had reasons for his actions and decisions that made sense on the other plane if not here. Followers and believers should simply follow and believe.

The eschatology of Aum Shinrikyo was a strange syncretism of Christian and Hindu–Buddhist beliefs mixed with the prophecies of Nostradamus. It predicted an apocalyptic end of the world, which was referred to as Armageddon or World War III. The expected apocalypse was at least partly a function of a vast international conspiracy, which involved the Freemasons as well as the American government. Early in the sect's history, the goal was to prevent this event from occurring. The work of the group, then, was to intercept the negative energy in the world and transform it into positive; for this work, thirty thousand members were needed, who had achieved their own enlightenment through the teachings of the guru.

However, as prevention began to seem more and more unlikely, the goal shifted to survival through and after it. The only avenue to such survival was participation in Aum Shinrikyo. By 1990 the sect was talking about and constructing communes and bomb shelters where they could isolate themselves from the ignorant society and prepare for and be saved from the inevitable Armageddon. These sole survivors of the mass destruction could then emerge to rebuild civilization—Aum Shinrikyo civilization—after the end. The similarity to American "survivalist" doctrines and practices, especially but not exclusively surrounding Y2K, as well as other apocalyptic movements like the Branch Davidians, should be clear.

The conflagration and the world-to-be afterward were vague in description, but it was specified that evil forces would attack the world with their ultimate weapons, including nuclear, biological, and chemical weapons, and gases like sarin would be among their tools. The group even began manufacturing, stockpiling, and testing its own supply of these agents, using sarin gas on the population of Matsumoto Nagano prefecture in Japan a year before the Tokyo attack (June 1994), with almost equally deadly results—seven fatalities, six hundred injuries.

When a doomsday cult's predictions begin to seem too real to its members or begin to seem not real enough, one possible and regular response is to act in ways to attempt to bring about the very things the cult predicts and supposedly dreads. This is one explanation for the assault on the Tokyo subway in 1995. It might have been an effort to jump-start Armageddon, or it might have been an attempt to make their prediction appear true, perhaps as a recruiting effort. That latter interpretation seems likely in view of Asahara's claim immediately following the attack that it was actually committed by the United States, which had begun its war against Japan and already seized the government.

One follower of the sect, interviewed by Juergensmeyer (2000), thought that the action was orchestrated by Asahara to give himself a feeling of power or perhaps was a reaction to the pressure he felt from authorities, who were increasingly attentive to the sect's movements (that the end of the group was near and he wanted to go out "with a bang"). One other suggestion was that the master wanted his chance to appear to be the last hope for humanity, that he "wanted to be seen as a savior" and "wanted to be like Christ" (112).

No matter what the motivation, the larger plan failed. Armageddon did not start, and recruits did not rush to the religion. Yet, Aum Shinrikyo could and did still justify the plan by appealing to spiritual conceptions. By twisting a Tibetan Buddhist term, *phoa*, which refers to the transfer of consciousness from the living to the dead to elevate their spiritual merit, Asahara could argue that some people were better off dead for the benefit of the living. In fact, Asahara wrote about the moral acceptability of "mercy killing," maintaining the "right of the guru and of spiritually advanced practitioners to kill those who otherwise would fall into the hells" (quoted in Juergensmeyer 2000: 114). Recall how the Christian thinkers Augustine and Aquinas basically concluded the same thing.

At any rate, death was all part of the plan: "The killers and their victims were simply actors in a divine scenario" (Juergensmeyer 2000: 15)—the most dangerous kind of scenario, as we have seen. Asahara himself stated that "the inhabitants of the present human realm do not recognize that they are fated to die" (109). Maybe we know we are going to die, just not at his hand and for his reasons. But the world was at war, he thought, whether we knew it or liked it or not—and not just any old war, but a cosmic war. "Once one is caught up in cosmic war, Asahara explained, the ordinary rules of conduct do not apply" (115).

Heaven's Gate: Self-Destruction for the Next Level

If self-mutilation, martyrdom, and suicide are forms of violence too—and by all rights they are, albeit self-inflicted—then the story of the Heaven's Gate sect is a noteworthy contribution to our analysis of the subject. Referring to itself as TELAH, or The Evolutionary Level Above Human, thirty-nine of its members acted on their convictions on March 26, 1997 and killed themselves with a mixture of sleeping pills, alcohol, and plastic bags placed over the head. The thirty-nine, including twenty-one women and eighteen men, most in their forties, lived together in a large home in Rancho Santa Fe, near San Diego, California. When they were discovered after their deaths, they were all wearing identical dark unisex outfits and cropped hair, obscuring their gender. Completing the obscurity, many of the men had been castrated.

What would make adult, professional (many cult members made a living designing websites), and apparently intelligent people commit group suicide after castrating themselves? The answer is a powerful authoritarian belief about cosmic struggle and an imminent eschatological conclusion to this struggle. The head of the group, an elderly man named Marshall Applewhite, who referred to himself as "Do" (pronounced "doe"), claimed to be the incarnation of a being from The Evolutionary Level Above Human, come to gather up his crew and prepare themselves and as many humans as possible to return to that higher realm. In fact, he suggested that this was not the first such visitation among humans but that the visits occurred at roughly two-thousand-year intervals, the last one being the mission of Jesus. According to TELAH's own website (www5.zdnet.com/yil/higher/heavensgate/index.html, accessed 3 March 1997):

> Two thousand years ago, a crew of members of the Kingdom of Heaven who are responsible for nurturing "gardens," determined that a percentage of the human "plants" of the present civilization of this Garden (Earth) had developed enough that some of those bodies might be ready to be used as "containers" for soul deposits. Upon instruction, a member of the Kingdom of Heaven then left behind His body in that Next Level . . . came to Earth, and moved into . . . an adult human body (or "vehicle") that had been "prepared" for this particular task. The body that was chosen was called Jesus.

Do himself writes: "Our mission is exactly the same. I am in the same position to today's society as was the One that was in Jesus then."

The process of evolution to this higher level of existence, then, involves the "incarnation" of a higher being into a human body through occupation or possession of that body; higher beings do not procreate, as it turns out. In fact, a 1995 statement from Heaven's Gate explains that previous missions to Earth identified and tagged specific bodies for occupation by placing "chips" in those bodies. "These 'chips' set aside those bodies for us." The chip, presumably like a computer chip, is the "soul" of the incarnated double being (human and TELAH) with "a program of metamorphic possibilities." The soul, a temporary resident in the body, is also itself a container with its own "brain" or "hard drive" that gradually fills through experience and instruction. As the "Next Level mind" fills, it expands and takes up more of the "space" that the human mind was originally occupying, until it displaces and "necessitates the abortion of the human mind." This is the process of metamorphosis by which the human "plant" becomes a higher being.

Humans therefore come in two varieties: those with "souls" or "deposits" placed there from TELAH and those without souls. The latter are "simple 'plants,'" physical bodies with mere human DNA and experiences. The former are potential, actual—but not yet always—higher beings, since they may be actively filling their hard drives through instruction from the present representative of TELAH on Earth (Applewhite, on this occasion) and thus progressing toward "metamorphic completion," or they may be not progressing either because they are not in communication with the representative or may "have chosen not to 'pursue.'" This creates the classic dichotomy between us and them, and another familiar dichotomy between the "active and faithful us" and the "passive or apostate us."

The urgency to all this is that the present civilization of the Earth is about to be recycled—"spaded under"—in order that the planet might be refurbished. The human "weeds" have taken over the garden and disturbed its usefulness beyond repair. The world is not salvageable any more and has become inadequate for its designed purpose, which was as a giant greenhouse for growing "human plants" that could become vehicles for TELAH souls. Thus the beings of TELAH are coming to end the experiment—shut down the nursery—and it was believed that they were coming in a spaceship that was hidden on the other side of the Hale-Bopp comet that swung near Earth around that time.

In preparation, progressing humans should be trying to extricate themselves from their lower, human, "mammalian" nature. They must strive to be truly "not of this world," and that entails full participation in the activities and teachings of the TELAH representative. As their self-prepared materials explain: "Unless you are currently an active student or are attempting to become a student of the present Representative from the Kingdom of Heaven [a synonym for TELAH]—you ARE STILL 'of the world,' having done *no significant* separation from worldliness, and you are still serving the *opposition* to the Kingdom of Heaven." But this mammalian nature that TELAH finds so distasteful includes naturally our carnal side, our materialistic and desiring side, and our gendered nature—our maleness and femaleness (TELAH beings are not procreative and therefore gender neutral). This explains the autocastration of the male members of the group. Finally, our mammalian nature includes conventional norms and morality—the lifestyle of the householder and worker, the obedient citizen, and the traditional religious believer.

All of this might be sufficient to drive a sect to self-destruction, but there is one other piece to the puzzle that was alluded to above—the struggle against the "opposition to the Kingdom of Heaven." Like so many other modern thought systems, this is one experiencing mortal conflict. Primarily it is up against conventional society, which sees the group and its mission as silly, if not satanic. But the real opposition is, of course, cosmic. A competing force of evil beings, "space alien races" called "Luciferians," threatens the cult's existence.

> These malevolent space races are the humans' GREATEST ENEMY. They hold humans in unknown slavery only to fulfill their own desires. They cannot "create," though they develop races and biological containers through genetic manipulation and hybridization. They even try to "make deals" with human governments to permit them (the space aliens) to engage in biological experimentation (through abductions) in exchange for such things as technically advanced modes of travel—though they seldom follow through, for they don't want humans of this civilization to become another element of competition. They war among themselves over the spoils of this planet and use religion and increased sexual behavior to keep humans "drugged" and ignorant (in darkness) while thinking they are in "God's" keeping.... These negative space races see to it, through the human "social norm" (the largest Luciferian "cult" there is), that man continues to not avail himself of the possibility of advancing *beyond* human.

The two particularly interesting aspects of this conception are that there is a superhuman contest going on in which the future of humans hangs in the balance (a familiar theme) and that human governments and even human religions are a party to the opposition side in the contest (a familiar theme with a twist). Predictably, since the Luciferians are in contact and alliance with the rich and powerful among the human race, the rich and powerful are co-conspirators.

> These powerful individuals have a loose-knit world-wide "club" that for the most part dictates who their primary "monopoly" players are—those leaders in the "significant" or strong societies or cultures. Government leaders, the very rich, and the world's righteous or "moral" leaders ... together really determine what is "right" and "wrong" for the populace as a whole.... Any little group that isn't naively, totally submissive to their social rules, or begins to see through this "control mechanism," or questions its rightness, is seen as subversive, radical, antisocial, a cult, or even treasonous—or potentially "terrorists."

Here, Heaven's Gate has found its way onto the oldest kind of conspiracy thinking in the world. But what they add is a fascinating condemnation of all of the world's conventional religions as Luciferian—which is not as unusual as it seems. Even Christianity has a tradition of branding non-Christian religions as "satanism" or "devil worship," and as we saw previously, Islam and Judaism also reject "idolatry," sometimes as the worst of all possible sins.

So, TELAH tells us that the Luciferian races "started all religions and masquerade as 'gods' to humans." It is the Luciferians who created the belief systems that most humans follow and who respond to the prayers and sins of humans, which are only supplications to or violations of the aliens and their ways. In actuality:

the Next Level abhors religions, for they bind humans more thoroughly to the human kingdom, using strong misinformation mixed with cosmic or universal consciousness of Creation, about which, in truth, they know nothing. . . . Only the Luciferians could have Christians believing that Jesus promoted family values, becoming better humans, establishing professional religious institutions, and looking for the Second Coming of some flowing-robed, peace-and-love manifestation of their artists' conceptions.

The ultimate message is all too clear and all too common. The world is a wicked place. It is all going to end soon. Only we have the truth. So only we see what is coming and only we will be saved or can save the world. So the only rational choice is joining us and surrendering what you thought was your individual mind. "The only way an individual can grow in the Next Level is to learn to be dependent on his Older Member as that source of unlimited growth and knowledge. So, any younger member in good standing forever remains totally dependent upon (and looks to) his Older Member for all things."

TELAH offers the final, indeed the only, answer: "If you have grown to hate your life in this world and would lose if for the sake of the Next Level, you will find **true** life with us—potentially forever. If you cling to this life—will you not lose it?" Those are the words that empower sacred suicide.

Soldiers for Christ   S. J.

A recent announcement described the latest initiative by the Christian group known as the Promise Keepers to attract younger males to their cause. Called "Passages," it consists of a set of programs for adolescent boys who are encouraged to "step up to the plate" and "become warriors for Christ." The announcement (available at http://www.thestate.com/mld/thestate/living/4817664.html, dated 27 December 2002) goes on to say:

> In ancient times as well as today, warriors have always fought together. Every fighting force is organized into platoons, squadrons, or units of some kind. By putting together this Passage group, we are forming a kind of fighting unit—a band of brothers. This unit has a single purpose of helping you learn to become a warrior for Christ and successfully navigate the passage into manhood.

Notice the deadly motifs of war and manhood, here organized and mobilized for a religious cause.

It is such thinking and such socialization that enabled, for example, Buford Furrow to shoot up a Jewish day-care center in California on August 10, 1999. It is the same thinking that has made a string of abortion clinic bombings and abortion doctor assassinations possible. Among many others, Reverend Michael Bray burned down a clinic in Dover, Delaware in February of 1984 and was eventually convicted of destroying seven clinics along the East Coast, and on July 29, 1994 Reverend Paul Hill (a friend of Bray) killed Dr. John Britton of Pensacola, Florida. Another associate of Bray, Rachelle Shannon, has also confessed to a series of bombings and to wounding Dr. George Tiller of Wichita, Kansas. From the Oklahoma City bombing by Timothy McVeigh to the string of attacks in 1998 and 1999 by Eric Robert Rudolph to Ruby Ridge and Waco, extremist and apocalyptic Christians have been involved in holy violence in this country.

For those who think these are isolated incidents (although dozens of incidents with the same theme and motivation cease to be "isolated"), some familiarity with the "Nuremberg Files" may suggest otherwise. Patterning their website (http://www.christiangallery.com/atrocity/) after the post-World War II trials of Nazi leaders for crimes against humanity, Christian anti-abortionists keep a list of abortion providers—including their work and sometimes home addresses—and judges, politicians, and "other blood flunkies" who support abortion rights. The language of the site is indisputably Christian and militant: "While we have every intention of fighting this until the day God's children are no longer legally slaughtered in this nation, we simply cannot effectively resist the evil at hand. . . . But because of the love God has for His slaughtered children, we have no doubt that the Living God will receive your donation as a sweet smelling savor arising to His nostrils and will bless you accordingly." Most disturbingly of all, when a pro-choice member of their list is killed, the name is crossed off with a thick black line.

There are other organized aspects to American Christian violence as well. A manual entitled *Army of God* is available online (http://www.armyofgod.com/AOGhistory.html) that gives instructions for conducting sabotage and violence against abortion clinics. Revered Bray himself wrote *A Time to Kill*, a justification of antiabortion violence. Of course, not all Christian violence in this country is directed against abortion providers. Some is targeted toward the government as a whole, to which we will return in the final chapter. Some is set against specific minorities (especially Jews and gays); the Westboro Baptist Church in Kansas maintains a website called Godhatesfags.com and travels to protest at funerals for gays and lesbians. Others stand against the general trend of "secularism" and "humanism" that some Christians, like Falwell and Robertson, perceive in this country.

The sources and inspirations for the violence are as varied as the targets, but they are all "cultural"—that is, aimed at resisting the current culture and at implementing a more Christian culture—and biblical. These groups, from the Ku Klux Klan to the "militia" movements to the extremist sects and churches, look to the Christian Bible for justification for their violence—and find it. There are too many groups and too many philosophies out there to discuss them all thoroughly here, which discussion would be further complicated by issues of communication and migration of membership, so we will choose one fairly significant and representative position to describe—the so-called Christian Identity movement.

Christian Identity (CI) is an example of extreme right-wing doctrine and its support of violence through the now-familiar language of cosmic struggle and eschatological consequences. The Kingdom Identity Ministries, for instance, takes as its motto "Conquer We Must, for our Cause is Just." They list their beliefs (http://kingidentity.com/doctrine.htm) as containing the usual biblical literalist claims about Jesus and the infallibility of scripture, but they also espouse the doctrine of "the elect," that is, that God "foreknew, chose and predestined the Elect from before the foundation of the world. . . . Only the called children of God can come to the Savior to hear His words and believe; those who are not of God, cannot hear his voice." In other words, not all Christians are even able to be Christians but merely those—the Kingdom Identity followers, we would presume—who are chosen by God to hear Christ's message.

After the familiar items of the creed, the beliefs turn to the issue of the "chosen people" and the "seedline" of the Christian people.

> We believe the White, Anglo-Saxon, Germanic and kindred people to be God's true, literal Children of Israel. Only this race fulfills every detail of Biblical Prophecy and World History concerning Israel and continues in these latter days to be heirs and possessors of the Covenants, Prophecies, Promises and Blessings YHVH God made to Israel. This chosen seedline making up the "Christian Nations" of the earth stands far superior to all other peoples in their call as God's servant race. Only these descendants of the 12 tribes of Israel scattered abroad have carried God's Word, the Bible, throughout the world, have used His Laws in the establishment of their civil governments and are the "Christians" opposed by the Satanic Anti-Christ forces of this world who do not recognize the true and living God.

Further, they assert, in a familiar refrain, that the Jews are spawn of the Devil—that they are literally his children through his sexual union with Eve that produced Cain. The "true Israel" is descended from Adam, who they claim was a white man. Thus, the white race was the one "created in God's image" (God being white, too, presumably) and the one that is a "separated people" from the world's wickedness and its other peoples. "This includes segregation from all non-white races, which are prohibited in God's natural divine order from ruling over Israel. Race-mixing is an abomination in the sight of Almighty God, a satanic attempt meant to destroy the chosen seedline, and is strictly forbidden by His Commandments." The appropriate Bible passages are cited.

Finally and predictably, homosexuality is condemned too. "We believe men and women should conduct themselves according to the role of their gender in the traditional Christian sense that God intended. Homosexuality is an abomination before God and should be punished by death." They cite Leviticus 20:13, which does in fact ordain: "If a man also lie with mankind, as he lieth with a woman, both of them have committed an abomination: they shall surely be put to death; their blood shall be upon them." For those who prefer New Testament sources, they mention Romans 1:32, which states "that they which commit such things are worthy of death."

In fact, CI followers have no trouble finding biblical support for their views; the statement of their creed is peppered with chapter-and-verse citations that appear to say precisely what they think it says. And the violent potential of these teachings, together with the remarkable level of conviction with which they are held, should not escape us, nor has it escaped the FBI. Christian Identity ideas and activities figured in the FBI's Project Megiddo on faith-based violence, a cause of concern for law enforcement, as indicated by director Louis Freeh's comment in 1994 that "With the coming of the next millennium, some religious/apocalyptic groups or individuals may turn to violence as they seek to achieve dramatic effects to fulfill their prophecies" (see http://www.religioustolerance.org/y2k_prob1.html).

Project Megiddo traces the roots of the Christian Identity movement to British Israelism, a movement from the nineteenth century that claimed the British were the direct descendants of the "ten lost tribes of Israel" and there-fore the true chosen people (although the British were hardly the first to make that claim). British Israelism came to America in the first decades of the twen-tieth century, and Wesley Swift is perhaps the most important leader in the early 1900s of what we might call American Israelism, or what would become the Christian Identity movement. From his church in California in the 1940s he mixed this latter-day "chosen people" theory with rampant anti-Semitism and extreme right-wing politics. In 1957 he changed the name of his church to the Church of Jesus Christ Christian, a name that is today associated with the Aryan Nations.

Swift's CI ideology was picked up and expanded by William Potter Gale, who added antigovernment (especially antitax) and paramilitary elements to it, giving it roughly the shape we see it in today. Since then, the CI movement has developed into a loosely organized collection of congregations and commu-nities, often with distinctly separatist views and practices—not just separation of their race from the other races, but separation of their "society" from the mainstream of American society. They have founded communes and practi-cally independent towns around the country, including "The Covenant, the Sword, and the Arm of the Lord" in Arkansas; Elohim City on the Oklahoma–Arkansas border; the Freeman Compound in Montana; the Aryan Nations compound in Idaho; the World Church of the Creator; the Worldwide Church of God; Randy Weaver's Ruby Ridge; and David Koresh's Waco Branch Davi-dian compound. Many of these settlements are heavily armed and ready to fight and die.

Folks like CI devotees obviously see themselves as a righteous minority in a sea of unrighteousness. They are quite literally at war; however, while other

Christians may be the "reserves" in the religious battle, Christian Identity members and other such organized factions are the "standing army." In fact, Kerry Noble, another CI spokesman, has written a booklet entitled *Prepare War!* that explains and justifies the Christian call to combat, evoking the famous passage in Exodus (15:3) in which Moses says that the Lord "is a man of war." Other CI personalities describe the entire Bible as "a book of war, a book of hate" (Juergensmeyer 2000: 146).

This war, like all religious wars, has two fronts. The first is temporal or material. The political and economic powers, in particular the government, are agents of evil, or at least of anti-Christianity (which is basically the same thing). The government, especially the judiciary, is seen as promoting secularism, gay rights, abortion rights, racial integration, feminism, and all the unbiblical things that CI enthusiasts hate so righteously. As such, Christianity is under attack, and this is a key to CI extremism and violence and much if not all of religious violence—they are already at war, they are not the aggressors. Rather, any force of resistance is purely *defensive*, defending themselves against the assaults of humanism and sinfulness. Abortion is an assault on Christian values. Gay, civil, and women's rights are assaults on Christian values. Separation of church and state is an assault on Christian values. The right-thinking Christian cannot help but respond to these assaults; they did not choose a war, but they have had one thrust upon them.

One front of the war, then, is to reconquer America for Christ—that is, to reinstill the Christian values upon which (they think) America was founded and from which it has drawn its strength. Even in less extreme circles of Christianity, this message is heard: political Christians, including what are called Reconstructionists, want to "reconstruct" American society with a biblical basis for both politics and culture. As Gary North puts it, it is "the moral obligation of Christians to recapture every institution for Jesus Christ" (Juergensmeyer 2000: 28). If a few people have to die in order to stop a greater evil, like abortion, then that is justifiable.

It is justifiable, of course, because there is a second and even higher front of the war, and this is the cosmic front. Christian Identity advocates, like many less militant Christians, believe in a literal and imminent end of the world, as foretold in Revelation. Somewhere in the course of the end (there is disagreement about the exact order of events), there will be a great, bloody, and final struggle between God's forces (Christians, whites in particular) and Satan's forces (non-Christians and nonwhites), which the forces of good must and will win. Defeat is inconceivable, and victory is already prophesied. But the slaughter will be almost unimaginable in its scope, and all will suffer.

Some Christians hold this apocalyptic view without much political motivation: Jesus will come, we should be on the side of right, and all will be well for us. However, many CI believers hold a particular interpretation of how events will proceed, one that calls for action here and now. Known as "postmillennialism," this view posits that the Second Coming of Jesus will only occur one thousand years *after* the creation of a godly, Christian kingdom on Earth. Premillennialists believe that Jesus will come before the creation of the godly kingdom and in fact create it. But postmillennialists, since the next era—the "next level"—cannot happen until the kingdom is already here for a millennium, are considerably more motivated to make changes *now*. Any delays or setbacks to Christian rule at the hands of the nonbeliever or nonchosen only postpone that much longer the return of the messiah. So action—even extreme action—is needed now.

This action may take the form of antiabortion violence, or of race baiting and race killing (even Charles Manson reportedly thought he was going to start a race war), or anti-Semitism and anti-Islamism, or pitched battles with government troops, or bombs aimed at civilian offices and installations. But one thing is certain: as long as such beliefs possess people, action will take some—more than likely, violent—form.

Case Study 4: Sikhism—Saint Soldiers

No nation, sect or community can survive and prosper unless it has a band of persons who are prepared to die, to uphold its faith, integrity, unity, its tradition and way of life. That is what the history of the world demonstrates clearly.
—*Sikh teaching*

Sikhism (from the Hindi for "disciple") is a religion that has glorified violent struggle and has been associated with armed conflicts in the Punjab region of northern India. In fact, it arose at a time and from an environment in which struggle and conflict were endemic and almost certainly to be ingrained into the tradition—namely, around 1500 C.E., during the confrontation between Muslim and Hindu cultures and forces, particularly in northern India. Today there are some 13 million Sikhs in India, constituting less than 2 percent of the population; however, they are concentrated in the Punjab area, where the 10 million local Sikhs make up 60 percent of the population.

The era of the 1500s in India was a time of political strife. In the 700s Muslims had first made their way into India, during their great expansion from Arabia that also carried them into Spain and to the southern border of France. By the 1500s there was a Muslim dynasty established in India, known as the Mughal (which gives us the English term "mogul" for someone of great power and influence). At roughly the same date, the future founder of Sikhism, Guru Nanak, had a mystical experience from which he concluded: "There is no

Case Study 4: Sikhism—Saint Soldiers (continued)

Hindu, there is no Muslim." Instead, the new discipline represented a sort of protest both against foreign domination and social injustice as well as a rejection of the more strident and restrictive aspects of both faiths. Guru Nanak simultaneously criticized what he perceived as the fanaticism and intolerance of Islam and the pointless ritualism and caste prejudice of Hinduism. Sikhism recognizes no caste distinctions and even includes women as social equals.

Guru Nanak died in 1539 and started a succession of gurus that would end in its human form but never really end, simply taking a different and non-human form. Meanwhile, around 1600 the Mughal rulers of India began to suppress Sikhism, and the Sikhs fought back; in particular, many members of the marshal Jat (farmer) caste joined the movement, affecting its course. In the late 1500s the Sikh temple at Amritsar, which became the holiest site in Sikhism, was constructed. However, the reigning guru, Arjan, was executed and martyred by Muslim authorities in 1606, setting a dangerous precedent. Subsequently, a religious movement evolved more and more into an armed struggle.

It was the tenth and final (human) guru, Gobind Singh (1675–1708) who put the finishing touches on the military development of Sikhism. In 1699 he created a new branch of the movement known as the Khalsa or "company of the pure." The Khalsa were to personify the ideal Sikh, the godly warrior, the saint soldier. As one modern Sikh website has put it:

> The essential condition for entry into the Sikh fold is self-surrender and devotion to the Guru and God. Readiness for the supreme sacrifice or of offering one's head on the palm of one's hand to the Guru is an essential condition laid down by the Gurus for becoming a Khalsa Sikh. Seeking death, not for personal glory, winning reward or going to heaven, but for the purpose of protecting the weak and the oppressed is what made the Khalsa brave and invincible. This has become a traditional reputation of the Khalsa. Right from the times of the Gurus till the last India–Pakistan conflict (1971), the Sikhs have demonstrated that death in the service of truth, justice and country, is part of their character and their glorious tradition. They do not seek martyrdom, they attain it. Dying is the privilege of heroes. It should, however, be for an approved or noble cause.

Accordingly, Khalsa Sikhs were given five symbols to bear as a sign of their purity, devotion, and readiness to take up arms. Known as the five "K's," they include *kirpan*, or the sword; *kesh*, or uncut hair; *kanga*, or comb; *kachh* or *katcha*, a type of undergarment; and *kara*, or steel bracelet. All of these are intended to set the Sikh in general and the Khalsa Sikh in particular apart from other people, and the *kirpan* is obviously intended as a literal weapon to defend the faithful and the weak.

Guru Gobind Singh's prediction of the need for Sikhs to fight in self-defense was realized in what are referred to as the "Lesser Holocaust" and the "Greater Holocaust," two defeats and massacres at the hands of the Muslim forces. Occurring in 1746 and 1762, respectively, these reverses included the

Case Study 4: Sikhism—Saint Soldiers (continued)

martyring of many Khalsa fighters and even the sack and defilement of the Golden Temple at Amritsar. Eventually, though, the Khalsa armies captured the city of Lahore (1799) and ruled the Punjab until their defeat at the hands of the British in 1849. Yet another foreign invader had come to deprive and defile the company of the pure.

The Sikh notion of evil and of apostasy (falling from the faith) will round out our discussion of their marshal spirit. Evil exists, of course, as no religion can deny. For Sikhism, evil, like everything else, is created by the one god, but it has a special purpose to serve—that is, to test the character of humans. "Suffering is the remedy and comfort the disease," Guru Nanak reportedly said. Evil challenges us—and the greater the person, the greater the evil he or she faces. Thus, evil and evil-minded people are to be avoided, as they are the only doorway to karma and the endless cycle of birth and death. The best defense against evil is the company of the good and the pious, that is, other Sikhs. Guru Arjan wrote that Sikhs should separate themselves from the godless. Or, as Guru Nanak expressed it: "Make Truth the knife. Let it be sharpened on the whetstone of 'The Name.' Keep it protected in a sheath of virtue."

This is why, as in most, if not all, religions, it is so important to reclaim those who have strayed from the flock. They, like all apostates, are the most imminent threat to any religion or movement, since they know the movement intimately and evidence the possibility of living happily without it. They are poisonous as an example of successful nonbelief. Therefore, like many faiths, Sikhism makes a special mission of "reconverting" such people, persuading them that it is somehow a shortcoming of theirs that they cannot see the group's truth. Many apostates, they argue, understand deep down that they have "wronged themselves and their community," and through encouragement, assistance, and "re-education" they can be brought back into the fold. Otherwise, they constitute perhaps the worst thing that can happen to any group—an "us" becoming a "them."

Case Study 5: Warrior Cults—Thugs and Assassins

As Elliott has described in his book *Warrior Cults* (1995), humanity has produced many religious sects that made violence a central if not sacramental aspect of their faith and practice. Many of these might seem unlikely, for example, the fighting monastic orders in Christianity such as the Knights Templar. Two particular groups, which have given their names to common English terms for antisocial violence, are Thuggee and Assassin.

Case Study 5: Warrior Cults—Thugs and Assassins (continued)

Thuggee was a killer cult in India, starting around 1200 C.E. and continuing until the 1800s, when it was brought to light and stamped out by British authorities. It was devoted to the Hindu goddess Kali, who is well known as the goddess of death. She is often represented as a black-skinned female with four arms—one holding a sword, another the severed head of a demon, a third making a gesture of peace, and the last grasping for power. Often she stands or dances on the body of her husband Siva and wears a necklace of severed heads and earrings of human corpses.

Practitioners of Thuggee believed that Kali ordered them to kill as a sacrifice to her. One of their legends states that during a mythical battle between her and a demon-lord, she brushed off sweat, which turned into two men. She gave these men the *rumal*, or yellow scarf, to use to strangle demons, but when the battle was over she insisted that they keep it to kill any strangers they would encounter. Yet another story tells of the goddess devouring the bodies of the victims of Thuggee and turning her own body into the symbolic Thuggee weapons—the magical pick-ax (*kussee*), the dagger, and the *rumal*.

The typical method of Thuggee ritual murder was to waylay a band of travelers or pilgrims. A small set of Thugs would meet and often join the travelers, perhaps accompanying them for several days, often picking up more Thugs along the way until they might outnumber the original travelers. At an opportune moment, they would select a spot to conduct their assault, and two members (*beles*, or grave diggers) would prepare graves with their *kussee*. Ideally three Thugs per traveler would attack the band, one strangling each victim with the sacred yellow scarf while the other two held him facedown. When all the victims were killed, the Thugs prayed to Kali, offered them to her as a sacrifice, and usually dismembered the bodies and pushed them into mass graves. Sometimes they camped on top of the graves and celebrated a feast called Tuponee. For this event, they spread a cloth in the tent and sat on it, placing a consecrated pick-ax, a piece of silver for an offering, and some special communion sugar on the cloth. They then dug a small hole in the ground and poured in the sugar and holy water, prayed, and then all the killers consumed some sugar in a kind of communion meal.

Naturally, the Thugs did not consider themselves to be psycho-killers or even deviants. Rather, they considered themselves to be good and pious men. Kali herself had ordained the murders and chosen the victims, for which members used omens to determine her wishes. When they were not killing, they were normal people, often policemen or doctors or government-officials. Some were even employees or servants of British colonial families. And they followed certain "rules" of killing, too. Women, for instance, were not to be killed, nor the handicapped or lepers or the blind. Specific craftsmen like carpenters, blacksmiths and masons were taboo also. Finally, members of the Kamal caste were

Case Study 5: Warrior Cults—Thugs and Assassins (continued)

left alone, as well as anyone herding a cow or female goat. Interestingly, it was forbidden to kill a tiger; Thuggee identified itself with tigers as fellow killers of humans (making the killing of tigers a kind of "self-violence"). During their attacks, Thugs also sometimes took property from their victims, but it should be obvious that robbery was not the motive for the killings.

The Assassins were a Muslim cult that functioned around the time of the Crusades (1100–1200 C.E.). They were, like the Ninjas of Japan, skilled at infiltration and surprise attack. They were especially feared because their fanatical devotion made them cold and efficient killers who could not be bribed or scared away from their appointed duties.

What we call today the Assassins were actually members of a Shi'ite Muslim sect known as Nizari Ismaili. Shi'ites ("partisans") generally believed and believe still that the leadership of Islam should be in the hands of a successor ("caliph") of Muhammad but that through political intrigues this succession had been corrupted by the worldly (and majority) Sunnis. Ismailis as a particular form of Shi'ism are devoted to Ismail, the supposed seventh successor who was passed over by Sunni authorities.

Around 100 C.E. Ismailis rose to power in Egypt, and a man named Nizar was in line to become the next caliph there, but he was overlooked in favor of his brother. Ismaili followers of Nizar—the Nizari Ismailis—split from the mainstream of the sect and organized their own "assassin" attackers to conduct operations against the government. They developed into an ascetic sect—no drugs or alcohol were allowed, and absolute loyalty to the leaders and the beliefs of the group was demanded. The discipline of the sect included seven "ranks" of initiation, from the pre-initiates (*fidai* or devoted ones) to Grand Masters (*dai'd-duat* or chief missionaries) and ultimately the *imam*, or holy leader himself. For some hundred and fifty years this group terrorized the Muslim world, although engaging in alchemy, astrology, and magic, until their reign of terror was crushed by authorities around 1260.

1951 - Hoffer

RETROSPECT AND PROSPECT

For the right cause, there is almost nothing that humans can—or should—do. And true believers always believe that theirs is the right cause. Give that group and its cause a higher authority, one that relieves them of responsibility, and put them in a situation of "war," and virtually all the bonds that hold humans back from extreme cruelty and destructiveness are sundered.

There are many other religious groups and doctrines that have engaged, and engage today, in violence, and there are also many religious groups and individuals that never engage in such violence. Our claim here is not that all religions at all times are hostile and hurtful but that religion provides the fertile circumstances for both.

We have one final point to make. We have already seen that, in relation to violence, there is nothing particularly unique about religion—that religious factors contribute to violence in the same way as other psychological and social factors. However, in addition to their spiritual motivations, religious movements—like families, villages, churches, and society in general—have quite practical (political and cultural) *interests*. When any interest identified as a distinct and crucial aspect of group activity mixes with issues of identity and ideolgy, what emerges is perhaps the most complete program for violence possible. This—political violence—is the subject of the next two chapters.

CHAPTER

8

POLITICAL VIOLENCE

Introduction

Much of the violence in the world is what we would call "interpersonal," that is, aggression toward individuals by individuals, as in the case of domestic violence or most criminal activity. However, a significant quantity of the world's violence—including the violence discussed in the last two chapters—is mass or group violence, carried out against members of a collective by members of a collective. As we have established, group violence was not invented in the twentieth century, and it was not even originated by humans; many species, especially "social" species, engage in group-based, or "intra-species," aggression (see Chapter 2).

What humans, especially humans in the modern world, add to the basic ingredient of intergroup hostility is a (more or less) conscious element of identity (a "name") and ideology (a "cause" or doctrine or belief). Group integration is sufficient to spawn all the violence we would ever care to see. Addition of identity and ideology turns up the heat. The final ingredient in the recipe is interest—something worth fighting over.

Interest is not absent in "nonpolitical" conflicts; it is not even absent in nonhuman conflicts. Individual animals may fight over food or mates. Aggregations of animals may fight over territory and such. These are surely matters of interest; and interest in the sense we are using it is any resource that an individual or group needs or wants. In situations containing finite resources and multiple groups, conflicts of interest stem from competition. No doctrines or ideologies are necessary to pit group against group in often deadly and even genocidal competition. And it is no surprise that individuals in one group would pursue their common interests in frequent indifference to the suffering of the other, since they are "other."

In the human case, groups tend to have names, cultures, histories, institutions, and typically a shared sense of "destiny," of going somewhere "together." These groups—societies, parties, classes, countries, ethnic groups, and so forth—engage in a form of communal competition and violence that

205

can only be called "political." And although "political" violence may be less common than interpersonal violence (that is, there are fewer wars every day than wife beatings or muggings), it is probably in sum the more destructive form; interpersonal violence may harm one or a few individuals at a time, while political violence can kill or maim thousands or millions at a time.

All violence is, to an extent, about interest and power, but political violence is an expression of a group's interests and its power to achieve those interests in a direct and explicit way. In fact, we may think of politics in general as the aspect of human society and culture concerning intergroup or intra-species power. As such, it is part of that pseudospeciation Lorenz (1966; Chapter 2) spoke of that we get from our primate heritage. It consists of features like xenophobia (a fear or dislike for members of other groups), territoriality, organization, and a heightened level of violence compared to "internal" violence, as illustrated in the case studies of Chapters 3 and 4.

This chapter, then, in coordination with the following one, will explore violence in its political context. We will look at war, revolution, terrorism, genocide, ethnic conflict, and other related forms of intergroup aggression—all united by the phenomenon of identity groups with ideologies pursuing their group interests. In the process we will raise and reinforce earlier ideas about dualistic ("us" versus "them") thinking, dehumanization and demonization, and legitimization/justification, introducing as well a few new ideas, such as the role of elites and of "identity politics."

POLITICS AS A MACROSOCIAL FACTOR IN VIOLENCE

As we know now, the occurrence of violence is very much related to other characteristics—macrosocial, microsocial, and psychocultural—of a society. We have already studied the connection between violence and one area of macrosocial structure: a society's economic system. Equally related to its level of violence (and to the economic system) is the second main macrosocial area: the political system. Anthropologists speak of political systems as falling along a continuum of *political integration*, each level of which is identified with a distinct level of violence. A society's level of political integration is determined by three factors:

1. Size of society—the larger a society, the more integrated it is.
2. Centralization of power—the more centralized the power in a society, the more integrated it is. That is, if only one or a few people control most or all of the power, then power is very centralized. If power is more dispersed, so that many or all people share power (or, in the extreme, if "power" as such is not even recognized at all), then power is decentralized.

3. Amount of *coercion*—the more coercion (force or threat of force) available to the "powerful" members of society, the more integrated it is. Power may also flow from *authority* (i.e., legitimate power based on skill, knowledge, office, or other social traits) or *persuasion* (i.e., the ability to influence people, usually either through effective speech or manipulation resources). However, leaders without coercion cannot compel their "followers" to follow and depend more on personal rather than formal means of directing the behavior of others.

In terms of level of political integration, then, there are four political systems, with very different attitudes toward and experiences of violence. These systems are *band, tribe, chiefdom,* and *state*. These are ideal types, and actual societies may fall between the ideals in practice.

1. *Band.* A band is a small, decentralized political unit without "formal" leadership. Bands are usually not even full "societies" but often the local residential groups of a society that is distinguished by its shared language, religion, and territory. For example, most foraging societies lived traditionally in discrete local bands, which traveled and hunted and camped independently of each other and only assembled on special (for instance, ritual) occasions and when food and water allowed. Each band was quite small—basically a family unit, often numbering no more than a handful of individuals and at most perhaps fifty or so—and without a distinct formal political structure. Ordinarily, a senior member (usually male) held some decision-making prerogative, but this "headman" could not coerce people into obedience to his will, and the culture tended to discourage such behavior. The Utku from Chapter 3 are a good example of a band-level society, as are the Australian aboriginals and the !Kung bushmen of the Kalahari. All such societies possess clear "leveling mechanisms," cultural traits that limit the power of any incipient "ruler" and that even proscribe leadership and domination as undesirable. Among these mechanisms is an attitude of egalitarianism within the group; also the very fluidity of the group makes coercive leadership difficult. If one member attempted to lord it over the others, the others could simply leave the band, join another band, or form their own. Band membership is not mandatory or permanent and is constantly fluctuating. Finally, there is little wealth or specialization of labor, so there is really nothing to be leader of. Consequently, band-level societies tend to be among the most nonviolent on earth.
2. *Tribe.* A tribe is a larger, somewhat more centralized political entity with the beginnings of some formal political structure. Tribes may number in the hundreds or even thousands and may consist of multiple local groups. Tribal-level organization is common among pastoral people and some horticulturalists. There may still not be any "leader" of the whole tribe,

but the society does have some institutions or agents of political power. A few examples of tribal "politics" would be a council of elders, a head of a lineage or other kinship grouping, an age set (normally men of a certain age, say, from late teens to early thirties, who function as the army and/or police force of society), a warrior club (as in the case of the Cheyenne from Chapter 4), or a religious specialist, who may act as mediator and problem solver. The point is that, with larger populations and more surplus wealth to defend (or maybe to steal from other societies), coordination and problem solving become more critical and permanent features of society. Hence, tribal-level societies, like the warlike pastoralists of East Africa or pre-Columbian North America, can be quite hostile and aggressive. Some, like the Cheyenne or the Yanomamo, value bravery, strength, and fearlessness in combat as high virtues.

3. *Chiefdom.* A chiefdom is a political system that organizes relatively large populations, often encompassing multiple local or regional groups, under the authority (symbolic and/or literal) of a chief or a hierarchy of chiefs. Chiefdoms are quite diverse, ranging from cases where the chief is a ritual figure with little practical power to cases where the chief is almost monarchical in his power. They are most common among horticultural societies with their fairly large populations, sedentary settlements, surplus wealth, and at least somewhat specialized division of labor; they can also occur among larger and more productive pastoralist societies. These characteristics unite to entail if not require formal leadership for coordinating economic activity, making decisions and settling disputes, and providing for defense. In the most formal cases, chiefs may be considered to the owners and managers of the land and other resources, and subjects may be compelled to contribute to the treasury of the chief(s) as well as to the labor, including military labor, of the chiefdom. In such instances, the chief or chiefs may have and need an armed contingent to enforce their will against outsiders and even insiders. Not all chiefdoms are equally violent and aggressive, but the potential for violence and aggression exists and is frequently developed. Certainly, the "natural" egalitarianism of bands is lost as society becomes stratified—giving people a justification for fighting and something to fight about.

4. *State.* A state is a highly centralized political system. It consists of a central government of formal and explicit leaders with power over a specific territory (often identified with a border, which is defended) to make laws, set the local currency and collect taxes, and maintain an army and fight wars. States are a relatively recent invention in human history, none existing before about five or six thousand ago. States depend on extremely productive economic systems, namely intensive agriculture, to produce the surplus and wealth necessary to finance the activities of the state. Additionally, the techniques required by intensive agriculture, such as

irrigation, contribute to the need for centralized administration; large building projects call for extensive coordination of labor, planning, supervision, and funding. Consequently, roles of leadership and authority arise to provide these functions. Some of the earliest states, as in Mesopotamia, were "temple communities" in which the priests served as the ritual and economic/political leaders of society. The state was often nothing more than a highly organized city, referred to as a city-state. Because of its sedentary population and wealth, the city-state was a natural target for the predations of other city-states or of nonstate societies such as tribes, so offense and defense were inherent elements in state political systems. As we know from the archaeological record, the first states were born at war with each other, and their local autonomy was soon lost as one or another state rose to dominate and even conquer neighboring states, creating "multistate" states, or *empires*. States, ultimately, are not "natural" or "objective" entities but are historical products—and generally products of violence and war. States are therefore perpetually made, unmade, and remade over the course of history as power shifts and wars are won or lost. The point is that states are almost innately violent, to which the historical experience of conquering and being conquered merely contributes. Regardless of the specific "political system" of the state—monarchy, oligarchy, democracy, or what have you—states always have enemies and must be prepared to defend against—or offend against—these enemies.

UNDERSTANDING POLITICAL VIOLENCE

> Intense political commitment is usually bad. It is bad in its motives.
> It is bad in its consequences.
>   —*Peter Berger*

The political system of a society, which is itself largely a product of the economic system, is therefore closely related to the attitude toward and incidence of violence in that society. In other words, in a way, politics helps to *explain* violence. Thomas Hobbes, the great early-modern political philosopher, theorized a relation between politics and violence, but in reverse: he suggested that before there was politics there was "war of all against all." In other words, war and violence resulted from too little politics. However, as we have seen, it is more the case that war and violence result from an abundance of politics—violence was constrained, and war virtually nonexistent, before fairly modern political systems evolved. On the other hand, Karl Marx argued that struggle, if not open conflict, was the natural order and motor of all societies; in particular, his theory was that class struggle was the defining force behind all history and all social change.

In other and more specific ways, politics serves to foment violence, since political conditions and factors meet all of the criteria we have identified for promoting violence. In fact, the nature of political violence makes it, along with religious violence, an almost perfect satisfaction of Zimbardo's and Baumeister's conditions for violence and an almost perfect manifestation of not only facile but legitimate violence. For one, essentially all perpetrators of political violence legitimize their actions as self-defense. Almost no warrior, even the most horrible one, deems himself or herself to the provocateur of violence but rather as having been provoked into it. Even the Nazis explained their aggression not as "evil" or belligerence but as "revenge" or restoration of fairness or justice after the punitive peace settlement of World War I, as the unification of the various German peoples into one state, and as the pursuit of *lebensraum* (living space) for the German people. Although we do not condone the violence of Nazi Germany, we cannot help but see the arguments for the legitimacy of war—restoration of fairness and justice, unification of a people, and land for that people—as those we ourselves could make and have made.

Further, as in the case of religious violence, political violence creates a classic us-versus-them situation, one that all too often collapses into a black-and-white way of thinking about the two sides. Warriors generally do not nor can they afford to see many shades of gray. War almost demands a certainty of action and right that shifts all light grays to white and all dark grays to black. Commitment to violence is much weaker when the issues are complex. Having thus dichotomized the world into "those who are with us" and "those who are against us," the group effect comes into play. We may even be encouraged if not required to give up our individuality—to de-individuate—in the name and the interest of the group. We call this kind of sacrifice of the self "patriotism," that is, commitment to or belief in the fatherland (*patrie*). To speak against one's own country and government is tantamount to treason in the eyes of many; once the bullets start flying, criticism and questioning must stop. To question one's own group is somehow to support the enemy group; it is unpatriotic.

An effective political group must have an effective leader, so the "leadership principle" arises. The leader not only heads but personifies the group; he not only gives voice to the group's interest but largely defines them and "sets the agenda" for the group. He may even be central to defining the group itself—who qualifies and what the qualifications are. He is certainly central to keeping the group integrated, focused, and mobilized. (We use the masculine pronoun here only because most such leaders have actually been male). He also commands more or less complete obedience, even adoration, especially depending on the level of crisis at the time; he is not unknown to create or exaggerate crisis. Overstreet and Overstreet (1964: 280) comment that for an extremist group or party or society a "sense of impending disaster is their most marketable ware. An understanding of this fact is vital to an understanding of their line and their tactics."

Such leaders—the fuehrers, duces, and other dictators—we can refer to as demagogues. Lowenthal and Guterman (1949) have summarized some of their common techniques, including the message of doom just mentioned. In addition, they may foment a sense of being cheated or deprived by some other group (e.g., the Nazi dogma that the Jews were responsible for their problems) or of being victims of a vast conspiracy. They may emphasize the corruptness of the existing regime or society, including sexual corruption. They tend to express a distrust for foreigners and a concern for polluting the "purity" of the group, ideologically or physically. They allow for no middle ground, no compromise, and no exceptions; the individual is either with them (on the side of right) or against them. Finally, the emergency is so dire that there is no time for the "luxury of thought"; now is a time for actions, not questions.

We should keep in mind, of course, that in any large and complex society in any particularly challenging situation, there will usually be competing "elites" vying for power and influence and offering to take the group in different directions. A good example is the contemporary Palestinians, divided as they are between the (comparatively) moderate al-Fatah PLO of Yasir Arafat (now deceased) and the much more extreme factions of Hamas, Hezbollah, and others. Within the Kurdish "nationalist" movement, various tribes, families, regions, and parties compete with each other for authority even as they compete with "enemy" forces. As we will see in the next chapter, in the emergencies of the French and Bolshevik revolutions there were dramatically different and opposed parties attempting to seize the day and impose their definitions and solutions on the conflicts.

Finally, in analyzing any instance of political violence, we should be aware of three overarching factors—the *claims*, the *grievances*, and the *passions*. All political violence is *about* something; it is goal oriented. Sometimes other forms of violence are goal oriented too, but none more so or more clearly so than political violence. The groups implicated in such violence are, among other things, *interest groups*—that is, they have shared interests and act in concert (although not always in unison) to achieve those interests. The elites may define those interests differently, as well as the path to achieving the interests, but political groups always have interests. When some force—especially another political group—obstructs those interests, conflict is likely to ensue. So, the claims of a group may include political power, land, wealth, resources, education and employment, cultural survival, even political independence and creation of its own state. The claim generally takes the form of "we demand/deserve/are entitled to X because we are Y," with Y being their name, shared identity, or shared culture and history.

The Y's in the argument are the "grounds" that the group advances for making the claim. In the modern world, "culture" is a particularly effective ground for arguing political claims. If the group can prove or show that it is a legitimate cultural group, with its own language, religion, customs, history, and so forth, the claim is often accepted. Other kinds of grounds include racial and national-origin issues, as well as "class" in some cases, although the latter is more controversial. So, for example, the Israeli–Palestinian conflict can be dissected for its claims and grounds. The Israelis claim a territory and a right to govern that territory. The Palestinians, unfortunately, claim much the same territory. The Israelis base their claim on various grounds: the biblical ground that their God promised that land to them, the historical ground that they once occupied and ruled it, and the political ground that they need a state of their own to be safe and self-determining in the world. The Palestinians base their claim on similar grounds: the historical ground that they conquered the land over a thousand years ago, the contemporary ground that they were the current occupants of the land (until a few decades ago), potentially even the religious ground that they too are descendants of the biblical patriarchs.

As is painfully clear, the claims and grounds of two different groups can be equally compelling but mutually exclusive, which is one reason why such conflicts can be particularly intractable. There simply is no political solution that can meet both claims simultaneously and satisfactorily. The result is almost guaranteed dissatisfaction with whatever outcome eventuates. This dissatisfaction is one of any number of grievances that the groups can have against each other. Again, in the same case, the Israelis' grievances against the Palestinians include old religious ones along with more present ones, such as the history of violence and terrorism between them. Every time a bus or café in Israel is blown up, another grievance is added; every time a peace settlement is vacated, another grievance is added. On the Palestinian side, their fundamental grievance is that their land was taken from them by a third party and given to their enemy. Each defeat in a subsequent war is an additional grievance, as are the housing developments built on occupied land, not to mention the generations of refugee life in Gaza and the West Bank. Such grievances make it much more difficult, if not ultimately impossible, to reach a resolution. In fact, quite honestly, many people on both sides no longer desire a peaceful resolution.

The third element in a political conflict, especially a more lasting and violent one, is passion. Political groups are interest groups, but they are not just interest groups; that is, they are not purely rational and unemotional groups. Groups in political conflict are often if not ordinarily *angry*, and their anger shows in their words and their actions. In the case of the French Revolution, discussed at some length in the next chapter, the language of the revolution was shot through with references to anger, vengeance, and almost apocalyptic hatred for the enemy (the privileged classes and the counterrevolutionaries). During the Cambodian revolution of Pol Pot in the 1970s (discussed later), people were encouraged to develop a "burning rage toward the enemy" and to resist them with "class ardor and fury." Indeed, people can be moved to extremes with, and cannot be moved to extremes without, whipping up their emotions. However, at the same time, maybe the sinister aspect of political violence is how these extreme emotions can be "institutionalized" or "bureaucratized" so that systematic violence becomes almost devoid of passion. Thus two uniquely human traits—passion and bureaucracy—combine all too easily into apparatuses of violence with all the qualities of enduring and extreme aggression.

A TYPOLOGY OF POLITICAL VIOLENCE

States are the major players on the international political scene in the modern age. Every part of the world has been absorbed into one state or another, some extraordinarily large (like the United States, Russia, or China) and some quite small. However, even in today's world, states have not succeeded in eradicating all other competing forms of identity, interest, and organization, and it would be a serious mistake to ignore this fact. Despite the efforts of state governments to "flatten" social and cultural difference, there still exist within (and sometimes across) states other groups and identities that command people's allegiances and motivate their actions. This is a conceptual and practical problem for states, as we will see below. First, states like to claim a monopoly on loyalty and "patriotism," not to mention resources, wealth, manpower, and "legitimate force." Second, states often face real and significant physical threats from these nonstate entities, to the point of being torn apart by them in some instances.

Therefore, we cannot speak exclusively of the "violence of states," let alone of the "violence between states." Accordingly, our typology identifies two types of "political players" and four types of political violence. The players will be called polities and peoples. A *polity* is a sovereign political entity, usually but not always a state. A *people* is a recognized and usually named political grouping, often an "ethnic group" but sometimes also a political party or class or other kind of social mass, that is not autonomous or sovereign but is often if not always struggling to be. The four types of violence, then, are polity versus polity, people versus polity, polity versus people, and people versus people. Although they share a variety of characteristics, each of these types generates a somewhat different dynamic of violence.

Polity versus Polity

> War is the continuation of diplomacy by other means.
> —*Clausewitz*

In the modern world, the most familiar type of political violence (and the only one that is considered truly "legitimate") is polity-versus-polity violence, or what we usually call *war*. It is "external" violence, since by definition a political system can only make war against an external enemy, not itself (the case of "civil war" will be discussed below). As we have seen, states reserve the right unto themselves to make war, and they have tended to use that right prolifically. Pitirim Sorokin, the famous Russian historian, calculated that his home country had only known one totally peaceful quarter-century in the last thousand years; another way of looking at this fact is that since the year 900, Russia had been at war in forty-six out of every hundred years of its history. Lest you conclude that Russia is uniquely violent, he computed that England was at war fifty-six out of every hundred years, and Spain even more often than that.

Of course, states did not invent external conflict. During the thousands of years of human history prior to states, groups often conducted violence against each other, although often in less lethal and more ritualized forms. As we saw in Chapter 4, intergroup violence between prestate societies could take the form of *raids, feuds, revenge attacks*, and *duels*. Some societies actually had or have physical contests between villages or societies, like wrestling matches or fights, into which all the hostility of the groups were funneled, leaving them relatively peaceful outside of these occasions. Prestate violence was often not about inflicting death, much less about conquest, although injury and death could and did occur.

However, state societies excel at intergroup violence, and these political systems were conceived in and by war. Originally, war was probably little more than organized and sustained raiding between states or city-states (and there are those who argue that it is little more today). However, already by the 2300s B.C.E., state raiding had transformed into state conquest and "empire building" by the first great leader and personality in history, Sargon of Akkad. The next four thousand years of human history would be roughly the story of the shifting fortunes of states and state leaders—kings, princes, generals, party chairmen, and presidents.

We can distinguish various kinds of war. *Wars of conquest* involve attempts to defeat an enemy so completely that its land, population, and wealth can be integrated into the conqueror's state. *Wars of exploitation*, on the other hand, tend to involve attempts to exploit a weakness in an enemy to wrest from it some concessions, such as land, tribute, labor, or positions of advantage; arguably, more wars have been fought for exploitation than for conquest. *Wars of interdiction* are fought to stop or prevent the enemy from doing something; for instance, the American war against the Barbary pirates was meant to interdict their piracy of American shipping. Similarly, the Iraq war of 2003 is claimed by some to interdict Iraq's ability to build and use destructive weapons and wage war on its neighbors. *Wars of liberation* are fought to free a friendly state or society from enemy aggression or domination or to bring that state some benefit or blessing (as seen by the liberator). During the French Revolution and the early Napoleonic era, the French perceived their European wars as bringing freedom from monarchs and tyrants to the peoples of Europe. The Soviet Union also saw its export of war as liberation of oppressed people from capitalism and colonialism. America's first Gulf war in 1991 was intended to liberate Kuwait.

The reference to the Soviet Union also brings up the issue of *cold wars* and *proxy wars*. Cold wars are conditions of hostility between societies that do not break into open conflict. Proxy wars are conflicts that major states fight indirectly, by supporting client or proxy states that fight each other or one of the major states. The Korean and Vietnam wars were proxy wars between the United States and the USSR or China, as were many of the local conflicts in Africa and Latin America.

The point here is that war is not an irrational action on the part of political system. As Clausewitz suggested, war is part of a state's diplomatic tool kit; states decide when it is in their interest to go to war and when it is not. They are not always correct, of course, but the decision is all the same one based on calculation and cost.

Finally, it should be recognized that, even in a world of states, not all polity-versus-polity violence is state-versus-state. For example, some of the most pivotal conflicts in human history have been nonstate-versus-state conflicts, such as the invasions of the Aryans into ancient India, the conquests of the Huns and Visigoths and other tribes that eventually toppled Rome, and the "world war" of the Mongols against every state from China to Austria. Similarly, states do not limit their aggression to other states. Much violence has been state-versus-nonstate, usually for two related purposes—conversion to Christianity and colonialism. We should think of all the conflicts between European states and the indigenous peoples of the world, from 1492 until the 1960s in some cases, as state-versus-nonstate wars. Interestingly, although there was ultimately no possible justification for such aggression—what had the American Indians or the Africans ever done to the Europeans?— Europeans nevertheless went to great lengths to justify and legitimize their conquests. One of the most famous, and most pathetic, attempts to do so was the reading of the "Requerimiento" by Spanish conquistadors to the peoples of America who were about to be colonized. This statement supposedly gave the people a chance to accept Spanish–Christian authority and avoid war, but its rejection was essentially taken as a declaration of war, making subsequent aggression fully justified. Never mind that the declaration was read in Latin, often not even within earshot of the natives. (See Box 8.1.)

8.1   *The Requerimiento (Abridged)*

On the part of the king and queen ... we their servants notify and make known to you, as best we can, that the Lord our God, living and eternal, created the heaven and the earth, and one man and one woman, of whom you and we, and all the men of the world, were and are descendants, as well as all those who come after us....

Of all these nations God our lord gave charge to one man called St. Peter, that he should be lord and superior to all the men in the world, that all should obey him, and that he should be the head of the whole human race, whenever men should live, and under whatever law, sect, or belief they should be; and he gave him the world for his kingdom and jurisdiction....

One of these pontiffs, who succeeded that St. Peter as lord of the world ... made donation of these islands and mainland to the aforesaid king and queen and to their successors, our lords, with all that there are in these territories, as is contained in certain writings which passed upon the subject as aforesaid, which you can see if you wish.

So their highnesses are kings and lords of these islands and mainland by virtue of this donation.... Wherefore, as best we can, we ask and require that you consider what we have said to you, and that you take the time that shall be necessary to understand and deliberate upon it, and that you acknowledge the Church as the ruler and superior of the whole world and the high priest called Pope and in his name the king and queen Dona Juana our lords, in his place, as superiors and lords and kings of these islands and this mainland by virtue of the said donation, and that you consent and permit that these religious fathers declare and preach to you the aforesaid.

If you do so you will do well, and that which you are obliged to do to their highnesses, and we in their name shall receive you in all love and charity, and shall leave you your wives and your children and your lands free without servitude, that you may do with them and with yourselves freely what you and think best, and they shall not compel you to turn Christians unless you yourselves, when informed of the truth, should wish to be converted to our holy Catholic faith, as almost all the inhabitants of the rest of the islands have done....

But if you do not do this or if you maliciously delay in doing it, I certify to you that with the help of God we shall forcefully enter into your country and shall make war against you in all ways and manners that we can, and shall subject you to the yoke and obedience of the Church and of their highnesses may command; and we shall take away your goods and shall do to you all the harm and damage that we can, as to vassals who do not obey and refuse to receive their lord and resist and contradict him; and we protest that the deaths and losses which shall accrue from this are your fault, and not that of their highnesses, or ours, or of these soldiers who come with us. . . .

Source: Sir Arthur Helps, *The Spanish Conquest in America and Its Relation to the History of Slavery and to the Government of Colonies* (London and New York: John Lane, 1900–1904), I, pp. 264–267.

People versus Polity

States claim a monopoly of legitimate force, but of course it is one thing to claim it and another thing to achieve it. In reality, states face a variety of "internal" threats; in fact, the remaining types of political violence are all "internal violence" in at least a sense. "A people" here may mean a "national" or cultural group, a regional group, a "party," a class, or a colonized group.

The first thing to consider in regard to people-versus-polity violence is that while polities, like states, purport to be homogeneous systems—that is, all the population of the polity identifies itself with the polity and holds allegiance to it—this is far from the truth. In the real world, the populations of states are usually if not always quite, even maddeningly, diverse, with different identities, loyalties, and interests. To fully understand this problem, we must distinguish between a state, a nation, and a nation-state. *State* we have already defined: it is a political system, a government, essentially the thing you find on a political map. A *nation*, on the other hand, is a *group of people* who share a common identity and interests. The two are not at all the same in principle and most often not the same in practice.

States seem like facts, but they are really *accomplishments*. The United States of America was "accomplished" through a series of successful wars, treaties, and land purchases. States also need to lay some foundations in order to realize or accomplish their statehood. States have to be "built," literally and figuratively. They must establish integrated systems—economic, political, and cultural—to link often far-flung populations into one. This entails communication and transportation systems (such as the railroad or highway systems), as well as common language, education, and other institutions.

Ultimately, states, being artificial and arbitrary, can be contested. That is, there is not always perfect agreement over what is and is not a state. The Confederacy of the South once claimed to be a state but could not defend that claim. Tibet used to consider itself a state but is today an administrative region of China. The best and most important example at present is Taiwan. The United States and much of the world community recognizes it as a state or a near-state. However, the People's Republic of China claims that Taiwan is nothing more than a rebel province, like the Confederacy in relation to the Union—one that will some day be returned to its place in a unified China. This is an unsettled—and unsettling— question for the future.

At any rate, nations are not the things you usually see on maps of the world. Instead, nations are social, but that does not mean that they are any more factual than states are. Anthony Smith (1991), one of the leading scholars of nationhood, lists the following as the main characteristics of a nation; not all nations have all of these characteristics, but most have most of them.

- A name, that is, a self-conscious awareness of their shared identity
- A historic territory or homeland
- Common myths and historical memory
- A mass public culture
- An integrated economy
- An integrated politics with common rights and duties for members

One of the crucial aspects of nationhood that Smith does not include on his list is probably a *shared sense of purpose or destiny*. The members of a nation are "in it together." They tend to think of themselves as, at least abstractly, a kind of family. Benedict Anderson (1983) has noted aptly that this is an imaginary kind of kinship, and he has accordingly called nations "imagined communities." Not everyone in the nation is actually related to, nor actually knows, everyone else; the point is that we feel closer to them than to other people in the world. If, say, an attack is made on citizens of Oklahoma or New York, other Americans tend to feel and react as if "they" have been attacked, in a way that they do not tend to feel and react if Toronto or Mexico City were attacked. A nation, therefore, is particular kind of self-conscious and mobilized group, one that sees itself making history together and working toward common ends. Among these ends—perhaps first among these ends—is politics. This brings us to the concept of nation-state, which refers to an entity that is at once political and social; let us define it, then, as "a state that consists of all of and only one nation." In other words, in a nation-state, the state and the nation are coterminous.

Why is this important? The answer is because so few, if any, of the states in the world today are nation-states. It has been proposed that Japan and Norway might qualify as nation-states, but even they are internally diverse—Japan contains Ainu and other groups, and Norway contains Lapps, among others. There may be no true nation-states in the world. And that would be okay, if the idea of nation-state were not so powerful. In fact, it is a relatively new idea, forming in Europe only in the seventeenth and eighteenth centuries. Prior to that time, throughout the world, politics tended to take the shape of empire, which is the polar opposite of nation-state. An empire, like the Roman

Empire, the Persian Empire, or the British Empire, is by definition a wild assortment of different societies and "nations" under the sovereignty of one society or nation. An empire is a state with many nations in it.

As late as the turn of the eighteenth century, nation-state status was not a secure achievement throughout Europe. Large parts of Europe were under the control of the Austrian Empire or the Russian Empire and so on. Even in the areas that would achieve (or claim) nation-state status first, like France and England, the process was far from complete. Rather than recognizing the equation between the French people and French state, Louis XIV famously proclaimed, "I am the state." In other words, the state under absolute monarchy *was the monarch*, and the people just came along for the ride—they were *subjects* to the sovereignty of the king, not sovereign in themselves.

Even when populations began to crystallize into nations and nation-states, the process was not inevitable or perfect. Not all people within the territory of France considered themselves "French." There were other local cultures and identities that had to be displaced and replaced before everyone in France felt French. Still today there are pockets of older non-French identities in France, including the Bretons in the north and the Basques in the south. And England is even worse, since the English were always aware that their "United Kingdom" was a (not altogether happy) union of English, Scottish, Welsh, and Irish, among other minor groups.

Thus, while nation-states are a kind of political ideal, they are not the reality. The reality is socially and culturally mixed states. We need, then, to distinguish two different versions of the overlap of nations and states. The first we will call *multinational states*, that is, states that contain all or parts of two or more nations. Most of the world's states are multinational states. The former Yugoslavia was certainly one. Modern Sri Lanka is one. Canada, depending on how you define nation, is one (English-speakers and French-speakers often refer to themselves as distinct nations, not to mention all of the native Canadian Indian societies and immigrant communities). The second type of arrangement we will call *multistate nations*, that is, nations that are cross-cut by two or more state boundaries. The archetypal case of a multistate nation is the Kurds, a group (not fully "national" even yet) that happens to fall across at least four state boundaries at the intersection of Turkey, Syria, Iran, and Iraq. Nations may become multistate nations by the conquest of part of their territory, by the redrawing of international boundaries, or by emigration or forced resettlement, such as the Jewish Diaspora.

The political issue is that nations, like states, have *goals and interests*. Among these goals and interests are (1) above all else, survival; (2) prosperity; (3) equality within the state with other groups—and sometimes superiority; (4) recognition by the state and possibly the world; (5) cultural rights, that is, the right and freedom to practice their culture; (6) self-determination, that is, the right and freedom to choose their own future; and (7) in the most extreme case, political independence and their own state. Thus, one of the goals of the nation may be precisely a nation-state. Why do nations pursue nation-states? The answer is basically to achieve the goals listed above *without the interference of other nations or by a state that they do not control*. Nations and other minority social groups within multinational states have discovered, much to their displeasure, that states often have dire plans for them. Not the worst of these plans is acculturation and assimilation; the worst of these is *ethnocide* (the eradication of their culture) or *genocide* (the eradication of their lives).

This, then, is why many nations feel at best alien and at worst oppressed and threatened in their host states. In the course of building and running the state, one language, religion, or history may be promoted and others ignored or suppressed. Entire nations may be forbidden to use their own languages or even their own names. At the very extreme but not unknown event, entire nations may find their existence threatened. It is only too predictable that such threatened groups would strike back. Hence, we see a set of people-versus-polity forms of violence, including nationalism, resistance movements, independence movements, revolution, class/party warfare, guerrilla war, and terrorism.

Nationalism is a particular kind of popular movement, one meant to advance the interests of a "nation" within or across a state. As we have seen, not all nations engage in nationalism, and not all nationalism pursues the same goals; however, it is always goal oriented, and it can easily slip into violence, especially if it is opposed by the state (see later discussion). One particularly common place for nationalism to appear is in *independence movements*, especially among colonized peoples. Prestate and state societies alike were brought under the heel of European powers from the late 1400s to the mid 1900s, and in most of those cases these societies had to struggle for their independence against a vastly superior force. Ceylon (or Sri Lanka) might be one of the few cases of little struggle and violence prior to independence—which is all the more ironic because of the extensive violence after independence. Political independence was by no means a panacea for former colonies.

This resistance took many forms. In India, Mohandas "Mahatma" Gandhi's principle of "passive resistance" and nonviolent, morality-based struggle defined the path to independence. Nevertheless, it was resistance and was occasionally met with violence. It was also not the only process going on within India at the time. In other places, and more often, the resistance was more violent and intentionally so. Algeria in the 1950s was one of the first societies to practice modern terrorism against French officials in the name of its anticolonial goals. In Vietnam and Angola and elsewhere *guerrilla* ("little war") armies fought protracted wars against European administrations to dislodge them from native homelands. And, as in Vietnam and Angola, as in many other colonies, communist ideology and even soldiers from other communist states led the way to independence.

For many, resistance and independence were and had to be violent processes. Practically speaking, the superior power of colonialist states meant that they would not leave without a fight. Theoretically or philosophically speaking, colonized peoples, especially when inspired by communist ideology, saw violent *revolution* as the only means of gaining their freedom. Marx himself had written about the struggle of the masses and the need for revolutionary action against the class forces that would certainly oppose them. It would require force to meet and beat force. Some representatives of the colonized peoples went even further, greeting revolutionary violence as the completion of the predicted world system and also as a kind of "cleansing" of the souls of the colonized. No one represents this position better than Frantz Fanon, the black revolutionary from Martinique, author of *The Wretched of the Earth* (1963). In this influential book, he maintains that "decolonization is always a violent phenomenon" because colonialism itself is a violent phenomenon. The colonialists' and colonized's "first encounter was marked by violence and their existence together— that is to say the exploitation of the native by the settler—was carried on by dint of a great array of bayonets and cannons." He continues:

> The violence which has ruled over the ordering of the colonial world, which has ceaselessly drummed the rhythm for the destruction of native social forms and broken up without reserve the systems of reference of the economy, the customs of dress and external life, that same violence will be claimed and taken over by the native at the moment when, deciding to embody history in his own person, he surges into forbidden quarters. To wreck the colonial world is henceforward a mental picture of action which is very clear, very easy to understand and which may be assumed by each one of the individuals which constitute the colonized people. To break up the colonial world does not mean that after the frontiers have been abolished lines of communication will be set up between the two zones. The destruction of the colonial world is no more and no less than the abolition of one zone, its burial in the depths of the earth or its expulsion from the country. (40–41)

This level of anger is very real, very comprehensible, and very important for grasping the long-term political and economic consequences for the world.

The French Revolution, discussed at length in the next chapter, is arguably the first truly modern revolution. It is the template for all later revolutions and would stand for them if it had the "theoretical" underpinning that later, especially communist, revolutions would develop. Class-based uprising was not invented by the French revolutionaries, much less by Marxist communists. The peasants of Europe rose in protest in the 1300s and again in the 1500s, this time thinking they had found a friend in Martin Luther. They were wrong. In the mid-1600s, during the English Revolution, communities of peasants and religious idealists had discovered a "communal" alternative to the unjust contemporary society in their "Digger" and "Leveller" movements, which were also squashed. Class warfare continued to evolve its methods, its discourse, and its theory throughout the nineteenth century, finding its purest expression perhaps in the brief document, "Catechism of a Revolutionary," by Sergie Gennadievich Nechayev (born 1847). Nechayev, like the Committee of Public Safety before him and many a revolutionary council after him, had one goal and one passion alone—the revolution. (See Box 8.2)

8.2   Nechayev, *The Catechism of a Revolutionary*

The Duties of the Revolutionary toward Himself

1. The revolutionary is a doomed man. He has no personal interests, no business affairs, no emotions, no attachments, no property, and no name. Everything in him is wholly absorbed in the single thought and the single passion for revolution.
2. The revolutionary knows that in the very depths of his being, not only in words but also in deeds, he has broken all the bonds which tie him to the social order and the civilized world with all its laws, moralities, and customs, and with all its generally accepted conventions. He is their implacable enemy, and if he continues to live with them it is only in order to destroy them more speedily.
3. The revolutionary despises all doctrines and refuses to accept the mundane sciences, leaving them for future generations. He knows only one science: the science of destruction. For this reason, but only for this reason, he will study mechanics, physics, chemistry, and perhaps medicine. But all day and all night he studies the vital science of human beings, their characteristics and circumstances, and all the phenomena of the present social order. The object is perpetually the same: the surest and quickest way of destroying the whole filthy order.
4. The revolutionary despises public opinion. He despises and hates the existing social morality in all its manifestations. For him, morality is everything which contributes to the triumph of the revolution. Immoral and criminal is everything that stands in its way.
5. The revolutionary is a dedicated man, merciless toward the State and toward the educated classes; and he can expect no mercy from them. Between him and them there exists, declared or concealed, a relentless and irreconcilable war to the death. He must accustom himself to torture.
6. Tyrannical toward himself, he must be tyrannical toward others. All the gentle and enervating sentiments of kinship, love, friendship,

gratitude, and even honor, must be suppressed in him and give place to the cold and single-minded passion for revolution. For him, there exists only one pleasure, one consolation, one reward, one satisfaction—the success of the revolution. Night and day he must have but one thought, one aim—merciless destruction. Striving cold-bloodedly and indefatigably toward this end, he must be prepared to destroy himself and to destroy with his own hands everything that stands in the path of the revolution.

7. The nature of the true revolutionary excludes all sentimentality, romanticism, infatuation, and exaltation. All private hatred and revenge must also be excluded. Revolutionary passion, practiced at every moment of the day until it becomes a habit, is to be employed with cold calculation. At all times, and in all places, the revolutionary must obey not his personal impulses, but only those which serve the cause of the revolution.

The Relations of the Revolutionary toward His Comrades

8. The revolutionary can have no friendship or attachment, except for those who have proved by their actions that they, like him, are dedicated to revolution. The degree of friendship, devotion and obligation toward such a comrade is determined solely by the degree of his usefulness to the cause of total revolutionary destruction.

9. It is superfluous to speak of solidarity among revolutionaries. The whole strength of revolutionary work lies in this. Comrades who possess the same revolutionary passion and understanding should, as much as possible, deliberate all important matters together and come to unanimous conclusions. When the plan is finally decided upon, then the revolutionary must rely solely on himself. In carrying out acts of destruction, each one should act alone, never running to another for advice and assistance, except when these are necessary for the furtherance of the plan.

10. All revolutionaries should have under them second- or third-degree revolutionaries—i.e., comrades who are not completely initiated. These should be regarded as part of the common revolutionary capital placed at his disposal. This capital should, of course, be spent as economically as possible in order to derive from it the greatest possible profit. The real revolutionary should regard himself as capital consecrated to the triumph of the revolution; however, he may not personally and alone dispose of that capital without the unanimous consent of the fully initiated comrades.

(continued)

8.2   Nechayev, *The Catechism of a Revolutionary (continued)*

11. When a comrade is in danger and the question arises whether he should be saved or not saved, the decision must not be arrived at on the basis of sentiment, but solely in the interests of the revolutionary cause. Therefore, it is necessary to weigh carefully the usefulness of the comrade against the expenditure of revolutionary forces necessary to save him, and the decision must be made accordingly.

The Relations of the Revolutionary toward Society

12. The new member, having given proof of his loyalty not by words but by deeds, can be received into the society only by the unanimous agreement of all the members.
13. The revolutionary enters the world of the State, of the privileged classes, of the so-called civilization, and he lives in this world only for the purpose of bringing about its speedy and total destruction. He is not a revolutionary if he has any sympathy for this world. He should not hesitate to destroy any position, any place, or any man in this world. He must hate everyone and everything in it with an equal hatred. All the worse for him if he has any relations with parents, friends, or lovers; he is no longer a revolutionary if he is swayed by these relationships.
14. Aiming at implacable revolution, the revolutionary may and frequently must live within society while pretending to be completely different from what he really is, for he must penetrate everywhere, into all the higher and middle classes, into the houses of commerce, the churches, and the palaces of the aristocracy, and into the worlds of the bureaucracy and literature and the military, and also into the Third Division and the Winter Palace of the Czar.
15. This filthy social order can be split up into several categories. The first category comprises those who must be condemned to death without delay. Comrades should compile a list of those to be condemned according to the relative gravity of their crimes; and the executions should be carried out according to the prepared order.
16. When a list of those who are condemned is made, and the order of execution is prepared, no private sense of outrage should be considered, nor is it necessary to pay attention to the hatred provoked by these people among the comrades or the people. Hatred and the sense of outrage may even be useful insofar as they incite the masses to revolt. It is necessary to be guided only by the relative usefulness

of these executions for the sake of revolution. Above all, those who are especially inimical to the revolutionary organization must be destroyed; their violent and sudden deaths will produce the utmost panic in the government, depriving it of its will to action by removing the cleverest and most energetic supporters.

17. The second group comprises those who will be spared for the time being in order that, by a series of monstrous acts, they may drive the people into inevitable revolt.

18. The third category consists of a great many brutes in high positions, distinguished neither by their cleverness nor their energy, while enjoying riches, influence, power, and high positions by virtue of their rank. These must be exploited in every possible way; they must be implicated and embroiled in our affairs, their dirty secrets must be ferreted out, and they must be transformed into slaves. Their power, influence, and connections, their wealth and their energy, will form an inexhaustible treasure and a precious help in all our undertakings.

19. The fourth category comprises ambitious office-holders and liberals of various shades of opinion. The revolutionary must pretend to collaborate with them, blindly following them, while at the same time, prying out their secrets until they are completely in his power. They must be so compromised that there is no way out for them, and then they can be used to create disorder in the State.

20. The fifth category consists of those doctrinaires, conspirators, and revolutionists who cut a great figure on paper or in their cliques. They must be constantly driven on to make compromising declarations: as a result, the majority of them will be destroyed, while a minority will become genuine revolutionaries.

21. The sixth category is especially important: women. They can be divided into three main groups. First, those frivolous, thoughtless, and vapid women, whom we shall use as we use the third and fourth category of men. Second, women who are ardent, capable, and devoted, but whom do not belong to us because they have not yet achieved a passionless and austere revolutionary understanding; these must be used like the men of the fifth category. Finally, there are the women who are completely on our side—i.e., those who are wholly dedicated and who have accepted our program in its entirety. We should regard these women as the most valuable or our treasures; without their help, we would never succeed.

(continued)

8.2 Nechayev, *The Catechism of a Revolutionary (continued)*

The Attitude of the Society toward the People

22. The Society has no aim other than the complete liberation and happiness of the masses—i.e., of the people who live by manual labor. Convinced that their emancipation and the achievement of this happiness can only come about as a result of an all-destroying popular revolt, the Society will use all its resources and energy toward increasing and intensifying the evils and miseries of the people until at last their patience is exhausted and they are driven to a general uprising.

23. By a revolution, the Society does not mean an orderly revolt according to the classic western model—a revolt which always stops short of attacking the rights of property and the traditional social systems of so-called civilization and morality. Until now, such a revolution has always limited itself to the overthrow of one political form in order to replace it by another, thereby attempting to bring about a so-called revolutionary state. The only form of revolution beneficial to the people is one which destroys the entire State to the roots and exterminated all the state traditions, institutions, and classes in Russia.

24. With this end in view, the Society therefore refuses to impose any new organization from above. Any future organization will doubtless work its way through the movement and life of the people; but this is a matter for future generations to decide. Our task is terrible, total, universal, and merciless destruction.

25. Therefore, in drawing closer to the people, we must above all make common cause with those elements of the masses which, since the foundation of the state of Muscovy, have never ceased to protest, not only in words but in deeds, against everything directly or indirectly connected with the state: against the nobility, the bureaucracy, the clergy, the traders, and the parasitic kulaks. We must unite with the adventurous tribes of brigands, who are the only genuine revolutionaries in Russia.

26. To weld the people into one single unconquerable and all-destructive force—this is our aim, our conspiracy, and our task.

Source: Translation available at http://www.spunk.org/library/places/russia/sp000116.txt.

The revolutionary, as Nechayev says, is four things: an angry person, a lonely person, a committed person, and a person willing to use any means—including other people—to achieve his ends.

Among these means are not only "political" techniques, such as party formation, oratory, and pamphleteering, but also acts of violence. Assassination is one tool of the desperate resister. Another, which has become all too familiar to us in the early twenty-first century, is terrorism. Of all the forms of modern political violence, terrorism is viewed ordinarily as the most disagreeable, the most irrational, the most illegitimate. It is of course not a new phenomenon; a group called the "sicarii" existed among the Jews of Roman-occupied Jerusalem at the turn of the Christian era, men who would conduct public daylight killings of Romans and Jewish collaborators to resist Roman rule and incite both sides to further violence. In the modern world, terrorists specialize in bombs, random shootings, attacks on civilians, and most recently in "weapons of mass destruction," whether these are potentially nuclear weapons, chemicals or biological agents, or hijacked airliners.

Terrorists are commonly thought to be insane, evil, and criminal in their conduct. Terrorists do not see themselves that way at all, nor do their supporters. The fact that they violate the "rules of war" highlights the fact that war, the zenith of violence and destructiveness, is itself "orderly" and "rule bound" and that those rules may be *some people's* rules but not others. Nevertheless, the rules of war (the Geneva Convention and the like) call for humane treatment of prisons of war, respect for neutral territory and civilian noncombatants, immunity for diplomats and government officials, and prohibition on the use of civilians as hostages. Terrorists may reject any or all of these conventions—to which they never agreed in the first place.

If terrorism were really insane and irrational, its study would belong under abnormal psychology rather than politics and sociology/anthropology. However, terrorism is a method, in many ways like any other political method. We might call it, paraphrasing Clausewitz, the continuation of war by other means: when diplomacy fails, and war fails, then terrorism is a likely step. Quite simply, *terrorism* can be defined as the practice of killing a few to frighten many. It is ordinarily seen as a tool of the weak and the desperate, and there is probably something to that. However, not all weak and desperate groups employ it, and not all groups that employ it are weak and desperate. As we will explore below, even states themselves have engaged in terrorism. It is in the end a strategy.

We can discuss terrorism in terms of its characteristics, its causes, and its goals. In regard to characteristics, Bruce Hoffman (2003a: 23) posits that it is:

- "ineluctably political in aims and motives"
- "violent—or, equally important, threatens violence"
- "designed to have far-reaching psychological repercussions beyond the immediate victim or targets"
- "conducted by an organization with an identifiable chain of command or conspiratorial cell structure (whose members wear no uniform or identifying insignia)"
- "perpetrated by a subnational or non-state entity"

Paul Pillar (2003) adds the following traits: premeditation and intention to harm and scare, political motivation, selection of noncombatants as targets, and subnational groups or clandestine agents as perpetrators. His list allows for the possibility of including "state terrorism" within the rubric.

In regard to the causes of terrorism—why people engage in such behavior, particularly as opposed to other kinds of resistance—Martha Crenshaw (2003) offers four considerations. The first is the specific concrete grievances, of the sort discussed above. The second is a sense of injustice about the conditions of the group. The third is a lack of opportunity for political participation—either exclusion from "ordinary" political processes or the failure of those processes. The fourth and final is state of passivity of the masses along with deprivation or dissatisfaction among the elites. Here she invokes the role of the elites, who are often some combination of "canaries in the coal mine" in relation to political injustice and a "vanguard party" who try to shape the thinking, feeling, and acting of the masses. Therefore, two things should not be too surprising to us: first, elite revolutionary leaders are often young educated middle-class professionals who feel the squeeze of injustice earliest, and second, the "common people" often fail to feel the gratitude these elites expect them to feel and consequently fail to follow them in revolution. Finally, in regard to goals, Crenshaw again offers some insight. In addition to or even in place of specific practical goals (that is, satisfying their unmet claims), they seek attention (they simply want to be seen and known), disruption or discrediting of the government (to show its unfairness and/or its ineffectiveness at protecting the population, influence on public opinion (especially creating outrage or sympathy for their cause), and provocation of a counterreaction (sometimes they actually want an escalation of conflict, either to bring attention to their cause or to hasten its achievement by drawing greater repression and violence down on themselves and their "constituents"), and group cohesion and expansion (in the form of morale building, enhancement of internal organization, and recruitment).

Terrorism, then, is a low-cost, relatively high-impact strategy, although one that has not shown much long-term effectiveness in international politics. Even so, it is at the start and at the finish political—about a cause and a goal. Hoffman goes so far as to assert that, far from being an egotist, the terrorist is an altruist, who "believes that he is serving a 'good' cause designed to achieve greater good for a wider constituency— whether real or imagined—which the terrorist and his organization purport to represent" (Hoffman 2003a: 23). Criminals and the insane perpetrate violence "without a cause," for personal gain or no good reason at all. The terrorist, Hoffman concludes, is a "violent intellectual," committing violence for the sake of his beliefs, ideas, and theories, who is "prepared to use and indeed committed to using force in attainment of his goals" (23).

Yasir Arafat, until the emergence of Osama bin Laden the poster child for terrorism, said the same thing in different words: "The difference between the revolutionary and the terrorist lies in the reason for which each fights. For whoever stands by a just cause and fights for the freedom and liberation of his land from the invaders, the settlers, and the colonialists, cannot possibly be called terrorist" (quoted in Hoffman 2003a: 11–12). And lest we think that only Palestinians and Arabs think this way, Menachem Begin, former Prime Minister of Israel and, before that, member of the Jewish insurrectionist group Irgun, said in 1944:

> What value in speeches?. . . No, there was no other way. If we did not fight we should be destroyed. To fight was the only way to salvation.
>
> When Descartes said: "I think, therefore, I am," he uttered a very profound thought. But there are times in the history of peoples when thought alone does not prove their existence. . . . There are times when everything in you cries out: your very self-respect as a human being lies in your resistance to evil. We fight, therefore we are! (1977: 46).

This self-perception, not entirely undeserved, as freedom fighters and liberators explains and is expressed by the names of many of these kinds of groups, such as the Palestine Liberation Organization, the National Liberation Front, Freedom for the Basque Homeland, the Justice Commandos of the Armenian Genocide, the Popular Liberation Army, and many others.

Polity versus People

States, as we have seen, all too readily turn their force outward against their neighbors. However, states also occasionally if not regularly turn their force inward against their "own kind." This is another kind of "internal violence," but an "official" kind rather than a resistance or protest kind. The state supposedly has a monopoly of legitimate force, as we have argued above, so when that force is turned against internal "enemies of the state," it ought to be that this is a legitimate response to a legitimate threat. It is difficult to maintain that this is always the case.

You will recall from Chapter 1 that Hannah Arendt (1969) theorized that any government, no matter how unpopular, must have some degree of legitimacy, or else even its use of force is doomed in the end. Further, she insists that, to the extent that a government has "power" (what we called "authority" above), it does not need force and that to the extent that it must use force it lacks power/authority. So, short of the situations where a paranoid and insane leader actually does control the state, most instances of state violence against "its own people" ought to have some analyzable sense to them.

We can identify a set of subtypes of polity-versus-people violence. One is *repression*, in which the government aims to quiet or dispel any criticism of its policies or to pacify one or more groups within its borders. Repression is mostly about conformity, obedience, and orthodoxy: do what the regime says and shut up. *State terrorism* takes this position even further and essentially

employs the means of a terrorist as an arm of internal political policy; the enemies of the state are to be frightened and crushed into submission. At the
extreme, ethnocide and genocide are intended as "final solutions" to internal
political problems; not content to silence protesters or minority groups, their
complete elimination is sought. We should also not forget the *structural violence* that preys on groups unequally, of the sort seen in our discussion of the
poor of Brazil in Chapter 5.

Repression is predominantly the tool of the unpopular or insecure government. It may take away the citizens' rights to free speech, free assembly, free
media, and the like (if these ever existed) to curtail any criticism of the government. It may also use arrests and even sporadic illegitimate violence to achieve
its ends. Unfortunately, one of the qualities of many states, especially but not
exclusively in the "Third World," is that they contain culturally diverse populations. So, in addition to political opposition, these regimes often encounter
"cultural" opposition. For instance, it is often the case that the government
represents one or another cultural or ethnic group disproportionately, so that
favors, offices, wealth, and other benefits are not shared equally among the
population. The state may also include colonized or defeated peoples, like the
Kurds in Turkey, the Chechens in Russia, or the various American Indian
societies in the United States. Herein lies one of the cautions in this discussion: while we said that the state may conduct violence "against its own," the
reality might be that the regime does not consider these other groups to be "its
own" at all. They are, to a considerable extent, "internal foreigners" who must
be kept in their place forcibly. Accordingly, when we think about Saddam
Hussein victimizing the Kurds in the north or the Shi'ites in the south of Iraq,
we must understand that, while they too are "inhabitants of Iraq," they may not
be thought of by the regime as "the same as" other Iraqis (that is, the kind
of Iraqis who man the regime). The same is the case in Rwanda, in Sri Lanka,
and in almost every culturally diverse state that has suffered internal, state-
sponsored violence.

State terrorism is in a way merely the intensification of repression, particularly in the conditions of perceived emergency. Stalin's regime in the Soviet
Union is probably a model for most people as a terrorist or police state; millions of "enemies of the state" were arrested, purged, shipped off to gulags, or
executed during his thirty-year reign. In some ways, during some moments,
communist China has acted like a terrorist state, most notably during the "Cultural Revolution," when violence was employed to jump-start a stalled rebuild-
ing of Chinese society. However, for sheer concentrated ferocity, none
matches the Khmer Rouge regime of Pol Pot, from its arrival in power in April
1975 until its overthrow by a Vietnamese army in January 1979. During that
less than four-year period, as much as one-fifth of the Cambodian population
died at the hands of the Cambodian government (1.5 million out of a total of
8 million). Many others were subjected to horrendous living conditions as

entire cities were emptied and their inhabitants sent to the countryside to work among the peasants, the "true Khmer," and to become "new people."

Khmer Rouge Cambodia (which the party renamed Kampuchea) is a classic example of revolutionary idealism and vengeance taken to extremes. The "killing fields" were the final resting places of counterrevolutionaries and those who merely looked like counterrevolutionaries—rich "capitalists," of course, but also professionals, intellectuals, civil servants, police, and soldiers, and sometimes even people with soft hands (indicating no hard manual labor) or glasses (indicating "liberal education" and counterrevolutionary ideas). Not only were the surviving Cambodians to become "new people"— remade in the ideals of the revolution—but they were treated with inconceivable cruelty and violence. They were given the least food and the longest and hardest work. No longer "pure" Khmer, they were dehumanized, made to do the tasks of animals and sometimes forced to go without clothing or shelter. A Khmer saying summed it up: "To keep you is no gain; to destroy you is no loss."

The Pol Pot regime intentionally promoted rage, fury, and vengeance, as we noted above. It reveled in the blood of the counterrevolutionary as exquisitely as the French Revolution had almost two hundred years before, but for several years longer. Like "The Marseillaise," the French anthem that sings of "impure blood" running in ditches, the Khmer song "The Red Flag" expressed its joy in bloodletting:

> Glittering blood blankets the earth—blood given up to
> Liberate the people: the blood of workers, peasants, and intellectuals;
> Blood of young men, Buddhist monks, and girls.
> The blood swirls away, and flows upward, gently into the
> Sky, turning into a red, revolutionary flag.
> Red flag! Red flag! Flying now! Flying now!
> O beloved friends, pursue, strike and hit the enemy,
> Red flag! Red flag! Flying now! Flying now!
> Don't leave a single reactionary imperialist (alive): drive
> Them from Kampuchea. Strive and strike, strive and strike,
> And win the victory, win the victory!

It might be tempting, based on this list of culprits, to blame leftist, Marxist revolutionaries for the greatest violence of the modern political era. This would be wrong, however, according to Hoffman (2003b), who declares that "Right-wing terrorism . . . has often been characterized as the least discriminate, most senseless type of contemporary political violence" (80). Obviously, the violence of Hitler and Mussolini must be placed under the heading of right-wing (statist, "conservative," anti-Marxist) violence. The death squads of Central and South America also fall in this category, as does the repression and state terrorism of a Hussein, a Franco, an Amin, and any number of other right-wing dictators, many of them supported by the United States as "enemies of my enemy."

One brief example will suffice in the form of the "dirty war" in Argentina during the late 1970s and early 1980s. Admittedly, Argentina had been rocked by leftist, student-led protesters and urban guerrilla warriors in Buenos Aires and elsewhere in the country in the 1960s. The response had been repressive from the government. By the 1970s the armed left was openly attacking security personnel and the upper classes, while the armed right (mostly under government control) was openly attacking both the armed and unarmed left. Kidnapping and murder were commonplace on both sides of this revolutionary struggle. Gradually ultra-right paramilitary organizations emerged, like the Anti-Communist Association of Argentina, which hunted down and killed leftist union leaders, politicians, and intellectuals. Sadly but predictably, this was actually one of the strategies of the left, like the People's Revolutionary Army, which hoped to unleash such repressive horror from the government that the people would have to rise up. Instead, they unleashed a horror that they could not imagine or withstand.

In 1976, a military coup replaced the government and made the way for the real rightist "dirty war." In the name of "national security," the Left was rooted out and effectively destroyed as an armed threat by 1978, but the terror did not end there. Not unlike the French Revolution, the state of emergency led to a general paranoia, one that saw an insurrectionist and enemy of the regime under every mattress. As Marcelo Suarez-Orozco put it (1992: 233), "The state rapidly underwent a metamorphosis from seeming unable to monopolize the use of violence to fully (and almost exclusively) relying on new kinds of political terror for social consensus." "Subversives" were rooted out and liquidated. The problem was that virtually anyone could be labeled a subversive. General Iberico Saint-Jean, a member of the ruling military, said it best: "first we will kill all the subversives; then we will kill their collaborators; then ... their sympathizers, then ... those who remain indifferent; and finally we will kill the timid" (quoted in Suarez-Orozco 1992: 235). Exactly like the French Revolution, it became a crime not only to be against the regime but to be insufficiently enthusiastic for it.

By 1983 when civilian rule returned to Argentina, between 9,000 (the official number) and 30,000 citizens had simply disappeared—or "had been disappeared," as they said, making a passive verb into an active one. During the terror, police or paramilitary units would break into houses, arrest suspects, and simply never release or refer to them again. Children were not spared the attacks, nor certainly were the professional and intellectual classes. Strangely—or not so strangely at all—the regime was unrepentant about its actions; as Minister of Foreign Affairs Admiral C. Guzetti stated, "When the social body of the country has been contaminated by disease which eats away at its entrails, it forms antibodies. These antibodies (death squads) cannot be considered in the same way as the microbes. As the government controls and destroys the guerrillas, the actions of the antibodies will disappear. This is already happening. It is only a reaction to a sick body" (Suarez-Orozco 1992: 239). Understandably, the "dirty war" was often referred to as a "cleaning." "We will clean you" was one of the utterances of the state terrorists and torturers.

In conclusion to this section, this language—of contamination and cleaning—should be very familiar by now. It dehumanizes the victim into dirt, bacteria, waste, pollution. It is the same language used by the Serbs in Bosnia ("ethnic cleansing"), and it is the same language used by Fascists in World War II. In answer to whether there was terror going on in Italy, Mussolini answered, "Terror? Never, simply . . . social hygiene, taking those individuals out of circulation like a doctor would take out a bacillus." As we know, reducing the "other" to a bacillus gives one the same clinical distance toward the one as the other, making it easy—even desirable, even necessary— to take the same measures against them both.

People versus People

Sometimes, the state itself is not involved in internal political conflicts at all or is involved only as an extension of one of the cultural-identity groups that occupies it. When the violence is entirely or essentially "group versus group," it is termed *ethnic conflict*. In the modern world, we all hear about ethnic groups and conflicts, and we all think we know an ethnic group or conflict when we see one, but in fact these social phenomena are more complicated than they first appear. To begin with, some ethnic conflicts are very old, and some are not. Some ethnic conflicts have remained essentially the same throughout their history, and some have changed dramatically over time. In some cases, ethnic groups themselves are very old, and some are not.

So, our first question should be, what is an ethnic group? The answer, as unsatisfying as it is, is that an ethnic group is a group organized on the basis of ethnicity. Ethnicity is an organizing principle in the modern world—not the only organizing principle by any means, but a particularly popular and successful one. Ethnicity has been defined in various ways, but the following two definitions raise important issues.

- Subjective symbolic or emblematic use of any aspect of culture [by a group], in order to differentiate themselves from other groups. [We should also add: to create cohesion within the group and to mobilize the group to action and to legitimize that action.] (DeVos 1975: 16).
- The character, quality, or condition of ethnic group membership, based on an identity with and/or consciousness of group belonging that is differentiated from others by symbolic "markers" (including cultural, biological, or territorial), and is rooted in bonds to a shared past and perceived ethnic interests (Burgess 1978: 270).

These two definitions, and many others like them, emphasize certain aspects of the processes of and behind ethnicity and its results that merit spelling out explicitly. Ethnicity is not purely "objective" or "factual" but at least partly "subjective"—in other words, it is not so much what is "true" as what people think is true and what they do with it. It is about identity—who we perceive ourselves to be, on the basis of those cultural "facts." It can base this identity on any part(s) of culture, including history, religion, language, race, land, or many others. Ethnicity is about differentiation—about specifying how and why "we" are not "them" and "they" are not "us." It is also about integration—about making us into an organized and effective "us." Finally, like the other types of political violence, it is about interests—about organizing and mobilizing us to achieve some goals(s) vis-à-vis other groups in our social environment.

We can illustrate this unfamiliar and counterintuitive point by recognizing a few facts:

- Groups can and do use any part(s) of their culture to organize their ethnicity—their language or religion or customs or history or physical traits or territorial attachments, and so forth—and that the part(s) they use may change over time.
- Groups can and do use the part(s) they choose for different purposes—to demand rights, wealth, land, power, jobs, education, political power, respect, self-determination, and even their own state.
- There is no one-to-one correspondence between the culture of a group and its "ethnicity." In other words, a small cultural difference can make a huge ethnic difference, and a huge cultural difference can make a small ethnic difference or none at all.

To further illustrate this last point, consider a particular cultural difference—say, Catholic versus Protestant—in relation to two distinct social contexts. In America Catholics and Protestants have generally coexisted peacefully. In Northern Ireland, they often fought and killed each other in the past and sometimes still do. In the 1500s and 1600s in Europe, they fought long and bloody wars over their cultural difference. Anthropologist Gregory Bateson (1979: 99), in a completely unrelated context, referred to a "difference that makes a difference" as opposed to a difference that does not. "Catholic versus Protestant" is the same difference in the United States and Northern Ireland, but in the former case it is not a "difference that makes a difference," whereas in the latter case it is.

What this means for us is that ethnic groups do not so much fight *about* culture as they fight *with* culture. Of course, not all ethnicity is violent, but it is all competitive. Ethnicity only applies when two or more groups exist and compete in a shared social context. In such situations, though, groups do not struggle or conflict *over* culture but *in the name of* or *under the banner of* culture. In other words, it is not even usually about who is "right" or "better."

Rather, ethnic groups are fighting about or over other things—wealth, power, jobs, education, land, and so forth—and culture is a useful tool or weapon in this fight. A group can say, "We deserve X because we are Y" and substitute any demand for X and any part of their name or culture for Y. Culture in conditions of ethnic conflict becomes the charter, the foundation, or the legitimation of the claims made by the group: we deserve land because we were here first, or we deserve employment or educational rights because we speak this language, or we deserve political power because we once had our own state, and so forth.

RETROSPECT AND PROSPECT

There are many, often well-meaning, people who want these sorts of political conflicts to end. They ask, as Rodney King did after his maltreatment at the hands of the Los Angeles police department, "Why can't we all just get along?" The answer to this question is, "Because we have unresolved, and maybe irresolvable, claims, grievances, interests, and passions." We could perhaps bring a halt to some particular political conflict—say, between Israelis and Palestinians, Turks and Kurds, Chechens and Russians, Northern Irish Catholic and Northern Irish Protestant—by forcing them to lay down their weapons and accept a truce. But would that really solve anything? We can perhaps pound Iraq into the ground or kill every member of al Qaeda, but will that really solve anything? Is that really peace?

The thesis here is that peace is much more than the absence of war or even the absence of violence. The evidence is that societies can be "at peace" one moment—like the Serbs and Muslims in Bosnia—and be at each others' throats the next. Unless people went suddenly insane (which is unlikely and not sociologically useful), there must have been preexisting claims and grievances lying dormant—or at least potentially exploitable by demagogues and hate mongers—before the explosion of violence. Imposing a "settlement" on warring parties may stop the fighting, but it does not remove the root cause of the war in the first place.

"Absence of war" is a negative definition, just as "absence of sickness" is a negative definition of health. Rather, health is a distinct condition with its own "symptoms" (positive ones), just as peace is a distinct condition with its own positive causes, characteristics, and goals. If political violence has goals, then political peace will not be achieved, unless and until those goals are either reached or redefined. This will not be easy—perhaps even possible—since different political groups may have contradictory interests and goals. However, focusing on the conflict itself and not the causes is like focusing on the fever and not the infection. You can bring the temperature down, but that is not a "cure." Rather, it smoothes the field down for a real cure. Unless we understand the real causes of political violence, we will never understand it, let alone address it, in a serious, useful, and lasting way.

In the next chapter, we will look in more depth at some moments of "social pathology" and the political—and near-religious, in some cases—violent responses that flowed from them. The reason to do so, beyond illustrating the analyses we have given so far, is to show that a simple ceasefire would not satisfy anyone, because the underlying causes of dissatisfaction, competition, and aggression—the conflicts of interest—would go unalleviated. Whether there was another, more nonviolent, possible solution is an interesting question. One of the answers is that the particular choices of individuals and parties, as much as the macrolevel circumstances in which people find themselves, determine the outcome.

POLITICAL VIOLENCE

Case Studies

> When it comes to revolutionaries, only trust the sad ones. The enthusiastic
> ones are the oppressors of tomorrow.
> —*Peter Berger*

In this chapter—the last before we turn finally to an in-depth study of violence in one particular society, namely, the United States—we will discuss four case studies of political violence in two major categories. The first category consists of the two most important and influential political revolutions in the modern era, the French and the Russian/Bolshevik. Each of these was not merely a change in rulers or governments but an attempt at "total revolution" and the complete redesign of society. The second category consists of two contemporary ethnic conflicts—Bosnia and Rwanda. These ethnic cases will not dwell on the details of the shooting portion of the conflict but rather on the background and buildup to conflict, particularly how the groups employed their cultures to establish identities and to define claims and grievances.

All of these and virtually all modern political activism and violence—and much of religious activism and violence— fall within the general conception of "mass movements," as numerous scholars have noted, including Le Bon and Hoffer (see Chapter 6). As we examine the cases in this chapter and reflect on previous cases and on instances we will encounter in the future, it may be useful to apply the analysis of Vejas Gabriel Liulevicius, a lecturer and author on twentieth-century political history. In his recorded lecture series, "Utopia and Terror in the Twentieth Century" (2003), he identifies four qualities, or elements, in mass movements of the age. These include

1. *The "masses."* Before we can have a mass movement, we must have a "mass" of humanity, particularly a frustrated and disappointed group. A mass of this sort, typically urban and often lower class, is usually the atomized remainder of the erosion or destruction of "traditional" or "authentic" communities (tribes, villages, etc.) in search of a new but necessarily artificial or "imagined" community.

2. *Machinery.* Mass movements are "practical" or "technical" phenomena that require tools or techniques to create and sustain them. This "machinery of revolution" includes literal machines of war (guns and bombs), machines of "information" (that is, "mass media," including a propaganda wing), and the very machinery or mechanization of the state itself.

3. *A master plan.* A modern movement needs a vision, a goal, even a "theory"—in other words, an *ideology*, as defined by its religious, political, or cultural identity. The master plan is a (more or less) all-encompassing discourse about the present and, even more so, about the future. What kind of society are we making? What is the "good society"? The twentieth century saw a surprising combination of apocalyptic righteousness and "scientific" inevitability in its major movements, often bringing strange bedfellows like economic/class justice, eugenics, and "blood and soil" identity into a single mix. Whatever else was true, the future was going to be better, maybe perfect. Hence a strong dose of idealism entered into such efforts.

4. *A mobster elite.* Leadership, an "elite" individual or party, has played a central role in mass movements, which all too often have evinced a "criminal" leadership willing to attain and maintain power through extralegal means and to place itself outside the law. Such elites see themselves as bound by no past law or as the creators of a new law. The movement itself may be above any law or morality and therefore beyond question. It is always right, always good, always *for* "the people" and always *against* the "enemies of the people." Using violence against enemies (and sometimes former friends) is acceptable, even virtuous. Anything for the movement.

These traits have lent to mass movements since the French Revolution (and probably those since the English Revolution of 1649, if not before), especially those of the twentieth century, a stark and chilling character. Those of the twenty-first century give no indication of being different.

Case Study 1: The "Reign of Terror" in the French Revolution

> If the spring of popular government in time of peace is virtue, the springs of popular government in revolution are at once virtue and terror: virtue, without which terror is fatal; terror, without which virtue is powerless. Terror is nothing other than justice, severe, inflexible; it is therefore an emanation of virtue; it is not so much a special principle as it is a consequence of the general principle of democracy applied to our country's most urgent needs.
> —*Robespierre*

Case Study 1: The "Reign of Terror" in the French Revolution (continued)

> All the arms of terrorism, however ultramodern and sophisticated, are descended from the same old model: the guillotine, fundamental symbol, in France, of the origin of institutions and the always possible recourse to state terrorism.
> —*Laurent Dispot, The Terror Machine*

Perhaps the first truly "modern" revolution was the French Revolution, commencing in 1789. This event is modern not only because it occurred just over two centuries ago, shortly before the turn of the nineteenth century but because it was not the first time a people had risen up against their king. The English Civil Wars of the 1640s had culminated in the execution of King Charles I and a brief experiment with "democratic" government. Also, the fledgling United States of America had just finished its successful war of independence against England and monarchy, although few persecutions and no high-profile executions accompanied that achievement. The French Revolution, and in particular the Reign of Terror (June 1793–July 1794), was "modern" and "revolutionary" in ways that these other moments were not. It was also modern in language, in goals, in methods, and in results. A true "revolution" aimed at much more than regime change, it sought a complete reinvention of nearly every aspect of society. It represents a distinct yet familiar discourse on violence, legitimization, otherness, and idealism that we have encountered throughout our analysis of violence, and it also depicts in fine detail Hoffer's (1966/1951) conception of the "true believer."

By the late 1780s, French society was in a state of ferment. Nobility living in opulence within the sight of poor commoners, especially those that crowded the streets of Paris, incensed the people. A spring drought in 1788, followed by a monumental hailstorm in July 1788 that wiped out much of the crop around Paris followed by the longest and coldest winter in memory, led to a serious food supply problem and a steep increase in the prices of grain, flour, and bread (the staple of the peasantry and urban poor). As much as 90 percent of the poorer people's income had to be spent to eat. This further led to a decline in "consumer spending" and a drop in production of nonfood goods of up to 50 percent. Simultaneously, after a long generation of royal wars under Louis XIV, followed by the campaign to aid America in its struggle for independence, the French government was deeply in debt. Between 1783 and 1787 it borrowed more than 653 million livres—more than its typical annual income. In 1786 alone the budget deficit was one-quarter of that year's revenues. In 1788 King Louis XVI ordered an additional loan of 420 million livres over four years. The upper classes resisted, and by August of 1788 the state was effectively bankrupt. There was only one choice left— one that almost everyone had tried to avoid—which was to call together

Case Study 1: The "Reign of Terror" in the French Revolution (continued)

the "Estates-General," the only body legally authorized to approve new taxes. However, Louis was already in a struggle over his power with the local magistrates, and everyone knew that the Estates-General would be a contentious body, considering itself representatives of the nation as its duly elected deputies. The Estates-General had not convened since 1614, and merely establishing meeting and voting procedures was sure to be provocative.

France at this time was an absolute monarchy, although a tenuous one. The Estates-General, roughly the equivalent of the English Parliament, although without its tradition of power sharing, consisted of three sections, or "estates"—the nobility, the clergy, and the "commons," or ordinary people. The commons numbered about 94 percent of the population but were entitled to only one "estate" and roughly the same number of deputies as the other two estates combined. Thus, if the sections voted as sections (that is, one vote per estate), the upper classes could always outvote the commons. However, if the voting was done "by head," then the commons, or lower classes, could win most of the decisions.

Naturally, the king ordered that the Estates-General vote by section. Also, although each deputy would bring a list of grievances from his constituency, only the grievances of the first two estates would be placed on the agenda. It is further worth noting that the "third estate" was not represented by any actual peasants or workers; its membership consisted primarily of lawyers and officials, with a few merchants.

Called to order in May 1789, the Estates-General quickly split over the voting issue. In June pamphleteering began, with one of the most influential published by Abbe Sieyes entitled, *What is the Third Estate?* The answer he gave to this question was, "Everything." In answer to the question, "What has it been heretofore in the political order?" he answered, "Nothing." He went on to claim that the French people, not the Crown, were sovereign and that the Third Estate was an assemblage of the French people.

Accordingly, on June 17, 1789 the Third Estate adopted the name "National Assembly" and declared itself the rightful representative of the French nation. The French Revolution had begun. Requiring weapons to protect itself against the king and his armies, on July 14 the National Assembly stormed two royal buildings (the Invalides and the Bastille) for guns, cannons, and ammunition (hence, Bastille Day). Already, in mid-July, counterrevolutionary individuals and officials were being seized and killed.

In August the National Assembly began to dismantle feudalism, depriving the nobility of various privileges and properties. It also intended to produce a constitution to which the king would be bound. The first step in this process was the Declaration of the Rights of Man and Citizen, a document reminiscent

Case Study 1: The "Reign of Terror" in the French Revolution (continued)

of the American Declaration of Independence; it too claimed that "men are born and remain free and equal in rights" and that these rights include "liberty, property, security, and resistance to oppression." It went on to say that the "source of all sovereignty is essentially in the nation; no body, no individual can exercise authority that does not proceed from it in plain terms." These words, although familiar to modern Americans, were an affront to royal sovereignty (recall that Louis XIV had declared, "I am the state"). Nevertheless, the contemporary Louis XVI condescended to accept the constitution that eventually emerged from this body in 1791—one that severely limited his power and referred to him merely as "king of the French."

Three problems faced the fledgling government. First, in the provinces, and even in the streets of Paris, the peasants and lower classes were in arms. Removing the old feudal powers set in motion a storm of pent-up anger and revenge. Second, a decree in August 1790 called the Civil Constitution of the Clergy had upset the Catholic priests, many Catholic Frenchmen, and the Pope himself. The Civil Constitution aimed only to bring the clergy under the civil authority, but it also imposed an oath of loyalty to the revolution, on pain of removal from office. Alienation of a large segment of society on the basis of religion was a dangerous development. Third, the international community was not at all pleased with the situation: Louis had family in other royal houses around Europe, and no monarch wanted the example of revolution to spread to his domain. France had become in effect an outlaw regime, at war with its near neighbors, in particular Austria and Prussia. Louis, although going along with the new circumstances, hoped to be restored to power by a counterrevolution.

So, the revolution was beginning to split. The revolutionary government was already divided against the church and the papists, and within the government itself there was a growing schism between the constitutional monarchists (known as the Feuillants) and the republicans (known as the Jacobins), who wanted to depose the king. With war abroad and counterrevolution at home, the guillotine was put to use as early as April 1792. Invented expressly as a "humane" form of execution by Dr. Joseph-Ignace Guillotine, it bore the inscription "THE JUSTICE OF THE PEOPLE." Makeshift courts were put together to try counterrevolutionaries, and more than a thousand people were executed within a week in early September 1792. At the end of that year, Louis himself was brought to trial and sentenced to death; he was guillotined on January 21, 1793.

The year 1793 began on an ominous and bloody note. By this time, the new government (now called the Legislative Assembly) had found itself eclipsed by new forces and leaders outside the "official" government. Not the

Case Study 1: The "Reign of Terror" in the French Revolution (continued)

least of these were the Paris mob, the "sans-culottes," or lower-class agitators, and their spokesmen, such as Marat. The agitators were drawing thousands of protesters to their street demonstrations, and men like Marat were calling for the massacre of enemies of the revolution. Also rising to prominence was Maximilien Francois Robespierre, whose name would become synonymous with the period known as the Terror.

As said above, war abroad and counterrevolutionaries at home had plunged France, and especially its leaders, into a state of paranoia, mania, and extremism. The discourse of the revolution more and more centered on vengeance, terror, and an almost apocalyptic mission for France in the world. Words like "salvation" and "regeneration" were on the lips of the revolutionaries, and France was "radically Other" in relation to all the nations on earth. As Robespierre himself uttered:

> The world has changed. It must change still more. What is there in common between what is and what was?. . . Everything of the physical order has changed; everything must change in the moral and political order. Half of the world revolution is already completed; the other half must be accomplished. . . . The French people seem to have moved two thousand years ahead of the rest of the human species: it is tempting even to see the French people in the midst of the others as a different species. . . . The Revolution . . . is but the transition from the reign of crime to the reign of justice. (Quoted in Haynal, Molnar, and de Puymege 1983: 90–92)

The world had never heard quite this kind of talk before—a world revolution, the creation of a new higher species of humans, a total transformation of morality and politics, and a "vanguard" party in the form of the French nation. It would not hear such talk again until Marx and Lenin.

Accordingly, enemies of the Revolution were much more than enemies of a party or even a nation. They were enemies of a cause, or even more than a cause, a holy mission—of humanity itself. The world was seen in starkly black-and-white terms—the good citizen and the bad citizen, the corrupt and the virtuous—and the whole conflict was imbued with practically religious significance. The Other was "impure" (a reference to "impure blood" occurs in the French national anthem, penned at this time). Anarcharsis Cloots, a fellow of Robespierre, said it clearly:

> The orthodoxy of the cult of equality must inspire in us a holy dread, and we must apply to man's true religion what a papist preacher criminally gave to his sect of lies. We are reproached for showing an inquisitorial severity, but does not zeal have its fury and religion its vengeance? Let us devote a civic hatred to all these denigrators of the universal republic: I look upon them as the executioners of the human race. . . . [A]ll these magnanimous republicans [of the past, like Brutus] had infinitely fewer reasons to sever the ties of friendship and consanguinity than

Case Study 1: The "Reign of Terror" in the French Revolution (continued)

> does the Orator of the Human Race [Cloots's title for himself], who tirelessly and relentlessly pursues the disorganizers, the dismantlers, the counterrevolutionaries, the advocates of political schism and perpetual war. (Quoted in ibid., 97–98)

One of the first acts of institutionalizing this policy of "tireless and relentless pursuit of counterrevolutionaries and advocates of political schism" was the formation of the oxymoronic Committee of Public Safety in the spring of 1793. An institution intended to oversee and coordinate the activities of the arms of the official government, it virtually functioned as the official government for about a year, from the summer of 1793 to the summer of 1794. The condemnation of "enemies of the people" came close at hand.

First to be condemned were the political enemies of the French at war. In early 1793, the war was not going well at all. Not only were the foreign enemies and their monarchist French allies advancing, but various parts of France were in revolt, both against the forced levy of troops and the apparent political domination of Paris over all of France. In particular, the region known as the Vendée, as well as Brittany and the cities of Marseilles and Lyon, were in open revolt. Robespierre advocated the death penalty for anyone who even suggested negotiation with the enemy. He and the committee also sent forces against the unruly provinces and against their own political adversaries, the group known as the Girondins. The Girondins were revolutionists too, but ones dedicated to the original principles of the 1789 Revolution rather than the evolving "people's revolution" and "republic of virtue" that Robespierre represented and personified; they also stood for decentralization of French government, which meant resistance to Parisian hegemony. To them, centralization was what the revolution had fought against, and Robespierre and the committee were beginning to act like a new monarchy.

In June 1793 the Girondins were purged from the government. Shortly thereafter, Marat was assassinated in what appeared to be a Girondin plot. The Committee of Public Safety turned decidedly more radical, voting off some of its prominent moderates and installing Robespierre as its virtual leader. With an iron will, not to mention fist, the full Terror was unleashed on the enemies of the revolution. To try to stabilize the food supply during the economic crisis, hoarding was made a capital offense. A general levy of soldiers was decreed, making essentially all Frenchmen members of the army. Brittany and Marseilles were subdued. Still the sans-culottes were not satisfied, so on September 17, 1793 the Law of Suspects was put into effect, creating surveillance committees with the power to name and arrest "suspects," who included "those who by their conduct, their connections, their remarks or their writings show themselves the partisans of tyranny or federalism and the enemies of

***Case Study 1: The "Reign of Terror" in the
French Revolution (continued)***

liberty," "those who cannot . . . justify their means of existence and the performance of their civic duties," "those to whom certificates of patriotism have
been refused," and of course "those of the former nobles, all of the husbands,
wives, fathers, mothers, sons, or daughters, brothers or sisters, and agents of
the Emigres who have not constantly manifested their attachment to the
revolution." In a word, the developing policy of the committee was, "He who
is not with the people is against the people, and consequently must be
exterminated."

In October 1793, the constitution was suspended indefinitely, and the
Committee of Public Safety was accepted as the temporary revolutionary
government. From this time until the fall of Robespierre in the summer of
1794, around sixteen thousand people were guillotined, mostly in Paris,
and many thousands more died in detention (out of the perhaps one-half
million who were arrested). On October 9, Lyon fell to the revolution.
With almost rapturous delight its utter obliteration was ordered, and all
buildings other than homes of patriots and the poor were pulled down.
Even its name was to be execrated, the site of its destruction marked by a
simple sign that read, "Lyon waged war on liberty; Lyon is no more."
Eventually, almost two thousand people were killed in Lyon, first by
guillotine until that process became too slow, and then by musket and
cannon.

On October 17, the king's wife finally followed him in death, and on
October 31 a group of Girondins were executed. The Terror continued to
spread. In December the city of Toulon was recaptured from the English and
almost a thousand of its people executed for collaborating with the enemy. The
eventual conquest of the Vendée left more than ten thousand dead in its wake.
Hundreds of priests across France were drowned for counterrevolutionary
activity. Thousands of others were forced to defrock, and around six thousand
were forced to marry. But perhaps the most extraordinary and emblematic
event of them all was the creation of a new calendar. In a symbolic break
from the past, the new revolutionary calendar ended the process of dating
years from the birth of Christ and set the beginning of the new age to
September 22, 1792 (thus 1794 was already Year II of the Revolutionary
Era). The familiar months were eliminated and replaced with twelve
thirty-day months with poetic seasonal names (Thermidor, Brumaire, Ven-
tose, for example), and the seven-day week was replaced with a ten-day
week ending in a day of rest called *decadi* instead of Sunday. Time itself
had been re-created anew.

On February 5, 1794, in his definitive statement of the goals of the revolution, Robespierre described the resultant "Republic of Virtue":

Case Study 1: The "Reign of Terror" in the French Revolution (continued)

> We desire an order of things in which all base and cruel feelings are suppressed by the laws, and all beneficent and generous feelings evoked; in which ambition means the desire to merit glory and to serve one's country; in which distinctions arise only from equality itself . . . ; in which all minds are enlarged by the continued conviction of republican sentiments and by the endeavor to win the respect of a great people. . . .
>
> We desire to substitute in our country, morality for egoism, honesty for mere honour, principle for habit, duty for decorum, the empire of reason for the tyranny of fashion, contempt of vice for scorn of misfortune, . . . the love of glory for the love of money. . .that is to say, all the virtues and the amazing achievements of the Republic for all the vices and puerilities of the monarchy. . . .
>
> We must crush both the internal and foreign enemies of the Republic, or perish with it. And in this situation, the first maxim of your policy should be to guide the people by reason and repress the enemies of the people by *terreur*. (Quoted in Gershoy 1957: 159–60)

How the guillotine would make for a more beneficent and loving society, isn't clear.

By April 1794, the Terror, having reached the peak of its ruinous fervor, had nowhere to turn but on itself. Rivals of Robespierre such as Danton and Mesmoulins were sent to the blade. On May 7, Robespierre made the curious, and perhaps fatal, choice of introducing a "Cult of the Supreme Being" to the Republic. The cult recognized the existence of a Supreme Being worthy of worship, as well as the immortality of the human soul. It established four annual festivals based on historic days in the Republic, as well as numerous *decadi* celebrations in honor of the Supreme Being itself, the French people, the Republic, truth, love, glory, stoicism, hatred of tyrants, disinterestedness, old age, and so forth. On June 8, the first public event was held, with Robespierre presiding over a ceremony of pomp and symbolism. Many people who formerly thought he only aspired to dictatorship now suspected him of aspiring to popehood, if not divinity.

In June came a reinvigoration of the Terror. In fact, of all guillotine executions in Paris during the Terror, more than half occurred in the final two months (June–July 1794). Indiscriminately targeted by Robespierre's virtue-inspired fury, no one felt safe. After a rambling but threatening speech to the National Convention on July 26, in which he insinuated that just about everyone was his enemy, everyone had had enough. Soldiers came for him on July 29, and he was made to bow to his own instrument of terror the next day. Within twenty-four hours more than eighty of his followers were executed as well, joining the estimated total of thirty thousand people who perished during the sacrificial bloodletting of the Reign of Terror.

Case Study 2: "Theoretical Revolution"— Bolshevism in Russia

> The scientific concept of the dictatorship [of the proletariat] means nothing else but this: power without limit, resting directly upon force, restrained by no laws, absolutely unrestricted by rules.
> —*Lenin, 1920*

> Everyone knows that we Bolsheviks do not confine ourselves to using weapons of terror, but go further—our aim is to liquidate completely the whole class of the bourgeoisie.
> —*Joseph Stalin to biographer Emile Ludwig*

By far the best-known and most significant revolution of the twentieth century was the communist revolution that began in 1917 in Russia; it defined the political struggles of the entire world, as well as much of the agenda of American policy, for eighty years. It also spawned or contributed to other historical upheavals like the Chinese communist revolution under Mao Tse-tung and the conflicts in Korea, Vietnam, Eastern Europe, and many other points on the globe. It was also, less familiarly, the first revolution with a real "theory" behind it. The French Revolution had been virtually "total," aiming, like Stalin above, to liquidate completely a "class" (the nobility) but also to redesign completely a society, from the religion to the calendar. That revolution failed for lack of time; however, the Russian revolution had nearly a century to accomplish its program.

It is also not widely appreciated how much "preparation" there was for the Bolshevik revolution of 1917; it was definitely not a streak of lightning out of a clear sky. In 1796, during the French revolution, Sylvain Marechal had predicted that it would be "but the precursor of another revolution, far greater, far more solemn, which will be the last" (quoted in Billington 1980: 77). Indeed the entire nineteenth century was distinguished by a series of political uprisings—most significantly in 1848 and 1871—that inspired revolutionaries and seemed in each case to augur the end of the current structure and the dawn of a new, more "populist" era.

The year 1848 was known as the year of revolutions, which broke out across Europe from France to Prussia to Austria. All ended with a restoration of "conservative"—what Marx would call "bourgeois" or "middle class"—and more or less autocratic government. The war between France and Prussia in 1870–71 brought such turmoil to defeated France that for a short time a latter-day Paris Commune was established once again. Marx observed these developments with interest, predicting that the Franco–Prussian war would eventually lead to a war between the two giants of the continent—Prussia and

Case Study 2: "Theoretical Revolution"—Bolshevism in Russia (continued)

Russia—and the ensuing (inevitable) revolution in the latter. In 1914 the first part of his prophecy was realized and three years later the second part. The failure of the 1848 and 1871 movements, like the 1789 movement before it, Marx attributed to the lack of realism and "theory" in each; rather than having a clear understanding of historical and social processes and a coherent goal, they were premature and "utopian," hoping to perfect society with the push of a few buttons rather than a revolutionizing the "grounds" of society, in particular the material grounds, or "modes of production," and the social relations that follow from them. Within Russia itself, the eventual revolution had a long lead-up and was by no means the first attempt at radical political and social change. One hundred years earlier, the Napoleonic war had introduced Russians to the revolutionary ideals and zeal of France. When Czar Alexander I died in 1825, an abortive coup led by Russian nobles, known as the Decembrist Revolution, revealed the level of dissatisfaction in the society. The immediate effect was a reactionary backlash under Nicholas I (1825–55), including censorship of the press, prohibition against travel outside the country, and restrictions on the availability and content of education. The social problems as well as the backwardness of the Russian system persisted; a year later it lost the Crimean War (1853–56) to the more advanced Western powers. Eventually serfdom was abolished in 1861, but the policy that replaced it required that peasants compensate landlords through a series of "redemption payments" over many years.

Under the influence of the new international communism of Marx (as well as other "socialist" parties) and a growing native Russian populism, social unrest began not only to coalesce but to radicalize. In the 1860s a movement known as nihilism or anarchism emerged that was hostile to all authority (aristocratic or bourgeois), to all "superstition" and religion, and virtually to all tradition. One organ of the movement, a journal called *Young Russia*, called for the violent overthrow of the government: a revolutionary party "should seize dictatorial powers and not refrain from taking any necessary steps. . . . Everything is false, everything is stupid, from religion . . . to the family. . . . [A] revolution, a bloody and pitiless revolution must change everything down to the very roots . . . we know that rivers of blood will flow and that perhaps even innocent victims will perish" (quoted in Billington 1980: 394–95). Out of this angry agitation emerged such thinkers and leaders as Michael Bakunin, Peter Tkachev, and Sergei Nechayev, the last of whom founded "The People's Justice" and composed the "Catechism" presented in the previous chapter (see Box 8.2).

Simultaneously, Russian populism—a commitment to, almost a fetishism of, the "Russian people," conceived of as the peasantry and to some extent the industrial workers—took shape around the term *narodnik* (from *narod*, for "people"). By the 1870s leaders who considered themselves

Case Study 2: "Theoretical Revolution"—Bolshevism in Russia (continued)

representatives or spokespersons for "the people" were organizing and acting "on behalf of the people" or "in the name of the people." However, as usual, most of these champions of "the people" were young intellectuals who knew little about "the people," so in 1874 thousands of young militants, using a strategy that would typify peasant communism in the twentieth century in such places as China and Cambodia, undertook a pilgrimage to the heartland of their country, to the villages, under the slogan *khozhdenie v narod*, or "going to the people." Another form of action that *narodnik* took was terrorism— bomb throwing and assassination. In fact, after several unsuccessful attempts, a terrorist group *Narodnaya Volya*, or People's Will, succeeded in assassinating Czar Alexander II.

Much of the anarchist movement was just that—anarchistic and disorganized, without any real commitment other than "the people" and without any real plan for the aftermath of revolution. However, Peter Tkachev, editor of *The Alarm*, foresaw the need for revolutionary discipline and even revolutionary leadership by an elite minority:

> The struggle can be conducted successfully only by combining the following conditions: centralization, severe discipline, swiftness, decisiveness, and unity of action. All concessions, all wavering, all compromises, multileadership, and decentralization of the fighting forces weaken the energy, paralyze their activity, and deprive the struggle of all chances of victory. (Quoted in Dmytryhsyn 1971: 24)

Thus, essentially all the pieces were in place for the Marxist–Bolshevik revolution a few decades later.

All that was missing now was a spark to light the fire. That spark almost came in 1905, after another humiliating military defeat, this time at the hands of Japan. The result was a workers' strike in the capital of Petrograd (St. Petersburg) in January of 1905, in which some two hundred thousand protesters marched to the palace and were shot down by government troops. The effect was to galvanize popular opposition to the monarchy and to further enhance tensions between the "masses" and the elite in Russian society. It was apparent that "the people" would have to take matters into their own hands, and they did so by forming a council or committee (*soviet* in Russian) in Petrograd to represent themselves. Other *soviets* soon organized, in Moscow, for instance, regarding themselves as the true grassroots government of Russia. In December 1905 the Moscow *soviet* conducted a general strike and actually seized control of part of the city for a few days until the army put down the revolt at the cost of more than a thousand lives and an undetermined number of arrests. Meanwhile, even elements of the military were showing their unhappiness, as with the mutiny on the battleship Potemkin in June of the same year.

Case Study 2: "Theoretical Revolution"—Bolshevism in Russia (continued)

Out of the peoples'/workers' and *soviet* movement there emerged a revolutionary leader with an iron will, a clear voice, and a definite plan. His name was Lenin, a pseudonym for Vladimir Illych Ulyanov. He was steeped in Marxist doctrine as well as the *narodnik* philosophy, particularly of the Tkachev variety. He recognized the necessity of a "core" or "corps" of "professional revolutionaries"; the "people" were not yet ready for revolution, not yet conscious of themselves as a class. An elite, an avant-garde, a "leading party" would be required to perform the revolution for the people while teaching revolution to the people. As part of the much wider Russian socialist revolutionary movement, Lenin urged revolutionary fervor, centralization, and discipline as early as 1902 in his influential tract *What Is To Be Done?* He insisted that only what he regarded as the "hards"—those who were willing to risk everything and to compromise nothing, who were willing to give their full energy and life to the cause—should be in the party, at least in the party leadership. His ideas were rejected at a party conference, but he was subsequently able to get his supporters elected to the central committee and the editorial staff (partly because some opponents had walked out), and from that time on he referred to his part of the socialist movement as the "bolsheviks" (from *bolshenstvo*, "majority"), although he was often really in the minority. His rivals became known as the "mensheviks," or "minority."

In January 1912 Lenin formed his own party based on the concept of a "revolutionary democratic dictatorship of the proletariat and peasantry" (Lindemann 1983: 198). However, he was still in no position to pull off a successful political overthrow of the establishment. The opportunity came when Russia entered another ill-fated war, World War I, in 1914. The war was incredibly unpopular and incredibly poorly prosecuted: Russian soldiers were thrown into combat with nonfunctioning weapons and sometimes literally no weapons at all. Throughout the duration, disastrous defeat after defeat, a German blockade, and an ongoing labor and supply shortage made living conditions intolerable and mass dissatisfaction acute. In early 1917, after almost three years of this situation, large-scale strikes and food riots started to break out, as in March of 1917 in Petrograd. On March 11, soldiers deployed to suppress the uprisings mutinied and actually joined the protesters. The members of the toothless parliament, the Duma, declared themselves to be the Temporary Committee and the new effective government, much as the Third Estate had done in revolutionary France. On March 16 Czar Nicholas II abdicated, and the Temporary Committee replaced itself with the Provisional Government, a conservative/liberal/bourgeois body. The first step of the revolution had transpired almost without incident.

Case Study 2: "Theoretical Revolution"—Bolshevism in Russia (continued)

Lenin had had nothing to do with developments so far, as he was not even in the country but rather in exile in Switzerland. However, at home the populist and socialist revolutionaries (like the French Jacobins) were hardly pleased with this first stage of the revolution. In Petrograd the Soviet of Workers' and Soldiers' Deputies ratcheted up again and also began to conduct itself as the "true" government of postczarist Russia. Still, the Provisional Government, under the direction mostly of Alexander Kerensky, did a fair enough job of running the state immediately, although it made two fatal mistakes: it agreed to continue the war, and it allowed agitators like Lenin, Leon Trotsky, and Joseph Stalin to return home.

In July 1917 a disastrous new campaign in the war led to a military revolt and a right-wing coup attempt, which emboldened the leftists under Lenin. He declared the time to be now. During the night of November 6 and 7, 1917, a Bolshevik coup almost effortlessly overthrew the Provisional Government, and Lenin's and Trotsky's Revolutionary Military Committee held the reins of power by early morning.

It is said that when the shooting stops the revolution begins (although in this case, there never was much shooting). Lenin pulled Russia out of the war and signed a unilateral peace with Germany. And the "legislation" of the "social revolution" began to pour out of the new government. Private property was abolished. Class and rank were eliminated. Factory workers were put in charge of their factories. All banks were declared a state monopoly. Marriage and divorce laws were changed, taking authority away from the Orthodox Church and more nearly equalizing gender power. Perhaps most ominously, on December 20 the All-Russian Commission for Struggle against Counter-Revolution and Sabotage, a secret police agency known as the CHEKA, was created. Resistance—even debate or internal dissension—was not to be allowed. The party was the voice of the people, and the people were always right, so the party was always right. Never mind that elections held in late 1917 (scheduled long before the Bolshevik coup) sent a majority of non-Bolsheviks to the Constituent Assembly. Lenin suffered it to meet once (January 18, 1918) and then dissolved it.

The attitude toward the people's revolution and party unity and infallibility was clear. As Lenin himself later said, "We must know and remember that the entire constitution of the Soviet Republic, both in legal and political matters, is based on the fact that the Party does everything, planning, building, and straightening out errors" (quoted in Heller and Nekrich 1986: 165). Trotsky echoed this sentiment when he stated: "None of us wishes to be or can be right against the Party. In the last instance the Party is always right" (quoted in Deutscher 1959: 139).

Case Study 2: "Theoretical Revolution"—Bolshevism in Russia (continued)

However, the unity Lenin sought did not exist in reality. On August 30, 1918 there was a near-successful attempt on his life, which led to the unleashing of the "Red Terror," in which the CHEKA arrested or executed known or suspected "enemies of the revolution." The Commissar of Justice, N. V. Krylenko, in a comment reminiscent of Robespierre and others yet to come, put it this way: "We must execute not only the guilty. Execution of the innocent will impress the masses even more" (quoted in Pipes 1990: 822). By some estimates the death toll was as high as 50,000 or even 150,000.

Many more died in the civil war that ensued. Lenin had seized power in a coup but did not command the support of the majority of Russians. He was also opposed, like the French revolutionary government in 1789, by all of his neighbors. England, France, Japan, and the United States landed troops on Russian soil in early 1918 to aid the "white Russians" who were fighting against Bolshevik communist rule. However, by the summer of 1920 the Bolshevik regime had survived the threat and emerged victorious. The cost had been staggering: by 1921 Russia had lost 26 million people—2 million had been war casualties; 7 million deaths were due to the terror and hunger and disease; 2 million emigrants had died; and 15 million inhabitants of the former empire had died in local independence movements. Another 35 million people lingered on in hunger (Dmytryshyn 1971: 113).

Then, on January 21, 1924, the fate of Russia—by now, the Union of Soviet Socialist Republics, or USSR—took another unexpected turn, when, after a series of debilitating strokes Lenin suddenly died. Without a process for orderly succession, over the next few years an unlikely candidate, Joseph Stalin (born Joseph Djugashvili), rose to the position not only of leader of the party but to that of *vozhd*, or "beloved leader" or "great genius," and became the first modern head of state to perfect the "cult of personality." He was much more of a bureaucrat than the revolutionary theorist Lenin had been. In fact, one of his key strategies was to virtually sanctify Lenin (including having his body embalmed and displayed) and to portray himself as the humble carrier of Lenin's cloak. However, he had very different ends in mind.

One goal was to "complete" the social revolution that the party had only inaugurated in 1917. This involved the "collectivization" of the peasantry and the eradication of any remnants of "capitalism" in the countryside. After the revolution, many peasants had expected, and many had managed, to acquire their own small holdings of land; that for them was the point of the revolution. But Stalin, part communist ideologue, part autocratic absolutist, wanted all private property eliminated and all private property holders eliminated with it. He began a merciless campaign against the so-called *kulaks*, the more prosperous peasants. They were not only to be dispossessed of their land but to be "liquidated as a class."

Case Study 2: "Theoretical Revolution"—Bolshevism in Russia (continued)

In 1927, in resistance to low commodity prices and plans for forced collectivization, the farmers began to withhold grain from the government. This move precipitated a food crisis and provoked Stalin's wrath: he declared "energetic measures" to compel farmers to supply the state, including "administrative arbitrariness, violation of revolutionary law, raids on peasant houses, [and] illegal searches" (quoted in Dmytryshyn 1971: 156). By the following spring, Stalin had called for an all-out campaign against the *kulaks* as counterrevolutionaries, traitors, and saboteurs; the army was used, along with forced resettlement and state-induced famines, to break the "enemies of the people." Thousands of peasants were killed, millions coercively collectivized, and millions more exiled or imprisoned in the new prison/workcamp system of *gulags*. Entire prison cities appeared in the middle of nowhere in Siberia and other bleak areas: Magadan was founded in 1932 with more than ten thousand slave laborers, and camps like Kolyma, Orotukan, and Solovetsky were supplied with a constant stream of political prisoners to replace the ones who died from exposure, malnutrition, or overwork. And there were plenty of suspects, as a 1930 party decree had identified three categories of *kulaks*: active enemies, the politically unreliable (including the kin of the enemies), and those who were considered "legal" but still removed to labor camps (numbering in the millions).

Meanwhile, to break the resistance of the Ukrainian people, Stalin had essentially engineered a famine in 1931. By demanding an ever-increasing amount of a shrinking harvest—even ordering peasants to send more food when there simply was no more—he managed to starve up to 5 million Ukrainian "enemies of the revolution." Over the entire period, estimates of those starved to death run as high as 20 million, although conservative estimates fall in the range of 10 million. For many of the survivors, austere diets, oppressive workloads, and constant fear were their lot.

Stalin did not only direct his cruelty toward the peasants and nonparty members. Starting in the mid-1930s, a series of purges of the party itself eventually left Stalin alone in power. In late 1934, a supporter named Kirov was assassinated, which set off a wave of arrests and trials (without defense). Within months thirty to forty thousand people had been arrested, and up to two hundred per day were being executed. In 1936 a purge, or *chistka* ("cleansing"), of the party began with the arrest of seventeen "Old Bolsheviks" from the revolutionary days; thirteen were executed, and the others were never heard from again. In 1937 thousands of army officers were tried and killed, and in 1938 some of the biggest names from the early days, including Bukharin, were tried and executed. By 1939 at the Eighteenth Party Congress, Stalin was the only Bolshevik remaining from the 1917 Revolution. Of the two thousand delegates at the Congress five years earlier, more than half had since

Case Study 2: "Theoretical Revolution"—Bolshevism in Russia (continued)

been arrested. Of the seventy-one Central Committee members, fifty-five had disappeared. About one-third of the entire party membership had been expelled, and millions had been "processed" by the legal system. Stalin was now a one-man government and an infallible leader; any and all mistakes and shortcomings of the society were "attributed to his opponents, who were described as 'wreckers,' 'spies,' 'saboteurs,' and 'enemies of the people'" (Dmytryshyn 1971: 183). Gone indeed were the idealist yearnings of 1917: the assassination of Leon Trotsky by Stalin's henchmen on the very eve of World War II marked, symbolically and actually, the end of an era.

Case Study 3: At War with History in Bosnia

The struggle over the political and ethnic fate of the fragmented and failed state of Yugoslavia—particularly its constituent republic, Bosnia—has given the world sharp images of hatred and cruelty, like the infamous "ethnic cleansing" of Bosnian Muslims from Serb territories. The main protagonists in the struggle—Serbs, Croats, and Bosnians—are members of a family of peoples called Slavs, which also includes the Bulgars, the Poles, and the Russians. The Serbs, Croats, and Bosnians are sometimes classified or classify themselves as southern, or "yugo," Slavs. All three speak roughly the same language; however, for historical reasons, the one language is written in two different scripts, in Latin by the Croats, in Cyrillic by the Serbs. Therefore, in at least two important senses, the peoples of the Balkans could be construed as one group. What would then lead them to think and act as disparate groups—and kill each other over it? The most significant difference is religious. Croats are predominantly Roman Catholic, Serbs largely Eastern Orthodox, and a considerable Muslim population lives in Bosnia.

The Slavs probably migrated to the Balkans in the sixth and seventh centuries C.E. Before that time, records refer to earlier inhabitants of the region known as Illyrians. The Slavs apparently arrived as a confederation of different tribes known as Slaveni; the Croats and Serbs established themselves in the region after 620. Christianity arrived in the Balkans in the ninth century from both the east and the west; Roman Catholicism had its best successes in the western Balkans, especially Croatia and Dalmatia, whereas Orthodox Christianity won most converts in the east, predominantly Serbia and Macedonia. Bosnia, the remote middle ground, was also the meeting point of these two traditions, so that neither faith developed a firm foothold in the territory. Well

Case Study 3: At War with History in Bosnia (continued)

into the eleventh century, there was no strongly organized church in Bosnia and few resident priests of either denomination.

The Ottoman Turks brought Islam to southeastern Europe during their territorial expansion in the early fourteenth and fifteenth centuries. The conquest of the Balkans is a key moment in Slavic, especially Serb, history. The crucial confrontation between Turks and Slavs was the famous Battle of Kosovo Polje (Field of Blackbirds) in 1389. Although both sides apparently suffered heavy losses, the Serbs in particular remember this episode as a bitter defeat, in which their Prince Lazar was killed. By 1392 all of Serbia was under Turkish control, but Sarajevo did not fall until 1451, and parts of northern Bosnia remained out of Ottoman jurisdiction until as late as 1527. As a result, Serbs withdrew to the north and east.

The Ottoman occupation had a serious effect on the "ethnic situation" in the Balkans. Understandably, strong forces existed to encourage assimilation if not conversion to Ottoman/Muslim culture, and without a deep Christian tradition or presence not much stood in their way. Bosnian Muslims enjoyed disproportionate, but not exclusive, benefits, such as access to feudal estates and titles. Conversion to Islam could also be interpreted as a political statement of the times, a confirmation of preference for Ottoman rule.

The opening years of the nineteenth century saw the first serious uprising in Serbia, which eventually led to Ottoman acceptance of limited autonomy for the province. In 1815 Serbia was granted its own Assembly and elected prince, which helped to define the outlines and fan the flames of Serbian nationalism. Bosnia too was restive in this period. At the same time, the economic conditions in Bosnia were deteriorating, and the entire economy and infrastructure remained relatively backward. Landlords used the disorder to attempt to utterly exploit their subjects. Although this burden may have seemed to fall disproportionately on the Christian population (the vast majority of landowners with serfs being Muslim, well into the twentieth century), it weighed heavily upon the Muslim peasants too. In essence, the real dynamic of stratification and inequality was not Muslim versus Christian but gentry versus peasant, but the latter could and would be translated into the former.

This process of ethnogenesis entailed a new equation of religious and "national" identities and boundaries. Specifically, in distinction to Muslim identity, Orthodox was coming to be coterminous with Serb, and Catholic with Croat. Thus the Serbs and Croats were the first among the southern Slavs to "awaken" to ethnic nationalism, which commenced as a sort of reunification and irredentism movement, to bring together the dispersed "national" community. One famous example of this is the document known as *Nacertanije* ("Outline") written in 1844, which expressed the belief that it is necessary to

Case Study 3: At War with History in Bosnia (continued)

"ensure national survival by a mission to unite Serbs in scattered parts of the Habsburg and Ottoman empires" (quoted in Dragnich 1992: 7).

Serb and Croat nationalisms presented alternative, and in some ways opposing, interpretations of "ethnic" identity and national destiny. Croat nationalists advanced the argument that "Croat" was not only a distinct identity in the Balkan region of the empire but *the* distinct identity. All southern Slavs were Croats, including the Serbs. For its part, Serb nationalism also had its extreme and exclusivistic side. The best-known early Serb nationalist was Vuk Karadzic, who in 1849 published a treatise entitled "Serbs All and Everywhere," in which he professed that Serb identity and culture was the primary and genuine southern Slavic one and that Croats were really Serbs.

These contests inevitably had their impact on a third group, the Bosnian Muslims. Both nationalisms attempted to claim the Muslims as well: Croats defined Muslims as Croats, Serbs defined Muslims as Serbs. For their part, the majority of Bosnian Muslims not only asserted their own unique identity but asserted it on different grounds, on the basis of religion rather than nationality. In other words, although they regarded themselves as a distinct group, they did not regard themselves as a *national* group; they were followers of a faith, not members of an "ethnic group."

A turning point in Balkan nationalism came in the 1870s, as the independence movement in Serbia gained momentum. In 1876 Serbia, which had enjoyed a degree of political autonomy within the Ottoman empire for decades, declared independence, which it achieved in 1878. It was only now that a modern Bosnian–Muslim nationalism began to emerge, based on the view that Bosnians were neither Serbs nor Croats but a distinct, though related, people and that both Croat and Serb claims to some sort of central or primordial status vis-à-vis the southern Slavs were fallacious.

The ethnopolitical activity among the Bosnian Muslims was matched by activity among the Serbs and Croats. A Serb political party, the Serbian National Organization (SNO), was founded, drawing most of its support from the upper classes. Croat nationalism had if anything an even smaller social base at first, emanating principally from the small intelligentsia and middle class and from the Franciscan order. Representing the two distinct interests of these segments of Croat society, two political parties took shape, one secular in outlook (the Croatian National Union) and one clearly religious (the Croatian Catholic Association). Like the SNO, the Croatian parties, particularly the former, sought and occasionally made alliances with the Muslim contingent.

Despite these separatist initiatives, a joint "Yugoslavism" came by the turn of the century to look like the best bet for "national" recognition and self-determination. The heightened nationalism(s) of the Slavs gave rise to a series of wars in the Balkans between 1912 and 1914 and ultimately sparked World War I

Case Study 3: At War with History in Bosnia (continued)

(touched off by the assassination of the heir to the Austrian throne by a Bosnian radical, Gavrilo Princip). It was clear that the political map would be redrawn after the war, and Yugoslavs wanted to be on that map. The growing consensus was for a Yugoslav state, based on a Yugoslav "national identity," in which Slovenes, Croats, and Serbs constituted a single linguistic, economic, and ethnic group. Accordingly, the authors of the peace treaty accepted the idea of a Yugoslav state, and on December 1, 1918 Serb Prince Alexander formally announced the creation of the "Kingdom of Serbs, Croats, and Slovenes."

However, in addition to the three named ethnic groups in the new state, other minorities—Slav and non-Slav—joined or were swept into it. To be precise, the "tripartite" kingdom was roughly 42 percent Serb and Montenegran, 23 percent Croat, 8 percent Slovene, 5 percent Macedonian, 5 percent Bosnian Muslim, and 4 percent Albanian; by religion, the population was about 47 percent Orthodox, 39 percent Catholic, and 11 percent Muslim. It should be clear that this tapestry of minorities would be a challenge to Yugoslav integration. For example, the Croatian Peasant Party maintained a Croat nationalist stance based on the "authentic" identity and traditions of rural Croatia. Similarly, the Serbian Popular Radical Party represented the extremists of Serb nationalism; in fact, its position on the "Bosnian problem" was as follows: "When our army crosses the Drina [River], we will give the Turks twenty-four hours, or even forty-eight hours, of time to return to their ancestral religion. Those who do not wish to do so are to be cut down, as we did in Serbia earlier" (quoted in Cigar 1995: 17). This did not mean that the Muslims would necessarily all be killed, but "There can no longer be any Turks in Bosnia. They can flee across the Sava [River, into Croatia], or wherever."

Bosnians, especially Bosnian Muslims, tried in various ways to adapt to the new Yugoslav reality: by founding their own "ethnic" organizations and parties, by welcoming Yugoslavism as an end to divisiveness, by attempting to play the middle position between the Serb and Croat factions in the government (thus making themselves a desirable political ally in the parliament to be courted by one side or the other), and by identifying with the lesser of the two evils from the Bosnian point of view, that is, the Croats.

But the Croats were a source of ethnic friction in themselves. Among the new generation of Croat leadership were those who pursued a course of action to expand if not liberate Croatia. Ante Pavelic organized the *Ustasha* ("Insurrectionists"), a Croat ultranationalist group which favored total independence for Croatia through the destruction of Yugoslavia. It was a *Ustasha* team that assassinated Yugoslavia's King Alexander on October 9, 1934.

After Yugoslavia fell to the Axis powers on April 17, 1941 the *Ustasha* was permitted to create an "Independent State of Croatia" with Pavelic as head of state. The treatment by the *Ustasha* state of its ethnic minorities, especially its

Case Study 3: At War with History in Bosnia (continued)

Serbs, became one of the principal grievances between Serbs and Croats in recent times. In fact, Pavelic is reputed to have championed a "one-third, one-third, one-third" policy in regard to Croatian Serbs: one-third would be killed, one-third would be pushed out of Croatia, and one-third would be converted to Catholicism. Whatever the policy underlying its actions, estimates of Serb casualties run between 500,000 and one million out of a total Croatian Serb population of something less than two million. In haunting anticipation of 1990s atrocities, whole villages or enclaves were depopulated or destroyed.

The postwar future of Yugoslavia was settled with the arrival of the Soviet army in Belgrade on October 20, 1944. In January 1946 a constitution for the new Yugoslavia was issued, with the Communist Party under Tito (Josip Broz) firmly in control. The new system created six republics, five of them "national" (Serbia, Croatia, Slovenia, Montenegro, and Macedonia) and the sixth Bosnia–Hercegovina, as well as two "autonomous regions" (Vojvodina and Kosovo) that were associated with Serbia.

Tito hoped and believed that a new supranational identity would develop, a true merger brought about by shared economic interests and progress and by socialist institutions. And it is true that in the 1940s and 1950s, and before and since, Bosnians were more inclined to self-identify as "Yugoslavs" than as any particular nationality. One caveat is that "Muslim" was not an available legal category with which to identify. However, in 1961, the census introduced a new category, "Ethnic Muslim," to which nearly a million Bosnians subscribed. In 1964, Muslims were declared a *narod* on par with Yugoslavia's five others—but the only one without a national republic. Finally, in 1968 came the fulfillment of the ethnogenesis of the Bosnian Muslims: the Bosnian Central Committee declared that it "has been shown, and present socialist practice confirms, that the Muslims are a distinct nation"(quoted in Malcolm 1994: 199).

Bosnian–Muslim ethnonationalism and Croat agitation stirred the Serbs, who were already aggrieved. Kosovo naturally was an acute issue; the Serb percentage of the population was declining and the Albanian majority was becoming restless about the dominance of the Serb minority, culminating in anti-Serb riots in 1968. As a consequence, Serbian communist Dobrica Cosic uttered these prophetic words in the same year: "One could witness even among the Serbian people a reignition of the old historic goal and national idea—the unification of the Serbian people into a single state"(quoted in Malcolm 1994: 205). Serbs also claimed their rights to a larger chunk of Yugoslavia's federal budget and a stronger voice in federal affairs, since the state was after all centered in and based upon their republic. Serbs suffered from a more backward economy than the northwestern republics of Croatia and Slovenia. And finally, "Serb culture" in the form of Orthodox Christianity was reawakening.

Case Study 3: At War with History in Bosnia (continued)

The death of Tito in 1980 left a political vacuum, which together with an undeniable economic crisis laid the foundations for factional competition. As early as 1981 Kosovo was showing signs of wear in its multiethnic population: the Albanian majority protested against the power and privilege of the Serb minority, while the Serbs "claimed that they were being subjected to 'genocide' and 'terror' by Albanian nationalists" who, presumably, wanted to separate Kosovo not only from Serbia but perhaps from Yugoslavia (Cohen 1993: 46). Serb and Croat nationalisms found a free arena for their claims and counterclaims. One of these claims was of a rampant and threatening "Islamic nationalism" operating in Bosnia. Bosnia's Muslims were lumped together by other radical nationalists with international Islam and even with "Eastern" culture or "primitive society." Accordingly, wrote Serb intellectual Dragos Kalajic, Bosnian Muslims do not belong to "the European family of nations"; instead, they are, culturally and genetically, the product of another, less savory people—of the five centuries of Ottoman rule during which, "in satisfying their sexual impulses . . . the Ottoman armies and administrators—drawn from the Near Eastern and North African bazaars—created a distinct semi-Arab ethnic group"(quoted in Cigar 1995: 26).

Still, these opinions lacked the endorsement of mainstream institutions and the weight and machinery of state until about 1986, the year of the "Memorandum" of the Serbian Academy of Arts and Sciences and the rise of Slobodan Milosevic to federal leadership. The Memorandum picked up and developed the Greater Serbia ideology. The writers perceived dangers to the Serb nation in the alleged assimilationist and "nationalist" policies in other republics, which threatened to identify, for example, Serbs in Croatia as Croats, or Serbs in Bosnia as Bosnians. One of the main objections of the Serb nationalists was the detachment of Kosovo from Serbia. In the ultimate symbolic gesture, Milosevic and a large number of pilgrims and politicians converged on Kosovo on June 28, 1989 for the six hundredth anniversary of the Battle of Kosovo. Milosevic cited that, all these years later and on the same ground, "we are again engaged in battles and quarrels. They are not armed battles, but this cannot be excluded yet"(quoted in Glenny 1994: 35). At around the same time, a troupe of Serbs traveled around Bosnia with what they alleged were the remains of Prince Lazar, the Serb martyr from the Battle of Kosovo; the party also proclaimed to the Muslims that "we will do our utmost to crush their race and descendants so completely that history will not even remember them" (quoted in Cigar 1995: 35). Government-controlled television broadcast such slogans as "For the Good Life: Partition and Separation" into Bosnia, and marches and rallies offered up their own slogans like "Oh Muslims, you black crows, Tito is no longer around to protect you!" "We love you Slobodan because you hate the Muslims!" and "I'll be first, who'll be second, to drink some Turkish blood?" (quoted in Cigar 1995: 34).

Case Study 3: At War with History in Bosnia (continued)

Meanwhile, alarm—and nationalism—in other republics was growing. Some of the alarm and the demands engendered by it were more or less strictly political: in the face of increasing Serbian centralism of Yugoslavian politics, Croatia and Slovenia in particular lobbied for more power sharing. Further, they wanted to keep a larger share of their wealth and stop subsidizing the poorer regions like Serbia and Bosnia. As early as June 1989 Slovenian party leaders warned that they would not accept a Serb-dominated government and hinted that such a system might eventuate in their withdrawal from the federation. By late 1990 Slovenia and Croatia had presented a draft of a confederal agreement that would essentially end the Yugoslavian confederation and replace it with an alliance of sovereign states. The Yugoslavian government and "Yugoslav" nationalists opposed this move; the most strident opposition came from those Serbs who lived outside Serbia proper, the 25 percent of the "nation" residing mainly in Croatia and Bosnia–Hercegovina. Slovenia and Croatia declared their independence from Yugoslavia on June 25, 1991. In less than a day, federal forces were sent into Slovenia.

The war in Slovenia was brief (troops were withdrawn by July 19), where the stakes for the federal government and the Serbs were not very high: few Serbs live in Slovenia. The stakes in Croatia were considerably higher. Some six hundred thousand "ethnic Serbs" lived within the borders of Croatia at the outset of conflict, and these Serbs had organized their own political party, the Serbian Democratic Party (SDS). When Croatia voted to secede from Yugoslavia, a war ensued between the Croats and the Yugoslavian army plus militias of the local Serbs, which cost over ten thousand lives and resulted in thirty thousand other casualties. A truce in early 1992 suspended the hostility in Croatia but allowed for its transfer to Bosnia.

One cause of the ensuing conflagration in Bosnia was the tug-of-war between Croatia and Serbia over their "co-nationals" and the territory they inhabited. Both Croats and Serbs were represented in large numbers in Bosnia, and they began to get mobilized as well. Bosnia's Muslims were the first to adopt a sectional party, the Party of Democratic Action or SDA, which alleged to recognize Serb and Croat rights in the republic but claimed Muslims as the "autochthonous Bosnian nation." Aliya Izetbegovic, leader of the SDA and a well-known "Muslim activist," became president of Bosnia. This alarmed the Bosnian Serbs, some of whom formed their own version of the SDS led by Radovan Karadzic. And when Slovenia and Croatia declared their independence, Bosnia began to contemplate doing the same.

Karadzic and the Bosnian Serb leadership declared their own "Serbian Autonomous Region of Hercegovina" in September 1991 with the help of the Yugoslavian army (which was by now basically the Serbian army). In the fragmenting context of multinational Bosnia, Bosnian Croats also organized their own party, the Croatian Democratic Alliance, which designated its own sphere of interest and influence in western Hercegovina, especially around the city of Mostar.

Case Study 3: At War with History in Bosnia (continued)

Bosnian Muslims were left holding the government of a dissolving republic and appearing to participate in its dissolution. On March 1, formal violence broke out.

Virtually all plans and proposals to bring the fighting to an end entailed some degree of ethnic partition. As Karadzic himself stated: "There is no return to a united Bosnia–Hercegovina. The time has come for the Serbian people to organize itself as a totality, without regard to the administrative [existing] borders" (quoted in Cigar 1995: 39–40). If this requires taking over half of Bosnia's land for less than one-third of its population, in order to create a "corridor" connecting disparate Serb regions, then so be it. Observers also noted that the conflict seemed to be more than a war of one nation against another nation. The war in Bosnia, with its atrocities and its ethnic cleansing, was a war against a multicultural ideal. Karadzic stated that in a Bosnian war the Muslims would "disappear from the face of the earth." He continued: "They are . . . threatened not only in the physical sense, and I did not think that they might disappear only physically; rather, this is also the beginning of the end of their existence as a nation" (quoted in Cigar 1995: 37).

Accordingly, the war for Bosnia included a war against culture and history in Bosnia, against the memory and symbols of Muslim culture and history. The attack was taken to mosques, for example, between eight hundred and a thousand of which were damaged or destroyed. Cemeteries, schools and their libraries, and old towns and neighborhoods were targeted. Major resources and collections of medieval and Ottoman history and culture such as the National and University Library and the Library of the Institute for Oriental Studies (both in Sarajevo) and the National Library in Mostar were destroyed; the Institute for Oriental Studies alone housed invaluable documents of historical, artistic, and political interest—all proof that a vibrant Muslim society once reigned there. Perhaps the single most symbolic casualty of the war was the old Mostar bridge between the Muslim and Croat sides of the city; its literal fall marked the failure of all attempts to "bridge" the combatants in their ethnic identities and hostilities.

Case Study 4: "Tribal" Genocide in Rwanda

> In the past our proper name was Bantu. We are Bantu. "Hutu" is no tribe, no nothing. Muhutu is a [Tutsi] word which means "servant.". . . It is a name that the Tutsi gave us.
> —*Hutu refugee in Tanzania*

Rwanda serves for many people as the very model of modern genocide. In the summer of 1994, Americans watched for weeks as Africans killed Africans,

Case Study 4: "Tribal" Genocide in Rwanda (continued)

often hand-to-hand with machetes and knives, and as bodies piled up on streets or floated down rivers. By the time it was over, perhaps half a million Rwandans, mostly "ethnic" Tutsis, had been killed by "ethnic" Hutus. Surely this was the face of "ethnic conflict."

Rwanda, and its sister-state Burundi, were new states created out of European colonialism in the early 1960s, as all of Africa was wresting itself free of colonial control. Both states have a roughly similar composition, around 85 percent Hutu and 15 percent Tutsi; there is also an extremely small (less than 1 percent) component of Twa or "bushman" people who get virtually no attention in either state. Tutsis had been the "traditional" dominant group in both states (with some qualification, as described below). However, to all appearances, this "traditional" domination did not go very far back into history and was never very complete. In fact, some anthropologists have argued that "Tutsi" and "Hutu" were not originally ethnic groups at all, as the opening quotation above suggests.

It seems quite likely that the Twa, a foraging people, were the first inhabitants of the area. The Hutu horticulturalists probably arrived some hundreds of years ago and displaced them. Most recently, in a process that was not finished when Europeans arrived, the Tutsi had migrated into the same area; pastoralists, they had established a kind of hegemony in a native "plural society" that is not uncommon when pastoralists and horticulturalists meet. The pastoral segment, being more warlike, tends to subdue the horticultural segment, being more sedentary, and establish itself as the elite or royal group, exploiting the previous population as servants and clients.

Three important qualifications to this picture must be mentioned. First, the penetration and subjugation of the local society was still under way and far from thorough in the late 1800s. Parts of Rwanda, especially the north, felt little intrusion of Tutsi power. King Rwabugiri had only brought parts of Rwanda under his control in midcentury. Second, the pictures in Rwanda and neighboring Burundi were not identical; in the former, the Tutsi had established a more distinctly "ethnic" system with Tutsi occupying leadership roles and Hutu occupying subordinate roles. However, in Burundi the situation was complicated by the rise of a unique "ruling class" of royal lineages that considered themselves neither quite Tutsi nor Hutu. Called *ganwa*, they outranked both Tutsi and Hutu, setting up a different kind of social dynamic. So, in Rwanda the important distinction was Tutsi versus Hutu, while in Burundi it was *ganwa* versus Tutsi and Hutu. This difference would make a difference as modern "ethnic" conflict unfolded.

Third, there are voices that characterize the Tutsi–Hutu split in traditional Rwanda not as an "ethnic" or "tribal" one at all but more as a class or caste separation. Jacques Maquet (1961) in particular likens Tutsi–Hutu relations to those of lords and serfs or patrons and clients, accordingly. Intermarriage between the groups was not unknown, although it was not common. Mythology

Case Study 4: "Tribal" Genocide in Rwanda (continued)

and ideology separated the groups into superior and inferior by what Maquet called the "premise of inequality," in which it was believed that "people born in different castes are unequal in inborn endowment, physical as well as psychological, and have consequently fundamentally different rights." This resembles the Indian caste case, with the Indian addition of spiritual "karmic" explanations of these inequalities, which make the classic "caste system" what it is.

Thus, Tutsi and Hutu, particularly in the Rwandan context, were conceived to be distinguishable physically, among other ways. Tutsi were theoretically taller and thinner, Hutu shorter and stouter, although in practice it was and is often difficult to detect the difference. Even more, "Tutsi" and "Hutu" were not closed identities; it was possible, by a process of *kwihutura*, or "shedding Hutu-ness," for a Hutu to become a Tutsi—that is, if he acquired wealth and especially cattle and adopted a "Tutsi" way of life. Finally, it is worth noting that not all Tutsi were rich and noble, nor did they even all own cattle. These are "ideal" descriptions, not actual ones.

Nevertheless, Hutu tended to be the "clients" of Tutsi superiors, and Rwandan society had a collection of different kinds of patron–client relations, all of which involved clients providing services to patrons and patrons providing access to resources or other advantages and securities to clients. These relationships were somewhat exploitative, like European feudal ones, but were limited in their exploitation by traditional rules and practical facts. They were not, to all appearances, violent nor completely resented or resisted. In conclusion, as Watson describes it (1991: 21), "'Tutsi' refers to a 'noble,' as 'Hutu' refers to a 'commoner' and not to different tribes.'"

The Europeans happened to stumble upon the scene in the late 1800s as the Tutsi upper class, particularly in Rwanda, was attempting to extend its hegemony into the society. German explorers characterized the scene as chaotic but one in which the Tutsi people were definitely predominant. As was the European habit at the time, German colonial administrators wanted to name the groups they encountered and to assign each individual to one and only one group, so the terms "Tutsi" and "Hutu" were natural choices. The people became either "Tutsis" or "Hutus," with the "Tutsis" in charge. Even worse, European observers, including anthropologists, saw distinctions where there were none and added the nasty element of "race" to the equation. Now "Tutsi" and "Hutu" were not just "group names" but also "races."

Race, as practiced by Europeans, is not just descriptive but evaluative, so Tutsis and Hutus were not only seen as different races but as *unequal* races. Tutsi were perceived as superior in every way; a colonial report from 1925 concluded that a Tutsi

> has nothing of the negro, apart from his color. He is usually very tall, 1.8 m. at least, often 1.9 or more. He is very thin. . . . His features are very fine: a high brow,

Case Study 4: "Tribal" Genocide in Rwanda (continued)

thin nose and fine lips framing beautiful shining teeth. Batutsi women are usually lighter-skinned than their husbands, very slender and pretty in their youth, although they tend to thicken with age. (Quoted in Prunier 1995: 6)

Their personalities and values were superior as well: "Gifted with a vivacious intelligence, the Tutsi displays a refinement of feelings which is rare among primitive peoples. He is a natural-born leader, capable of extreme self-control and of calculated good-will." (ibid.) Hutu, on the other hand, were less attractive to Europeans in every regard. The same report states that the Hutu "display very typical Bantu features. . . . They are generally short and thick-set with a big head, a jovial expression, a wide nose, and enormous lips." (ibid.) As people they were seen as "hardworking, not very clever, extrovert, irascible, unmannerly, obedient" (ibid.)—all normal qualities of the lower class. The reader does not even want to know what was thought of the Twa.

The point is that Europeans applied their own conceptions of beauty and superiority to peoples who had never been so compared and described before. And, being more beautiful, more intelligent, more refined, lighter-skinned— in short, *more European*—the colonialists had a fellow feeling for the Tutsis that they did not have for the more "African" Hutus. One missionary went so far as to call them "European under a black skin." Contemporary science, including anthropology, and Christian mythology combined to offer an account of the ancestry of these black Europeans: they were "Hamites," descendants of Ham the son of Noah, "pastoral Caucasians" who had intermixed with "the two more primitive African stocks, the Negro and the Bushman" to produce African civilization but who were "better armed as well as quicker witted than the dark, agricultural Africans." And this from an early anthropologist, Charles Seligman (1930).

After World War I, the joint colony of Rwanda–Urundi fell into the hands of Belgium, to add to their holdings along with the neighboring (and much larger) Congo. The Belgians began to institute economic and administrative reforms to make the colony more efficient and profitable, including intensification of production and streamlining of the political system. Many of the chiefly offices occupied by Tutsi were eliminated; in one province the 119 chiefs were reduced to 5. Certain kinds of patron–client relations were also ended, replaced by other traditional or modern ones. And the remaining native administrators were brought under the control of Belgian authorities, in a typical condition of "indirect rule," in which it was the natives' job to collect the taxes and organize the labor.

These changes had a mixed effect on traditional society. In some ways, Tutsi authorities lost power, and in other ways they gained it. Their exploitation of clients could become more "modern," more purely economic, and therefore more complete. Hutus felt the pressure from above more but also had options to

Case Study 4: "Tribal" Genocide in Rwanda (continued)

escape clientage and seek out their own wage-paying employment. But Tutsi privilege was still present and in some aspects growing. From 1929 Tutsis were favored in mission schools and thus advantaged in their access to education and religion. Attempts to install some Hutu chiefs were met with stiff resistance; in fact, some existing Hutu chiefs were deposed as colonial authorities moved the society to a more Tutsi-oriented administration than had ever existed before.

Independence was in the air, but not until the early 1950s. And as in many settings, a class of educated and acculturated natives, both Hutu and Tutsi, had formed over the decades. Known as *evolués* (the "evolved"), they were prepared for placement in modern colonial and postcolonial society, but they were out of touch with the rural and more "traditional" segments of society as well as frustrated by their lack of opportunity in a very segregated colonial system. At the same time, Belgian sentiments began to favor a more "democratic" society—that is, one in which the majority (here, Hutu) determined their own course. So colonial authorities opened new political, educational, religious, and economic avenues to the traditionally subservient Hutu.

The result was the rise of Hutu "ethnic" and political consciousness. In late 1956, a predominantly Hutu party, TRAFIPRO (acronym for "Travail/Fidelité/Progrès"), was formed. Even more significantly, in March 1957 a group of Hutu intellectuals issued the "Manifesto of the Bahutu," in which they asserted that the social problem in the colony "lies in the political monopoly of one race, the Tutsi race, which, given the present structural framework, becomes a social and economic monopoly." The manifesto called for reforms to address the poverty and oppression of the Hutus as well as their "political and economic emancipation." Shortly thereafter, one of the signers of the document, Gregoire Kayibanda, founded the Mouvement Social Muhutu (MSM); however, opinions and ambitions varied, and other parties like APROSOMA (Association pour la Promotion Sociale) came on the scene.

The initial Tutsi response was condescending. One statement included the following provocative language:

> the relations between we [*sic*] (Batutsi) and they [*sic*] (Bahutu) have always until the present been based on servitude. There is, therefore, between we and they no foundation for brotherhood. . . . Since it was our kings who conquered the Bahutu country and killed their petty kings and thus subjugated the Bahutu, how can they pretend to be our brothers? (Quoted in Webster 1966: 43)

The Tutsi thus drove Kayibanda to reorganize his party into the Parti du Mouvement de l'Emancipation Hutu (PARMEHUTU) in 1959. The Tutsi royalists answered with the Union Nationale Rwandaise (UNAR), which was supposedly a "national" party although it was really mostly Tutsi.

Violence broke out in late 1959, and the response of Belgian authorities was demonstrably pro-Hutu. Thus emboldened, PARMEHUTU became

Case Study 4: "Tribal" Genocide in Rwanda (continued)

more militant and anti-Tutsi, and on January 28, 1961 declared itself the government of Rwanda (Burundi having been set on its separate independence course), with Kayibanda as prime minister. The outside world could see the dangerous path Rwanda was treading; a U.N. commission in 1961 reported that "a racial dictatorship of one party has been set up in Rwanda, and the developments of the last eighteen months have consisted in the transition from one type of oppressive regime to another. Extremism is rewarded and there is a danger that the [Tutsi] minority may find itself defenseless in the face of abuses" (quoted in Lemarchand 1970: 194–95).

Physical attacks on Tutsi grew until some 120,000 or more—somewhere between 40 percent and 70 percent of the entire Tutsi population—fled the country into neighboring states. There they settled into refugee camps, integrated themselves into local politics, and festered until their eventual return. Some refugees and their descendants organized themselves into paramilitary bands of *inyenzi* (cockroaches) to plan and execute raids and ultimate invasion and reconquest of their lost homeland. Their initial efforts were stymied, and they laid low for about a generation.

By the early 1990s, the *inyenzi* were in a position to push their demands, so a wise Hutu president of Rwanda, Juvenal Habyarimana, had entered into negotiations with an expatriate Tutsi leader, Paul Kagame. Kagame had risen to some power in Uganda and organized the Rwandanese Patriotic Front (RPF) with a military wing, the Rwandanese Patriotic Army (RPA) and launched attacks in late 1990. In August of 1993, the two leaders agreed to the Arusha Accord, calling for the disarming of the RPA, its integration into the Rwandan national army, and the transition to a multiparty government over time. However as in many such cases, not all Hutus welcomed this conciliatory development, especially the extremists known as the *interahamwe* (those who attack as one), who desired no peace with nor return of the defeated Tutsis.

And so it happened that on April 4, 1994, a plane carrying Habyarimana and the Burundian president, Cyprien Ntaryamira, was shot out of the sky over Rwanda's capital city. The RPF was instantly blamed, but it was almost certainly not guilty. The Hutu response was fast—too fast. Government radio stations began to broadcast urgings to "kill the Tutsis," and prepared lists of Tutsi and Tutsi-sympathetic targets were distributed by armed Hutus, including government soldiers. What was widely seen as a "spontaneous" outbreak of "ethnic hatred" was probably actually a well-orchestrated campaign of intimidation and murder for political ends. In the process, hundreds of thousands of Tutsis and people who supported (or even just failed to hate) Tutsis were killed.

Ironically, the RPF emerged as the saviors of the situation while the world watched and dithered. The Hutu government forces were swiftly defeated and sent into their own exile in refugee camps in Zaire and elsewhere. There, they no doubt wait their turn to avenge their honor, deem their dead, and reclaim their homeland. "Ethnic conflict," which did not exist at all as a recognizable phenomenon before colonialism, has evolved to a point where its next incarnation is practically assured.

RETROSPECT AND PROSPECT

The stories recounted in this chapter are a small but representative sampling of the grievance- and identity-inspired violence of the "modern era." Identity, ideology, and interest have become so entwined in many parts of the globe that it is virtually impossible to separate them and, so it seems, virtually impossible to address the violence stemming from them. The solutions offered are often of the "idealist" or "totalistic" sort—that is, they are no more than visions of a future in which all problems—and all "others" that cause problems—vanish. Benjamin Barber (1996) has recognized this as one of the two opposing processes operating in the modern world, which he (unfortunately) calls "jihad." Jihad in his view (not the original Muslim view) is a fragmentation of the world, a retribalization around "traditional" or even lost identities and cultures in the name of cultural "authenticity" and self-determination. This form of politics and political movement, however, is much more "self-conscious" as a political movement; it is not simply tradition, or even tradition remembered, but tradition agitated and mobilized.

Whether these mass movements and the violence they engender are focused on a past or a people or a class, they are *focused*, and they tend to let nothing stand in their way of achieving the future they pursue. In this sense, as Le Bon (1896) argued, even the most secular movements take on some of the nature of religion—the goodness of the cause, the wisdom of the leader or the group he leads and personifies, the wickedness of those who provide obstacles to the goal, the voluntary and aggressive segregation of "us" from "them." There is every reason to expect that, although the language of particular movements may vary in the near future, the general dynamics of such phenomena—the pursuit of interests under the banner of identities and ideologies—will be a feature of political and cultural life for a long time to come.

We turn our attention one last time to the society that most of us know best and that, for good or ill, manifests every species of violence that we have noted so far in this book. From domestic violence to violent crime to "normal" violence and competitiveness to ideological and political violence to international war, America evinces essentially the whole range of possible types and motives for violence. For that reason, and because we have to live there, it deserves our special attention. Such analysis had to wait until we had developed the tools to make sense of what we see, and now we are ready to proceed.

Violence in American Society

Introduction

> America has always been a relatively violent nation. Considering the tumultuous historical forces that have shaped the United States, it would be astonishing were it otherwise.
> —*National Commission on the Causes and Prevention of Violence,*
> *1969*

The Gisu of Africa (see Chapter 4) are a society that bemoan their own violent tendencies, yet they repeatedly produce the kind of people who have violent tendencies. Likewise, Americans bemoan their own violent tendencies, but clearly something they are doing repeatedly produces the kind of people who participate in violence.

The United States of America is a rich and free country. It is also has the highest rate of violence in the Western industrialized world and one of the highest rates worldwide. Wealth and freedom apparently do not guarantee peace; in fact, their existence may depend on the very lack of such a guarantee. From what we have learned about the macrosocial, microsocial, and psychocultural foundations of violence and nonviolence, it is not hard to conclude that America has few of the characteristics related to nonviolence and many of those associated with violence. It is a large, complex, differentiated, intensive agricultural, state-level, competitive, male-dominated society, whose behavior is marked by the group- (integrative), ideology-, identity-, and interest-based factors that contribute to violence. Perhaps more than anything else, we find a high level of "normal" violence and an acceptance that violence is a good way to respond to certain kinds of situations and problems.

In any society that engages in widespread violence, there must be values, ideologies, and institutions that allow and promote it. There must also be "training grounds" where individuals can observe, acquire, and practice those values and ideologies in order to take their place in the institutions. There must be a certain degree of "background violence," some or much of it even perhaps below the consciousness of most members of the society. It is only when the cumulative effect of the background, or "normal," violence reaches a critical level, or when exceptional instances of violence exceed the background level, that violence is recognized as a problem—as "abnormal," as antisocial, as pathological and culturally disruptive. America seems to have reached that point.

In the final two chapters of this book, we will turn our focus onto ourselves, employing the tools and concepts we have developed and used on other societies in an attempt to understand our own. On this journey we will look at unique aspects of American history, culture, and psyche to try to find the causes of—and perhaps some potential cures for—our distinctive national version of violence. Those of us looking for and hoping for answers will discover meaningful points of entry for intervention and change.

THE SCOPE OF VIOLENCE IN THE UNITED STATES

Violence in America encompasses such a broad range of behaviors that it is impossible to describe all at once—from interpersonal and "domestic" violence to gang violence to hate crimes to serial killing to international war: the list is seemingly endless. Let us then start with a basic introduction to the violence internal to our society, as measured by the incidence of violent crime. As we mentioned in the first chapter, there are various ways to determine the incidence of crime in a society, and we described two major techniques in American law enforcement—the Uniform Crime Report (UCR) and the National Crime Victimization Survey (NCVS). Let us begin, then, with an overview of what these instruments tell us about ourselves.

The Uniform Crime Report

Established in 1929, the UCR records statistics on seven "index crimes," four of which are violent (murder/nonnegligent manslaughter, rape, robbery, and aggravated assault) and three of which are property (burglary, larceny/theft, and auto theft). In 1979, arson was added as an eighth category. The year 2002 is the most recent for which complete figures are available. Before we continue, stop and ask yourself, "What is the situation for crime and violence in the country today?" Many Americans in the late 1990s and early 2000s were under the impression that they were in the midst of a crime explosion. Widely reported cases of school shootings, child abductions, bewilderingly irrational violence like "wilding," and random sniper attacks made it appear that the country was under siege. However, the reality is that crime has *decreased sharply* over the last decade and that by some measures it is at a thirty-year low.

According to the UCR, there was a total of just under 12 million (11,877,218) index crimes in 2002 for a population of over 288 million. This number is virtually unchanged from the year before (less than 600 crimes more).

TABLE 10.1	VIOLENT INDEX CRIMES, 2002			
	Murder	**Rape**	**Robbery**	**Assault**
Number	16,204	95,136	420,637	894,348
Rate/100,000	5.6	33.0	145.9	310.1

Source: Uniform Crime Report, a publication of the F.B.I.

That works out to a rate of 4,119 crimes per 100,000 of population, a decrease of 1.1 percent from the previous year. Far and away, the majority of these crimes (almost 10.5 million) were property crimes that arguably threatened little or no physical violence. That leaves around 1.4 million violent crimes, which is still a large number but only a rate of 495 per 100,000, again down (2 percent) from 2001. The specifics of violent index crimes are presented in Table 10.1.

More than 16,000 murders sounds like a lot, and it is: it represents one murder every 33 minutes in this country (we also add on average one assault every thirty-five seconds, one robbery every 1.2 minutes, and one rape every 6 minutes). However, this homicide rate is actually 4.5 percent less than that for 1998 and represents a remarkable 34 percent decline from 1991, when a record-high 24,700 murders took place. In fact, Table 10.2 presents the data showing that the incidence of violent crime in the United States today is lower than at almost any time in the last twenty years. Notice, regrettably, that there has been a small (1 percent) increase in murder in 2002, on top of the 2.5 percent increase in 2001. However, there was also a 1 percent growth in population, so the murder rate remained unchanged relative to population.

Apparently, then, civilization is not about to crumble in the United States. In fact, we need to ask ourselves—assuming that human nature has not changed much in the last two decades—how to account for this steep decline in criminal violence. Certain trends are interesting.

- The Northeast and Midwest regions reported a disproportionately low rate of violent crime. The Northeast, with 18.8 percent of the country's population, provided only 15.8 percent of the violent crime, while the Midwest experienced 19.4 percent of the violence with 22.6 percent of the population. The West reported a roughly proportionate rate (22.8 percent of population, 23.4 percent of violent crime), but the South was disproportionately high (35.8 percent of population, 41.4 percent of violent crime).
- Not surprisingly, cities suffered a higher violent crime rate (624.6) than suburbs (352.1) or rural areas (232.2). Larger cities suffered higher rates (1,029.9) than smaller cities (326.5). However, most of these numbers still represent decreases over the past year: urban violent crime was down 1.9 percent (and a whopping 3.9 percent in cities between half a million

TABLE 10.2	VIOLENT INDEX CRIMES, 1982–2002			
Year	Murder	Rape	Robbery	Assault
1982	21,010	78,770	553,130	669,480
1983	19,308	78,918	506,567	653,294
1984	18,692	84,233	485,008	685,349
1985	18,976	87,671	497,874	723,246
1986	20,613	91,459	542,775	834,322
1987	20,096	91,111	517,704	855,088
1988	20,675	92,486	542,968	910,092
1989	21,500	94,504	578,326	951,707
1990	23,438	102,555	639,271	1,054,863
1991	24,703	106,593	687,732	1,092,739
1992	23,760	109,062	672,478	1,126,974
1993	24,526	106,014	659,870	1,135,607
1994	23,326	102,216	618,949	1,113,179
1995	21,606	97,470	580,509	1,099,207
1996	19,645	96,252	535,594	1,037,049
1997	18,208	96,153	498,534	1,023,201
1998	16,974	93,144	447,186	976,583
1999	15,522	89,411	409,371	911,740
2000	15,586	90,178	408,016	911,706
2001	15,980	90,491	422,921	907,219
2002	16,204	95,136	420,637	894,348

Source: Uniform Crime Report, a publication of the F.B.I.

and a million in population), and rural violence was down 1.2 percent, even though suburban violence was up 1 percent.

- Minors (under age eighteen) accounted for 14.9 percent of violent crime arrests, and those under twenty-five years of age made up a full 43.7 percent.
- Men accounted for 82.6 percent of the violent-crime arrests.
- Over half (59.7 percent) of violent-crime arrests were whites, 38 percent black. However, in the area of homicide, black Americans constituted 50 percent of the arrests.
- There was a total of 8,832 "hate crime" offenses reported (down nearly 10 percent), involving 9,222 victims. As opposed to other kinds of crime, hate crimes tend to be overwhelmingly committed against persons rather than property by a ratio of 2 to 1 and therefore more violent by definition. Of these incidents, 49.7 percent were race-related (most antiblack), 15.2 percent ethnicity related, 17.8 percent religion related (mostly anti-Jewish), and 16.6 percent sexual-orientation related (mostly anti–male homosexual). Less than 1 percent were disability related.

The National Crime Victimization Survey

The National Crime Victimization Survey (NCVS) was instituted in 1973 by the Department of Justice Bureau of Justice Statistics to fill in missing information from the tools and methods of the UCR. It is based on surveys and interviews of approximately fifty thousand households to determine how many of them have been victims of certain sorts of crimes in the previous year, whether or not those crimes were ever reported to the police. In the year 2002, the NCVS gave the following general results:

- U.S. citizens experienced some 23 million crimes (down from 25.9 million in 2000), of which 76.1 percent (17.5 million) were property crimes and 23.2 percent (5.34 million) were violent crimes.
- As would be expected, the rates of most crimes were much higher by this measure than by the UCR. For instance, among citizens age twelve and over, the rate of rape or sexual assault (including attempted rape) was 110 per 100,000, assault (aggravated and simple) 1,980 per 100,000, and robbery (including attempted robbery) was 220 per 100,000.

The NCVS confirms what the UCR indicates about long-term trends in violent crime: that they have been steadily decreasing for a decade or even longer. In fact, it shows that the violent crime rate declined 15 percent in the year 1999–2000 alone to reach the lowest level in the twenty-seven-year history of the survey.

More interesting and innovative than the general results are specific measures of the characteristics of victims. For example, the following facts are highlighted in the research:

- Age—as a rule, the younger the person, the greater likelihood of experiencing violent crime. The age range of 12–24 suffered violence at the highest rate of any age group. Teenagers (16–19) were the very highest, with a 5,820 per 100,000 rate of violent victimization—550 rape, 400 robbery, and 4,860 assault. In most categories they were about three or four times as likely to be victimized as someone aged thirty-five to forty-nine and often ten times or more as likely as someone over sixty-five.
- Race and ethnicity—African Americans have a higher chance of being victimized by violence than white Americans. The victimization rate was 2,790 for blacks (down from 3,500 in 2000), 2,280 for whites, and 1,470 for other races. Hispanics, on the other hand, were victims of rape and sexual assault at rates lower than whites and blacks, although Hispanics and blacks experienced similar rates of robbery and aggravated assault. Of all groups, however, American Indians had the very highest violent victimization rate—more than twice that of blacks, two and a half times that of whites, and four and a half times that of Asians.
- Gender—males continue to be victimized at a higher rate than females, although the difference has been shrinking over the years (and males are usually the victimizers, too). Males experienced a total violent crime rate of 2,550, while the rate for women was 2,080. The obvious exception is sex crimes, which are disproportionately (6 to 1) committed against women.

However, men are three times as likely to be killed and 50 percent more likely to be the victim of carjacking.

- Household income—there is a nearly linear inverse correlation between household income and violent crime, that is, the richer the household the less likely the household is to experience violent crime. Very poor families (income less than $7,500) had the highest rate of violence of all income groups (4,550). Conversely, families with incomes over $75,000 suffered only about one-third the rate of violence. The pattern is true although less dramatic for black households.
- Marital status—individuals who are single and have never been married encountered more violence than any other marital category—four times greater than married people and more than six times greater than widowed people.

The NCVS also tells us something about the crimes and the perpetrators themselves. For instance:

- Victim/offender relationship—males were more likely to be victimized by a stranger, whereas females were more often victimized by someone they knew or were in a relationship with. About 60 percent of rapes and sexual assaults were perpetrated by a friend, acquaintance, or familiar. In terms of crimes in which young people were killed, family members were most likely to murder a young child (one in five child murders being committed by a family member), whereas a friend or acquaintance was most likely to kill an older child (age 15–17). For all murders, 45 percent were committed by someone who knew the victim and only 15 percent by strangers, with 40 percent undetermined. Finally, about 40 percent of victims of workplace violence knew their offender.
- Intimate violence—violence committed at the hand of an intimate partner is predominantly a problem for women; they experienced 72 percent of the murder by intimate partners and about 85 percent of nonlethal intimate violence. Intimate violence, like other forms of violence, has been decreasing over recent years, but the decrease has been more rapid for male victims (4 percent per year) than female (1 percent per year). The range of intimate violence as a proportion of all violence in selected cities spanned 42 percent (Tucson) to 74 percent (Los Angeles).
- Time of occurrence—on the whole, violent crime was more likely to take place during the day than at night; however, two-thirds of all sexual crimes occur at night.
- Place of occurrence—one in four violent crimes happened in or near the victim's home. The workplace accounted for about 18 percent of violent crime. Schools were another location where considerable violence occurred: 186,000 serious violent crimes in 1999, with around 7 percent of students reportedly carrying a dangerous weapon to school. Still, like

other forms of violence, school violence declined throughout the 1990s, as did gang-related activities in schools (going from 29 percent in 1995 to 17 percent in 1999).

- Region—the West and Midwest reported the highest rates of violent victimization in 2002 (2,940 and 2,570, respectively), 1,970 for the South, and 1,880 for the Northeast, somewhat contradicting the UCR on this issue.
- Urban versus rural—urban residents experienced the highest violent victimization rate, followed by suburban and then rural. A survey of twelve urban centers showed that blacks were more likely than whites to see violent crime in most cities.
- Weapon use—in 26 percent of violent crimes, a weapon was used, although it varies highly with the type of crime. Robbers presented a weapon 55 percent of the time, whereas rapists only did so 6 percent of the time. Not surprisingly, murder most often involved a gun (51 percent handguns, 14 percent other guns) but frequently employed knives (13 percent) and other weapons (16 percent).
- Alcohol—among respondents who commented on alcohol use related to their victimization, 35 percent claimed that the offender had been drinking. However, the number rises dramatically for intimate violence, where about two-thirds of victims reported alcohol as a factor. When the perpetrator was a spouse, the number jumped to 75 percent. Only about 31 percent of stranger-crimes were perceived to be alcohol related. Finally, one in five victims also reported possible drug use by their victimizer.

EXPLAINING AMERICAN VIOLENCE

As we argued in the first chapter of this book, there are two reasons to be cautious about the kind of information we have just been perusing. First, there is the issue of research error and omission: operationalization of variables, overreporting or (more commonly) underreporting, statistical problems, and the like. Any type of large-scale research will suffer from these limitations. Second, there is the issue of other forms of "noncriminal" violence that will not show up in crime reports. Some of this violence may even be "normal" or "legitimate" or "justified" to the members of society, but it may be violent and destructive and hurtful to people —and above all else, anathema to real peace and nonviolence. Along with this matter goes the matter of explanation: viewing the statistics of crime and violence does not give us any real insight into why Americans indulge in this behavior and why they repeat the patterns of behavior—and the patterns that generate the behavior—over and over again.

To get some perspective on these questions, we must go deeper, employing all of the tools and concepts we have developed throughout this book.

In considering a wide range of violent and nonviolent societies and scenarios, we have acquired some sense of what contributes to violence and nonviolence in each in terms of macrosocial, microsocial, and psychocultural factors. We can now apply our analysis to our own society, with surprising and often disturbing results.

The Psychocultural Dimension

Years ago I watched Fred Rogers, the "Mr. Rogers" of children's television, sing a song to children as he often did. In this song, he sang about how you the individual are special, how there is no one else like you and how everyone likes you for being you. We recognize the sentiments in the song as distinctly and familiarly American and as generally positive and laudable. But we might also want to consider the relation between the messages we give to children, the personalities they develop, and the propensity to violence in our society. In this case, he is instilling a strong sense of self and of "self-esteem," the kind that we know can lead to trouble and that is exactly the opposite of what comparatively nonviolent societies like the Semai and the Utku do.

Before we proceed, stop for a moment and reflect on the typical or ideal American personality. Ask yourself the following question: What are the personality traits of a good American? Or, if it is easier, put the question this way: What traits would I like to have, or what traits would I like my children to have? Personality in any society is a complex and even contradictory notion. There is no doubt that we would like American citizens to be fair, tolerant, considerate, cooperative, and so forth—to have characteristics we know from experience and from research to be supportive of nonviolence. At the same time, the American personality has other characteristics, some of them highly prized, that we know to be supportive of violence.

For instance, the typical or ideal American citizen is *competitive*, and we think this is a good thing. Our society is shot-through with competition, which we enjoy watching and participating in. We tell ourselves continuously that competition is good for everyone—that it makes people stronger, products better and cheaper, and life more interesting. We turn everything into a competition—children learn to play and invent competitive games early on—and we praise winners and disparage losers. In fact, one of the worst things you can be called in America is a loser. One of the main venues for inculcating this value and habit is sports, and many commentators have mentioned it. Sports is a "school for competition" as well as other fundamental values and traits. As Beal has noted (2001: 462), sports is "one of the most significant institutions of male bonding and male initiation rites." Even more enlightening is the opinion of John Carroll, who wrote in 1986 that sports is an expression of masculine "virtue and grace" that creates and conserves "the moral and the religious" values of competitive manliness; women should thus be banned from sports because they represent "the values of tenderness, nurture, and compassion, and this most important role must not be confused with the military and political values inherent in sport" (quoted in Messner 2003: 669). These values center on competition, which is apparently not tender or compassionate.

While Americans do work and play in teams (and we often say that "there is no 'I' in team"), our focus is on the individual. Americans are very *individualistic*—not in the sense that Bonta (1997) used the term (as solitary or separatist) but in the sense of egoistic or self-centered. Even when we are working in teams, we are doing so for our own personal interest. Americans tell themselves, as Fred Rogers does, that it is good to be unique, that there is no one like you, and that people like an individual better than a "conformist" or "follower." We feel that there is something not quite genuine about one who conforms or marches to someone else's drummer.

Along with competition and individualism goes *achievement seeking*. We want to be the best and we want to be recognized as the best. We want to rise to the top and be praised and rewarded for our individual achievements. We devise all kinds of ways to give ourselves accolades (awards shows, testimonials, etc.), and we bask in the attention. In fact, at the extreme, we are hungry for individual fame and will do almost anything to attain it, as evidenced by the recent spate of "reality television" programs, which pit mundane people in strange competitions with each other—for money, prizes, even spouses. Many people enter these virtual "reality" situations hoping for real fame as actors or celebrities, and many viewers watch the shows for some sort of vicarious pleasure or other (inexplicable) reasons. Together, these three items indicate the highly *self-oriented* nature of American personality. Everything we talk about concerns the self. Cosmetics are about having a more beautiful self, exercise is about having a more fit self, and even therapy is about having a more mentally adjusted self. In fact, we refer to the ensemble of these kinds of endeavors as our "self-help" or "self-improvement" industry. In addition, not only are we self-oriented but we are *self-assertive* and *egoistic*. "I am going to be me no matter what anyone else says or does" is what matters. "Don't tread on me" was the first American motto. We like to be "in your face" with our own views, values, and opinions.

In being self-oriented and self-assertive, we are naturally *antiauthority* and *nonconformist*. We highly value *independence, freedom, and liberty*. This roughly means that I will be and do what I want and you can be and do what you want, as long as we do not get in each other's way too much. We distrust government, experts, and anyone who claims to be our "superior." As we said above, conformity feels confining and more than a little inauthentic, which is why we see people striving to be "different" in all sorts of ways, from painting their hair blue to trying to enter the *Guinness Book of World Records*. At the same time (because we are a contradictory people and because no society can truly support real nonconformity), we struggle for our uniqueness within specific limits—as Dr. Pepper used to sing, we tend to be "part of an original crowd." We put heavy pressures on each other to assimilate to whatever the group norms are, and we carefully and critically judge each other's performances against the standards of whatever group we join. There are correct ways to be "Goth" or "club" or "hip hop" just as surely as there are to be Republican or Christian.

Because we compete and judge, we are very *differentiated* and even *hierarchical* in the end. We rank ourselves and everyone else, and we know exactly what the pecking order is, even while we disclaim any status differences in our society (if I were of lower status than you, it would offend my self-esteem). Everything is ranked—beauty, intelligence, wealth, power, entertainment, you name it. We even enjoy a harsh and degrading judge, like Simon Cowell on the hit TV show *American Idol*. Although we cringe in a way at the brutal things he says to untalented singers (after all, doesn't everybody have a right to sing— even to be a "great singer"—if they want to?), we also delight in such trashing of our fellow citizens. Given that we both indulge in and delight in vilifying and humiliating our fellows (injuring their "self-esteem," in other words), we are more than a little *callous* and *unempathetic* toward the suffering of others. Why else would we still giggle at a pie in the face or a bat to the crotch?

A part of the American culture and personality that must not be overlooked or discounted is its *moralism* and *idealism*. We are a practical people, but we also tend to see people and events through moralistic lenses, particularly Christian morality. We see the world in terms of "good guys" and "bad guys," who are usually distinguishable by surface qualities (the color of their clothes is one obvious sign, but their beauty and overall sanity are other powerful indicators—"evil" people are most often ugly and crazed). Of course, in any interpersonal dispute, we tend to see ourselves as the good guys, the ones in the right, and in any international dispute, we tend to see America collectively as the good guy. Note the descriptions of our enemies as not only bad but evil in such recent phrases as "evil empire" (Ronald Reagan on the Soviet Union) or "axis of evil" (George W. Bush on terrorists and specifically Iran, Iraq, and North Korea). Never mind that those enemies might have their own motivations and their own perspectives (Iran once called America the "great Satan"). We habitually see the world in black-and-white, us-versus-them, absolute terms.

Our idealism tends to suggest to us that we do things, personally and nationally, not for petty practical reasons but for high-minded, even religious, principles. We only fight "just wars"; we do not go to war for oil but for human rights and freedom. We do not seek regime change to oust a bad man but to foster international peace and world stability. We see ourselves as virtuous and fair and principled, and this habit goes back a long way: the first European American settlers almost four hundred years ago saw themselves as seekers of religious truth (although not necessarily tolerance) and founders of an ideal new civilization of good and right. In modern times, we have our own cham-

pions of virtue: Ronald Reagan referring to the "shining city on ↑
Superman's announcer speaking of "truth, justice, and the American ...,
are even more than a little self-righteous, regarding ourselves as the "chosen
people" and the "guardians of democracy and liberty"—once upon a time, the
"policemen of the world."

For a variety of reasons (our individualism, our distrust of authority, our
"Wild West" heritage, etc.), we also communicate in our culture that *force is
an acceptable, even a valuable, way to solve conflicts*. People have glorified war
for a very long time, and we have perhaps detached some of the glory from killing and getting killed on the battlefield. However, we still incline toward sentiments like "bombing them back to the Stone Age" if our enemies will not
capitulate to our terms, and our popular figures—like Rambo, James Bond, or
John Wayne—often sort things out with guns a-blazing, producing countless
casualties in the process. Our most popular movies are usually in the "action"
category, which means lots of guns, explosions, and death. Some elements of
our society complain about all the violence, but in general we see it and we like
it—and we learn from it. Indeed our entertainment, from movies and television to music to video games, is soaked in violence. A 1972 report from the
U.S. Department of Health, Education and Welfare observed the obvious fact
that in America "violent material is popular" (5), which says a couple of important things about our culture. First, we like violence: we as a society make violent entertainment because we find violence entertaining, and in the course of
the socialization process (which includes entertainment) we acquire a taste for
violence that we seek to continuously feed with more of it. Second, as a consequence of this aspect of our pleasure-seeking behavior, we provide ourselves
with a high level of what we term "background" violence, which must rise to
significant proportions before we notice and condemn it.

Finally, while we compliment ourselves on our individualism and our freedom, we also value *order and structure*. We, increasingly in the early twenty-
first century, are a no-nonsense law-and-order society, with little sympathy for
incarcerated folks, welfare mothers, or other disadvantaged types. Because we
believe so strongly in personal achievement, we often blame victims for their
own plight, since "you can accomplish anything if you put your mind to it."
Therefore, the poor, the unsuccessful, the "losers" must not have applied
themselves adequately or worked hard enough to succeed like the rest of us.
They got what they deserved, so what am I supposed to do about it?

These are some of the standard traits of the American personality. Of
course, this is not an exhaustive list, and we have other traits that run counter to
these. However, these are recognizably American, and they are the ones that
create a foundation for violence. Another way to think about American "style"
is to look at it through the eyes of other societies. One particularly interesting
study of U.S. negotiating behavior in international settings, prepared by
the United States Institute of Peace, describes a style of interaction that

incorporates many of these characteristics. It finds, for instance, that American negotiators tend to be "forceful, explicit, legalistic, urgent, and results-oriented." It goes on to say that Americans are "uncomfortable with silence and ignore body language. They enter negotiations with their own time frame and usually press for an early agreement, especially if the issue at stake has political significance at home." They tend to see themselves as "tough but fair bargainers," but other countries often perceive them to be "less concerned to negotiate than . . . to persuade, sermonize, or browbeat negotiating counterparts into acceding to American positions." Ultimately Americans are pragmatic and businesslike, more interested in results than in relationships.

The point here is not, of course, that watching TV or playing video games creates a generation of violent deviants. There is no simple cause-and-effect relationship, and there is certainly no such relationship between watching any one TV show or video game and violence. Rather, the point is that altogether they create a psychocultural environment in which the conditions for violence are met. It might not even be—and probably is not—the case that Americans want to be as violent as they are. It is simply that, like the Gisu, we do things, sometimes unconsciously, that foster violence.

Let us turn now to "violent personality" proper, that is, unacceptable or illegitimate violence. A number of researchers have studied violent personality in America, and their findings are fairly consistent. Goldstein (1996), for instance, has described the following characteristics of a typical violent personality:

1. Is self-centered—the kind of person who "does what I want" and "does not care what other people say or who gets hurt"
2. Views others as being hostile, whether they are or not—misreads or misinterprets social interaction, for example, seeing a threat or challenge in getting bumped or looked at, and so forth.
3. Assumes the worst and that honor or "face" is at stake—thinks that he or she must respond or retaliate or else he or she will "look weak."
4. Externalizes blame—excuses or rationalizes violence with claims such as, "He was asking for it."
5. Sees false consensus of values—thinks that "everyone thinks/acts like I do."
6. "Anchors" his or her thought process—resists changes in thinking, even in light of new information.

Further, Goldstein associates violence with the ability to avoid feelings of guilt and responsibility, which is associated with

- Minimizing the reality or impact of the aggression by comparing it to even worse behavior (for example, saying things like, "At least I didn't use a knife")
- Justifying aggression in terms of higher moral principles
- Blaming the victim

- Diffusing the responsibility (for instance, blaming the violence on crowd behavior or alcohol rather than on personal choice)
- Dehumanizing the victim
- "Graduated desensitization" (with each act of aggression, additional aggression becomes easier)
- "Hygienic positioning" (creating emotional or physical distance from the victim, for example, by using derogatory euphemisms for violence).

Moving along the continuum of violence, in 1968, the American Psychology Association published its standards on the "antisocial personality," which it defined as

> reserved for individuals who are basically unsocialized and whose behavior pattern brings them repeatedly into conflict with society. They are incapable of loyalty to individuals, groups, or social values. They are grossly selfish, callous, irresponsible, impulsive, and unable to feel guilt or to learn from experience. Frustration tolerance is low. They tend to blame others or offer plausible rationalizations for their behavior. (Quoted in Conrad and Dinitz 1977: 22)

Conrad and Dinitz (1977), building on the work of Cleckley, offer an even more extensive account of the "sociopath," who typically exhibits

- Superficial charm and good intelligence
- Absence of delusions and other signs of irrational thinking
- Absence of nervousness and other psychoneurotic traits
- Unreliability
- Insincerity or lack of truthfulness
- Lack of remorse and shame
- Poor judgment and failure to learn from experience
- Pathological egocentricity and incapacity for love
- General impoverishment of emotional relations
- Specific loss of insight
- Unresponsiveness in interpersonal behavior
- Sex life impersonal, trivial, and poorly integrated
- Failure to follow any life plan
- Rarely suicidal

Still further along the continuum is what DiIulio and his colleagues termed the "super-predator," the new breed of highly aggressive, usually youthful, offender that appeared in the 1970s and 1980s. These people are characterized as

> radically impulsive, brutally remorseless youngsters, including ever more preteen-age boys, who murder, assault, rape, rob, burglarize, deal deadly drugs, join gun-toting gangs, and create serious communal disorder. They do not fear of the stigma of arrest, the pains of imprisonment, or the pangs of conscience. They perceive hardly any relationship between doing right (or wrong) now and being rewarded (or punished) for it later. (Quoted in Brownstein 2000: 120)

Finally at the extreme of pathological violence is the serial killer, described by Ressler (see next chapter) as usually sexually dysfunctional, unable to maintain consensual relationships (as many as 50 percent have never had consensual sex), emotionally distant, often quite intelligent, sometimes personable and popular, but frequently mentally ill, especially from delusional schizophrenia. We will return to this ultimate expression of American violence in the final section of the book.

The Macrosocial Dimension

Personality and culture do not exist in a vacuum; they only exist and persist because of the specific social realities that embed and embody them. Throughout this book, we have considered many kinds of social factors and forces that contribute to violence and nonviolence, from basic economic and political systems to family patterns, religious groupings, and ethnic identities. The United States, as we posited at the beginning of this chapter, contains many of the violence-promoting institutions and few of the violence-inhibiting ones. Most obviously and fundamentally, America is a state-level society based on intensive agriculture with a complex and differentiated social and class system and a male-dominated tradition and structure. We have noted some of the following social characteristics that typify violence in America as well:

1. Gender plays an important role in violence. Males are much more likely to be both victims and perpetrators of violence than females. In 1990, one out of every one hundred white females was in the criminal justice system at any given time, as opposed to one out of every sixteen white males. For Hispanics, the numbers were one out of fifty-six of females and one out of ten of males, and for African Americans, one out of thirty-seven females and a staggering one out of four of males. A 1996 Bureau of Justice Statistics report concluded that around 5 million women and 6.6 million men were victims of violence but that women were much more likely to be victims of people they knew, in their own home, or injured during an assault.

2. Race plays an important role in violence, or at least in the prosecution of violence. Black Americans tend to be overrepresented in violence, whereas whites and Asians are underrepresented and Hispanics are roughly proportionately represented. Whites account for about 54 percent of arrests for violent crime, whereas blacks account for about 44 percent, while their percentage in the population is only 12 percent. Homicide is the most common cause of death for black men and women: young black women are four times as likely to be killed as nonblack women, and young black men are eleven times as likely to be killed as nonblack men.

3. One other factor closely correlated with race is poverty. Nonwhites are more likely to be poor and to live in poor parts of cities, and the poor are more likely to be implicated in violence. There are in turn a variety of possible explanations for this fact. For one, the poor tend to be less educated and prone to greater frustrations and inequities. It is also conceivable that

their elevated exposure to social-service agencies makes their behavior easier to observe and to report. Also, the types of crimes that tend to get reported to police—like the "index crimes" above—are the type that the lower class is more likely to commit (notice that "white collar crimes" are not on the list). Finally, some analysts blame a "culture of violence" on the poor and the ghetto dwellers.

4. Young people are more likely to be both victims and perpetrators of violence. Youths in their teens and twenties contribute more than their share to the total violence of society, and violence from adults over thirty is comparatively rare—although some extreme cases (such as mass murderers and mass child abusers) are an exception to the trend.

We now examine a variety of other large-scale social facts and institutions in America that can be seen to contribute to the trajectory of violence in society.

Urbanization   One of the first sources of violence, perceived as social or institutional dysfunction or breakdown, that was identified in the sociological literature was *anomie*, the failure of social control and attendant social disorder that follows particularly from the collapse of old stable social forms (see Chapter 2). Durkheim and others attributed this phenomenon to *urbanization*. Even before Durkheim, in the works of Charles Dickens and other social critics of the nineteenth century, cities—especially industrial cities—were condemned for their dirt, vice, and class stratification. As far back as ancient Rome, the city was recognized as the place where the restless and often poor masses met the satisfied and rich elite—a place of uncomfortable contrasts, dizzying diversity, and potentially explosive inequality. Recall how the streets of Paris became the fertile ground, and then the battleground, of the French Revolution.

The urban sociologists who appeared in the early twentieth century to analyze and criticize the new phenomenon of urbanization found much to dislike. They tended to distinguish (perhaps a little romantically) the informal, personal, and small-scale quality of rural or village society with the formal, impersonal, and large-scale quality of urban life. The effect of urbanization was seen as a loss of community and an alienation from neighbor and fellow citizen. Cities, Louis Wirth (1964) said in his classic essay "Urbanism as a Way of Life," were characterized by superficiality, anonymity, and transitoriness; relationships between urbanites were "segmental" or partial. This person was our butcher, that person was our baker, and the other person was an irrelevant stranger in our path, but none of them was a significant member of our personal life. As a result, the ordinary bonds of sociality and mutual obligation that ordered traditional society frayed and disappeared, allowing us to treat each other as means to an end or worse. This anonymity, alienation, "virtual impotence as individuals," flagrant class contrast, and ugly struggle for survival loosened the mores of society and created the perfect breeding conditions for violence.

However, this development does not explain the extraordinarily high level of American violence either in the cities or the noncities. Recall from our synopsis of the UCR above that cities do in fact have a higher violent crime rate than suburbs or rural areas. However, even the rural rate is quite high, and the fluctuations over the years in crime rates cannot be attributed strictly to urbanization. Also, some of the most urbanized parts of the country, the Northeast and Midwest, actually evidenced a disproportionately low rate of violent crime. The West reported a roughly proportionate rate, while one of the traditionally most rural areas, the South, suffered from a disproportionately high crime rate (although the NCVS casts some doubt on this observation). Finally, it is impossible to say that the violence in American society only began when urbanization began; we were a violent society long before we became an urban society (the United States only became predominantly urban in the twentieth century).

Race and Ethnic Stratification and Competition   In an important way, it could be said that the United States was born and sustained by violence. The first acts of settlement by immigrants were violent acts against the native population, continuing as such—often in the form of outright war—for almost three hundred years. Among the earliest other acts of nation building was the creation of a slave society, founded on the violent expropriation and exploitation of another group of human beings, which also continued for more than two hundred years and was succeeded by another hundred years of hostile (and often violent) segregation and discrimination. The westward expansion of American society toward the Pacific coast merely created new arenas for violence and new images of violent heroes and villains, from Indian-fighters and Texas Rangers to gunslingers and bank-robbing gangs. In fact, if there was extreme anomie anywhere in early American society, it was not in the eastern cities but in the frontier towns and camps.

Traditions and institutions like *Indian wars* and *slavery* could not help but make America a meaner place. Christian attitudes about Americans being "God's chosen people" and America being the "New Jerusalem," together with systems of male domination and a rampant gun culture, enshrined in the Bill of Rights, only contributed to this anomie. And the unrestrained competitiveness of American society, especially but not exclusively in the cities, made confrontation and conflict almost inevitable.

Prominent in the development of American society and its culture of violence is the more or less continuous flow of new immigrants from the founding of the country until World War II. No one is saying that immigrants caused violence; rather, we are saying that attitudes toward immigrants and the fact of competition between immigrant groups and between immigrants and

"natives" (even if those "natives" had only been here for a couple of generations or more) contributed to an ethos of competition and, often enough, violence. Public figures and politicians in the nineteenth century were sometimes
openly vocal about the threat to American culture and society posed by immigrants, supposedly based on their racial characteristics. Charles Davenport, a
biologist of the day, actually predicted that the "great influx of blood from
Southeastern Europe" would make America "darker, smaller, more given to
crimes of larceny, kidnapping, assault, murder, rape, and sex-immorality"
(quoted in Kevles and Kevles 1998: 25). If there was any truth to the latter, it
may have had more to do with the hostility of the white Americans than the
bad habits of the immigrants—that is, the immigrants may have been more
the victims than the perpetrators of such violence. And history bears this out
to a degree. Routinely, violence has been directed against the latest bunch of
immigrants—first the Irish, then the Chinese, Koreans, Mexicans, and of
course continually against the Africans. Immigrants have almost always
entered American society at the bottom of the class structure, where conditions are meanest and competition most fierce for jobs, housing, women, and
almost all resources. The recent Hollywood film *Gangs of New York* purports
to illustrate some of those living conditions.

Gender Relations   However, one way to look at the conflict that ensued
from immigration and settlement of the United States is not in terms of race
but of gender. That is, for most of the history of immigration, the vast majority
of immigrants—up to 90 percent in some cases—have been male. Often males
from other countries migrated to this country as (at least ideally) temporary
workers, who would send money back to their families overseas and hope to
return to them some day. Some arrived alone but with the intention to stay. A
relatively small minority came with their families or brought their families over
later. This created a surplus of young single males in the American population
for every year until 1946.

What such a male surplus can lead to is well demonstrated in the California
gold rush of 1849. A case of "internal migration" for the most part (some
Chinese immigrants did arrive to work the fields, but most prospectors were
Americans from the east), the forty-niners were 95 percent male, and within six
months one-fifth of them were dead, some no doubt from the hardships
involved in that life, but many from violence. In such a predominantly male
society, men indulged profligately in what have been called the "bachelor
vices," such as gambling, drinking, frequenting prostitutes, and of course fighting. Some mining towns in California had a murder rate of more than 80 per
100,000 of population in the 1850s (compared to a rate of 5.6 in 2001). Interestingly, when women began to arrive on the frontier, the men began to settle
down. One observer, Alfred Jackson, commented: "The wives of some of the
wildest boys on the creek have come down to join their husbands, and it has

sobered them down considerably" (quoted in Courtwright 1998: 9). It appears, then, that women have a "civilizing," or pacifying, effect on men, and it becomes possible to extrapolate that at least some of the "urban" problems we have talked about may actually be better understood as gender problems. If cities concentrate males the way mining camps did, then the predictable violence will follow.

In general, and from a variety of sources, males have dominated the culture and society of America, not only denying women their equal place in its economy and polity (recall that women did not have their rights, including their voting rights, guaranteed to them until 1920 with the ratification of the Nineteenth Amendment to the Constitution). Men have also shaped the competitions that turned into conflicts in most cases. Finally, and perhaps most pervasively, men organized themselves into networks to pursue or maintain their interests, forming those male–male bonds that we have discovered are common to aggressive societies—human and nonhuman.

History and Geography   Other sources of macrosocial variation are also identifiable. For instance, American violence has shown itself to be cyclical to an extent. There have been three clear cycles in the last century and a half, of about fifty years' duration each. The first cycle or wave of violence crested around the 1860s, the second around 1900–1910, and the third in the 1960s, with an arguable fourth wave cresting in the early to mid-1990s. The first wave coincides with the introduction of improved handgun technology and the obvious effects of the Civil War, the emancipation of slaves, and the outbreak of the final Indian wars. The first decade of the 1900s is notable for the climax of immigration, with the prohibition of alcohol in 1919 contributing historically to the rise and institutionalization of organized crime. Finally, the 1960s witnessed the Vietnam War, the decline of the old northern industrial cities (the so-called rust belt), and urban and racial unrest. Violence in the 1990s may be attributable to the economic downturn in the late 1980s, the "war on drugs" and the proliferation of gangs, and possibly even the Gulf War. There is in fact evidence to suggest that periods of war increase violence at home.

Another noteworthy variable in American violence is the regional one. As we have seen, certain areas of the country, namely the South and West, have consistently higher rates of violence, contrary to what simple urbanization/anomie theories of violence would predict. Surely, some of this tendency can be linked to the history and culture of these areas—the South with its tradition of slavery and race inequality, its old concepts of honor and opposition to outside (i.e., northern) government, its lower incomes and lower levels of education; the West with its history of violence toward Indians, of hostility toward Hispanics, and of "manly" violence toward everyone, its resistance to "eastern" interference, and its general frontier mentality. Both of these regions have the makings of their own "cultures of violence." Consequently, murders in the

South are much more likely to be "expressive" or "primary" (that is, seeking to do harm to a particular individual) than in other parts of the country, where the killing is often "instrumental" or "secondary" (that is, committed in the course of another criminal act).

Regional violence has been studied in such investigations as the Legitimate Violence Index and the Violence Severity Ratio. In the former, the researchers measured cultural support for violence in the forms of mass media images of violence, government use of violence (e.g., corporal punishment, execution, etc.), and socially approved violence (e.g., hunting, violent sports like football, and former practices like lynching). Their results showed the highest levels of legitimation of violence—that is, attitudes that violence is good—in the South and the Rocky Mountain West. Also significantly, legitimate violence, poverty, and social inequality were all correlated to violence. Which of these relations are causal we are not able to say. The Violence Severity Ratio asked subjects to rate various types of violence in terms of their degree of severity, and in this study the South, along with the Northeast (basically an arc from Texas to New York), scored highest.

The Microsocial Dimension: Family

Macrosocial factors do and must exist to give a society its structure, but those defining or overarching institutions and social facts must "come down" into the lives of individuals and directly interacting groups to shape their interactions. The way that dyads and triads and such "face-to-face" groups instantiate the higher-level social realities will determine the microsocial quality of a society.

For our present purposes, we will focus on the most important and common of the microsocial relations, the family. Family in America in the twenty-first century receives a lot of attention. There are those who think that family and "family values" are the panacea to all of America's problems. However, some scholars point to family as a big part of the problem. As we saw in Chapter 5, the family is actually a dangerous and violent place in many parts of the world, including the United States. Richard Gelles, whom we met earlier in the book, has said that the family is "one of society's most violent institutions" and that our desire "to idealize family life is partly responsible for a tendency either not to see family and intimate violence or to condone it as being a necessary and important part of raising children, relating to spouses, and conducting other family transactions" (1997: 1). The American Medical Association in 1991 went so far as to say that the home in America is "more dangerous to women than city streets" (quoted in Henderson 2000: 47). Facts support this claim all too starkly. According to the NVCS, the single greatest circumstance of victimization (aside from being robbed in a parking lot by a stranger) is at home and by someone you know: 26.8 percent of all violent crimes occurred in the home at the hands of a nonstranger, including 34 percent of all rapes, 44.1 percent of all robberies, and 25.3 percent of all assaults. About 1 in 8 murders occurs within the family.

Gelles (1997: 124–25) summarizes the features of the family that make it a haven for interpersonal harm. For one thing, people spend a great amount of time together and engage in a wide variety of activities together. The intensity of their mutual interactions, day in and day out, and the competition over those activities (for instance, which TV show they will watch, when they will eat, or when they will have sex) breed hurt feelings and power struggles. Age and sex differences establish power inequalities. A key feature we noted in other societies is the enclosed or "private" nature of the family, in which outsiders (including the police or the government) have no right to interfere. The significance of "traditional" and ascribed roles cannot be overstated, especially when those roles disadvantage women from the outset. For the parent–child relationship, the "involuntary" nature of membership is important; that is, you cannot choose your parents or children, and you cannot (ordinarily) escape them either. Finally, the intimate knowledge that members have of each other makes it easy to prolong conflicts, reopen old wounds, and "push each other's buttons."

Of course, it should not surprise us that the American family is violent, any more than that the American workplace or school is violent (see the next chapter). If a society is violent, we have discovered, it is usually violent in more than one way and in more than one locus in the society. The home and the family unit is a microcosm of the larger society as well as a "training ground" for the individuals who will take their place in public society in the future.

The two main issues to consider in regard to any family, not just American families, as we have seen, are child-rearing practices and domestic gender (i.e., spousal) relations. Naturally, these two issues cannot be completely separated, because what parents do to or with each other is an instrinsic part of the child-rearing environment. Children use their parents as models for appropriate adult behavior, and adults have to learn their behaviors somewhere.

Parenting and Child Abuse   Let us begin with American parenting. Few if any of us set out to be a bad parent, and few of us believe that we are. Behaviors like child abuse are condemned (although they are also committed), and some people even worry about corporal punishment (especially when someone else is administering it to our children). Parenting styles have definitely evolved over recent generations as "baby boomers" have become parents and their children have become parents in turn. The general sense is that parents are more indulgent and more liberal than in the past. They are also much busier, with both partners working (if both live in the home). What specific impact the "normal" American household—with divorce, "blended" families, latch-key kids, day care, video games, and the like—might have on the psyche of children is too early and convoluted to say. However, we do have some sense of what "bad" parenting is and what its consequences might be.

Psychologists have identified specific characteristics of bad parenting that have negative consequences. For instance, the Oregon Social Learning Center coined the term "coercive parenting" to describe a style that is inconsistent and often irritable; in particular, they note that coercive parenting vacillates between too harsh and too lenient, or anomic, discipline. Sometimes parents take strong note of and quick action against children for misbehavior, meting out severe punishment, while at other times they seem not to notice or not to care about such behavior, indirectly encouraging it. One result is children who "stop misbehaving" in response to the punishment often enough to reward parents for their harsh style but who, in Pavlovian form, learn that they can get away with it a large portion of the time. A second outcome is children who learn to be coercive themselves, who engage in antisocial behaviors like yelling and hitting, whining, and temper tantrums. The poor models of self-control they observe become poor structures of self-control internally.

Again, in the very worst cases, of killers and serial killers, family pathology plays a remarkable role. About half of such families have a history of parental mental illness or crime, and 70 percent exhibit substance abuse. Ressler suggests that 100 percent of dangerously violent repeat murderers were subjected to serious emotional abuse in the home. The forms he mentions include distant and cold relationships with their mothers (relationships that are "unloving, neglectful, [with] little touching, emotional warmth, or training in the ways in which normal human beings cherish one another and demonstrate their affection and interdependence" [Ressler and Schachtman 1992: 83]), coercive parenting of the sort described above, abandonment of children in front of the television or in their rooms, and absentee fathers (either literally or emotionally). The outcome of these circumstances is lack of empathy for and emotional attachment to other humans, violent fantasies, and even mental illness in the child.

America has a long history of force being applied "appropriately" to children, stretching to sources as far back as the biblical admonition not to spare the rod and the Roman concept of *patria potestas* discussed in Chapter 5, among others. Pleck, in her study of the history of the American family, argues that the colonists, particularly the Massachusetts Puritans, brought with them a tradition of "legitimate force" by fathers against children (and also husbands against wives) and that the *Book of Liberties* written in 1641 called for death for "a child over the age of sixteen who cursed or struck at a father or mother" (1987: 25). She further finds that "stubborn child laws" remained on the books for decades, even centuries, although it is difficult to determine when and if they were enforced. If anything, she suggests, corporal punishment became more severe in the late 1700s, although actual whipping was eventually replaced with spanking—although not completely, apparently, as she mentions Robert E. Lee, whose aunt described her parenting child-rearing style as "whip and pray and pray and whip" (47).

At a certain point, poor parenting crosses the line into actual child abuse (unfortunately, this is a blurry and shifting line). The National Center for Victims of Crime estimates that in the year 2000 some 879,000 American children were abused, at a rate of 1,200 per 100,000. According to their calculations, 63 percent of these cases were neglect, 19 percent were physical abuse, 10 percent were sexual abuse, and 8 percent were psychological or emotional abuse. Other interesting aspects of their findings include:

- Among child victims 51.9 percent were female and 48.1 percent were male.
- The younger the child, the higher the rate of victimization—children under age three were victimized at the highest rate.
- Among child victims 50.6 percent were white, 24.7 percent were black, 14.2 percent were Hispanic, and 1.6 percent were American Indian/ Alaska natives.
- Fully 79 percent of victimizers were parents, while 8.5 percent were other relatives.
- Women actually accounted for more than half (59.9 percent) of abusers.

At the most serious end of the child abuse spectrum, the federal Administration for Children and Families calculates 1,400 child fatalities due to abuse in 2002. The UCR shows 449 indexed cases of murder of a son or daughter (239 and 210, respectively). It also lists 107 cases of sibling murder and 223 cases of matricide/patricide.

Domestic Violence and Spouse Abuse   The home is a dangerous place for wives in many societies, including America. In Chapter 5 we studied some of the forms and some of the causes of domestic or intimate violence. Still, it should come as something of a surprise and a shock that people, particularly women, are so unsafe among their loved ones. For example, around 10 percent of all murders are spouse murders, 90 percent of which take place in the home; the Department of Justice reports that four women per day are killed by a husband or boyfriend. These violent acts almost never occur without prior, nonlethal violence preceding them. The DOJ also found that 671,110 women were victims of intimate violence in 1999, at a rate of 580 per 100,000. The National Morbidity Study from 2001, using Gelles' Conflict Tactics Scale as its instrument, cites that 17.4 percent of women experienced minor physical violence and 6.5 percent experienced severe violence, while 18.4 percent and 5.5 percent of men reported experiencing minor and severe intimate violence, respectively. These facts make spousal abuse a critical issue: although not necessarily a sign of greater violence to come, this greater violence, when it occurs, almost never happens without warning. Men are the more likely sex to kill their mates. Women, when they commit violence in the home, are more likely to commit it against young children—the younger, the more vulnerable. Men, instead, are more likely to kill older children or *the whole family*. And, although women are more likely to abuse children than men are, men are more likely to *sexually* abuse children.

Like child-directed violence, spouse- or intimate-partner-directed violence has a long pedigree. Early American attitudes emphasized the authority of the husband and the importance of preserving the marriage at almost any cost. In colonial families, women who were hit by their husbands were often regarded as having done something to deserve it. Except in the most extreme cases, men were left to discipline their family members, including their wives. As colonial leader John Winthrop put it:

> The woman's own choice makes . . . a man her husband; yet being so chosen, he is her lord, and she is to be subject to him, yet in a way of liberty, not of bondage; and a true wife accounts her subjection her honor and freedom, and would not think her condition safe and free but in her subjection to her husband's authority. (Quoted in Jones 1980: 36)

And of course the concept of "marital rape" did not even exist until recent years; before then, sexual congress was considered a man's right, and "rape" was defined as a "criminal" act, usually perpetrated by a stranger but always by someone who did not have sexual "rights" to the woman. Incredibly enough, Myers et al. (2002) quote two articles from the 1950s that claim that rape is less of a problem than "the problem of the psychopathic woman" (37) and that what appears to be rape often is not because "resistance during preliminary love-making greatly increases the sexual pleasure of some women" (38).

Something is not treated like a problem until it is considered to be a problem, and male coercive authority in the family was not considered a problem until recently (and occasionally is not today). Today we can distinguish a variety of types of domestic or spousal or intimate abuse, including physical abuse (battering), sexual abuse, emotional abuse, and what we might call "social" abuse, involving isolation of the partner from other people and things that she would normally enjoy freely otherwise. This latter suggests that, although the violence between partners may be related to specific events (from infidelity to failing to have supper on the table), it is more often than not usually one piece of a power struggle in which the man expresses his control or feels the need to reestablish his control. Accordingly, such factors as power imbalances, the threatened male ego, psychological (and sometimes physical) entrapment, social isolation, and what has been called "traumatic bonding" tend to underlie a violent relationship. Lenore Walker found, consistent with this view, that when men were feeling in control their abuse would subside, only to reemerge when that control felt threatened. Then, they would rely on anything from beating to verbal humiliation as "coercive techniques" to establish power (1979: 166).

Since this violence is "situational" as well as episodic and cyclical, we should expect to find certain circumstances that lead more dependably to spousal violence. For example, new marriages experience a higher rate of abuse than more settled ones; the DOJ study mentioned earlier found that the highest rate of intimate violence occurred among women aged sixteen to twenty-four, at an astounding 1,500–1,600 per 100,000. When the man loses his job, risk of violence increases. Also, sadly, when the woman becomes pregnant she enhances her risk for violence, as a few recent news-making cases have demonstrated, namely the murders of Laci Peterson and Lori Hacking, allegedly by their husbands.

Victim and victimizer alike can find ways to rationalize the unpleasant situation in which they find themselves. For instance, when men are asked to explain why they abused their partners as they did, they often offer excuses by which they deny full responsibility for their acts. They may blame alcohol, drugs, or some kind of frustration in their lives for their temporary loss of control, or they may blame the victim herself; sometimes they claim that she was physically or verbally aggressive or abusive first, as if that somehow validates their own usually much more intense violence. On other occasions, they accept responsibility for their actions but minimize or trivialize their consequences. They may deny that they "really hurt" their partner, or they may point to her own failure to be a "good wife" as sufficient provocation for a little "discipline."

Women, for their part, often permit this abuse to continue much longer than they should. There are many reasons for this inertia. Sometimes they really do feel as though it is somehow their fault. In other cases, they feel powerless or even fearful to do anything about it. In yet others, they think the abuse is "manageable" or that the man does not "really mean" to do it and that his behavior can be contained or fixed eventually.

A final reason why spousal abuse continues—as well as why it occurs in the first place—lies in the religious ideology of marriage and spousal roles. Patriarchal religious views of the world, including gender relations and marriage, can contribute to the "legitimization" of abusive behaviors and bonds by both husband and wife, as well as by society at large. Of course, not all religions or religious followers perceive or act this way. The problem is that at least some elements and agents of religion do encourage women to be subservient to men, even if those men are abusing them, and to avoid any step to avoid or escape such abuse, including divorce. A text used by many clergy in the United States for premarital counseling actually instructed readers to think this way:

> Suppose a woman feels God is leading her definitely opposite from what her husband has commanded? Whom should she obey? The Scriptures say a woman must ignore her feelings about the will of God and do what her husband says. She is to obey her husband as if he were God himself. She can be as certain of

God's will when her husband speaks as if God has spoken audibly from heaven. (Quoted in Pagelow and Johnson 1988: 6)

The evidence to indicate that this attitude contributes to justified and tolerated spousal (and child) abuse is anecdotal, but even a few cases is a few cases too many. Pagelow and Johnson cite the case of a woman who actually left her husband and sought refuge in a woman's shelter. Her minister called the director of the shelter and said that if she did not return home immediately " 'she would be excommunicated from the church because it was her duty to keep the family together and submit to her husband in all things' despite the fact that the children were also abused" (Bussert, quoted in ibid.: 6). Along the same lines, Pagelow did a study that included several wives of ministers. One told the story that she had left but returned "despite life-threatening abuse, partly because of her personal commitment to her marriage and religion which taught her that she was to 'submit' to her husband and partly because he 'needed' her" because his ministry would suffer or end with her departure (Pagelow and Johnson 1988: 4). In fact, in a study of 350 abused women, 28 percent reported seeking assistance from clergy, and the primary help they got was

> (1) a reminder of their duty and the advice to forgive and forget, (2) a reference elsewhere to avoid church involvement, and (3) useless advice, sometimes on religious doctrine rather than their own needs. Some were reminded of their vows of "for better or for worse" and admonished to pray more and live more worthy lives. One, scolded by her minister for "betraying" her husband by revealing what had occurred in the privacy of their home, was beaten harder by her husband when the pastors told him of her visit. (Pagelow and Johnson 1988: 5)

Finally, the experience of spousal violence appears to vary depending on race in this country. The Department of Justice determined in a 1996 study that the intimate murder rate for black women was 451 versus 134 for white women (and 283 versus 36 for black versus white men). A study by Beadell, Baker, Morrison, and Knox in 2000 concluded that 31 percent of black women suffered no abuse (versus 52 percent of white), 51 percent suffered emotional abuse (versus 35 percent of white), and 19 percent suffered physical abuse (versus 13 percent of white) (quoted in Malley-Morrison and Hines 2004: 132). Results for other groups are less certain, although at least some evidence suggests that Hispanics do not experience disproportionate spousal violence: the DOJ's 2000 report entitled *Intimate Partner Violence* states that Hispanic and non-Hispanic female victimization was virtually identical (800 versus 850 per 100,000). Asian American groups tend to report the lowest rates of domestic abuse, and Native American groups the highest. Two different studies employing the Conflict Tactics Scale yielded almost incredible numbers for Native American families: in one 75 percent and in the other 91 percent of women asserted that they had encountered domestic abuse in their lifetimes, and men asserted rates nearly as high (quoted in ibid.: 86).

RETROSPECT AND PROSPECT

American society is a violent one, and although we are not completely happy with that reality, we nonetheless somehow perpetuate it. If people did not do violence, people would not see violence and learn to do it. And if people did not accept and even to an extent enjoy violence (at least as entertainment), then they would not have a taste for it, and entertainers would produce less of it. Where though can one break into the cycle to change it?

As we have observed, there are many mutually interlocking and reinforcing elements that feed America's violent tendencies. No one piece of the psychological and social puzzle is completely responsible, and no one piece could be altered or eliminated to make it all different. In fact, one might ask whether it is possible and ultimately desirable among most Americans to do so: how would it be the "world's only superpower" unless it could muster a fair amount of force and aggression—and feel good about it? However, the cost of such constant low-grade mobilization of aggression is likely to be a high tolerance for "normal violence" and the occasional and regular "spilling over" of violence where we do not want it. But human values and institutions tend to have such unintended consequences. Are we doomed to accept a high rate of "collateral damage" to ourselves?

The question, I suppose, is whether America is serious enough about rejecting its own violence to take the hard steps to reduce it—and to accept the consequences of doing so. What are those steps, and what are those consequences? The second part of the question we cannot answer now, but the first part we can approach. Gelles (2000) suggests a set of initiatives to prevent family violence, perhaps the linchpin of the entire violent system. His five recommendations, are:

1. Eliminate the norms that legitimize and glorify violence in the society and the family . . .
2. Reduce violence-provoking stress created by society. . . .
3. Integrate families into a network of kin and community. . . .
4. Change the sexist character of society. . . .
5. Break the cycle of violence in the family (22–23; numbering added)

In the next and final chapter, we will examine in more detail several types of violence in America. In the process, we will apply the understanding we have gained throughout the course of the book, analyzing specific instances of violence within the context of American values, groups, and institutions. Before we move on, we might also want to revisit Table 10.2 and, in reflecting on its contents, try to determine precisely what the effects would be of actually putting Gelles' program into action.

CHAPTER 11

VIOLENCE IN AMERICAN SOCIETY

Case Studies

We know that there are many more ways to be violent than to be nonviolent, and the United States of America exploits many of them. It also combines all of the factors that contribute to violence—integration into groups, identity, ideology, and interest—with the interpersonal relations and forces that foster violence. Finally, it promotes many of the values and practices—competition, hierarchy, male dominance, honor, idealism, and so forth—that we have established as foundations for violence.

More particularly, U.S. society presents a constellation of "niches" in which violence is either more prevalent or more prominent. It is not always the case that violence is actually more common in these corners of society, and it would be surprising if it were less common; in a society steeped in violence, each institution and gathering place of citizens will be a unique opportunity to explore the possibilities of violence. We are familiar with many of these niches. Clearly one is the family, which we have discussed already. Others include situations in which conditions of stress, competition, and anonymity collide to "license" violence in ways that other situations do not.

For instance, we all know that driving has become a process fraught with violent potential. When people are stressed by traffic or the behavior of other commuters, when they are already "wound up" by the demands of driving, and when strangers not only offend us but endanger us, violence is likely to erupt in the form of "road rage." Sporting events and parties, where people mingle, get excited, and often drink, are occasions for potential violence. Work and school constitute high-pressure circumstances in which high-profile violence takes place. In fact, every social situation in America has the potential to turn into a violent encounter, especially when we factor in access to deadly weapons; drugs and alcohol; passions; and real or perceived threats to the body, or "respect."

In this last chapter, we will base our discussion on a representative sampling of the myriad situations and forms of violence in modern American society. It is not the case that America is unique in the expression of these violent behaviors, but it certainly excels at them and perhaps even "exports" them by its example. One of the tasks of the chapter will be to examine the causes and "justifications" behind such behaviors. In most cases, they will not be difficult to find.

Case Study 1: Workplace Violence

All Americans are familiar with the concept of violence at work, and we have all heard about—and even joke about—"going postal," a phrase based on several well-known instances of deadly violence in U.S. Postal Service worksites.In fact, the American workplace is a location of considerable violence. According to the NCVS (National Crime Victimization Survey; see previous chapter), between 1992 and 1996 over 2 million acts of violence were committed at work in an average year. The Bureau of Justice Statistics (BJS) reported 1,063 workplace homicides in 1992 alone, and the Bureau of Labor Statistics counted 23,225 worker injuries from assaults and other violence in 1999.

Two comments are worth making at the outset of our discussion. The first is that, given America's general penchant for violence, it should not be surprising that this violence occurs at work too. Why should the workplace be immune? If the typical American spends eight hours a day at work (more than any other single location except bed), we would expect the workplace to account for a substantial part of the violence in society. The second is that, although violence and injury are common in the workplace, they are *not*—contrary to popular impression—usually the result of direct worker-on-worker violence. Rather, as the same BJS study cited above indicates, of the 1,063 workplace murders, only 5 percent, or 59, of those killings involved co-workers. The National Violence Against Women Survey, for instance, found that only 1.7 percent of respondents had experienced violence from a co-worker in their lifetime. In actuality, the vast majority of workplace homicide and other violence is committed by nonworkers in the course of the commission of other crimes, including robbery and burglary.

So, to get a useful handle on workplace violence, let us develop a typology of such violence. Remember also that discussing such violence is subject to all the problems we considered in Chapter 1—that is, the definition of violence, the classification of violence, and the reporting of violence. Which things shall we count as workplace violence? A police officer getting wounded in the field? A customer punching a salesperson in the face? A boss saying an unkind or threatening word to an employee? It is almost certain that much "violence" goes unreported, either because of fear of reprisal (especially if the perpetrator is a supervisor) or because of doubt that the incident really qualifies as violence.

Case Study 1: Workplace Violence (continued)

At any rate, the Occupational Safety and Health Administration (OSHA) offers a three-part typology of workplace violence, including "intrusive," "consumer-related," and "relationship" versions. Vaughan Bowie (2002), analyzing the real incidence of such violence, suggests a fourth category, "organizational." Let us then adopt this four-category system.

Type 1: Intrusive Violence

Intrusive violence involves a nonworker who invades the workplace for purposes of committing a crime. The crime may be one of violence but is more often one of property. Violence, then, is incidental to, or at least separate from, the main criminal intent in most cases. Examples of such violence include crimes resulting in injury, mental-illness or drug-related aggression, protest violence, and terrorist acts. There are obviously some very clear risk factors for this kind of violence. According to Mayhew (2000), four core risk factors are

1. Workplaces where there is face-to-face contact with customers
2. Workplaces where the business exchanges money with the public
3. Workplaces where there are few workers on site
4. Workplaces that are open in the evening and at night

Not unexpectedly, then, some of the institutions that are at highest risk are bars, liquor stores, gas stations, convenience stores, grocery stores, hotels/ motels, and restaurants. It has been suggested that up to 80 percent of all work-related homicides and at least 30 percent of nonfatal assaults occur in the course of robberies or other crimes in such locations.

Type 2: Consumer-Related Violence

Consumer-related violence occurs when workers perform their duties in relation to members of the public who are not in the process of committing crimes but who are dangerous nonetheless. Examples include injury to workers by customers, clients, or patients with whom they must interact, "vicarious" trauma to such workers, and injury to customers or clients or patients at the hand of workers. *Vicarious trauma* is defined as the psychological and interpersonal damage that is done to workers from the exposure to the violence or horror of their jobs; this can be particularly powerful for police and prison workers, medical (especially emergency medical), mental-health, and social-service staff. It can lead to burnout and the transmission of violence to their personal lives, including their homes and families.

Any workplace that puts workers in contact with the public runs the risk of this sort of violence. Of course, not every workplace is equal to another

Case Study 1: Workplace Violence (continued)

(presumably, shoe store customers are not as likely to become violent as prison inmates); therefore, we find that the highest-risk jobs in this regard are police officer, security/prison guard, fire fighter, healthcare provider (especially mental healthcare provider), teacher, and social worker. Healthcare workers, particularly those involved in in-patient care, are among the most at risk, since they are interacting with and handling difficult people daily. It has been found that young male patients with psychoses and a history of violence are most likely to assault their caretakers. Hospital staff, especially in high-crime areas, also face a dangerous situation; one study showed that 25 percent of trauma patients in emergency rooms have weapons in their possession.

Type 3: Relationship Violence

We are now entering the more stereotypical world of worker-on-worker violence. Relationship violence, which involves people who know each other or who at least work together, includes staff-on-staff assault and bullying as well as domestic violence at work. Some recent high-profile cases have involved estranged husbands carrying guns to their wife's workplace and shooting her and sometimes other employees; this behavior qualifies as workplace and relationship violence, although only one of the two people concerned occupied the workplace.

Employee at-risk factors for violence include the following (Kenny 2002: 81–82):

- A history of violence or run-ins with the law
- Frequent anger, frustration, or inflexibility
- Recent talk of or attempt at suicide
- Prior personal threats or interpersonal conflicts
- Recent attempts to obtain weapons
- Drug or alcohol abuse
- Personality disorders
- Social isolation
- Frustration over having complaints or grievances ignored or dismissed
- Defensiveness or paranoia
- Low self-esteem and hopelessness
- Lack of self-control

Not all of the dangers are internal to the employees, however. Some of the risk factors that have been identified as contributing to Type 3 violence have more to do with the experience of work, such as "management toleration of bullying, job insecurity, workers facing unemployment with little chance of re-employment, workers with a strong sense of entitlement who feel cheated, vengeful

Case Study 1: Workplace Violence (continued)

workers, a loss of self-esteem and stability amongst workers, and disciplinary suspensions" (Mayhew, 29). We are not, then, talking about violence that is "unprovoked" in many cases. We might not accept the violence as a desirable response to the provocation, but neither can we dismiss it as "senseless" or "indiscriminate."

Type 4: Organizational Violence

Like the "structural violence" we identified in many societies, whereby circumstances, practices, or systems committed their own kind of violence against people, organizational violence exists when the circumstances, practices, or systems of the business or even of the wider society impact workers in negative ways—inadvertently fostering violent responses. Bowie counts violence against staff and violence against consumers/clients/patients as two subtypes of organizational violence.

As we know, companies have their distinctive "organizational cultures," and the experience of work in America has general features, shaped partly by overarching economic and social realities. A company's organizational culture is set largely by its management. Thus, the quality of the interactions between employees and supervisors is critical for understanding the responses of employees. Allcorn (1994: 100–103) has identified several types of management style that can contribute to the frustration of workers, including:

- "Expansive" or "mastering" leadership style, which encompasses the perfectionist boss, the arrogant-vindictive boss, and the narcissistic boss
- "Self-effacing" leadership style, whereby the boss tries to be loved by subordinates by not making any tough choices and avoiding responsibility
- "Resigned" leadership style, in which the boss detaches himself or herself from workplace conflict and performance problems, allowing them to fester and leaving workers feeling abandoned and frustrated

Leaders themselves can introduce anger, condescension, and even violence into the workplace.

Apart from the more personal aspects of the workplace, it is important to consider the structural characteristics of particular workplaces and general characteristics that all workplaces have in common. For instance, work in general tends to be hierarchical and rigid, unlike other aspects of American society, where we are all made to feel (or are at least told) that we are all equal and free. Based on power and authority, work promotes dependency on superiors and even peers. Individual companies may suffer from labor–management conflict, reorganization and downsizing, ineffective or nonexistent grievance

Case Study 1: Workplace Violence (continued)

processes, threats to pay and benefits, inconsistency, poor working conditions, and even ethnic and gender tensions (Kenny 2002: 83).

More and more in the modern era, working conditions, largely determined by macroeconomic and macrosocial conditions, have become negative for workers, including longer working hours; higher pressures and expectations; constantly changing skill requirements or deskilling; fluctuating wages; and, at the extreme, job insecurity. Job insecurity, especially in times of economic slowdown and massive layoffs, is one of the greatest instigators of employee frustration and violence. Catalano found that "job loss was associated with a higher risk of violent behavior than many of the characteristics cited as the leading predictors of violence. In our study losing a job increased the odds of a violent episode more than having a history of psychiatric disorder . . . or of being male, young or of low socioeconomic status" (quoted in Bowie 2002: 12). And it is not even necessarily the fact of losing one's job but the process by which it transpires that may be the culprit: Benison states that "time and time again, disgruntled workers who have become violent have said that what impelled them was not the fact that they were demoted, fired or laid off, but the dehumanizing way the action was carried out" (quoted in ibid.: 13).

In other words, except for the clearly psychologically troubled worker, staff-on-staff violence is situationally explicable. Workers who feel their egos, their self-respect, and of course their livelihoods frustrated and threatened are the most likely to lash out. Williams (quoted in Bowie 2002: 13) states that "workplace violence becomes a response or reaction to an unexpected, unexplained, unwarranted change in policy, procedure or practice that creates trauma among employees and in the organization itself." The more this situation traumatizes the worker, and the more arbitrary and "unjust" it seems, the greater its potential to spark violence. This assessment is borne out by a study of human-resource professionals conducted by Arway (2002), who asked these front-line specialists on workplace violence what factors contributed to the violence they had seen in their companies. The single largest set of factors (44 percent) were "organizational issues" like job termination or layoff, worker recognition, working hours or environment, supervision, and job assignments (52). In the final analysis, then, workplace violence, although it may be maladaptive, is not irrational or incomprehensible. It is like all other nonpathological violence: "At the heart of almost all aggressive and bizarre behaviors is an attempt to achieve or maintain justice, or correct or prevent some wrong" (Kenny 2002: 77).

A word is in order about gender and workplace violence. Like other occasions of violence, men continue to be the predominant victims and perpetrators. In the NCVS study, from 1992 to 1996 men outnumbered women as

Case Study 1: Workplace Violence (continued)

victims of such violence by 2 to 1. However, women have been cau
lately. Still, men are the victims of 81 percent of workplace homicide ʌ
often shot during a robbery), and men are three times more likely to be tʌ
victim of robbery and assault than women. Of course, in victimization by sexual violence and "intimate" violence women still lead men. Over 83 percent of
workplace rapes and sexual crimes are committed against women, and over 6
percent of all workplace violence against women involves rape or sexual
assault. Women experience higher rates of workplace violence when they work
in liquor stores, gas stations, and grocery stores, as well in the mental-health
field. However, women remain ten times more likely of being assaulted by a
family member than a co-worker, and the home remains one of the most dangerous places for them.

Case Study 2: School Violence

Since some of the newsworthy school violence in the mid- to late-1990s, concern over the dangerous and even deadly conditions in American schools has
reached a fevered pitch. Kip Kinkel's shooting spree in Springfield, Oregon
(May 21, 1998) cost four lives and 22 injuries, not counting his parents, whom
he had murdered the day before, and Eric Harris's and Dylan Klebold's assault
on Littleton, Colorado (April 20, 1999) was even more deadly, leaving thirteen
dead and twenty-three wounded. Incidents in West Paducah, Kentucky, and
Jonesboro, Arkansas led Americans to conclude that there was an epidemic of
murderous violence in the schools.

There is in fact a great deal of violence in American schools, as there is in
American workplaces. This should not surprise us. There is a great deal of violence in America, and schools and workplaces are microcosms of American
society. Furthermore, just as adults spend a large part of their lives at work,
children spend a large part of theirs at school, so incidents are likely to occur
in both places. However, as a microcosm of American society, schools tend to
follow the same patterns of violence as other parts of society—in fact, there
has been a decrease in such violence in recent years, the high-profile cases
notwithstanding.

Sadly, or not so sadly, violence and other antisocial behavior in schools is
not a 1990s phenomenon, nor even a twentieth-century phenomenon. Crews
and Montgomery, in their book *Chasing Shadows: Confronting Juvenile Violence in America* (2001), show that discipline problems (if not mass shootings) existed in seventeenth- and eighteenth-century schools, including

Case Study 2: School Violence (continued)

rebelliousness and disobedience; they also point out that some of the colonies officially proscribed the death penalty for rebellion against parents (following scriptural example), although they did not enforce it. Violence, of course, went both ways: children were subjected to "corporal punishment" from teachers and administrators in the form of blows with a rod, cane, ruler, or hand; boxed ears; and more unusual forms, such as being locked in closets or forced to kneel on peas or blocks of wood. Parent–child hostility at school prepared children for the hostile adult society that awaited them. Those of us older Americans can remember the principal's paddle, the "board of education."

In the 1960s and 1970s, as staff violence against students began to recede, student violence began to grow and intensify; movies like *The Blackboard Jungle* capture some sense of the change. A study called "The Unruly School" (Rubel 1977) also supports this conclusion: from 1964 to 1968, the number of homicides at school increased 73 percent (15 versus 26), the number of assaults on students increased 167 percent (1,601 versus 4,267), and the number of assaults on teachers increased 7,100 percent (25 versus 1,801). By the late 1970s sufficient attention had been drawn to school violence to motivate the congressional study known as "Violent Schools—Safe Schools: The Safe School Study Report to Congress" (U.S. Department of Health, Education and Welfare 1978). This research found the following:

- Each month 13 percent of students were victims of crime at school.
- Homicides at school increased 19.5 percent from 1970 to 1973.
- Incidents of rape and attempted rape increased 40.1 percent.
- Student-on-student assaults increased 85.3 percent.
- Student-on-teacher assaults increased 77.4 percent.
- The number of weapons confiscated at school grew 54.4 percent.
- Millions of students were afraid while at school and deliberately avoided certain locations within the school out of fear.

Another study in mid-decade documented the surge of gangs and gang activity, especially in the country's largest cities (see the section on gangs below).

Again, analysis of school violence confronts us with the standard problems of analyzing violence in context. First, there is the issue of definition and operationalization: what will count as violence, and what will count as school? "Violence" can include anything from bullying and teasing to vandalism to hate crimes against specific groups (especially gays and lesbians), gang activity, dating violence, and mass murder. Further, it can include staff-on-student or even staff-on-staff violence (and because the latter could be construed as workplace violence, perhaps it should it be counted twice, once in each category). "School violence" can also cover incidents occurring on school property as well as on the way to and from school, plus incidents at school-sponsored or

Case Study 2: School Violence (continued)

school-sanctioned events and to and from them. Second, there is the issue of reporting. As a result of the lack of a federal requirement to report violence at schools as a distinct phenomenon of "school violence" and the failure of students to report every incident to their teachers or parents, most of what we know about school violence comes from victimization studies conducted by social scientists or from their efforts to glean school-related information from crime statistics. There are comparatively few such studies, their methods and operationalizations differ widely, and many of them are fairly old.

Nevertheless, researchers have made useful discoveries about school violence. First of all, although it is widespread and disturbing, it is not growing at the epidemic rate that intensive media coverage of a few extreme cases would suggest. In the area of homicide, the rate doubled in the decade from 1984 to 1994; on a typical day in 1992, seven juveniles were killed. The high point of school violence was also reached at that time: in the 1992–93 school year, there were fifty-five violent deaths at school, and in the 1993–94 year about fifty. Of these, around 80 percent were homicides and 20 percent were suicides. According to the *Journal of the American Medical Association*, seventy-six of the victims were students, twelve were staff, and the rest were not associated with the school. Two-thirds of the incidents involved personal conflict or gangs, and 77 percent of them involved guns. They were twice as likely to take place in urban environments as suburban ones.

However, there has actually been a 50 percent decrease in school homicides since the 1992–93 school year. In 1997–8 there were 32–35 (depending on the source) juvenile murders on school grounds and the numbers continue to shrink. Interestingly, in the same year there were 2,717 juvenile murders off of school grounds, suggesting that school is not the most dangerous place for our children. Similarly, the Department of Education (National Center for Education Statistics 1998) reports that fights on school grounds declined during the same period and that the number of students carrying guns to school fell from 12 percent to 7 percent (with 11 percent of boys and 3 percent of girls carrying the weapons). The overall victimization rate dropped from 144 per 1,000 in 1992 to 101 per 1,000 in 1998. Despite these facts, the perception often continues to be that schools are increasingly less safe: a report by the Centers for Disease Control in 2003 showed that 5.4 percent of students skipped school at least once out of fear for their safety compared to 4.4 percent in 1993.

A few regular characteristics of juvenile and school violence have emerged from years of observation and research. For one thing, bullying and constant low-grade hostility appear to figure prominently in outbreaks of violence and in fact contribute to the total number of reports of violence. Bullying, a familiar phenomenon to anyone who went through school, is essentially repeatedly victimizing another person or persons, usually by teasing—verbal or

Case Study 2: School Violence (continued)

physical—but often with actual assaults on the person(s). Bullies are most often boys (up to two-thirds), and they tend to be physically mature and athletic (even if not actual athletes), dominant and domineering, impulsive individuals with poor self-concepts, little empathy for others, and an inclination to see hostile intent in others whether it is there or not. This constellation of traits, as we have seen repeatedly, tends to spawn, perpetuate, and enhance violence in all contexts.

Girls are known to bully as well, although their activities tend to be more "covert" and "social," including gossip and ostracism. Whoever is doing the bullying, some locations in school are more conducive to the behavior—the lunchroom, playground, hallways and bathrooms, as well as during the commute to and from school. In other words, situations in which there is little structure or adult supervision see more antisocial behavior. Finally, the victims of bullying (and sometimes subsequent aggression, although they may turn into aggressors themselves as a result) tend to be physically smaller and weaker, often overweight or underweight, younger, and less popular or with inferior social skills.

Predictably, gender, race, and age are aspects of school violence. Boys commit and suffer more violence than girls. Boys get in most of the fights, carry most of the weapons, and in general get into trouble more than girls. Girls are of course far more likely to be the victims of violent sexual behavior, but in other types of assaults, boys are more likely to be the victim of other boys. A 1995 study showed that boys were two and a half times more likely to be the victim of an armed attack than girls; the same study showed that blacks were twice as likely to be victims as whites. Other studies and research support the latter conclusion. The Youth Risk Behavior Surveillance System (2000) reported that 18.7 percent of black students have gotten into fights at school as opposed to 12.3 percent of white students. And a 1998 study indicated that Hispanic students have a rate of violent school death five times the white rate, while black students have a rate *nine* times the white rate.

One of the most striking aspects of school and juvenile violence is the age factor. We already know that youths are more likely to commit crimes and other violence than adults; a NCVS study concluded that youths aged sixteen to nineteen have a victimization rate of violent crime four and a half times greater than adults aged thirty-five to forty-nine (which is a considerably wider age range, too). Teenagers in the age range of sixteen to seventeen have the highest rate of serious violence of any age group, which then drops precipitously until 80 percent of them cease such activity by age twenty-one (Hamburg 1998: 32). However, in terms of school violence, it has been repeatedly observed that the age group with the highest rate of infraction is younger

Case Study 2: School Violence (continued)

teens, from the seventh to the tenth grades. Crews and Montgomery report that, between 1985 and 1988, adolescents aged twelve to fifteen were twice as likely to commit crimes on school grounds as well as to victims of such crimes (2001: 52). Goldstein similarly calls seventh grade the most aggressive grade, and junior high a more aggressive age than senior high (1996: 115). A 1993 study by the National Education Goals Panel claimed that 9 percent of eighth graders, 10 percent of tenth graders, and only 6 percent of twelfth graders carried a weapon to school in the previous month and that the highest rate of victimization of school violence (19 percent) occurred among eighth graders. Finally, a study of fighting at school showed that in 1999, 21 percent of ninth graders got into fights as opposed to 10 percent of twelfth graders. Although it is possible that some of these consistent discrepancies are related to the "bigger world" of the older teen, who spends more time in public venues other than school, it may also be related to developmental issues of early adolescence.

So far we have essentially looked at school violence in isolation—the perpetrators and victims as isolated individuals and the school as an isolated institution. However, there is plenty of evidence to suggest that we cannot understand school violence properly in this manner. Schools are necessarily part of the wider American society, and school children have critical experiences in settings other than school. In fact, Sheley, McGee, and Wright have asserted that "a dangerous environment outside the school, as opposed to a dangerous environment inside the school, was a better predictor of weapon-related victimization at or during travel to and from school" (quoted in Loeber and Stouthammer-Loeber 1998: 143). Margaret Hamburg states (1998: 35): "Evidence suggests that violence in schools derives mainly from factors external to schools, but may be precipitated or aggravated by the school environment." Elliott, Hamburg, and Williams (1998: 16) together posit that "Most of the known risk factors for violence [at school] reside in the family and larger community." In other words, it is not schools that cause violence but domestic and social factors; schools are just where the violence plays out.

What are these risk factors? Surveying the literature, the following items repeatedly crop up:

FAMILY (MICROSOCIAL) RISK FACTORS

- Child abuse in the home
- Other domestic violence
- Harsh and inconsistent discipline
- Poverty
- Substance abuse

Case Study 2: School Violence (continued)

- Parental criminal behavior
- Aggression between siblings
- Inadequate parenting skills or adult supervision
- Disruptions to family functioning, such as divorce

In general, then, these factors create bad models for behavior and bad environments in which to learn and practice social interaction.

COMMUNITY (MACROSOCIAL) RISK FACTORS

- Poverty
- Unemployment or lack of opportunity
- Gangs
- Neighborhood violence and crime
- Poor or nonexistent community services (day care, recreation, etc.)
- Unstable neighborhoods—ones with high rates of population change
- Neighborhoods with many single-parent families
- Inadequate housing
- Easy availability of guns and other weapons
- Prevalence of alcohol and drugs
- Violence in the mass media

It should be obvious that these factors not only contribute to school and juvenile violence but to all forms of violence in America.

In conclusion, Fagan and Wilkinson (1998) make some noteworthy comments about "rough play" that help to put American youth violence into perspective. We all know that American children, especially boys, like to play rough and are encouraged to do so. This play may entail dodge ball, wrestling, or structured competitive games. You will recall from Chapter 3 that the truly nonviolent societies of the world—the Semai, the Utku, and the like—do not include and do not encourage rough or competitive play. Fagan and Wilkinson offer as "functions" of rough play (1) formation of affiliations and friend selection, (2) development of fighting skills, and (3) "initial establishment of one's position in a dominance hierarchy" (1998: 63). The question is whether we want children learning fighting skills and forming dominance hierarchies. These may be exactly the qualities that breed violence, in schools and everywhere else. The authors even extol the functions of violence: achieving and maintaining status, materialism and the search for social identity, power, "rough justice" (that is, retribution, restitution, or compensation for past perceived wrongs by a "law of the jungle/playground"), defiance of authority, and socialization into risk taking. Precisely so. As long as we enculturate young people to seek status and power, pursue their own retribution, and defy authority, we should expect nothing other than violent youths who grow into violent adults.

Case Study 3: Gang Violence

Bangin' ain't no part-time thang, it's full-time, it's a career. It's bein' down
when ain't nobody else down with you. It's gettin' caught and not tellin'.
Killin' and not caring, and dyin' without fear. It's love for your set and hate
for the enemy. You hear what I'm sayin'?
—*A gang leader, quoted by Sanyika Shakur*

Americans are very familiar with gangs and gang violence; we have alternately
glorified it and been horrified by it. In a way, gangs are an extension and intensification of youth violence of the sort seen in schools and elsewhere. In
another way, they are a microcosm of the general violence in America and
especially the "political" or "identity" aspect of violence that we have emphasized throughout this book. They also mirror for us our society's race, class,
residential, and even gender distinctions and hierarchies.

Our first problem, as always, is a definitional one: what exactly do we mean
by "gang"? Any group of people who hang around together and interact for
some purpose could be construed as a gang, but that would not be a very useful definition. Is, for example, participation in violence inherent in the nature
of "gangs"? Are gangs specifically juvenile-oriented kinds of entities? The definition, as always, will affect what we "count" as a gang and what we count as
gang violence.

Numerous scholars have taken their turns at defining gangs. Thrasher, one
of the first researchers to study gangs systematically, described a gang as

> an interstitial group, originally formed spontaneously, and then integrated
> through conflict. It is characterized by the following types of behavior: meeting
> face to face, milling [hanging out], movement through space as a unit, conflict,
> and planning. The result of this collective behavior is the development of tradi-
> tion, unreflective internal structure, esprit de corps, solidarity, morale, group
> awareness, and attachment to a local territory. (Quoted in Weisel 2002: 17)

Moore called gangs "unsupervised peer groups who are socialized by the
streets rather than by conventional institutions. They define themselves as a
gang or 'set' or some such term, and have the capacity to reproduce themselves, usually within a neighborhood" (quoted in Hagedorn 1998: 367).
Notice that neither of these accounts makes criminality central to the
existence of a gang. Others, like Miller (quoted in Covey, Menard, and
Franzese 1997: 5) have put crime and violence in the very definition:

> A youth gang is a self-formed association of peers, bound together by mutual
> interests, with identifiable leadership, well-developed lines of authority, and other
> organizational features, who act in concert to achieve a specific purpose which
> generally includes the conduct of illegal activity and control over a particular terri-
> tory, facility, or type of enterprise.

Case Study 3: Gang Violence (continued)

Similarly, Klein (quoted in Shelden, Tracy, and Brown 2001: 18–19) conceives of a gang as

> any denotable ... group [of adolescents and young adults] who (a) are generally perceived as a distinct aggregation by others in their neighborhood, (b) recognize themselves as a denotable group (almost invariably with a group name), and (c) have been involved in a sufficient number of [illegal] incidents to call forth a consistent negative response from neighborhood residents and/or enforcement agencies.

However we choose to define gangs, note that certain key characteristics arise, including a sense of identity, internal organization or even "culture," and shared purposes or ends. We will have more to say about this below.

Gangs are often seen as a new and unprecedented menace to society, but in reality they are not a new phenomenon at all. In a way, and at least from a certain perspective, Robin Hood and his merry men could be viewed as a gang. There have been gangs of bandits, "highwaymen," train robbers, and bank robbers as long as there have been highways, trains, and banks. The earliest American gangs operated on the East Coast in the early 1800s and can be associated with various immigrant groups who often clustered—or found themselves clustered—in ethnic enclaves in New York and Philadelphia and nearby cities. The very first recorded gang may have been the "Forty Thieves," a New York Irish group from the turn of the nineteenth century. A Philadelphia newspaper claimed that the city was "plagued" with gangs prior to the Civil War (1861). In New York in particular, gang activity was often associated with politics, and the "political machines" like the one working out of Tammany Hall depended on gangs to "get out the vote," that is, manipulate local elections; a report from 1855 estimated that 30,000 men in the city were loyal to gang leaders. Simultaneously, a report by the New Children's Aid Society in 1854 commented on the delinquent juvenile gangs roaming the streets:

> Crime among boys and girls has become organized, as it never was previously. The police state that picking pockets is now a profession among a certain class of boys. They have their haunts, their "flash" language, their "decoys," and "coverers," as they are called, or persons who will entice others where they can be plundered, and protect the thieves if they are caught. (Quoted in Covey, Menard, and Franzese 1997: 119)

By the late 1800s, East Coast gangs had formed into more coherent and well-known organizations as the Pug Uglies, the Dusters, the Roach Guards, and the Bowery Boys. Already as early as the 1860s juvenile gangs were engaging in violent conflicts between each other over "turf" in New York City. Of course, the first few decades of the twentieth century, especially the years of Prohibition, saw the emergence of more organized "criminal syndicates,"

Case Study 3: Gang Violence (continued)

specializing in the bootlegging of alcohol and other criminal activities, including bank robbery. These were the days of Al Capone, Bonnie and Clyde, Ma Barker, and other colorful and often popular "gangland" figures. The same years—the 1920s and beyond—found the first gang appearances on the West Coast, particularly in Los Angeles where marginalized Mexican immigrants or Cholos often formed themselves into conspicuous, even ostentatious, groups clad in "zoot suits." These immigrants formed an underclass and found themselves subject to discrimination and even deportation (as during the Depression of the 1930s). The so-called Zoot Suit riots of 1943, along with increased police attention to and suppression of such groups, made the Chicano "gangs" more self-conscious and more unified: as one commentator put it, those men who fought against the authorities in the riots "were seen by their younger brothers as heroes in a race war" (quoted in Shelden, Tracy, and Brown 2001: 9). This led to the further institutionalization of the groups.

Thus "ganging" was initially a primarily white and white-ethnic phenomenon until the early twentieth century, when Hispanics entered the gang landscape. In fact, up to the 1950s, gangs, as depicted in movies like *The Wild Ones* and *Rebel Without a Cause*, were still predominantly populated by angry young white men. Also, their activities were relatively benign, other than an occasional "rumble," as in the film *West Side Story*. African Americans were somewhat late to join, probably because of their complete repression until the 1950s. However, the Watts riot in California in 1965 and the development (and perceived stalling) of the civil rights movement changed all that. "Political" gangs like the Black Panthers were supplemented and supplanted by "regular" or delinquent gangs such as the Vice Lords in Chicago. The Vice Lords supposedly formed among jailed youths seeking protection and grew into an enterprise that expanded into the territory of other gangs through violence— although much milder violence than we see today. Fighters would often not even use weapons, aiming to show their toughness in fistfights; homicide was not their goal.

By the 1970s, two "nations" of largely African American gangs—the Crips and the Bloods—had crystallized. Each was really a "supergang" composed of more or less loosely associated local gangs or *sets*, something like chapters although they were not all "officially" attached to the supergangs. The Crips and the Bloods each adopted their own distinctive signs and language: for example, Crips would wear blue while the Bloods wore red, each developed its unique hand signs and greetings (Crips called each other "cuzz" while Bloods called each other "blood"), and so on. Intergang competition and "warfare" occasionally broke out and escalated, and, especially within the Crip "nation," intragang violence was also common.

Case Study 3: Gang Violence (continued)

A good occasion to transition from this discussion of the history of gangs to the causes and consequences of gang activity is the autobiography of the former Crip member Sanyika Shakur, also quoted at the top of this section. Born Kody Scott (and nicknamed "Monster" on the streets), Shakur joined a local set of the Crips, the Eight Trays of South Central Los Angeles, in 1975 at the age of eleven. Coming from a female-headed household in a rough ghetto neighborhood riddled with crime and the presence of gangs, he enlisted in his neighborhood division and was "jumped in" with a physical beating and an assignment to carry out some gang-related violence. Most of the violence that the Eight Trays perpetrated, he makes very clear, was aimed at other gangs, not the general public. And although guns were ubiquitous in his set, the purpose of the gang was not crime (especially drug dealing) or even so much violence for the sake of violence, but rather violence for the sake of protection and respect.

In Shakur's account, gangs exist, in a word, because gangs exist: "My participation came as second nature. To be in a gang in South Central when I joined—and it is still the case today—is the equivalent of growing up in Grosse Pointe, Michigan, and going to college: everyone does it. Those who don't aren't part of the fraternity. And as with everything from a union to a tennis club, it's better to be in than out" (Shakur 1993: 138). This confirms one of Thrasher's points about gangs and a general truism in the analysis of gangs. Thrasher asserts that "ganging"—that is, forming identity and interest groups—is normal adolescent peer behavior; in fact, it is normal *human* peer behavior. Everywhere that they inhabit, humans gather into various kinds of named collectivities and distinguish themselves from other named collectivities; this is the essence of "us-versus-them" identification. Such collectivities also, as is generally recognized, evolve their own "subcultures" in the form of language, symbols, and such. Therefore, in a way, the gang phenomenon constitutes a subculture, and each individual gang or set has its own variant of that subculture, as did the Crips and the Bloods, for example. That is, in the end, we might think of gangs as an alternative vehicle of socialization and enculturation for certain types of youths—or perhaps even the primary vehicle of socialization for some.

Thus, ganging for Shakur amounted to the commitment to an identity and a corporate body—the gang functions essentially as a male interest/political group. He goes so far as to say that gangs "tend to function as 'states' in regard to taking or colonizing territory" (1993: 19). States, as we saw in Chapter 8, are competitive and even predatory political systems, for which power and the control of land, population, and wealth can be an end in itself. Also, any rival state is a potential enemy (or at best a temporary friend). Shakur even likens gang expansion to the territorial conquest of states:

Case Study 3: Gang Violence (continued)

> The mechanics involved in taking a street, or territory, is not unlike any attempt, I would assume, on behalf of early Euro-American settlers. Send in a scout, have him meet the "natives," test their hostility level, military capabilities, needs, likes, and dislikes. Once a military presence is established, in come the "citizens"—in this case, gang members. Those who are not persuaded by our lofty presence will be persuaded by our military might. All who are of fighting age become conscripts. The set expands, and so does our territory. Sometimes there is resistance, but most of the time our efforts are successful. (1993: 36)

One almost wonders whether a Requerimiento was read to the natives.

No one, it seems, will truly understand gangs unless they can see them in this context—as political institutions. In fact, he admits that his "state" acts like any other state and that his "wars" are like any other war; the difference, he says, "is not legality, but cause. Some causes are righteous and in accord with human nature, while others are reactionary and repressive. Gang wars fall somewhere in between. I can quite easily justify the retaliation on enemies for killing one of my comrades. But simultaneously I will condemn the murdering of noncombatants" (Shakur 1993: 57).

Undoubtedly, not all gang bangers concur, but the point is that gang violence is not necessarily any more "irrational" or "disorganized" than any other form of violence. It is done usually by and for a group, and we know that humans are more violent when they are acting on behalf of a group than when they are not. When the groups are armed and threatened, or actively in conflict, the violence intensifies. Thrasher, in his definition earlier, recognized this in relation to gangs: that they are integrated through conflict. Elsewhere he argues that a gang "develops through strife and thrives on warfare." Shakur echoes this sentiment:

> With each new generation of Crip and Blood bangers comes a more complex system, which is now reaching institutional proportions. It is precisely because of this type of participation in the development and expansion of these groups' mores, customs, and philosophies that gangbanging will never be stopped from without. The notion of the "war on gangs" being successful is as realistic as the People's Republic of China telling Americans to stop being American. When gang members stop their wars and find that there is no longer a need for their sets to exist, banging will cease. But until then, all attempts by law enforcement to seriously curtail its forward motion will be in vain. (Shakur 1993: 79)

This is a depressing assessment but probably a sensible one; just as there is no institution or system superior to states to curb state violence, so there is no institution or system superior to gangs to curb gang violence. Law enforcement is to gangs as the United Nations is to sovereign states.

Case Study 3: Gang Violence (continued)

In the divided and therefore divisive world of gangs, the typical us-versus-them mentality reigns; when the guns start firing, the mentality seems uniquely appropriate and self-reinforcing. However, if humans tend to think in all-or-nothing, us-or-them terms much of the time, gangs are even more prone to it since the gang system appears so "total" to the members. Gangs exist—that is, they are a social reality—and you belong to one or another, or you can take your chances and not belong. But there are no alternatives and no "retreat." "There was no gray area, no middle ground. You banged or held strong association with the gang, or else you were a victim, period" (Shakur 1993: 100). Every non-us is a them; the system is closed. As Shakur exclaims, "Fence sitters disgusted me" (87). So, although gangs did not target noncombatants, noncombatants were like the victims of the French Reign of Terror, the Argentine "dirty war," or Nechayev's vengeance—guilty of insufficient enthusiasm for and commitment to the gang.

Finally, Shakur notes that the main attraction of a gang, aside from protection from other gangs (a self-fulfilling prophecy), is the pursuit of individual honor and respect. Each male—or at least the one who works hard to rise in the gang system—wants to become a "ghetto star," esteemed for his fierceness and his organizational ability. It is a male status game, like any other male status game. "The principle [behind gangs and gang killing] is respect, a linchpin critical to relations between all people, but magnified by thirty in the ghettos and slums across America" (102). In a world where little opportunity to gain honor exists, gangs provide a medium of self-esteem and esteem of others. A reputation is a main goal, if not the main goal; it is achieved by first building your own individual name, then associating your name with your particular set and ultimately establishing yourself as a player and promoter at the level of the "supergang"—Crip or Blood, respectively. This name is acquired through daring acts of violence, by surviving daring acts of violence against yourself, by spending time in juvenile hall and eventually adult prison, and other "steps" on the ladder to status. Death, Shakur notes, is the ultimate honor, which is why the fear of a premature death is no disincentive to the dedicated banger: "Though never verbally stated, death was looked upon as a sort of reward, a badge of honor, especially if one died in some heroic capacity for the hood. The supreme sacrifice was to 'take a bullet for a homie' (103). Perhaps the last thing we can say about the psychology of gangs is the next thing that he says: "The set functioned as a religion."

This phenomenon would be distressing enough to Americans if it existed in some far-away neighborhood, but gangs and gang violence have grown in recent decades both in number, penetration, and destructiveness. Thrasher, in his classic study, purported to study 1,313 gangs in Chicago alone in 1927. More temperate calculations still put the number of gangs today in the

Case Study 3: Gang Violence (continued)

thousands. A U.S. Justice Department report from 1999 (Egley 2000) estimated the number of gangs at over 30,000, with over 80,000 members. A 1995 survey announced 4,927 gangs in California, 3,276 in Texas, 1,363 in Illinois, and 1,304 in Colorado. Perhaps more troubling than the absolute numbers is the distribution of those numbers: more and more cities, and even towns, report gangs and gang violence than ever. By some estimates, there were only 54 cities in the country with active gangs before 1960, then 94 by 1970, 172 by 1980, and 766 by 1992. By the mid-1990s gangs were present in over eight hundred cities and towns, including more than ninety towns with populations under ten thousand people. At the same time, for various reasons, gang deadliness has surged periodically, perhaps related to guns, drugs, the resumption of "gang wars," and the institutionalization of some gangs into virtual businesses. In the years 1987 to 1994, gang-related homicides doubled in Los Angeles and quintupled in Chicago.

There are many different types of gangs (or at least many different types of activities that gangs engage in at various times in their lives), and there are many different factors that contribute to the existence, perpetuation, and violence of gangs. We cannot in this limited space discuss all the types, but we should give some attention to the factors that underlie them. Drawing together converging sources on gangs and demographic and social-structural factors, the following repeatedly appear as significant contributors:

- *Gender.* Gang members are overwhelmingly male. This was even more true in the past, when probably 90 percent were male; today, an increasing number of females are participating, either as members of "auxiliaries" to male gangs or as members of coed gangs or as members of all-female gangs. Also, female gang members seem to commit fewer and less serious criminal offenses than their male counterparts.
- *Age.* Gang activity, of the sort discussed here, is a youthful phenomenon. Membership concentrates in the under-eighteen age category; by the early twenties, most males have "outgrown" (or died from) gangs. Not surprisingly in light of what we learned about school violence in the last section, very young adolescents participate in larger numbers than older ones: a 1992 study by Lashley showed that more than half of gang members were aged fourteen to seventeen, while less than 30 percent were eighteen and nineteen, and less than 15 percent were over twenty. However, there is an emerging tendency for gangs to retain their older members, rather than have them "age out," which may account for some of the growth in gang membership. Of the newer gangs, 90 percent of members are under eighteen, but of the older more established gangs, only 25 percent of members are so young.

Case Study 3: Gang Violence (continued)

- *Class.* Although not restricted to lower-income individuals and neighborhoods, gangs certainly thrive in these conditions. A number of subfactors play a part here. Poverty, often due to lack of jobs and opportunity in certain neighborhoods, can lead to alternate ways of making a living. At the macroeconomic level, the change to a service economy in recent decades has drained the inner cities of manufacturing jobs and replaced them with low-paying service jobs. An overall decline in real wages has hit some groups and neighborhoods harder than others. Gangs and other types of "deviant careers" can become attractive to people, especially men, with few other options. In fact, having seen their self-respect threatened by poverty, gangs can fill in as surrogate sources of respect and honor.

- *Race.* Although whites still participate in gang activities of various sorts (not the least of which are the motorcycle gangs like the Hell's Angels), it is a fact that gang members are disproportionately nonwhite or minority. Many gangs are actually racially exclusive (that is, exclusively black, Hispanic, or Asian American), although some are racially mixed. Again, the "white flight" out of inner cities and the isolation of minorities in crumbling segregated neighborhoods has only exacerbated the problem. Faced with discrimination, lack of opportunity, and threatened (especially male) egos, gangs hold some allure. Of course, to understand the proliferation, migration, and even "franchising" of gangs, including their spread into affluent middle-class neighborhoods or small towns, some other explanation will be necessary.

- *Family issues.* Although not wanting to harp on the damage of single-parent families, especially families with a female head of household, it appears to be a fact that only a minority of gang members live in households with both parents present, and 40 percent live with a single female parent. This of course does not prove that women are inferior parents; rather, it parallels the observation that single-mother households tend to be more impoverished than two-parent homes, and when she or both parents must work outside the home, children are left with little or no adult supervision. Also, such children tend to see violence, criminality, and other kinds of deviance—including gang membership—in the home, exposing them and desensitizing them to such behavior.

As unpleasant as it is to think about, then, gangs may represent "rational" adaptations to certain conditions that America produces all too often—especially given the well-established forces of competitiveness, binary/oppositional thinking, threatened egoism, and young-male traits that contribute to violence in all human settings.

Case Study 4: Right-Wing/Militia Violence

[W]e the militiamen of the Southeastern United States, do affirm before God that we have entered an alliance against tyranny. . . . We will consider it an act of war to surrender any more of the sovereignty of this nation to the United Nations. Thus, the Southeastern States Alliance will fight the New World Order, and any of its proponents, to the bitter end.
> —*from the "Articles of Alliance" of the Southeastern States Militia (quoted in Snow 1999: 164)*

I'm ready to get my gun and my clips and take off my safety and pull my trigger with my finger. I don't care anymore. This is the beginning of a revolution, a war.
> —*supporter of Randy Weaver (quoted in Stern 1996: 19)*

No, folks, it is not a perverse joy I take in the impending doom of the enemy. It is a righteous joy!
> —*pastor James Bruggemann, Stone Kingdom Ministries, Asheville, North Carolina (quoted in Dees 1996: 21)*

In this section, we will examine a distinctly American form of violence that combines and exhibits all of the traits of organized, politically or even religiously motivated, group-based, anger-powered aggression that we have explored throughout this book and that also displays the uniquely American proclivity for guns, antiauthoritarianism, and often racism, anti-Semitism, and homophobia. We are talking about the right-wing or "hate" groups, ranging from the Ku Klux Klan, formed at the end of the Civil War, to the "militia" or "patriot" groups, formed at the beginning of what members consider to be the next great war.

The precursor to all violent "conservative" groups in the United States is considered to be the Ku Klux Klan (KKK), founded on Christmas Eve, 1865, in Tennessee, eight months after the end of the Civil War. In the beginning ostensibly a social club for former Confederate soldiers, it evolved quickly into the first serious "terrorist" group in American history. Before "Jim Crow" laws were passed creating legalized segregation in the South, the KKK and its "night riders" used fear and intimidation to prevent emancipated blacks from challenging the social order, for example, by voting. The Klan employed lynching, tarring, cross burning, rape, and other forms of hostility to terrorize blacks and any white sympathizers, and as is well known, they adopted mysterious and symbolic trappings like white hoods and titles such as "Exalted Cyclops" and "Grand Imperial Wizard." At its height, the group claimed over half a million members. It was in effect a private vigilante terrorist army.

Its activities having attracted considerable attention and condemnation from American society, President Grant suppressed the KKK in 1871. The

Case Study 4: Right-Wing/Militia Violence (continued)

group faded from public view, as the institution of segregation served to accomplish its main objectives anyway. However, it reemerged in the early 1900s (especially the 1920s) with a bigger agenda—the opposition of immigration, particularly Catholic and Jewish immigration. Membership in that era may have reached 3 or 4 million, and a major KKK rally was held in Washington, D.C. in 1925. The third incarnation of the Klan began in the 1960s, in response to the civil rights movement. Black residences and churches were fire-bombed, and civil rights activists were attacked. When three such activists—James Chaney, Andrew Goodman, and Michael Schwerner—were found dead, the Klan came under withering criticism and investigation and began to recede. Klanwatch, an arm of the Southern Poverty Law Center, estimates that there are some 5,500–6,000 Klan members today in 109 local groups, mostly but not exclusively in southern states (Alabama alone has 13, and even Ohio has 7).

What is plain to see about the Klan is that, despite its violent activities and virulent philosophy, it has a "cause" or, as we said in an earlier chapter, a *grievance*. Klansmen are upset and angry about something, and although we might not share their anger, we need to understand it in order to defuse it. Ungrasped and unchecked, this kind of anger festers and mutates into multifarious forms, as we will see in the discussion that follows.

The 1960s was a historical moment of cultural upheaval and, to many people, cultural corruption. Blacks, gays, women, communists, and even atheists seemed to be "coming out of the closet" and threatening the patrimony—the very values and existence—of white heterosexual Christian male society. The Klan responded as described earlier. Other groups arose too, such as the Minutemen, a private army stoked with the teachings of the John Birch Society and the Christian Identity movement (discussed in Chapter 7). Their goal was to fight communism by organizing guerrilla cells of ten to twenty-five members to conduct an "underground resistance"—apparently on the assumption that the communists had already won, or at least succeeded to such an extent that direct struggle was useless. As their document *The Principles of Guerrilla Warfare* stated, "the communists now have such complete control over this nation's news media and the political processes that it is no longer possible for the American people to change their government's policies by normal democratic means" (quoted in Stern 1996: 48). The main agents of this surreptitious cultural and political takeover were, naturally, the blacks, Jews, and internationalists, especially the United Nations (an institution that really seems to gall many conservative activists); the three were often bundled into one, as when Reverend William Potter Gale said (pardon the offensive language), "You got your nigger Jews, you got your Asiatic Jews, and you got your white Jews. They're all Jews and they're all offspring of the Devil. . . . Turn a nigger inside

Case Study 4: Right-Wing/Militia Violence (continued)

out and you've got a Jew" (quoted in ibid.: 47). Furthermore, the Minutemen's newsletter in November 1963 claimed that American soldiers had already been lent to the United Nations to occupy American cities in order to disarm the populace and begin the reign of "one world."

The Minutemen were highly ready to use force, including bombs, grenades, Molotov cocktails, booby traps, and other terrorist favorites in a campaign of sabotage and assassination. Stern (1996) even maintains that they had developed chemical and biological weapons, and naturally they were well stocked with guns, as all paramilitary groups are. The group began to fall apart after the arrest of their leader in 1970, to be replaced by others. For instance, the Posse Comitatus appeared in 1969, although it was most active in the 1980s. It had an apocalyptic and anti-Semitic program, as evidenced by these words of National Director of Counter-Insurgency James Wickstrom: "Yahweh our father is at work setting the stage for the final act against the Christ-murdering Jews and their father, Satan" (quoted in Stern 1996: 50). In fact, the war was already on and not going well: "Our nation is now completely under the control of the International Invisible government of the World Jewry. Our United States Constitution, our Bill of Rights, and our Christian Law have been trampled beneath the mire and filth of the International Money Barons of high finance who now control the government of these United States." (Quoted in ibid.)

These comments highlight some common features of recent and contemporary right-wing paramilitary groups. First, they hold the Constitution and the Bill of Rights in almost fetishistic esteem; they sometimes refer to those items as the "organic Constitution," in such a way as to discredit all subsequent amendments—especially the thirteenth and fourteenth, that establish racial equality—and all extra-constitutional law, particularly tax law and gun law. Naturally, they are particularly adamant about the Second Amendment, protecting the right to bear arms. Second, they object to the expanded powers of the modern federal government, sometimes calling for a return to state sovereignty or even to lower-level government, such as county government. Third, they tend to be exaggeratedly hostile to "internationalism" or (since the first President Bush) the "new world order." Finally, and related to the previous, they tend to see conspiracies everywhere in which the internationalists, one-worlders, and new-world-order agents have already penetrated and undermined American society and independence, sometimes in the form of "international Jewry," sometimes in the form of international communism, and sometimes (quite seriously) in the form of extraterrestrials.

Many of these groups add to this volatile mix a dose of racism and fundamentalist Christianity. The KKK was a clear example of this phenomenon, although it evolved before the communist and internationalist threat was

Case Study 4: Right-Wing/Militia Violence (continued)

identified. A more modern version is the Aryan Nations, a neo-Nazi group formed in the 1970s that provides the following creed on its website:

> We believe in the preservation of our Race, individually and collectively, as a people as demanded and directed by Yahweh (Aryan Nations members do not call the supreme being God because God is dog spelled backwards).... We believe that Adam, man of Genesis, is the placing of the White Race upon this earth. Not all races descend from Adam. Adam is the father of the White Race only.... We believe that the Cananite [sic] Jew is the natural enemy of our Aryan (White) Race. . . . The Jew is like a destroying virus that attacks our racial body to destroy our Aryan culture and the purity of our Race.... (Quoted in Snow 1999: 2)

The affinity between this attitude and the Christian Identity movement, and also Hitler's Nazi rants, is obvious. Finally, an offshoot of the Aryan Nations (which still functions today) is The Order, a terrorist group that takes its inspiration from the alarmist novel *The Turner Diaries*, written in 1978 by William Pierce (head of the National Alliance, another neo-Nazi group). In it, Pierce describes a white supremacist race war against blacks (who are even portrayed as cannibals) and the federal government (which among other things is trying to deprive citizens of their guns). White terrorists, as part of their antigovernment campaign, detonate a truckload of ammonium nitrate to destroy a federal building on October 13, 1990. What follows is a war between white Americans and the forces of ZOG (the Zionist Occupation Government) in which masses of minorities and other "undesirables" are killed before the final triumph of the Aryan race in 1999. It should be no surprise that Timothy McVeigh knew this book well.

One last group worth mentioning is the White Aryan Resistance, whose name appears redundant until you realize that it is necessary to create the acronym WAR. On the organization's website, aptly named www.resist.com, they post a graphic of a slathering, rabid wolf with the embedded message, "Lone wolves are everywhere. We're in your neighborhoods, financial institutions, police departments, military, and social clubs."

The site also sells paraphernalia such as t-shirts with the slogan "Some people are alive simply because it's illegal to kill them." No doubt.

In WAR's literature they invoke many of the conventional arguments in favor of the white race and against contemporary government and society. They represent themselves as the oppressed minority, only 15 percent of the world's population. Thus, they are "defending" their "family" against what would be "the eventual extinction of Nature's finest handiwork." They distinguish themselves from the mainstream Right, though, in the sense that the Right is nationalistic ("America first"), whereas they are race separatist ("White first"). America, they gripe,

Case Study 4: Right-Wing/Militia Violence (continued)

is not a real nation. This is a bastard nation, with almost no roots, where millions of non-Whites can claim only one generation on the land. That land usually being the asphalted big metropolis. . . . The metropolises being the gaping anal cavities of a sick and dying nation. To those unclean places flock the worst of all races. Only the most degenerate of the White race struggle to stay on top of the maggot pile in such unnatural settings. (www.resist.com)

A natural concomitant of this plan is "states rights," and they rail against government: "All governments are oligarchies, which means rule by the few. Some oligarchies have facades, such as the Congress and the Senate." Hearkening back to the previous section, they argue that national governments

are gangs, no less, no more. Gangs, by their nature, strive to becoming syndicates (or as we know them to be now, transnational corporations). Remember, the goal of international Socialism and International Capitalism, was to destroy smaller states, or to absorb them into the "Super Gang." Soviet Russia was a good example, and the term "the West" as opposed to "the East" was another. (ibid.)

However, they are unique in the sense that they attack conventional religion too, positing that "all loyalty to any entity that doesn't serve our race should perish, especially Christianity." Indeed, they are opposed to Christian government and Christian models of gender relations.

Our views must be futuristic and not tied to myths of Asiatic cult religions. Imagine determining today's actions, by adhering to the crazy ramblings of ancient religious dervishes, who sit in the desert, babbling at the moon. It is simply not productive. . . . Let's not help our enemies by putting up Middle Eastern and Asiatic based roadblocks to male/female unity. (ibid.)

Thus, White Aryan Resistance represents the most unalloyed race-based program out there, eschewing everything that does not advance race first, last, and only.

There are many many violent right-wing paramilitary groups in America today, and contrary to some opinion, they do not predominate in the West (that is, survivalists hiding out in the Rocky Mountains). Rather, they are concentrated in the Southeast and Northeast, from west Texas, Louisiana, Arkansas, and Missouri eastward, almost continuously. They also embody a variety of ideological positions with a variety of underpinnings. Of particular interest is a distinct permutation of the right-wing agenda in recent years, known as the militia movement.

The militia movement shares much with the organizations and efforts we have just seen—its antigovernment policy, its conspiracy-filled mentality, its pro-gun and pro-Constitution stance. Still, it has a history and a trajectory all its own. Before 1992 precursors certainly existed: tax protesters, gun activists, survivalists, states rights proponents, and separatists of various kinds. However, a federal attack on Randy Weaver's Ruby Ridge compound in the

Case Study 4: Right-Wing/Militia Violence (continued)

summer of 1992 galvanized the movement. The shoot-out that took place in this northern Idaho forest left Weaver's wife Vicki and her son Samuel dead. Many previously agitated right-wing types saw this as merely proof of their beliefs—that the government meant to disarm and suppress resisters and would stop at nothing (including killing innocent women and children) to do so.

In response, about two months later (October 23–25, 1992), Pastor Pete Peters of the LaPorte Church of Christ, a Christian Identity sect, called a meeting of organization leaders of all sorts. This gathering, which occurred at Estes Park, Colorado and which has been dubbed the Rocky Mountain Rendezvous, brought together 160 activists from Christian Identity, Aryan Nations, Gun Owners of America, Christian Crusade for Truth, CAUSE (an acronym composed of the first letters of the major white countries or regions—Canada, Australia, United States, South Africa, and Europe), and more. Two important outcomes from the meeting were an agreement to tone down the racist and anti-Semitic rhetoric to attract more mainstream members and a plan for a "leaderless resistance" movement, which coalesced into the militia movement of the 1990s. The attendees drafted a letter to the Weavers, which read in part:

> Impelled by the spirit of our Heavenly Father, We, 160 Christian men assembled for three days of prayer and counsel, at Estes Park, Colorado.
> At our gathering the sad events of Ruby Creek [*sic*] were recounted. . . .
> We have not the power to restore to you the loved ones who were cruelly stolen from you!
> But as Christian men, led by the word of our Heavenly Father, we are determined to never rest while you are in peril and distress!
> We are determined to employ HIS strength and to work continually to insure that Vicki and Samuel's mortal sacrifices were not in vain!
> We call for Divine Judgment upon the wicked and the guilty who shed the blood of Vicki and Samuel! (Quoted in Dees 1996: 65–66)

The faith-based nature of the meeting, the communiqué, and the resultant action cannot be dismissed and in fact speaks to the nature of religious-inspired violence as discussed in Chapter 6 and 7. At any rate, the action to come was presaged in Louis Beam's document, "Leaderless Resistance": "It is clear, therefore, that it is time to rethink traditional strategy and tactics when it comes to opposing a modern police state. America is quickly moving into a long dark night of police state tyranny, where the rights now accepted by most as being inalienable will disappear. Let the coming night be filled with a thousand points of resistance" (quoted in Dees 1996: 207). These "thousand points of resistance" were the symbolic equivalent of numerous independent armed militia groups. Then, as if the Weaver incident had not been sufficient provocation, in early 1993 the Branch Davidian standoff in Waco, Texas occurred,

Case Study 4: Right-Wing/Militia Violence (continued)

which ended on April 19 with the deaths of more than eighty occupants of the compound—in some minds, at the hands of the federal government, while in other minds, at their own hands. In the summer of 1993, the Brady Bill—establishing a waiting period for gun purchases and a criminal background check—was enacted, followed by a ban on assault weapons. The grievances of the radical right were all in place.

The first militia group to emerge was the Militia of Montana, in early 1994. It was led by John Trochmann, who had already declared his "sovereignty" (in other words, renounced his citizenship) from the United States in 1992. It organized itself in a classic cell structure (i.e. "leaderless") for the purpose of armed opposition to the federal government (i.e., resistance). The goals of MOM, as they sometimes referred to themselves, were clearly violent; in fact, they prepared a training manual that called for "guerrilla warfare that included such acts as raiding armories, kidnapping prominent individuals, executing government officials, and bombing both government and private installations . . . [with] 'greatest coldbloodedness'" (Snow 1999: 103). MOM also took much of its inspiration from the infamous *Protocols of the Elders of Zion*, a well known forged manuscript that purported to outline a world Jewish plot.

Other militias developed apace. By spring of 1994 the Michigan Militia had appeared. Founded by Ray Southwell and Reverend Norman Olson, its stated goal was to "stand against tyranny, globalism, moral relativism, humanism, and the New World Order threatening to undermine these United States of America" (quoted in Stern 1996: 97). Reverend Olson's at-war mentality was clearly expressed in his words: "If this country doesn't change, armed conflict is inevitable. . . . Who is the enemy? Anyone who threatens us" (quoted in ibid.). Within a year there were militia groups in at least 36 states, sometimes multiple groups in a state. The Southern Poverty Law Center estimates that between 1994 and 1996 there were at least 441 militia outfits in the country, with every state harboring at least one. There were an additional 386 "patriot" units in existence.

Lest one think that these are harmless war games played by overzealous boys, it is well to remember that deaths have occurred. Far back in 1983, Gordon Kahl of the Posse Comitatus killed three law enforcement officers. In June of 1984 members of The Order shot dead Denver radio personality Alan Berg at his own home. Also in 1984 Richard Wayne Snell, of the "Covenant, Sword, and Arm of the Lord" organization, killed a black Arizona state trooper, and in 1985 David Tate killed a Missouri police officer on the way to the "Covenant, Sword, and Arm of the Lord" compound. Federal officers died at Ruby Ridge and Waco. But 1995 would be much different.

For some reason, the militias went on "red alert" in early 1995. Rumors spread among camps that a major federal assault was about to occur, perhaps

Case Study 4: Right-Wing/Militia Violence (continued)

in March. While the concern was part paranoia, it was also part reaction to the events in Japan surrounding Aum Shinrikyo (see Chapter 7); just as some Japanese blamed that attack on America, some Americans were tying Japan to the expected countermilitia attack. This heightened tension would have come to nothing if not for the militia-inspired bombing in Oklahoma City merely days later. The Alfred P. Murrah Federal Building was destroyed with a truck-load of ammonium nitrate explosive on a weekday morning, killing more than 160 people. This American-on-American terrorist act, for which Timothy McVeigh was found guilty, had two other significant aspects: it was exactly as described in *The Turner Diaries*, and it was carried out on April 19, 1995, the second anniversary of Waco.

The story does not end there. Klanwatch claimed in 1997 that it was moni-toring 523 patriot groups, 221 of which were armed militia groups. Right-wing attacks have taken other forms as well, including attacks on abortion clinics and doctors who perform abortions; the so-called "Nuremburg Files" contain a list of doctors, politicians, and other public figures who support abortion rights; it crosses off the names of those who have been executed. But violent right-wing political groups continue to exist because the conditions that breed them continue to exist. In particular, these conditions include negative eco-nomic circumstances, especially for lower-educated and non-urban white men, who blame much of their lack of success on the surge of minority rights and government efforts to promote minorities; undesired social change, including the secularization and liberalization of society and the loss of what they consider "traditional values"; the expansion of the federal government, especially into areas which were formerly regarded as state prerogatives; and new and supposedly invasive legislation in such domains as gun control and environmental standards. Not all militia and right-wing group members are angry, poor, rural, underemployed white men, of course, but a sufficient num-ber are for this to be a cause of concern and a focus of attention.

Ultimately, to understand the mentality of these people, one must under-stand the mentality of the warrior, for that is how militia members and right-wing activists see themselves. They are at war. Furthermore, they are the good guys in the war; they often liken themselves to the patriots of the Revolution-ary War, even inaugurating a Third Continental Congress and referring to themselves as "we the people." In this way too (and others) they remind us of the *sans-culottes* of the French Revolution—idealistic, violent masses who were willing to do anything, including killing and dying, for the cause of "liberty" and good government. Mix this war mentality and patriotic fervor with religious (even apocalyptic) vision, righteous anger, real economic/social/political grievances, group mobilization (leading to an extreme us-versus-them sensibility), and terrorist tactics and technologies, and you have a potent recipe for violence indeed. From our analysis in Chapter 8, we would call this a classic case of people-versus-polity violence, not so different from any case seen anywhere in the world. In fact, as some observers have noted, Americans not only participate in what could only be considered as political or terrorist violence on each other, but they also export this terrorism: as Ingo Hasselbach, a former neo-Nazi leader in Germany, stated, "Virtually all our propaganda and training manuals came from right-wing extremist groups in [America]." (Quoted in Stern 1996: 239)

"Psycho"
— films —

Case Study 5: American Psycho—Serial Killers and Psychopaths

We will now take a look at the most extreme and "irrational" type of violence in America, that of the serial killer, the motivation of which is essentially psychological (as opposed to social or political). The United States of America did not invent the serial killer (after all, "Jack the Ripper" was killing prostitutes in England over a century ago), but we do, sadly, produce them in extraordinary numbers. Jeffrey Dahmer, John Wayne Gacy, the "Boston Strangler," the "Green River Killer"—these are only a few of the names representing the many infamous and outlandishly violent cases of torture and murder (and, in the case of Dahmer, cannibalism) that have graced the American media in recent decades. America, for some reason, has become especially good at producing what most of us would consider "monsters"—humans who prey on other humans without remorse and with, in many cases, a fair amount of pleasure.

And of course not all multiple murders fit the category of serial killer. Criminal justice scholars distinguish serial killing from mass murder and "spree killing." Mass murder is a form of homicide in which several people are killed at one time or in a short period. Goldstein has identified five types of mass murderer: the "disciple," the family annihilator (usually a male in the household), the pseudocommando (the type who climbs a tower to shoot at passers-by), the disgruntled employee (see our earlier discussion in Case Study 1), and the "set and run" killer, or bomber (1996: 139). Spree killing is something like serial killing although without the "waiting period" between instances; serial killers sometimes go weeks, months, or even years between murders, whereas spree killers kill in rapid succession without "cooling off." Serial killers themselves can be classified according to four basic types: the visionary (hallucinatory or delusional), the mission killer (on a self-defined crusade against some social type, like prostitutes), the hedonist (thrill killer), and the power-and-control killer.

Case Study 5: American Psycho—Serial Killers and Psychopaths (continued)

Robert Ressler (Ressler and Schachtman 1992) was an FBI agent who virtually created the field of criminal profiling and who did invent the term *serial killer*. In dealing with and interviewing many of the most notorious killers of the twentieth century, he arrived at a general portrait of the most pathological of all violent Americans. His first comment is that some of our more precious notions about serial killers—that they come from broken homes, are victims of poverty, of have low IQs—are myths. In fact, of the thirty-six killers he interviewed, most had normal intelligence and about a third (eleven) had IQs over 120. Rather, he attributes their criminally violent personalities predominantly to psychocultural factors, some of which we discussed in the last chapter. In particular, he emphasizes family mental illness, violence, and substance abuse, along with the coercive and negligent parenting that was identified by the Oregon Social Learning Center. Perhaps most important of all the factors, the early life experience of subsequent serial killers provided no models for or training in warm and empathetic interpersonal relationships.

Therefore the first years of the child's life are marked by shallow or cold or nonexistent emotional bonds to the parents. Ressler found that, around ages eight to twelve, this crisis was often exacerbated by the fragmentation of the family; commonly, the father would leave or end up in jail or simply detach himself emotionally from the family, vacantly watching television or reading the newspaper. With no place to turn emotionally, the child (almost always a boy) would develop anger and sexual perversity, particularly violent sexual fantasies. This latter factor became key: "Sexual maladjustment is at the heart of all the fantasies, and the fantasies emotionally drive the murders" (Ressler and Schachtman 1992: 96).

Outwardly, adolescent soon-to-be serial killers do not always present as pathological or even abnormal. Some appear on the surface to be friendly, sociable, and intelligent; however, inside they are increasingly lonely, angry, and emotionally/sexually deviant. As they enter adulthood, they often cannot keep a job or a relationship, especially with the opposite sex: around 50 percent never have consensual sex with another adult. The vast majority are male and white and commit their first murders in their twenties or thirties. A few are female, but their crimes tend to be different—"spree" murders rather than systematic serial killings. Many of the serial killers are clinically mentally ill, in particular schizophrenic, and all have extreme fantasies linking sex and violence.

Ressler talks about these fantasies in detail because they seem so central to the etiology of multiple murder. "The fantasies are characterized by strong visual components, and by themes of dominance, revenge, molestation, and control. . . . Therein lies the key: In these sorts of fantasies, the other person is

Case Study 5: American Psycho—Serial Killers and Psychopaths (continued)

depersonalized, made into an object" (Ressler and Schachtman 1992: 97). However, these ideas and images do not remain only in the head very long; eventually they become goals, rehearsals for action, and eventually real behaviors. "What begins as fantasy ends as part of a homicidal ritual" (99), he writes, concluding that it is "because these murderers deal in fantasy that we characterize serial murders as sexual homicides" (95).

By the time the killer commits his first actual murder, he has done it many times in his imagination. This is one of the most important and powerful aspects of the serial-killer mentality: the real murder is not "new" to the murderer but something he has become intimately familiar and comfortable with. It constitutes only a small step to go from fantasy to reality. However, the reality is never as satisfying as the fantasy; the victim does not act the way the imagined victims always did, or the expected feeling is not the same. Since the satisfaction is imperfect—and temporary—the killer is driven to repeat it, perhaps to perfect it. Also, the execution of the first murder makes it easier to commit the second and third. Since he got away with it, he becomes bolder, and, as we noted in Chapter 2, engaging in your first violence always makes your next violence easier. Each actual murder is practice for the next. The killer even fancies himself smarter than the authorities and plays a game of cat-and-mouse with them until he is caught.

Not all serial killers are alike, however. Ressler divides them into two categories, which he calls "organized" and "disorganized." Disorganized killers, who make up about one-third of the total, usually commit spontaneous, unplanned, "opportunistic" crimes. Often they attempt to attack "high risk" targets and thus expose themselves to much greater danger of detection or even danger to themselves. Since they have usually not intended in advance to murder and have not thought the action through, they use whatever weapon is available to kill their victim. They do not try to cover up the evidence of their crime by taking simple measures like wiping off fingerprints or taking away the murder weapon. Their attacks are often more brutal than those of organized killers, their victims enduring particularly heinous wounds; overall, the crime scene and the crime itself seem "chaotic or symbolic." One distinctive calling card of the disorganized killer is the preservation of a body part of the victim as a souvenir. Not too surprisingly, the living space, like the mental space, of the killer is often messy and disordered.

The majority of serial killers (two-thirds), however, are organized killers. They plan their operation, often meticulously. They usually choose low-risk targets, typically strangers selected on the basis of specific criteria important to the killer. The murder is often the endgame of a deceit or con perpetrated

Case Study 5: American Psycho—Serial Killers and Psychopaths (continued)

against the victim. The killer brings along his own weapon of choice, sometimes as part of a "murder kit," and he tends to clean or destroy the crime scene afterward. He may restrain the victim and often carries off one or more personal items of the victim as "trophies." The organized killer is more thoughtful and premeditated than his disorganized counterpart, often demonstrating good intelligence and good verbal and problem-solving skills. He tends to be harder to catch.

Not surprisingly, then, the personality and childhood of the two types tend to be different. The disorganized killer typically had a father who was often unemployed or unable to keep a job. Household discipline was harsh, and alcohol, drugs, and mental illness are common. The future disorganized killer is a repressed child who internalized his pain or anger or fear and who cannot express emotions well. Unfortunately, he was usually not a very successful, popular, or even attractive child, and he felt inferior and inadequate throughout childhood. He eventually withdrew from human company, becoming a loner or recluse. Acquaintances from school remember him as quiet, even nice, and never causing any trouble. He tends to be less intelligent and less motivated, without a life plan; after finishing school, he wanders from one low-paying job to another or is unemployed altogether. Among his failures is relationships with women. In the final analysis, his disillusionment is turned on himself first and on the world second.

The organized killer starts down a different path. His father was usually present in the household, and employed, but discipline was inconsistent. He himself was often intelligent, attractive, and even popular in school. He may actually have some success with girls, but he is superficial and shallow and does not sustain any meaningful relationships. He has high self-esteem; he feels superior to his colleagues but frustrated that his intelligence, charm, or talent do not get him the success or attention he thinks he deserves. Accordingly, he externalizes his pain or anger or fear, punishing others rather than himself. He tends to "act out" early on and to be disruptive and violent even while still in school. His anger is particularly directed against women, and he will be the more intentional and elusive killer when he finally crosses that line.

Finally, not only serial killing but extreme pathological violence in general have become so prevalent that psychologists have looked for ways to diagnose it dependably. One such attempt is the Psychopathy Checklist (Hare 1991), which consists of twenty items that measure the personality of the presumed psychopath. Each item is scored with a value of 0 ("does not apply"), 1 ("applies somewhat"), or 2 ("definitely applies"). The closer the total score to the maximum of 40, the greater "the degree to which an individual resembles

Case Study 5: American Psycho—Serial Killers and Psychopaths
(continued)

the prototypical psychopath." The following list of test items serves us as a summary of the danger signs of the violent personality:

1. Glibness/superficial charm
2. Grandiose sense of self-worth
3. Need for stimulation/proneness to boredom
4. Pathological lying
5. Conning/manipulative behavior
6. Lack of remorse or guilt
7. Shallow affect
8. Callousness/lack of empathy
9. Parasitic lifestyle
10. Poor behavioral control
11. Promiscuous sexual behavior
12. Early behavior problems
13. Lack of realistic, long-term goals
14. Impulsivity
15. Irresponsibility
16. Failure to accept responsibility for one's own actions
17. Many short-term marital relationships
18. Juvenile delinquency
19. Revocation of conditional release from prison
20. Criminal versatility

If this test has real validity—and it has been used extensively on adult males and increasingly on females and adolescents—then we have here a long list of traits that indicate and enable highly violent behavior. Societies that contain a large number of violent individuals and that have structures and practices that produce and encourage them—in particular, by valuing the traits listed above—have good reason to beware. They may pretend to promote peace and nonviolence but are doing the exact opposite.

RETROSPECT AND PROSPECT

In examining the disturbing panorama of human violence, we have noted the creative range of American violence. It is in the light of American cultural values that this chapter—indeed this text—poses the following question: "How do you hurt someone and not feel guilty about it?' Or, even more to the point: How do you hurt someone and actually feel good about it—or perhaps feel nothing at all? Arnold Goldstein asks this same question in his book *Violence in America*, a short chapter of which bears the question as its title. Reference to the study enables us a brief review of the processes that breed violence. Of the nine Goldstein lists, how many can we identify at work in modern American society and in how many guises?

- Minimization of one's own aggression by comparing it with worse behavior in others
- Justification of one's own aggression in terms of higher moral principles
- Displacement of responsibility
- Diffusion of responsibility
- Dehumanization of victims
- De-individuation
- Attribution of blame to victims
- Graduated desensitization
- Hygienic positioning (i.e., keeping oneself at a distance, physically and psychologically, from the violence and its victims, for example, by using disparaging terms for the victims or euphemisms for the violence)

Truly, as long as our world is full of these habits of hurtfully effective people, and as long as we ourselves practice and teach and model them, our world will be full of violence and we ourselves will excel at it.

Glossary

Bilateral   a kinship system in which individuals do not consider themselves as belonging to only one descent group (father's or mother's) but rather equally to both "sides" of the family.

Bridewealth *or* **brideprice**   the institution in which wealth is given by a potential groom to the family (usually the father or brother) of a potential bride in order to make a marriage. Sometimes viewed as a means of compensating the bride's family for the loss of her labor and childbearing, it is also sometimes construed as "buying" a wife.

Dowry   the institution in which wealth is given by the family of a potential bride to the potential husband (or occasionally his family) in order to make a marriage.

Endogamy   literally "inside marriage," the marriage principle whereby a person should marry someone "in the same" category as oneself, in regard to such categories as age group, race, religion, language, nationality, or whatever category is relevant to the particular individuals or society.

Exogamy   literally "out marriage," the marriage principle whereby a person should marry someone "not in the same" category as oneself, in regard to such categories as family, gender, or whatever category is relevant to the particular individuals or society.

Hypergamy   the practice of attempting to "marry up" by achieving a marriage to a member of a higher class or higher-status family and thereby acquiring some of the status of the in-law family.

Levirate   a kinship practice in which a family provides another male if the first male offered in marriage is unsatisfactory (for instance, dies young, is unacceptable to the spouse, or cannot produce children).

Matrilineal descent   a kinship practice in which group membership is traced through a line of related females. Children belong to the descent group of their mother. Sons belong to the group too, but their children do not (they belong to his wife's/their mother's group). The groups so created are referred to as *matrilineages*, and the rule for creating such groups is called matrilineality. This system tends to promote female prestige.

Matrilocal residence   the residence model whereby a married couple lives in or near the household of the wife. The resulting household contains related women (mothers and daughters, sisters, etc.) and the husbands they bring in.

Neolocal   the residence pattern whereby a married couple starts a new household apart from the extended family of either partner. This pattern is the norm in about 5 percent of the world's societies.

Patrilineal descent   a kinship practice in which group membership is traced through a line of related males. Children belong to the descent group of their father. Daughters belong to the group too, but their children do not (they belong to her husband's/their father's group). The groups so created are referred to as *patrilineages*, and the rule for creating such groups is called *patrilineality*. This system tends to promote male dominance and prestige.

Patrilocal residence   the residence model whereby a married couple lives in or near the household of the husband. The resulting household contains related men (fathers and sons, brothers, etc.) and the wives they bring in.

Polyandry   the marriage practice whereby a woman can or should have two or more husbands. This practice is the norm in less than 1 percent of the world's societies.

Polygamy   the general marriage practice whereby one person can or should marry two or more spouses and which differentiates into *polygyny* and *polyandry*.

Polygyny   the marriage practice whereby a man can or should have two or more wives. This practice is the norm in 70 percent to 80 percent of traditional societies.

Sororate   a kinship practice in which a family provides another female if the first female offered in marriage is unsatisfactory (for instance, dies young, is unacceptable to the spouse, or cannot bear children).

Bibliography

Abbink, Jon. 2001. "Violence and Culture: Anthropological and Evolutionary-Psychological Reflections on Inter-Group Conflict in Southern Ethiopia." In Bettina Schmidt and Ingo Schroder, eds., *Anthropology of Violence and Conflict*. London: Routledge, 123–42.

Allcorn, Seth. 1994. *Anger in the Workplace: Understanding the Causes of Aggression and Violence*. Westport, CT: Quorum Books.

Anderson, Benedict. 1983. *Imagined Communities: Reflections on the Origin and Spread of Nationalism*. London: Verso.

Archer, D., and P. McDaniel. 1989. "Violence and Gender: Differences and Similarities Across Societies." Paper presented to the American Sociological Association Annual Meeting, San Francisco.

Arendt, Hannah. 1969. *On Violence*. New York: Harcourt, Brace, and World.

Arway, A. Giles. 2002. "Causal Factors of Violence in the Workplace: A Human Resource Professional's Perspective." In Martin Gill, Bonnie Fisher, and Vaughan Bowie, eds., *Violence at Work: Causes, Patterns, and Prevention*. Devon, UK: Willan, 41–58.

Bacon, M. K., I. L. Child, and H. Barry III. 1963. "A Cross-Cultural Study of Correlates of Crime." *Journal of Abnormal and Social Psychology* 66: 291–300.

Barber, Benjamin. 1996. *Jihad vs. McWorld: How Globalism and Tribalism Are Reshaping the World*. New York: Ballantine Books.

Bateson, Gregory. 1979. *Mind and Nature: A Necessary Unity*. New York: Dutton.

Baumeister, Roy. 2001. *Evil: Inside Human Violence and Cruelty*. New York: Barnes and Noble.

Beal, Becky. 2001. "Alternative Masculinity and Its Effects on Gender Relations in the Subculture of Skateboarding." In Michael Petracca and Madeleine Sorapure, eds., *Common Culture: Reading and Writing about Popular Culture*, 3d ed. Upper Saddle River, NJ: Prentice-Hall, 460–78.

Becker, Howard. 1963. *Outsiders: Studies in the Sociology of Deviance*. New York: Free Press.

Begin, Menachem. 1977. *The Revolt*, revised ed. Los Angeles: Nash.

Benokraitis, Nijole. 1993. *Marriages and Families*. Englewood Cliffs, NJ: Prentice-Hall.

Billington, James H. 1980. *Fire in the Minds of Men: Origins of the Revolutionary Faith*. New York: Perseus Books.

Bonta, Bruce D. 1997. "Cooperation and Competition in Peaceful Societies." *Psychological Bulletin* 121: 299–320.

Bourdieu, Pierre. 1977. *Outline of a Theory of Practice*. Cambridge: Cambridge University Press.

Bowie, Vaughan. 2002. "Defining Violence at Work: A New Typology." In Martin Gill, Bonnie Fisher, and Vaughan Bowie, eds., *Violence at Work: Causes, Patterns, and Prevention*. Devon, UK: Willan, 1–20.

Bowlby, John. 1969. *Attachment and Loss*. Vol. 1, *Attachment*. New York: Basic Books.

Bowman, Glenn. 2001. "The Violence of Identity." In Bettina Schmidt and Ingo Schroder, eds., *Anthropology of Violence and Conflict*. London: Routledge, 25–49.

Briggs, Jean. 1970. *Never in Anger: Portrait of an Eskimo Family*. Cambridge: Harvard University Press.

Brown, Judith. 1999. "Introduction: Definitions, Assumptions, Themes, and Issues." In Dorothy Ayers Counts, Judith K. Brown, and Jacquelyn C. Campbell, eds., *To Have and to Hit: Cultural Perspectives on Wife Beating*. Urbana: University of Illinois Press.

Brown, Judith. 1997. "Agitators and Peace-Makers: Cross-Cultural Perspectives on Older Women and the Abuse of Young Wives." In Aysan Sev'er, ed., *A Cross-Cultural Exploration of Wife Abuse: Problems and Prospects*. Lewiston, NY: Edwin Mellen Press, 79–99.

Brownstein, Henry H. 2000. *The Social Reality of Violence and Violent Crime*. Needham Heights, MA: Allyn and Bacon.

Burgess, M. Elaine. 1978. "The Resurgence of Ethnicity: Myth or Reality?" *Ethnic and Racial Studies* 1: 265–85.

Buset, Mila, and Debra Pepler. 2002. "Canada." In Randal W. Summers and Allan M. Hoffman, eds., *Domestic Violence: A Global View*. Westport, CT: Greenwood Press, 13–24.

Chagnon, Napoleon. 1968. *Yanomamo: The Fierce People*. New York: Holt, Rinehart, and Winston.

Cigar, Norman. 1995. *Genocide in Bosnia: The Policy of "Ethnic Cleansing."* College Station: Texas A&M University Press.

Cohen, Lenard. 1993. *Broken Bonds: The Disintegration of Yugoslavia*. Boulder, CO: Westview Press.

Conrad, John, and Simon Dinitz, eds. *In Fear of Each Other: Studies of Dangerousness in America*. Lexington, MA: Lexington Books.

Copet-Rougier, Elisabeth. 1986. "'Le Mal Court': Visible and Invisible Violence in an Acephalous Society—Mkako of Cameroon." In David Riches, ed., *The Anthropology of Violence*. Oxford: Basil Blackwell, 50–69.

Coser, Lewis A. 1956. *The Functions of Social Conflict*. New York: Free Press of Glencoe.

Covey, Herbert, Scott Menard, and Robert J. Franzese. 1997. *Juvenile Gangs*. Springfield, IL: Thomas.

Counts, Dorothy Ayers. 1999. "'All Men Do It': Wife Beating in Kaliai, Papua New Guinea." In Dorothy Ayers Counts, Judith K. Brown, and Jacquelyn C. Campbell, eds., *To Have and to Hit: Cultural Perspectives on Wife Beating*. Urbana: University of Illinois Press, 73–86.

Courtwright, David T. 1998. "Violence in America." In Frank McGuckin, ed., *Violence in American Society*. New York: Wilson, 3–15.

Cowley, Geoffrey. 2002. "A Deadly Passage to India." *Newsweek*, 25 November 2002, 38–43.

Crenshaw, Martha. 2003. "The Logic of Terrorism: Terrorist Behavior as a Product of Strategic Choice." In Russell D. Howard and Reid L. Sawyer, eds., *Terrorism and Counterterrorism: Understanding the New Security Environment*. Guilford, CT: McGraw-Hill/Dushkin, 55–67.

Crews, Gordon A. and Reid H. Montgomery, Jr. 2001. *Chasing Shadows: Confronting Juvenile Violence in America*. Upper Saddle River, NJ: Prentice-Hall.

Daly, Martin and Margo Wilson. 1984. "A Sociobiological Analysis of Human Infanticide." In Glenn Hausfater and Sarah Blaffer, eds., *Infanticide: Comparative and Evolution-ary Perspectives*. New York: Aldine, 487–502.

De Rougemont, Denis. 1956 [1940]. *Love in the Western World*. Trans. Montgomery Belgion. New York: Harper and Row.

Dees, Morris, with James Corcoran. 1996. *Gathering Storm: America's Militia Threat*. New York: Harper Collins.

Dentan, Robert Knox. 1968. *The Semai: A Non-violent People of Malaya*. New York: Holt, Rinehart, and Winston.

Deutscher, Isaac. 1986. *The Prophet Unarmed: Trotsky, 1921–1929*. New York: Random House.

DeVos, George. 1975. "Ethnic Pluralism: Conflict and Accommodation." In George DeVos and Lola Romanucci-Ross, eds., *Ethnic Identity: Cultural Continuities and Change*. Palo Alto, CA: Mayfield, 5–41.

Dickeman, M. 1975. "Demographic Consequences of Infanticide in Man." *Annual Review of Ecology and Systematics* 6: 107–37.

Divale, W. T., and M. Harris. 1976. "Population, Warfare and the Male Supremacist Com-plex." *American Anthropologist* 78: 521–38.

Dmytryshyn, Basil. 1971. *USSR: A Concise History*, 2d ed. New York: Scribner's.

Dragnich, Alex. 1992. *Serbs and Croats: The Struggle in Yugoslavia*. New York: Harcourt Brace Jovanovich.

Draper, Patricia. 1999. "Room to Maneuver: !Kung Women Cope with Men." In Dorothy Ayers Counts, Judith K. Brown, and Jacquelyn C. Campbell, eds., *To Have and to Hit: Cultural Perspectives on Wife Beating*. Urbana: University of Illinois Press, 53–72.

Dunn, Richard S. 1970. *The Age of Religious Wars, 1559–1689*. New York: Norton.

Dunning, Eric, Patrick Murphy, and John Williams. 1986. "'Casuals,' 'Terrace Crews,' and 'Fighting Firms': Towards a Sociological Explanation of Football Hooligan Behavior." In David Riches, ed., *The Anthropology of Violence*. Oxford: Basil Blackwell, 164–83.

Dutton, Donald. G. 1995. *The Batterer: A Psychological Profile*. New York: Basic Books.

Delbert S. Elliott, Beatrix A. Hamburg, and Kirk R. Williams. 1998. "Violence in American Schools: An Overview." In Delbert S. Elliott, Beatrix A. Hamburg, and Kirk R. Williams, eds., *Violence in American Schools: A New Perspective*. Cambridge: Cambridge Univer-sity Press, 3–28.

Egley, A. 2000. *Highlights of the 1999 National Youth Gang Survey*. Washington, DC: U.S. Department of Justice, Office of Juvenile Justice and Delinquency Prevention.

Elliott, Paul. 1995. *Warrior Cults: A History of Magical, Mystical, and Murderous Organi-zations*. London: Blandford.

Ember, Carol R., and Melvin Ember. 1993. "Issues in Cross-Cultural Studies of Interpersonal Violence." *Violence and Victims* 8: 217–33.

Evans-Pritchard, E. E. 1951. *Social Anthropology.* Glencoe, IL: Free Press.

Fackler, Martin. 2002. "Chinese Women See Suicide Only Way Out." *Denver Post*, 14 April 2002.

Fagan, Jeffrey, and Deanna L. Wilkinson. 1998. "Social Contexts and Functions of Adolescent Violence." In Delbert S. Elliott, Beatrix A. Hamburg, and Kirk R. Williams, eds., *Violence in American Schools: A New Perspective.* Cambridge: Cambridge University Press, 55–93.

Fanon, Frantz. 1963. *The Wretched of the Earth.* Trans. Constance Farrington. New York: Grove Press.

Fernandez, Marilyn. 1997. "Domestic Violence by Extended Family Members in India: Interplays of Gender and Generation." *Journal of Interpersonal Violence* 12(3): 433–55.

Fortes, Meyer, and E. E. Evans-Pritchard, eds. 1940. *African Political Systems.* London: Oxford University Press.

Freke, Timothy, and Peter Gandy. 1999. *The Jesus Mysteries: Was the "Original Jesus" a Pagan God?* New York: Harmony Books.

Gartner, Rosemary. 1993. "Methodological Issues in Cross-Cultural Large-Survey Research on Violence." *Violence and Victims* 8: 199–215.

Geertz, Clifford. 1973. *The Interpretation of Cultures.* New York: Basic Books.

Gelles, Richard J. 2000. "Violence between Intimates: Historical Legacy—Contemporary Approval." In Helene Henderson, ed., *Domestic Violence and Child Abuse Sourcebook*, 1st ed. Detroit: Omnigraphics, 3–26.

Gelles, Richard J. 1997. *Intimate Violence in Families*, 3d ed. Thousand Oaks, CA: Sage.

Gelles, Richard J., and Claire Patrick Cornell, eds. 1983. *International Perspectives on Family Violence.* Lexington, MA: Lexington Books.

Gelles, Richard J. and Murray A. Straus. 1988. *Intimate Violence.* New York: Simon and Schuster.

Gershoy, Leo. 1957. *The Era of the French Revolution 1789–1799.* Princeton, NJ: Van Nostrand.

Girard, Rene. 1977. *Violence and the Sacred.* Trans. Patrick Gregory. Baltimore: Johns Hopkins University Press.

Glenny, Misha. 1994. *The Fall of Yugoslavia: The Third Balkan War.* New York: Penguin Books.

Gluckman, Max. 1956. *Custom and Conflict in Africa.* Oxford: Basil Blackwell.

Goldberg, Jeffrey. 2000. "Inside Jihad University: The Education of a Holy Warrior." *New York Times Sunday Magazine*, 25 June 2000.

Goldstein, Arnold P. 1996. *Violence in America: Lessons on Understanding the Aggression in Our Lives.* Palo Alto: Davies-Black.

Gondolf, Edward W. 1989. *Man Against Woman: What Every Woman Should Know about Violent Men.* Blue Ridge Summit PA: TAB Books.

Hagedorn, John M. 1998. "Gang Violence in the Postindustrial Era." In Michael Tonry and Mark H. Moore, eds., *Youth Violence.* Chicago: University of Chicago Press, 365–420.

Gilligan

Hamburg, Margaret A. 1998. "Youth Violence is a Public Health Concern." In Delbert S. Elliott, Beatrix A. Hamburg, and Kirk R. Williams, eds., *Violence in American Schools: A New Perspective*. Cambridge: Cambridge University Press, 31–54.

Hanson, Victor Davis. 1999. *The Wars of the Ancient Greeks*. London: Cassell.

Hare, Robert. 1991. "The Psychopathy Checklist—Revised (PCL-R)." Http://www.criminology.unimelb.edu.au/victims/resources/assessment/personality/psychopathy_checklist.html., accessed 1 June 2003.

Harris, Marvin. 1974. *Cows, Pigs, Wars, and Witches: The Riddles of Culture*. New York: Random House.

Hausfater, Glenn, and Sarah Blaffer, eds. 1984. *Infanticide: Comparative and Evolutionary Perspectives*. New York: Aldine.

Haynal, Andre, Miklos Molnar, and Gerard de Puymege. 1983. *Fanaticism: A Historical and Psychoanalytic Study*. New York: Schocken Books.

Heald, Suzette. 1986. "The Ritual Use of Violence: Circumcision among the Gisu of Uganda." In David Riches, ed., *The Anthropology of Violence*. Oxford: Basil Blackwell, 70–85.

Hegland, Mary Elaine. 1999. "Wife Abuse and the Political System: A Middle Eastern Case Study." In Dorothy Ayers Counts, Judith K. Brown, and Jacquelyn C. Campbell, eds., *To Have and to Hit: Cultural Perspectives on Wife Beating*. Urbana: University of Illinois Press, 234–51.

Heller, Mikhail, and Alexander Nekrich. 1986. *Utopia in Power: The History of the Soviet Union from 1917 to the Present*. New York: Summit Books.

Henderson, Helene, ed. 2002. *Domestic Violence and Child Abuse Sourcebook*, 1st ed. Detroit: Omnigraphics.

Hoebel, E. Adamson. 1960. *The Cheyennes Indians of the Great Plains*. New York: Holt, Rinehart, and Winston.

Hoffer, Eric. 1966 [1951]. *The True Believer: Thoughts on the Nature of Mass Movements*. New York: Harper Perennial.

Hoffman, Bruce. 2003a. "Defining Terrorism." In Russell D. Howard and Reid L. Sawyer, eds., *Terrorism and Counterterrorism: Understanding the New Security Environment*. Guilford, CT: McGraw-Hill/Dushkin, 3–24.

Hoffman, Bruce. 2003b. "The Modern Terrorist Mindset: Tactics, Targets, and Technologies." In Russell D. Howard and Reid L. Sawyer, eds., *Terrorism and Counterterrorism: Understanding the New Security Environment*. Guilford, CT: McGraw-Hill/Dushkin, 75–96.

Johnson, Chalmers. 1966. *Revolutionary Change*. Boston: Little, Brown.

Jolin, Annette, and Steffen Webke. 2002. "Germany." In Randal W. Summers and Allan M. Hoffman, eds., *Domestic Violence: A Global View*. Westport, CT: Greenwood Press, 39–53.

Jones, Ann. 1980. *Women Who Kill*. New York: Fawcett Group.

Juergensmeyer, Mark. 2000. *Terrorism in the Mind of God: The Global Rise of Religious Violence*. Berkeley: University of California Press.

Kempe, C. Henry, Frederic N. Silverman, Brandt F. Steele, William Droegemuller, and Henry K. Silver. 1962. "The Battered-Child Syndrome." *Journal of the American Medical Association* 181: 17–24.

Kenny, James F. 2002. "The Process of Employee Violence: The Building of a Workplace Explosion." In Martin Gill, Bonnie Fisher, and Vaughan Bowie, eds., *Violence at Work: Causes, Patterns, and Prevention*. Devon, UK: Willan, 76–89.

Kerenzsi, Klara. 2002. "Child Abuse in Hungary." In Michael Freeman, ed., *Overcoming Child Abuse: A Window on a World Problem*. Aldershot, UK: Dartmouth, 189–204.

Kevles, Bettyann, and Daniel Kevles. 1998. "Scapegoat Biology." In Frank McGuckin, ed., *Violence in American Society*. New York: Wilson, 23–28.

Kishwar, Madhu. 1986. "Dowry: To Ensure Her Happiness or to Disinherit Her?" *Manushi* 34: 2–13.

Kreisberg, Louis. 1982. *Social Conflicts*, 2d ed. Englewood Cliffs, NJ: Prentice-Hall.

Lateef, Shireen. 1999. "Wife Abuse among the Indo-Fijians." In Dorothy Ayers Counts, Judith K. Brown, and Jacquelyn C. Campbell, eds., *To Have and to Hit: Cultural Perspectives on Wife Beating*. Urbana: University of Illinois Press, 216–33.

Le Bon, Gustave. 1896. *The Crowd: A Study of the Popular Mind*. New York: Macmillan.

Leach, Edmund. 1954. *Political Systems of Highland Burma*. Boston: Beacon Press.

LeBlanc, Steven A., with Katherine E. Register. 2003. *Constant Battles: The Myth of the Peaceful, Noble Savage*. New York: St. Martin's Press.

Lemarchand, Rene. 1970. *Rwanda and Burundi*. New York: Praeger.

Lemert, Edwin. 1951. *Social Pathology*. New York: McGraw-Hill.

Levinson, David. 1983. "Physical Punishment of Children and Wifebeating in Cross-Cultural Perspective." In Richard J. Gelles and Claire Patrick Cornell, eds., *International Perspectives on Family Violence*. Lexington, MA: Lexington Books, 73–77.

Levy, Leonard W. 1993. *Blasphemy: Verbal Offense against the Sacred, from Moses to Salman Rushdie*. New York: Knopf.

Lindemann, Albert S. 1983. *A History of European Socialism*. New Haven: Yale University Press.

Liulivicius, Vejas Gabriel. 2003. "Utopia and Terror in the Twentieth Century." Chantilly, VA: The Teaching Company.

Loeber, Rolf and Magda Stouthamer-Loeber. 1998. "Juvenile Aggression at Home and at School." In Delbert S. Elliott, Beatrix A. Hamburg, and Kirk R. Williams, eds., *Violence in American Schools: A New Perspective*. Cambridge: Cambridge University Press, 94–126.

Lorenz, Konrad. 1966. *On Aggression*. Trans. Marjorie Kerr Wilson. New York: Harcourt, Brace, and World.

Lowenthal, L. and N. Guterman. 1949. *Prophets of Deceit: A Technique of the American Agitator*. New York: Harper.

Malcolm, Noel. 1994. *Bosnia: A Short History*. New York: New York University Press.

Malley-Morrison, Kathleen, and Denise A. Hines. 2004. *Family Violence in a Cultural Perspective*. Thousand Oaks, CA: Sage.

Maquet, Jacques. 1961. *The Premise of Inequality in Rwanda: A Study of Political Relations in a Central African Kingdom*. London: Oxford University Press.

Markham, Edwin, Benjamin B. Lindsey, and George Creel. 1914. *Children in Bondage*. New York: Hearst's International Library.

Marton, Kati. 2004. "The Worldwide Gender Gap." *Newsweek*, 10 May 2004, 94.

Marvin, Garry. 1986. "Honor, Integrity, and the Problem of Violence in the Spanish Bull-fight." In David Riches, ed., *The Anthropology of Violence*. Oxford: Basil Blackwell, 118–35.

Matsushima, Yukiko. 2000. "Child Abuse in Japan: The Current Situation and Proposed Legal Changes." In Michael Freeman, ed., *Overcoming Child Abuse: A Window on a World Problem*. Aldershot, UK: Dartmouth, 231–56.

Mayhew, Claire. 2002. "Occupational Violence in Industrialized Countries: Types, Incidence Patterns, and 'At Risk' Groups of Workers." In Martin Gill, Bonnie Fisher, and Vaughan Bowie, eds., *Violence at Work: Causes, Patterns, and Prevention*. Devon, UK: Willan, 21–40.

McDowell, Nancy. 1999. "Household Violence in a Yuat River Village." In Dorothy Ayers Counts, Judith K. Brown, and Jacquelyn C. Campbell, eds., *To Have and to Hit: Cultural Perspectives on Wife Beating*. Urbana: University of Illinois Press, 87–99.

Meadow, Roy. 1977. "Munchhausen Syndrome by Proxy: The Hinterland of Child Abuse." *Lancet* 2: 343–45.

Merton, Robert K. 1949. *Social Theory and Social Structure*. New York: Free Press.

Messner, Michael A. 2003. "Power at Play: Sport and Gender Relations." In Sonia Maasik and Jack Solomon, eds., *Signs of Life in the USA: Readings on Popular Culture for Writers*, 4th ed. Boston: Bedford/St. Martin's, 668–79.

Michell, Humfrey. 1964. *Sparta*. London: Cambridge University Press.

Milgram, Stanley. 1963. "Behavioral Study of Obedience." *Journal of Abnormal and Social Psychology* 67: 371–78.

Miller, Barbara Diane. 1999. "Wife Beating in India: Variations on a Theme." In Dorothy Ayers Counts, Judith K. Brown, and Jacquelyn C. Campbell, eds., *To Have and to Hit: Cultural Perspectives on Wife Beating*. Urbana: University of Illinois Press, 203–15.

Mishima, Yukio. 1977. *The Way of the Samurai: Yukio Mishima on* Hagakure *in Modern Life*. Trans. Kathryn Sparling. New York: Basic Books.

Mitchell, William E. 1999. "Why Wape Men Don't Beat Their Wives: Constraints Toward Domestic Tranquility in a New Guinea Society." In Dorothy Ayers Counts, Judith K. Brown, and Jacquelyn C. Campbell, eds., *To Have and to Hit: Cultural Perspectives on Wife Beating*. Urbana: University of Illinois Press, 100–109.

Moeran, Brian. 1986. "The Beauty of Violence: *Jidaigeki, Yakuza*, and 'Eroduction' Films in Japanese Cinema." In David Riches, ed., *The Anthropology of Violence*. Oxford: Basil Blackwell, 103–17.

Morris, Desmond. 1977. *Manwatching: A Field Guide to Human Behavior*. New York: Abrams.

Mushanga, Tibamanya mwene. 1983. "Wife Victimization in East and Central Africa." In Richard J. Gelles and Claire Patrick Cornell, eds., 1983. *International Perspectives on Family Violence*. Lexington, MA: Lexington Books, 139–45.

Myers, John E. B., Susan E. Diedrich, Devon Lee, Kelly Fincher, and Rachel Stern. 2002. "Prosecution of Child Sexual Abuse in the U.S." In John Conte, ed., *Critical Issues in Child Sexual Abuse: Historical, Legal, and Psychological Perspectives*. Thousand Oaks, CA: Sage.

Newman, G. 1976. *Comparative Deviance: Perception and Law in Six Cultures*. New York: Elsevier.

National Center for Education Statistics. 1998. *Violence and Discipline Problems in U.S. Public Schools: 1996–97*. Washington, DC: U.S. Department of Education, Office of Educational Research and Improvement.

Overing, Joanne. 1986. "Images of Cannibalism, Death, and Domination in a 'Non-Violent' Society." In David Riches, ed., *The Anthropology of Violence*. Oxford: Basil Blackwell, 86–102.

Overstreet, Harry, and Bonaro Overstreet. 1964. *The Strange Tactics of Extremism*. New York: Norton.

Pagelow, Mildred Daley, and Pam Johnson. 1988. "Abuse in the American Family: The Role of Religion." In Anne L. Horton and Judith A. Williamson, eds., *Abuse and Religion: When Praying Isn't Enough*. Lexington, MA: Lexington Books/D. C. Heath, 1–12.

Pagon, Milan, Gorazd Mesko, and Branko Lobnikar. 2002. "Slovenia." In Randal W. Summers and Allan M. Hoffman, eds., *Domestic Violence: A Global View*. Westport, CT: Greenwood Press, 111–24.

Pickering, Sharon. 2002. "Australia." In Randal W. Summers and Allan M. Hoffman, eds., *Domestic Violence: A Global View*. Westport, CT: Greenwood Press, 1–12.

Pillar, Paul. 2003. "The Dimensions of Terrorism and Counterterrorism." In Russell D. Howard and Reid L. Sawyer, eds., *Terrorism and Counterterrorism: Understanding the New Security Environment*. Guilford, CT: McGraw-Hill/Dushkin, 24–46.

Pipes, Richard. 1990. *The Russian Revolution*. New York: Knopf.

Pleck, Elizabeth. 1987. *Domestic Tyranny: The Making of Social Policy Against Family Violence from Colonial Times to the Present*. New York: Oxford University Press.

Propper, Alice. 1997. "Measuring Wife Assault by Surveys: Some Conceptual and Methodological Problems." In Aysan Sev'er, ed., *A Cross-Cultural Exploration of Wife Abuse: Problems and Prospects*. Lewiston, NY: Edwin Mellen Press, 51–77.

Prothrow-Stith, Deborah. 1991. *Deadly Consequences*. New York: Free Press.

Prunier, Gerard. 1995. *The Rwandan Crisis: History of a Genocide*. New York: Columbia University Press.

Ranstrop, Magnus. 2003. "Terrorism in the Name of Religion." In Howard, Russell D. and Reid L. Sawyer, eds., *Terrorism and Counterterrorism: Understanding the New Security Environment*. Guilford, CT: McGraw-Hill/Dushkin, 121–35.

Rawstone, Shirley. 2002. "England and Wales." In Randal W. Summers and Allan M. Hoffman, eds., *Domestic Violence: A Global View*. Westport, CT: Greenwood Press, 25–38.

Ressler, Robert, and Tom Schachtman. 1992. *Whoever Fights Monsters*. New York: St. Martin's Press.

Reitman, Valerie. 2002. "Self-immolation on Rise in Afghanistan." *Denver Post*, 18 November 2002.

Riches, David, ed. 1986. *The Anthropology of Violence*. Oxford: Basil Blackwell.

Ritual Abuse Task Force. 1989. *Ritual Abuse: Definitions, Glossary, the Use of Mind Control*. Los Angeles: Los Angeles County Commission for Women.

Rosaldo, Michelle. 1980. *Knowledge and Passion: Ilongot Notions of Self and Social Life*. Cambridge: Cambridge University Press.

Ross, Marc Howard. 1993. *The Culture of Conflict*. New Haven: Yale University Press.

Rubel, Robert. 1977. *The Unruly School*. Lexington, MA: Heath /Lexington.

Scheper-Hughes, Nancy. 1992. *Death without Weeping: The Violence of Everyday Life in Brazil*. Berkeley: University of California Press.

Schwandner-Sievers, Stephanie. 2001. "The Enactment of 'Tradition': Albanian Constructions of Identity, Violence, and Power in Times of Crisis." In Bettina Schmidt and Ingo Schroder, eds., *Anthropology of Violence and Conflict*. London: Routledge, 97–120.

Seligman, Charles. 1930. *The Races of Africa*. London: Thornton Butterworth.

Sen, Mala. 2001. *Death by Fire: Sati, Dowry Death, and Female Infanticide in Modern India*. New Brunswick, NJ: Rutgers University Press.

Seward, Jack. 1968. *Hara-kiri: Japanese Ritual Suicide*. Rutland, VT: Tuttle.

Schmidt, Bettina, and Ingo Schroder, eds. 2001. *Anthropology of Violence and Conflict*. London: Routledge.

Shakur, Sanyika (Kody Scott). 1993. *Monster: The Autobiography of an L.A. Gang Member*. New York: Penguin Books.

Shelden, Randall G., Sharon K. Tracy, and William B. Brown. 2001. *Youth Gangs in American Society*. Belmont, CA: Wadsworth.

Simmel, Georg. [1908] 1955. *Conflict and The Web of Group-Affiliations*. Trans. Kurt H. Wolff and Reinhard Bendix. New York: Free Press.

Smith, Anthony. 1991. *National Identity*. Reno: University of Nevada Press.

Smith, Lacey Baldwin. 1997. *Fools, Martyrs, Traitors: The Story of Martyrdom in the Western World*. New York: Knopf.

Snow, Robert L. 1999. *The Militia Threat: Terrorists Among Us*. New York: Plenum.

Sorel, Georges. [1908] 1961. *Reflections on Violence*. New York: Collier Books.

Stern, Kenneth. 1996. *A Force upon the Plain: The American Militia Movement and the Politics of Hate*. New York: Simon and Schuster.

Stone, Linda, and Caroline James. 1995. "Dowry, Bride-Burning, and Female Power in India." *Women's Studies International Forum* 18(2): 125–34.

Suarez-Orozco, Marcelo. 1992. "A Grammar of Terror: Psychocultural Responses to State Terrorism in Dirty War and Post-Dirty War Argentina." In Carolyn Nordstrom and JoAnn Martin, eds., *The Paths to Domination, Resistance, and Terror*. Berkeley: University of California Press, 219–59.

Summers, Randal W., and Allan M. Hoffman, eds. 2002. *Domestic Violence: A Global View*. Westport, CT: Greenwood Press.

Sutherland, Edwin H., and Donald R. Cressey. 1978. *Criminology*, 8th ed. Philadelphia: Lippincott.

Tajfel, Henri. 1981. *Human Groups and Social Categories: Studies in Social Psychology*. Cambridge: Cambridge University Press.

Tajfel, Henri. 1978. *Differentiation between Social Groups*. London: Academic Press.

Tannenbaum, Frank. 1938. *Crime and the Community*. New York: Columbia University Press.

Taskinen, Sirpa. 2000. "Dealing with the Problems of Sexual Abuse of Children in Finland." In Michael Freeman, ed., *Overcoming Child Abuse: A Window on a World Problem*. Aldershot, UK: Dartmouth, 155–65.

Todorova, Velina. 2000. "Child Abuse: The Bulgarian Case." In Michael Freeman, ed., *Overcoming Child Abuse: A Window on a World Problem*. Aldershot, UK: Dartmouth, 39–61.

Tsunetomo, Yamamoto. 2002 [1979]. *HAGAKURE: The Book of the Samurai*. Trans. William Scott Wilson. Tokyo: Kodansha International.

U.S. Department of Health, Education and Welfare. 1978. *Violent Schools—Safe Schools: The Safe Schools Report to the Congress*. Washington, DC: U.S. Government Printing Office.

U.S. Department of Health, Education, and Welfare. 1972. *Television and Growing Up: The Impact of Television Violence*. Rockville, MD: National Institutes of Mental Health.

Uzodike, Eunice. 2000. "Child Abuse: The Nigerian Perspective." In Michael Freeman, ed., *Overcoming Child Abuse: A Window on a World Problem*. Aldershot, UK: Dartmouth, 329–52.

van der Dennen, Johan M. G. 2002. "Nonhuman Intergroup Agonistic Behavior and Warfare." http://rint.rechten.rug.nl/rth/dennen/animwar.htm, accessed 29 May 2002.

van der Hoven, Anna Elizabeth. 2002. "South Africa." Randal W. Summers and Allan M. Hoffman, eds., *Domestic Violence: A Global View*. Westport, CT: Greenwood Press, 125–41.

Voigt, Lydia, and William E. Thornton. 2002. "Russia." In Randal W. Summers and Allan M. Hoffman, eds., 2002. *Domestic Violence: A Global View*. Westport, CT: Greenwood Press, 97–110.

Walker, Lenore. 1979. *The Battered Woman*. New York: Harper and Row.

Wallace, Anthony F. C. 1966. *Religion: An Anthropological View*. New York: Random House.

Wallace, Harvey. 1999. *Family Violence: Legal, Medical, and Social Perspectives*. Boston: Allyn and Bacon.

Watanabe, Noriyoshi. 2002. "Japan." In Randal W. Summers and Allan M. Hoffman, eds., 2002. *Domestic Violence: A Global View*. Westport, CT: Greenwood Press, 83–95.

Watson, Catharine. 1991. *Exile from Rwanda: Background to an Invasion*. Washington, DC: American Council for Nationalities Service.

Webster, John. 1966. *The Political Development of Rwanda and Burundi*. Syracuse, NY: Syracuse University Press.

Weisel, Deborah Lamm. 2002. *Contemporary Gangs: An Organizational Analysis*. New York: LFB Scholarly Publishing.

Wiesel, Elie, and Michael de Saint Cheron. 1990. *Evil and Exile*. Trans. Jon Rothschild and Jody Gladding. Notre Dame, IN: University of Notre Dame Press.

Wirth, Louis. 1964. *Urbanism as a Way of Life*. Chicago: Chicago University Press.

Zimbardo, Philip. 2000. "The Psychology of Evil." *Psi Chi* 5: 16–19.

Zimbardo, Philip. 1973. "The Mind is a Formidable Jailer: A Piradellian Prison." *New York Times Magazine*, 8 April 1973, 38–60.

Index

Abakiga, 123
Abasoga, 123
Afghanistan, 139
African Network for the Prevention and
 Protection Against Child Abuse and
 Neglect, 135
Agoge, 101
Ahimsa, 81
Ahura Mazda, 160
Angra Mainyu, 160–61
Al-Qaeda, 148, 183, 184, 235
Albania, 103–05
 Albanians in Yugoslavia, 256–58
Alexander, King of Yugoslavia, 256
Alexander the Great, 99, 103
Alexander I, Czar, 247
Alexander II, Czar, 248
Alfred P. Murrah Federal Building, 320
Allah, 124, 164, 167–69, 186
Allcorn, Seth, 297
American Association for Protecting
 Children, 117
American Idol, 276
American-Israelism, 197
Amritsar, 200–01
Anabaptism, 180–82
Ankole, 123
Anomie, 45, 281, 282, 284
Anonymity, 14, 16, 152, 281, 293
Ants, 37
Applewhite, Marshall, 191
APROSOMA, 264
Aquinas, Thomas, 165, 178, 190

Arafat, Yasir, 211, 228
Arendt, Hannah, 7, 9, 10, 19, 153, 229
Argentina, 232, 310
Arianism, 177, 180
Aryan Nations, 197, 316, 318
Asahara, Shoko, 188–90
Augsburg, Peace of, 181
Augustine, Saint, 165, 167, 178, 190
Aum Shinrikyo, 188–90, 320
Australia, 28, 130, 318
 Australian aboriginals, 47, 86, 207
 child abuse in, 137, 138

"Bachelor vices," 283
Bakunin, Michael, 247
Band, 64, 75, 77, 82, 95, 207–08
Bandura, Albert, 44
Barber, Benjamin, 266
Bateson, Gregory, 234
Battered-child syndrome, 136
Baumeister, Roy, 7, 9, 11, 14, 16, 20,
 210
Begin, Menachim, 229
Benokraitis, Nijole, 115
Berg, Alan, 319
Berger, Peter, 209, 237
Bhagavad Gita, 161, 169–70
Black Panthers, 307
Bloods, 307–09
Blue Eyes, Brown Eyes, 47
Bolshevik, 153, 211, 237, 246–52
Bom Jesus da Mata, 142–46
Bonta, Bruce, 70–71, 78–79, 275

FGM
Circumcisio

—

Book of Liberties, 287
Bourdieu, Pierre, 113
Bowie, Vaughn, 295
Bowlby, John, 17
Branch Davidian, 189, 197, 318
Bray, Reverend Michael, 194, 195
Brazil, 138, 142–47
Bride burning. *See* India
Briggs, Jean, 77–79
Britain, 106–08, 120, 130, 219, 239, 240, 251, 321
British-Israelism, 197
Britton, Dr. John, 195
Bruggemann, Pastor James, 313
Buddha/ism, 33, 80, 108, 110, 159, 189, 190, 231
Buid, 73
Bulgaria, 136–38
Bullfight, 105–06
Bun, 123
Bureau of Justice Statistics, 294
Bureau of Labor Statistics, 294
Bush, George H. W., 315
Bush, George W., 184, 276
Bushido, 109–11

Cambodia, 133, 213, 230–31, 248
Canada, 28, 120, 130, 219, 318
   Utku in, 77–80
Carroll, John, 275
Chagnon, Napoleon, 88
CHEKA, 251
Cherubino, 131
Chesterton, G. K., 174
Chewong, 72
Cheyenne, 94–7
Chi, 33
Chief(dom), 65, 92, 93, 96, 97, 208, 263
Chimpanzees, 37–38
China/Chinese, 74, 139, 140, 188, 213, 215, 217–18, 230, 246, 248, 283, 309
Cholos, 307
Christian Crusade for Truth, 318
Christian Identity (CI), 196–98, 314, 316, 318
Christian(ity), 32, 33, 124, 130, 140, 151, 155, 161, 163–69, 171, 173, 174, 176, 182–84, 187, 194–98, 215, 227, 276, 282, 317, 318
   Aum Shinrikyo and, 189, 190

Balkans and, 253–57
dualism in, 160
eschatology in, 187–88
fighting monastic orders in, 201
fundamentalism, 148, 315
Hamites and, 263
Heaven's Gate and, 193
Ku Klux Klan and, 314
persecution of heretics, 177–82
scriptures, 156–59
City of God (St. Augustine), 165
Civil War
   American, 26, 284, 306, 313
   English, 239
   Russian, 251
Clausewitz, 214, 215, 227
A Clockwork Orange, 72
Cloots, Anarcharsis, 242
"Coercive parenting," 287, 322
Cognitive dissonance, 18, 19, 153
Committee of Public Safety, 222, 243–44
Communist/ism, 16, 41, 76, 150, 151, 154, 163, 220, 221, 230, 314, 315
   Albania and, 103–05
   Anti-Communist Association of Argentina, 232
   Chinese Communist revolution, 246
   Communist Manifesto, 41
   revolution in Russia, 246–48, 251
   In Yugoslavia, 257
Comparative Crime Data File, 28
Conflict Tactics Scale (CTS), 28, 117, 288, 291
Conrad, John and Simon Dinitz, 279
Contrary, 95, 97
Cooley, Charles, 44
Coser, Lewis, 48–49
Counting coup, 97
Covenant, the Sword, and the Arm of the Lord, The, 197, 319
Cowell, Simon
Crime Trends and Criminal Justice Surveys, 28
Crips, 307–9
Crusade, 21, 148, 164, 165–67, 184–85, 203, 321
Cult of the Supreme Being, 145
Cyprian, 173

Davenport, Charles, 283
Dehumanization, 14, 17, 21, 82, 206, 326
Deindividuation, 14, 326
Demonization, 14, 17, 176, 206
Dentan, Robert Knox, 74, 76
Desensitization, 19, 279, 326
Devil, 7, 17, 32, 33, 153, 160, 175,
    187. *See also* Satan
  Jews as spawn of, 196, 314
  worship, 193
Dickens, Charles, 133, 281
Diffusion of responsibility, 14, 15, 326
Diggers, 181, 221
DiIulio, John, 280
Dollard, John, 43
  and Neal Miller, 43
Dowry death, 126. *See also* India
Dukkha, 159
Durkheim, Emile, 46–49, 45, 139, 281
Dutton, Donald, 119

Eichmann, Adolf, 7
Electroconvulsive therapy, 35
Elliott, Jane, 47
Elliott, Paul, 201
Ellis, Albert, 44
Elohim City, 197
Ember, Carol and Melvin, 23–28
England. *See* Britain
Estes Park, Colorado, 318
Ethology, 35
Evans-Pritchard, E.E., 40
  and Meyer Fortes, 40
Exodus, Book of, 155, 198

Falwell, Jerry, 182–84, 195
Fanon, Frantz, 221
Fascist/ism, 16, 150, 233
Federal Bureau of Investigation (FBI),
    21, 23, 197, 322
Fiji, 124, 132
Finland, 138
Foraging, 64, 74, 77, 113, 121, 134, 207, 261
Four Noble Truths, 159–60
Free Spirits, 179
Free will, 33, 155, 156
Freeh, Louis, 197
France/French, 181, 199, 219, 220, 246,
    247, 248, 250, 251. *See also* French
    Revolution
  French speakers, 219

French Revolution, 43, 153, 211, 212, 215,
    221, 231, 232, 237, 238–45, 246,
    251, 281, 320
Freud, Sigmund, 40–41
Frustrating socialization, 25
Frustration-aggression hypothesis, 43
Fulani, 133
Functionalism, 46–51, 43
Furrow, Buford, 194

Gale, William Potter, 197, 314
Gandhi, Mohandas "Mahatma," 220
Gangs, 1, 19, 45, 105, 268, 273, 279, 282,
    284, 300, 305–12, 317
  African American gangs, 307
  Chicano gangs, 307
  definitions, 305–06
  gang rape, 37
  Gangs of New York, 283
  Hooliganism and, 107, 108
  Japanese film and, 112
  school violence and, 301, 304
Ganwa, 261
Gartner, Rosemary, 27, 30
Geertz, Clifford, 11
Gelles, Richard, 115, 116, 285, 286, 288,
    292
  and Conflict Tactics Scale, 288
  and Cornell, Claire Patrick, 120
  and Straus, Murray, 115, 117, 118, 122
General strike, 43
Genesis, Book of, 131, 156, 254
German(y), 131, 210, 250, 321
Girard, Rene, 171–2, 174
Girondin, 243–4
Gisu, 91–2
Gluckman, Max, 40
Gobind Singh, 200
God/gods, 3, 33, 42, 80, 83, 109, 126,
    150–61, 163–67, 170–71, 173–5,
    177–82, 185–7, 193, 195–202, 212,
    216, 282, 290–91, 313, 316
  city of, as religion's goal, 151
Goldstein, Arnold, 278, 303, 321, 326
Gondolf, Edward, 119
Goodall, Jane, 37

Habyarimana, Juvenal, 265
Hagakure, 108–11, 113
Hairesis, 177

Genital

Gilligan →

Hamas, 221
Hamites, 263
Hara-kiri. See Seppuku
Hare, Robert, 324
Harris, Eric and Dylan Klebold, 299
Harris, Marvin, 47
Hell's Angels, 312
Helots, 100
Heraclitus, 99
Hezbollah, 211
Hill, Reverend Paul, 195
Hindu(ism), 80, 124–5, 139, 161, 169,
    188–89, 199–200, 202
Hitler, 231
HIV, 141
Hobbes, Thomas, 209
Hoffer, Eric, 150–3, 174, 176, 186, 237,
    239
Hoffman, Bruce, 227, 229, 231
Holism, 62
Homoioi, 101
Homosexual(ity), 102, 196, 270
Honor, 12, 16, 21, 87, 97, 101, 119, 120,
    123, 139, 178, 223, 245, 266, 278,
    284, 289, 293
  in Albanian culture, 104–05
  in bullfight, 105–06
  in gang culture, 310, 312
  honor killing, 124
  in samurai, 109, 111–13
Hoplites, 100
Horticulture, 47, 64, 74, 84, 88, 92, 121
Human Relations Area Files, 117
Hungary, 137
Huss, Jan, 179

Idealism, 14, 16, 20, 21, 149, 231, 238,
    239, 276, 326
Ideology, 10, 14, 19, 30, 42, 48, 62, 80,
    114, 149, 174–76, 204, 205, 266,
    290, 293
  Christian Identity, 197
  communist, 103, 220, 221
  Greater Serbia, 258
Ifaluk, 72
Ilongot, 84–85
In-group, 17, 44, 93, 104
India, 120, 123, 124, 199, 215, 219, 220,
    262
  Asahara and, 188

AIDS, 141
  Kadar society, 72
  Nayaka society, 73
  Sati, 125–26
  Sikhism in, 200–02
  Thuggee in, 202
  violence against women in, 125–29
Indians, American, 94–97, 215, 230, 271,
    282, 284, 288
Infanticide, 25, 36, 37, 47, 89, 133, 134,
    135, 140
  in India, 127, 129
Inhibiting mechanisms, 37, 39
Intensive agriculture, 65, 113, 208, 267,
    280
Intergroup agonistic behavior (IAB), 36–38
International Crime Survey, 28
International Criminal Police
    Organization (INTERPOL), 28
International Women's Health
    Coalition, 138, 141
Iran, 123–24, 132
Irgun, 229
Isaiah, 155, 159
Islam, 164, 167, 173, 174, 183–8, 193, 199,
    254, 258. *See also* Muslim
  Sikhism and, 200
  assassins and, 203
Israel, 148, 156–9, 183, 185–86, 196–97,
    212, 229, 235
Izetbegovic, Aliya, 259–60

Jacobin, 241, 250
Jain(ism), 80–82, 86
Japan(ese), 99, 108–13, 120, 130, 137,
    203, 218, 248, 251
  Aum Shinrikyo in, 188–90, 320
  child abuse in, 138
  gender abuse in, 140
Jerome of Prague, 179
Jesus, 171, 173, 177, 179–80, 183, 196,
    198–99
  Heaven's Gate and, 191, 194
Jews/Jewish, 165, 179, 181, 184, 194–96,
    211, 227, 229, 270. *See also* Judaism
  Diaspora, 219
  militia movement and, 314–16,
    319
Jihad, 80, 164, 167, 185–86
  Benjamin Barber on, 266

Job, Book of, 155, 160
John Birch Society, 314
Johnson, Chalmers, 149
Juergensmeyer, Mark, 149, 190, 198
Judaism, 171, 177, 179, 188, 193. *See also*
    Jews/Jewish
Just war, 164–66

Kadar, 72
Kagame, Paul, 265
Kahl, Gordon, 319
Kali, 202
Kaliai, 122
Kanun, 104–05
Karadzic, Radovan, 259–60
Karadzic, Vuk, 255
Karma, 33, 42, 80–81, 188, 201
Kayibanda, Gregoire, 264–65
Kempe, C. Henry, 136
Kenny, James, 296, 298
Kerensky, Alexander, 250
Khalsa, 200–01
King, Rodney, 235
Kinkel, Kip, 299
Klan, Ku Klux (KKK), 195, 313–15, 320
Klanwatch, 314, 320
Koestler, Arthur, 164
Koresh, David, 197
Kosovo, 257–58
    Battle of, 254
Kreisberg, Louis, 48
Kulaks, 251–52
!Kung, 72, 86, 121, 122, 207

LaPorte Church of Christ, 318
Le Bon, Gustave, 150, 176, 237, 266, 274
Leach, Edmund, 40
Lee, Robert E., 288
Legitimate Violence Index, 285
Lemert, Edwin, 46
Lenin, 246, 249–51
Levelers, 181, 221
Leveling mechanism, 71, 207
Levinson, David, 132
Leviticus, Book of, 156, 196
Levy, Leonard, 177–9
Limira, 91–92
Liulevicius, Vejas Gabriel, 237
Lobotomy, 35
Lord's Resistance Army, 135

Lorenz, Konrad, 17, 39, 206
Louis XIV, 219, 239
Louis XVI, 239, 241
Luciferians, 193–4
Luther, Martin, 180–82, 221

Macrosocial, 62–4, 66, 87, 113, 116, 119,
    122, 124, 139, 140, 147, 206, 267,
    274, 280, 284, 285, 298, 304
Madrasa, 174
Magnitude gap, 11
Manifesto of the Bahutu, 164
Manson, Charles, 7, 199
Maquet, Jacques, 261–62
Maring, 47
Marton, Kati, 141
Martyr(dom), 139, 173–74, 185, 190
    Sikh, 200–01
    Serb, 258
Marx, Karl, 41–2, 209, 221, 242, 246–47
Marxist/ism, 43, 149, 221, 231, 249
Masada, 173
McVeigh, Timothy, 195, 316, 320
Mead, George Herbert, 44
Merton, Robert, 45
Microsocial, 62–64, 87, 113, 116, 119,
    147, 206, 267, 274, 285, 303
Milgram, Stanley, 7, 8, 13
Militia of Montana, 319
Milosevic, Slobodan, 258
Minutemen, The, 314–15
Mkako, 92–94
Morris, Desmond, 176
Mostar, 260
Mouvement Social Muhutu (MSM), 264
Muhammad, 183–84, 186, 203
Munchhausen syndrome by proxy, 137
Muslim, 124, 139, 166, 169, 183–88, 199,
    200, 203, 235, 266. *See also* Islam
    Bosnian, 253–60
Mussolini, 231, 233

Nacertanije, 254
Nacheyev, Sergei, 174, 222, 226, 247, 310
Nagovisi, 121–22
Narod, 247–49, 257
National Alliance, 316
National Center for Elder Abuse, 117
National Center for Injury Prevention and
    Control, 14

National Center for Victims of Crime, 288
National Coalition against Domestic
    Violence, 117
National Commission on the Causes and
    Prevention of Violence, 267
National Crime Victimization Study
    (NCVS), 23, 268, 270–72, 282, 294,
    298, 302
National Morbidity Study, 288
National Victim Center, 117
National Violence Against Women Survey,
    294
Nayaka, 73
Nazi(sm), 7, 150, 151, 154, 195, 210, 211,
    316, 321
Nicaea, Council of, 177
Nigeria, 133, 137, 138
Nuremburg Files, 320

Occupational Safety and Health Adminis-
    tration (OSHA), 295
Olson, Reverend Norman, 319
Operant conditioning, 43
Operationalization, 22–24, 26, 28, 61, 116,
    117, 273, 300, 301
Order, The, 316
Oregon Social Learning Center, 287, 322
Osama bin-Laden, 183, 186–87, 228
Out-group, 7, 17, 44, 45
Overing, Joanne, 82

Pascal, Blaise, 148
Palestine/Palestinian, 148, 184, 211–12,
    229, 235
    Palestine Liberation Organization
        (PLO), 221
PARMEHUTU, 264
Pastoralism, 64, 65, 113, 124
Patria potestas, 130, 287
Pavlov, Ivan, 42, 287
Peters, Pastor Pete, 318
Phrenology, 35
Piaroa, 82–84
Pierce, William, 316
Pleck, Elizabeth, 287
Posse Comitatus, 315
Pot, Pol, 213, 230–31
Potemkin, 248
Princip, Gavrilo, 256
Principles of Guerrilla Warfare, The, 314

Project Megiddo, 197
Promise Keepers, 194
Protest masculinity, 25
Prothrow-Sith, Deborah, 115
Protocols of the Elders of Zion, 319
Pseudo-speciation, 39, 206
Psychocultural, 63, 64, 69, 71, 77, 86, 87,
    113, 116, 147, 206, 267, 274, 278,
    322
Psychopath(y), 19, 20, 117, 321–25
    Psychopathy Checklist, 324–25
    psychopathic wife assaulters, 119
    "psychopathic woman, problem of,"
        289

Quakers, 181
Qur'an, 124, 167–68, 185

Ranstrop, Magnus, 176
Ranters, 181
Reagan, Ronald, 276–77
Rebel without a Cause, 307
Reconstructionists, 198
Reference group, 44, 69
Reign of Terror, 238, 239, 245, 310
Requerimiento, 166, 215–16, 309
Ressler, Robert, 280, 287, 322–23
Riches, David, 11, 12
Ritual Abuse Task Force, 133
Robertson, Pat, 182, 195
Robespierre, Maximilien, 238, 242–45,
    251
Rocky Mountain Rendezvous, 318
Rogers, Fred (Mr. Rogers), 274
Rome/Roman, 10, 130, 165, 173, 215,
    218, 227, 281. See also Patria
    potestas
    Roman Catholic, 253
    Twelve Tables, 134
Rosaldo, Michelle, 84
Ross, Marc Howard, 66–69
Ruby Ridge, 195, 197, 317–19
Rudolph, Eric Robert, 195
Rwabugiri, King, 261

Saint-Jean, General Iberico, 232
Samurai, 108–13
Satan(ic), 32, 133, 160, 161, 165,
    168, 187, 193, 196, 198,
    276, 315. See also devil

Sati, 125–26. *See also* India
Scheper-Hughes, Nancy,
   142-46
Self-esteem, 20, 21, 133, 274, 276, 296,
   297, 310
   threatened, 21
   battered wives', 119
   serial killers and, 324
Seligman, Charles, 263
Semai, 72, 74–6, 82, 121, 122, 274, 304
Seppuku, 111–12
September, 11 (9/11), 1, 174, 176,
   182–84
Shakers, 181
Shakur, Sanyika (Kody Scott), 305–10
Sicarii, 227
Significant others, 44
Sikh(ism), 199–201
Simmel, Georg, 48–49
Skinner, B. F., 42–43
Slovenia, 131, 257
Smith, Anthony, 218
Smith, Lacey Baldwin, 173
Sorel, Georges, 42–43
Spain/Spanish, 105, 178, 181, 199, 214,
   215
Sparta(n), 99–103
Spencer, Herbert, 47
Stalin, Joseph, 230, 246, 250–53
Stanford prison experiment, 56
Stone Kingdom Ministries, 313
Structural violence, 4, 140–42, 144, 147,
   230
Sulaiman Abu Ghaith, 184
Supernatural, 32–34, 61, 149, 150, 154,
   173
Suri, 97–98
Swift, Wesley, 197

Taiwan, 217–18
Tajfel, Henri, 17, 44, 47, 108, 114
Tannenbaum, Frank, 46
Tertullian, 173, 177, 178
Testosterone, 35, 36
Thirty Years War, 166, 181
Thorndike, E. L., 42
Thrasher, James, 305, 308–10
Tito, 257–58
Tkachev, Peter, 247–48
Tonnies, Ferdinand, 46

TRAFIRO, 264
Tribe, 39, 49, 43, 207–08, 215, 226, 237,
   253, 260, 262
Trotsky, Leon, 250, 253
Truchmann, John, 319
Turks, 235, 254, 256, 258
Turner Diaries, The, 316, 320
Twins, 134

Ujelang Atoll, 123
Ulyanov, Vladimir Illych. *See* Lenin
Uniform Crime Report (UCR), 23, 24,
   268, 271, 273, 282, 288
United Kingdom. *See* Britain
United Nations, 28, 141, 309
   and militia movement, 314
"Unruly School, The," 300
U.S. Child Abuse Prevention and
   Treatment Act, 135
Ustasha, 256
Utku, 76–80

Van der Dennen, Johan, 36, 38
Vesta, 160
Vice Lords, 307
Vietnam, 246
   army in Cambodia, 230
   War in, 26, 215, 220, 284
Violence Severity Ratio, 285
"Violent Schools—Safe Schools: The Safe
   School Study Report to Congress,"
   300

Waco, 195, 197, 318–20
Waldo, Peter, 179
Walker, Lenore, 119, 289
Wape, 121–22
Weaver, Randy, 197, 313, 317–18
Weinberg, Stephen, 148
West Side Story, 307
Westboro Baptist Church, 195
Westphalia, Peace of, 181
White Aryan Resistance (WAR),
   316–17
Wickstrom, James, 315
Wiesel, Elie, 154
Wild Ones, The, 307
Wilson, E. O., 36
Winthrop, John, 289
Wirth, Louis, 281

World Church of the Creator, 197
World Health Organization (WHO), 28, 140
World War I, 26, 41, 210
  Slavs and, 255
  Russia and, 249
  Rwanda and, 263
World War II, 1, 7, 15, 26, 103, 150, 195, 233, 282
  Japanese and, 109, 112
World War III, 189

Worldwide Church of God, 197
Wycliffe, John, 179

Yanomamo, 7, 47, 82, 88–90, 104, 114, 121, 132, 208
Youth Risk Behavior Surveillance System, 302
Yugoslavism, 255

Zarathrustra/Zoroaster, 160, 164, 165
Zimbardo, Philip, 13, 46, 82, 210
Zoot Suit riots, 307